An Expanding World
Volume 6

Scientific Aspects of European Expansion

AN EXPANDING WORLD

The European Impact on World History, 1450–1800

General Editor: A.J.R. Russell-Wood
with the assistance of Mark Steele

EXPANSION, INTERACTION, ENCOUNTERS
1   **The Global Opportunity** *Felipe Fernández-Armesto*
2   **The European Opportunity** *Felipe Fernández-Armesto*
3   **The Globe Encircled and the World Revealed** *Ursula Lamb*
4   **Europeans in Africa and Asia** *Anthony Disney*
5   **The Colonial Americas** *Amy Turner Bushnell*

TECHNOLOGY AND SCIENCE
6   **Scientific Aspects of European Expansion** *William Storey*
7   **Technology and European Overseas Enterprise** *Michael Adas*

TRADE AND COMMODITIES
•   **Merchant Networks in the Early Modern World** *Sanjay Subrahmanyam*
•   **The Atlantic Staple Trade** (Parts I & II) *Susan Socolow*
•   **European Commercial Expansion in Early Modern Asia** *Om Prakash*
•   **Spices in the Indian Ocean World** *M.N. Pearson*
•   **Textiles: Production, Trade and Demand** *Maureen Mazzaoui*
•   **Interoceanic Trade in European Expansion** *Pieter Emmer and Femme Gaastra*
•   **Metals and Monies in a Global Economy** *Dennis O. Flynn and Arturo Giraldéz*
•   **Slave Trades** *Patrick Manning*

EXPLOITATION
•   **From Indentured Servitude to Slavery** *Colin Palmer*
•   **Agriculture, Resource Exploitation, and Environmental Change** *Helen Wheatley*
•   **Plantation Societies** *Judy Bieber*
•   **Mines of Silver and Gold in the Americas** *Peter Bakewell*

GOVERNMENT AND EMPIRE
•   **Theories of Empire** *David Armitage*
•   **Government and Governance of Empires** *A.J.R. Russell-Wood*
•   **Imperial Administrators** *Mark Burkholder*
•   **Local Government in European Empires** *A.J.R. Russell-Wood*
•   **Warfare and Empires** *Douglas M. Peers*

SOCIETY AND CULTURE
•   **Settlement Patterns in Early Modern Colonization** *Joyce Lorimer*
•   **Biological Consequences of the European Expansion** *Kenneth Kiple, with Steve Beck*
•   **European and non-European Societies** (Parts I & II) *Robert Forster*
•   **Christianity and Missions** *J.S. Cummins*
•   **Families in the Expansion of Europe** *Maria Beatriz Nizza da Silva*
•   **Changes in Africa, America and Asia** *Murdo MacLeod and Evelyn Rawski*

THE WORLD AND EUROPE
•   **Europe and Europe's Perception of the World** (Parts I & II) *Anthony Pagden*

Please note that unnumbered titles are provisional and titles may change before publication.

An Expanding World
The European Impact on World History 1450–1800

Volume 6

Scientific Aspects of European Expansion

edited by
William K. Storey

VARIORUM
1996

Published by VARIORUM
Ashgate Publishing Limited
Gower House, Croft Road
Aldershot, Hampshire GU11 3HR
Great Britain

Ashgate Publishing Company
Old Post Road
Brookfield, Vermont 05036
USA

ISBN 0–86078–524–6

British Library CIP data
Scientific Aspects of European Expansion. — (An Expanding World: The European Impact on World History, 1450–1800; Vol. 6)
1. Science—History. 2. Civilization, Modern—European Influences. 3. Europe—History. 4. Europe—Civilization. 5. Europe—Colonies. I. Storey, William K. II. Series
303. 4' 83' 094

US Library of Congress CIP data
Scientific Aspects of European Expansion / Edited by
William K. Storey.
p. cm. – (An Expanding World: Vol. 6)
ISBN 0–86078–524–6 (cloth: alk. paper)
1. Science—Europe—History—19th century. 2. Research—Europe—History—19th century. 3. Science—Political aspects—Europe—History—19th century. 4. Engineering—Political aspects—Europe—History—19th century. 5. Europe—Politics and government—1989.
I. Storey, William K. II. Series
Q127.E85359 1996   95–44266
509. 4' 09034–dc20   CIP
Printed and bound by Athenaeum Press, Ltd., Gateshead, Tyne & Wear.
This book is printed on acid free paper.
AN EXPANDING WORLD 6

Contents

Acknowledgements   vii

General Editor's Preface   ix

Introduction   xiii

1   The Spread of Western Science
George Basalla   1

2   On Visiting the 'Moving Metropolis': Reflections on the
Architecture of Imperial Science
Roy MacLeod   23

3   Viajes, comisiones y expediciones científícas españolas a
ultramar durante el siglo XVIII
Francisco de Solano   56

4   Science for Political Purposes: European Explorations of the
Pacific Ocean, 1764–1806
Alan Frost   67

5   Seapower and Science: The Motives for Pacific Exploration
Daniel A. Baugh   85

6   Anthropological Analysis of Exploration Texts: Cultural
Discourse and the Ethnological Import of Fray Marcos de
Niza's Journey to Cibola
Daniel T. Reff   140

7   Silences and Secrets: The Hidden Agenda of Cartography in
Early Modern Europe
J.B. Harley   161

8   English Charting of the River Amazon *c.* 1595–*c.* 1630
Sarah Tyacke   181

9   The Influence of Father Ricci on Far Eastern Cartography
Helen Wallis   198

10   Amerindian Contributions to the Mapping of North America:
A Preliminary View
Louis De Vorsey   211

11 Indicators of Unacknowledged Assimilations from Amerindian
    Maps on Euro-American Maps of North America: Some
    General Principles Arising from the Study of La Vérendrye's
    Composite Map, 1728–29
    G. Malcolm Lewis   219

12 Ayurvedic Medicine in Goa According to the European Sources
    in the Sixteenth and Seventeenth Centuries
    John M. de Figueiredo   247

13 The Pre-History of Modern Science in Japan: The Importation
    of Western Science During the Tokugawa Period
    Yabuuti Kiyosi   258

14 Chinese Astronomy and the Jesuit Mission: An Encounter of
    Cultures
    Joseph Needham   283

15 Western Mathematics in China, Seventeenth Century and
    Nineteenth Century
    Catherine Jami   305

16 Ottomans and European Science
    Ekmeleddin Ihsanoglu   315

Index   327

Acknowledgements

The chapters in this volume are taken from the sources listed below, for which the editor and publishers wish to thank their authors, original publishers or other copyright holders for permission to use their material as follows:

Chapter 1: George Basalla, 'The Spread of Western Science', *Science* CLVI (5 May 1987, 611–622. © 1987 by the American Association for the Advancement of Science.

Chapter 2: Roy MacLeod, 'On visiting the "Moving Metropolis": Reflections on the Architecture of Imperial Science', in eds. Nathan Reingold and Marc Rothenberg, *Scientific Colonialism: A Cross-Cultural Comparison* (Washington, D.C., 1987), 217–249. © 1987 by the Smithsonian Institution Press.

Chapter 3: Francisco de Solano, 'Viajes, comisiones y expediciones científicas españolas a ultramar durante el siglo XVIII', *Cuadernos Hispanoamericanos* II (1988), 146–156.

Chapter 4: Alan Frost, 'Science for Political Purposes: European Explorations of the Pacific Ocean, 1764–1806', in eds. Roy MacLeod and Philip F. Rehbock, *Nature in its Greatest Extent: Western Science in the Pacific* (Honolulu, 1988), 27–44. © 1988 by the University of Hawaii Press.

Chapter 5: Daniel A. Baugh, 'Seapower and Science: The Motives for Pacific Exploration', in ed. Derek Howse, *Background to Discovery: Pacific Exploration from Dampier to Cook* (Los Angeles, Calif., 1990), 1–55. © 1990 by the University of California Press.

Chapter 6: Daniel T. Reff, 'Anthropological Analysis of Exploration Tests: Cultural Discourse and the Ethnological Import of Fray Marcos de Niza's Journey to Cibola', *American Anthropologist* XCIII (September 1991), 636–655. © 1991 by the American Anthropological Association.

Chapter 7: J.B. Harley, 'Silences and Secrets: The Hidden Agenda of Cartography in Early Modern Europe', *Imago Mundi* XL (1988), 57–76. © 1988 The Society for the History of Cartography.

Chapter 8: Sarah Tyacke, 'English Charting of the River Amazon *c.* 1595–*c.* 1630', *Imago Mundi* XXXII (1980), 73–89. 73–89. © 1980 by The Society for the History of Cartography.

Chapter 9: Helen Wallis, 'The Influence of Father Ricci on Far Eastern Cartography', *Imago Mundi* XIX (1965), 38–46. © 1965 by The Society for the History of Cartography.

Chapter 10: Louis De Vorsey, 'Amerindian Contributions to the Mapping of North America: A Preliminary View', *Imago Mundi* XXX (1978), 71–78. © 1978 by The Society for the History of Cartography.

Chapter 11: G Malcolm Lewis, 'Indicators of Unacknowledged Assimilations for Amerindian Maps on Euro-American Maps of North America: Some General Principles Arising from the Study of La Vérendrye's Composite Map, 1728–29', *Imago Mundi* XXXVIII (1986), 9–34. © 1986 by The Society for the History of Cartography.

Chapter 12: John M. de Figueiredo, 'Ayurvedic Medicine in Goa According to the European Sources in the Sixteenth and Seventeenth Centuries', *Bulletin of the History of Medicine* LVIII (1984), 225–235. © 1984 by The John Hopkins University Press.

Chapter 13: Yabuuti Kiyosi, 'The Pre-History of Modern Science in Japan: The Importation of Western Science During the Tokugawa Period', *Cahiers d'histoire mondiale* IX, no. 2 (1965), 208–232.

Chapter 14: Joseph Needham, 'Chinese Astronomy and the Jesuit Mission: An Encounter of Cultures', Pamphlet published by the China Society (London, 1958), 1–20.

Chapter 15: Catherine Jami, 'Western Mathematics in China, Seventeenth Century and Nineteenth Centuries', in eds. Patrick Petijean, Catherine Jami and Anne Marie Moulin, *Science and Empires: Historical Studies about Scientific Development and European Expansion* (Dordrecht, 1992), 79–88. © 1992 by Kluwer Academic Publishers.

Chapter 16: Ekmeleddin Ihsanoglu, 'Ottomans and European Science', in eds. Patrick Petijean, Catherine Jami and Anne Marie Moulin, *Science and Empires: Historical Studies about Scientific Development and European Expansion* (Dordrecht, 1992), 37–48. © 1992 by Kluwer Academic Publishers.

Every effort has been made to trace all the copyright holders, but if any have been inadvertently overlooked the publishers will be pleased to make the necessary arrangement at the first opportunity.

General Editor's Preface

A.J.R. Russell-Wood

An Expanding World: The European Impact on World History, 1450–1800 is designed to meet two objectives: first, each volume covers a specific aspect of the European initiative and reaction across time and space; second, the series represents a superb overview and compendium of knowledge and is an invaluable reference source on the European presence beyond Europe in the early modern period, interaction with non-Europeans, and experiences of peoples of other continents, religions, and races in relation to Europe and Europeans. The series reflects revisionist interpretations and new approaches to what has been called 'the expansion of Europe' and whose historiography traditionally bore the hallmarks of a narrowly Eurocentric perspective, focus on the achievements of individual nations, and characterization of the European presence as one of dominance, conquest, and control. Fragmentation characterized much of this literature: fragmentation by national groups, by geography, and by chronology.

The volumes of *An Expanding World* seek to transcend nationalist histories and to examine on the global stage rather than in discrete regions important selected facets of the European presence overseas. One result has been to bring to the fore the multicontinental, multi-oceanic and multinational dimension of the European activities. A further outcome is compensatory in the emphasis placed on the cross-cultural context of European activities and on how collaboration and cooperation between peoples transcended real or perceived boundaries of religion, nationality, race, and language and were no less important aspects of the European experience in Africa, Asia, the Americas, and Australia than the highly publicized confrontational, bellicose, and exploitative dimensions. Recent scholarship has not only led to greater understanding of peoples, cultures, and institutions of Africa, Asia, the Americas, and Australasia with whom Europeans interacted and the complexity of such interactions and transactions, but also of relations between Europeans of different nationalities and religious persuasions.

The initial five volumes reflect the changing historiography and set the stage for volumes encompassing the broad themes of technology and science, trade and commerce, exploitation as reflected in agriculture and the extractive industries and through systems of forced and coerced labour, government of empire, and society and culture in European colonies and settlements overseas. Final volumes examine the image of Europe and Europeans as 'the other' and the impact of the wider world on European *mentalités* and mores.

An international team of editors was selected to reflect a diversity of educational backgrounds, nationalities, and scholars at different stages of their professional careers. Few would claim to be 'world historians', but each is a recognized authority in his or her field and has the demonstrated capacity to ask the significant questions and provide a conceptual framework for the selection of articles which combine analysis with interpretation. Editors were exhorted to place their specific subjects within a global context and over the *longue durée*. I have been delighted by the enthusiasm with which they took up this intellectual challenge, their courage in venturing beyond their immediate research fields to look over the fences into the gardens of their academic neighbours, and the collegiality which has led to a generous informal exchange of information. Editors were posed the daunting task of surveying a rich historical literature and selecting those essays which they regarded as significant contributions to an understanding of the specific field or representative of the historiography. They were asked to give priority to articles in scholarly journals; essays from conference volumes and *Festschriften* were acceptable; excluded (with some few exceptions) were excerpts from recent monographs or paperback volumes. After much discussion and agonizing, the decision was taken to incorporate essays only in English, French, and Spanish. This has led to the exclusion of the extensive scholarly literature in Danish, Dutch, German and Portuguese. The ramifications of these decisions and how these have had an impact on the representative quality of selections of articles have varied, depending on the theme, and have been addressed by editors in their introductions.

The introduction to each volume enables readers to assess the importance of the topic *per se* and place this in the broader context of European activities overseas. It acquaints readers with broad trends in the historiography and alerts them to controversies and conflicting interpretations. Editors clarify the conceptual framework for each volume and explain the rationale for the selection of articles and how they relate to each other. Introductions permit volume editors to assess the impact on their treatments of discrete topics of constraints of language, format, and chronology, assess the completeness of the journal literature, and address *lacunae*. A further charge to editors was to describe and evaluate the importance of change over time, explain differences attributable to differing geographical, cultural, institutional, and economic circumstances and suggest the potential for cross-cultural, comparative, and interdisciplinary approaches. The addition of notes and bibliographies enhances the scholarly value of the introductions and suggests avenues for further enquiry.

I should like to express my thanks to the volume editors for their willing participation, enthusiasm, sage counsel, invaluable suggestions, and good judgment. Evidence of the timeliness and importance of the series was illustrated by the decision, based on extensive consultation with the scholarly community, to expand a series, which had originally been projected not to exceed eight volumes, to more than thirty volumes. As General Editor, my task has been facilitated by the tireless assistance of Dr Mark Steele who was responsible for the 'operations' component of the series, and of John Smedley whose initiative gave rise to discussion as to the viability and need for such a series and who has overseen the publishing, publicity, and marketing of *An Expanding World*.

The Department of History,
The Johns Hopkins University

Introduction

William K. Storey

In the past thirty years scholars have begun to pay closer attention to the role of science and technology in cross-cultural relations. Historical research along these lines has focused mainly on the ways in which Europeans 'transferred' technologies from their own countries to the non-Western world during the period of 'high imperialism', roughly 1870 to 1919. The present collection of articles addresses the role of science in cross-cultural relations during an earlier and relatively neglected period, 1450 to 1800.

The standard interpretations in this field relate the politics of European domination closely to the distribution of new kinds of science and technology. Daniel Headrick argues that many of today's former European colonies lag behind the West because imperialists introduced new technologies without imparting the scientific knowledge needed to produce and maintain these technologies independently.[2] During the nineteenth and twentieth centuries, the resulting inability of colonies to match Europe's industrialization only reinforced European ideologies of superiority and domination. Michael Adas contends that before Europe's industrial revolution, European cultural chauvinism derived mainly from a sense of physical and religious superiority. During the industrial revolution, Europeans came to base their self-serving analyses of foreign cultures increasingly on technological standards. This in turn slowed the rate at which Europeans introduced technological knowledge, creating a self-fulfilling prophecy of 'backwardness'.[3] All the while, according to Jack Kloppenburg, Europeans extracted important information and technology from non-Europeans in order to fuel their own prosperity and power.[4]

Historians have not yet thoroughly addressed the role of science and technology in cross-cultural relations between 1450 and 1800, even while producing a number of excellent studies concerning the nineteenth and twentieth centuries. Perhaps some of the sciences which were most important to the earliest

---

[1] The author wishes to thank fellow editors Michael Adas and John Russell-Wood for their helpful comments and suggestions.

[2] Daniel Headrick, *The Tentacles of Progress: Technology Transfer in the Age of Imperialism, 1850–1940* (Oxford, 1988). See also Headrick's *The Tools of Empire: Technology and European Imperialism in the Nineteenth Century* (Oxford, 1981).

[3] Michael Adas, *Machines as the Measure of Men: Science, Technology, and Ideologies of Western Dominance* (Ithaca, 1989).

[4] Jack R. Kloppenburg, *First the Seed: The Political Economy of Plant Biotechnology, 1492–2000* (Cambridge, 1988).

European empire-builders, such as astronomy, cartography, and navigation, seem irrelevant to contemporary problems in the non-Western world. However, surface appearances are deceptive. The production and distribution of knowledge and tools in these fields set the tone for later scientific and technological interaction across cultural boundaries. In any case, other sciences covered within this volume, such as botany, ethnography, mathematics, and medicine, are obviously relevant to today's issues.

This collection does not seek to review the vast literature devoted to the development of science and technology within specific cultural settings.[5] This is despite evidence presented here showing how cross-cultural relations have played a more important role in the development of various sciences than many scholars have assumed. Rather, this collection is an effort to encourage the further study of scientific interaction across cultures by presenting the most significant interpretative problems in this field. Its companion volume in the *Expanding World* series, edited by Michael Adas, addresses technological interaction across cultures.[6]

The best-known interpretation of Europe's scientific and technological interaction with the rest of the world is George Basalla's 1967 article, 'The Spread of Western Science', included as the first article in this collection.[7] Basalla elaborated a three-stage model for cross-cultural scientific relations which was closely related to modernization theory. In the first stage, Western scientists explored non-Western countries and appropriated their resources for study. These scientists were concerned not only with collecting and classifying objects for the sake of improving their knowledge, but they also sought exportable natural resources. In the second phase, Europeans established familiar scientific institutions in their colonies. Expatriate Europeans and westernized local scientists provided the staffs of these organizations, and may or may not have had formal training in Europe. Most often, they depended upon institutions in the European metropolis for guidance and also for a sense of tradition. In the third phase, colonial scientists developed independent scientific traditions based upon Western professional standards.

Basalla's article was influential until the 1980s, when new research cast doubt upon his model. His definition of science is too Eurocentric and restrictive

---

[5] The literature on western European science is extensive; a serviceable but anecdotal introduction to the field is Daniel Boorstin, *The Discoverers: A History of Man's Search to Know His World and Himself* (New York, 1983). For an extensive survey of Chinese science, see Joseph Needham, with Wang Ling, *Science and Civilization in China* (Cambridge, 1954–). On Africa, see Jack Goody, *Technology, Tradition, and the State in Africa* (Cambridge, 1980). On India, see D.M. Bose, S.N. Sen, and B.V. Subarayappa, *A Concise History of Science in India* (New Delhi, 1971).

[6] Michael Adas, ed., *Technology and European Overseas Enterprise*. An Expanding World, vol. 7 (Aldershot, 1996).

[7] *Science* CLVI (5 May 1967), 611–622.

to encompass the cross-cultural exchange of ideas which occurred between 1450 and 1800. He focuses exclusively upon the ways in which 'modern Western scientific culture' spread throughout the world, and upon scientists who were 'heirs to the Scientific Revolution, that unique series of events that taught Western man the physical universe was to be understood and subdued not through unbridled speculation or mystical contemplation but through a direct, active confrontation of natural phenomena'.[8] However, the meaning of science can vary a great deal from culture to culture, and can change over time within the same culture.

This collection of articles will suggest a more flexible definition of science in order to take cross-cultural interaction into account. Here, science will mean the systematic production of knowledge. In addition, the boundaries between one culture's science and another's cannot be conceived as fixed and formal. Scientific interaction between different cultures does not resemble a game of billiards, in which one cultural ball rolls occasionally and knocks another ball in a different direction. Instead, scientific information spreads in many ways at differing rates, depending upon the geographical, social, and educational status of the people involved.

Although Basalla's definition of science is too narrow to suit a broad investigation of cross-cultural relations, he made an important contribution by placing European science abroad within a social context. According to Basalla, 'What is important is the fact that the observer is a product of a scientific culture that values the systematic exploration of nature'.[9] Earlier historians of science emphasized the individual decisions and actions of scientists, without examining the social structure of their institutions. Basalla was adopting the viewpoint of Thomas Kuhn, who argued earlier in the 1960s that institutional pressures caused scientists to conform to dominant intellectual paradigms.[10] The thesis that the social dynamics of the research environment reduced scientific objectivity opened up the possibility that society itself influenced scientists in various ways. Although neither Kuhn nor Basalla would endorse this view wholeheartedly, many studies have now shown how exigencies from the outside world impinge upon scientific objectivity. This 'externalist' or 'social constructivist' position has itself become the dominant paradigm within the history of science. It provides a powerful tool for examining the scientific aspects of cross-cultural relations.

Some of the articles in this collection show how European states used science overseas as an instrument to increase their power. Roy MacLeod (see chapter 2 below) has attempted to revise Basalla's taxonomy with particular reference to British scientific efforts at home and abroad. While MacLeod deals with the

---

[8] Basalla, 'The Spread of Western Science', 2–3.

[9] Basalla, 'The Spread of Western Science', 611.

[10] Thomas Kuhn, *The Structure of Scientific Revolutions* (Chicago, 1962).

eighteenth through the twentieth centuries, his detailed criticism of Basalla and his 'architecture' of imperial science might be stretched backward in time and compared with other colonial powers. He gives wider credence to the ways in which local and metropolitan politics affect scientists, stating that 'science became a convenient metaphor for empire'.[11] MacLeod's structure links the ethos of each kind of imperial scientific institution closely to its own society and government, and stresses its economic and technological role.

Three scholars whose works are included below have shown a particular interest in the relationship between science and early-modern European statebuilding. The Spanish historian Francisco de Solano (see chapter 3 below) has noted how ostensibly scientific expeditions could take on roles more associated with political, commercial, diplomatic, and intelligence gathering objectives. Alan Frost (see chapter 4 below) demonstrates how scientific expeditions to the Pacific during the late eighteenth century had significant political overtones.[12] Daniel Baugh (see chapter 5 below) argues that little Pacific exploration occurred between 1640 and 1760 because interstate rivalries distracted and deterred European powers from undertaking difficult voyages to distant, unknown regions. Even when trade picked up during the late seventeenth century, it was safer and more lucrative to sail to proven destinations rather than to risk an exploratory voyage. However, Baugh's main point is that the Pacific explorations which occurred at the end of the eighteenth century were substantially different from earlier missions. While the explorers themselves continued to demonstrate scientific curiosity as well as maritime prowess, the motivations of states in financing their voyages changed completely. From 1492 to 1800, European states were interested in enlarging their treasuries and overseas territories. Over the course of these three centuries, governments grew to appreciate the importance of seapower in protecting colonies and trade. But according to Baugh, the main difference between late-fifteenth and late-eighteenth century European maritime powers was that the latter believed science should be an instrument of statecraft. This new conception of science

> held that knowledge of the natural world should be pursued not only for the glory of God and man but also because such knowledge translates to prosperity

---

[11] Roy MacLeod, 'On Visiting the "Moving Metropolis": Reflections on the Architecture of Imperial Science', in eds. Nathan Reingold and Marc Rothenberg, *Scientific Colonialism: A Cross-Cultural Comparison* (Washington, D.C., 1987), 244. Originally published in *Historical Records of Australian Science* V, no. 3 (1982).

[12] Francisco de Solano, 'Viajes, comisiones y expediciones científicas españolas a ultramar durante el siglo XVIII', *Cuadernos Hispanoamericanos* II (1988), 146–156; Alan Frost, 'Science for Political Purposes: European Explorations of the Pacific Ocean, 1764–1806', in eds. Roy MacLeod and Philip F. Rehbock, *Nature in Its Greatest Extent: Western Science in the Pacific* (Honolulu, 1988), 13–26.

and power. In this view, any society whose capacity for acquiring knowledge is inferior or merely derivative must therefore expect to hold an inferior and derivative role in global affairs.[13]

The Pacific explorers were also the heirs to another intellectual tradition of the early European explorers: the new science of ethnography. While early travel narratives often lacked analytical rigor, it is clear that they provided useful information about the world outside of Europe. In this collection's next article (see chapter 6 below), Daniel T. Reff examines the early texts of Marcos de Niza, a Spanish friar who visited the present-day southwestern United States during the late 1530s. Going beyond questions of whether or not the friar wrote accurately about what he saw, Reff shows the complexity of the construction of the friar's account. Both the politics of Spanish America's administrators and De Niza's interaction with the indigenous population influenced his writing. His journey may have abetted the Spanish conquest of the region, but the Zuni, Yaqui, and Hopi all influenced his description.[14]

State-enhancing exploration can have positive spinoffs, but it can also have negative side-effects. The history of cartography shows that sometimes the production of knowledge does not lead to its further distribution, but rather to its restriction. In the present volume's next article (see chapter 7 below), J.B. Harley views early modern European cartography as 'primarily a form of political discourse concerned with the acquisition and maintenance of power'.[15] Relying on the work of Michel Foucault, he argues that mapmaking was not objective and empirical, but an instrument of power. In turn, maps can tell a great deal about struggles for power. In a related piece included here (see chapter 8 below), Sarah Tyacke relies primarily on cartographic evidence to reconstruct the rivalry of European merchants to control the Amazon basin between 1595 and 1630.[16]

Furthermore, maps from this period contain deliberate silences, errors and omissions that served a political purpose. For example, Harley cites the world map which Matteo Ricci presented to the Chinese court. The map indicated the importance of Christian holy cities, but did not attach any significance to Islam's holy cities. Ricci and the mapmaker feared that any sign of religious rivalry might

---

[13] Daniel A. Baugh, 'Seapower and Science: The Motives for Pacific Exploration', in ed. Derek Howse, *Background to Discovery: Pacific Exploration from Dampier to Cook* (Berkeley and Los Angeles, 1990), 4–5.

[14] Daniel T. Reff, 'Anthropological Analysis of Exploration Texts: Cultural Discourse and the Ethnological Import of Fray Marcos de Niza's Journey to Cibola', *American Anthropologist* XCIII (September 1991), 636–655.

[15] J.B. Harley, 'Silences and Secrets: The Hidden Agenda of Cartography in Early Modern Europe', *Imago Mundi* XL (1988), 57.

[16] Sarah Tyacke, 'English Charting of the River Amazon *c.*1595–*c.*1630', *Imago Mundi* XXXII (1980), 73–89.

detract from his mission's proselytizing goals.[17] Of course, the Chinese would pay the price for Ricci's insecurities. In other cases, maps might not contain crucial details in order to protect commercial and military secrets. There could also be 'unintentional silences'. At a time when Europeans knew more about the world around them, mapmakers applied greater standards of uniformity to their work. Maps became more abstract, silencing the illustrations and descriptions of places which older maps often contained. Maps lost their human touch, and in the process rulers might have felt less empathy for the residents of visually sterile locations.

Historians of cartography have pioneered new methods in the study of how cultural interaction can produce new forms of knowledge. In the next article included in this collection (see chapter 9 below), Helen Wallis shows how Matteo Ricci and other Jesuit missionaries brought globes to China. On the one hand, their globes contained state of the art cartographic information which was new to the Chinese. European conceptions of longitude and latitude were also more practicable than Chinese methods of determining position, which relied on calculating surface distance. The division of the Earth into tropical, temperate, and polar zones was also a revelation to the Chinese. On the other hand, the missionaries believed that the concept of the earth's sphericity was new to the Chinese too, which Wallis proves to be incorrect. As early as the 4th Century B.C.E. Chinese astronomers knew that the Earth was round, and in 1267 a Persian astronomer presented Kublai Khan with a globe. The missionaries also learned a great deal from the Chinese about magnetism and compasses. The Chinese largely ignored Jesuit science, although the Japanese eventually proved more receptive. Therefore, it is altogether conceivable that the Europeans learned more about cartography from the Chinese during this encounter than vice versa.[18]

European expansion resulted in more non-European knowledge flowing to Europe than most people realize. Again, our strongest awareness of this issue comes from the research of historians of cartography. Louis De Vorsey (see chapter 10 below) writes that Amerindian mapmakers provided cartographic information to Europeans in North America throughout the period of exploration and early settlement. De Vorsey analyzes the early settlement of the Chesapeake, and finds that Captain John Smith learned much of what he knew about the region from Amerindians. In turn, he passed this information on to his superiors in London, where it became incorporated into European cartographic knowledge. In later years, surveyors and explorers such as George Washington continued to

---

[17] Harley, 'Silences and Secrets', 59.
[18] Helen Wallis, 'The Influence of Father Ricci on Far Eastern Cartography', *Imago Mundi* XIX (1965), 38–46.

benefit from Amerindian knowledge. Information flowed back and forth between Europeans and Amerindians, not just from Europeans to Amerindians.[19]

G. Malcolm Lewis pursues this point further (see chapter 11 below). He agrees that there was much cross-cultural assimilation in early North American cartography, but argues that Amerindians and Europeans had fundamentally different ideas about how to map their worlds. Analyzing the maps and reports of La Vérendrye, the French military commander of the north shore of Lake Superior during 1728 and 1729, Lewis finds that local Amerindians influenced French mapmaking. Furthermore, the French included Amerindian spatial concepts into their maps when describing territories which Europeans had never visited. The French assumed that Amerindians drew maps to scale, when they were actually drawing diagrams of connections between several points, much like a modern-day map of a public transport system. Amerindians also caricatured unusual topographical features, which the French translated literally to their maps. Traces of these cross-cultural miscommunications can be found in La Vérendrye's maps, as well as in other maps from the era of European exploration in North America.[20]

The interchange of ideas could take place in a number of ways. In the next piece (see chapter 12 below), John M. de Figueiredo shows that before the Portuguese takeover in 1510, Goa was a center of both Ayurvedic and Arabic medical learning. The Portuguese brought European medical ideas to Goa, and the city became a center of European medicine, too. Nevertheless, even high-ranking Portuguese officials preferred to call upon doctors trained in the Ayurvedic and Arabic traditions, in part because the Portuguese believed that these Indians understood tropical illness better than Europeans. Impressed with the treatments of Indian doctors, some Europeans attempted to bring home their knowledge and medicinal plants. Even after the Portuguese restricted Ayurvedic medical practice in the early seventeenth century, it still flourished thanks in part to the patronage of Portuguese officials. However, by the late seventeenth century enough Ayurvedic practitioners had converted to Catholicism or fled to other provinces that this kind of medicine, which was linked to Hinduism, began to die out in Goa.[21]

Yabuuti Kiyosi has also conducted a detailed examination of the introduction of European science to an Asian country, in this case Japan (see chapter 13

---

[19] Louis De Vorsey, 'Amerindian Contributions to the Mapping of North America: A Preliminary View', *Imago Mundi* XXX (1978), 71–78.

[20] G. Malcolm Lewis, 'Indicators of Unacknowledged Assimilations from Amerindian Maps on Euro-American Maps of North America: Some General Principles Arising from a Study of La Vérendrye's Composite Map, 1728–29', *Imago Mundi* XXXVIII (1986), 9–34.

[21] John M. de Figueiredo, 'Ayurvedic Medicine in Goa According to European Sources in the Sixteenth and Seventeenth Centuries', *Bulletin of the History of Medicine* LVIII (1984), 225–235.

below). He refutes the thesis that the Tokugawa shogunate stopped the flow of western knowledge into Japan. On the contrary, the shogunate manipulated selected kinds of knowledge for its own political advantage. Kiyosi goes so far as to argue that the Tokugawa's selective adaptation of western scientific knowledge laid the foundation for Japan's subsequent industrialization. Interestingly, Kiyosi demonstrates that the dissemination of European science in Japan rested upon the prior assimilation of Chinese science. Although his views about science seem Whiggish at times, Kiyosi shows the complexity involved in the cross-cultural transmission of scientific thought.[22]

Sometimes European knowledge encountered even stronger cultural barriers to diffusion. Joseph Needham (see chapter 14 below) shows that although the Jesuits introduced many of the most recent European technologies to China, their interpretation of Catholicism led them to teach Aristotle and Ptolemy's theory that the Earth was at the center of the universe, surrounded by crystalline spheres. The Jesuits used Western science as a proselytizing tool, associating it strongly with their religion. For this reason, the Chinese did not regard Western science as normative, but rather as a new way of thinking that might be blended with Chinese methods and knowledge. Some Chinese scientists collaborated with the Jesuits, others pursued an independent course, with the result that Chinese contributed to the world's knowledge of nature.[23] Building on Needham, Catherine Jami (see chapter 15 below) argues that the Jesuit mission coincided with a small revival in China of 'concrete studies', such as mathematics, astronomy, and geography. The Jesuits did not necessarily initiate an interest in reforming these subjects, but their arrival did coincide with a growing indigenous movement. By and large these Chinese scholars rejected the Jesuits' social and religious writings. The assumption that the Chinese should have embraced the 'essence' of Western science derives more from the imperialism of the nineteenth and twentieth centuries than the actual situation of the early seventeenth century.[24]

In many ways the Chinese considered their knowledge superior to the West's. Ekmeleddin Ihsanoglu (see chapter 16 below) shows that the Ottomans felt much the same way. During the fifteenth and sixteenth centuries, the Ottomans absorbed information and technology from the West which they considered to be useful, but rejected Western methods of investigation and conceptualization. During the

---

[22] Yabuuti Kiyosi, 'The Pre-History of Modern Science in Japan: The Importation of Western Science during the Tokugawa Period', *Cahiers d'histoire mondial* IX, no.2 (1965), 208–232.

[23] Joseph Needham, 'Chinese Astronomy and the Jesuit Mission: An Encounter of Cultures'. Pamphlet published by the China Society (London, 1958).

[24] Catherine Jami, 'Western Mathematics in China, Seventeenth Century and Nineteenth Century', in eds. Patrick Petitjean, Catherine Jami, and Anne Marie Moulin, *Science and Empires: Historical Studies about Scientific Development and European Expansion* (Dordrecht, 1992), 79–88.

seventeenth, eighteenth, and nineteenth centuries, Ottomans began to send students to Europe and to copy Western institutions. Cultural bias against Western ideas diminished, and some of the most novel new pieces of knowledge, such as the heliocentric universe, met with no dogmatic resistance from Islamic religious experts. The Ottoman government hired Western advisers to educate civilian administrators and military officers. Nevertheless, Ottoman ways of thinking continued to be dominant, and Western approaches to knowledge did not take hold until the twentieth century.[25]

These articles challenge historians to look beyond the standard Eurocentric scholarship on the history of science in cross-cultural relations. People from many different cultures have produced knowledge in many different ways. When these cultures interacted during the period of expanding European hegemony, the resulting knowledge was a complex blend of influences. If different people from around the world can learn to share knowledge in a more productive fashion, there might be grounds to hope that solutions to many ecological and social problems could come nearer to hand. It is hoped that this collection of articles will encourage further scholarship in this field.

---

[25] Ekmeleddin Ihsanoglu, 'Ottomans and European Science', in eds. Patrick Petitjean, Catherine Jami, and Anne Marie Moulin, *Science and Empires: Historical Studies about Scientific Development and European Expansion* (Dordrecht, 1992), 37–48.

1

The Spread on Western Science

George Basalla

A small circle of Western European nations provided the original home for modern science during the 16th and 17th centuries: Italy, France, England, the Netherlands, Germany, Austria, and the Scandinavian countries. The relatively small geographical area covered by these nations was the scene of the Scientific Revolution which firmly established the philosophical viewpoint, experimental activity, and social institutions we now identify as modern science. Historians of science have often attempted to explain why modern science first emerged within the narrow boundaries of Western Europe, but few if any of them have considered the question which is central to this article: How did modern science diffuse from Western Europe and find its place in the rest of the world?

The obvious answer is that, until fairly recent times, any region outside of Western Europe received modern science through direct contact with a Western European country (*1*). Through military conquest, colonization, imperial influence, commercial and political relations, and missionary activity the nations of Western Europe were in a position to pass on their scientific heritage to a wider world. This simple explanation is essentially correct, but it is entirely lacking in details. Who were the carriers of Western science? What fields of science did they bring with them? What changes took place within Western science while it was being transplanted? By what means is a flourishing scientific tradition fully recreated within societies outside of Western Europe? In this article I undertake to incorporate all these questions into a meaningful framework through the means of a model designed to aid our understanding of the diffusion of Western science.

The Model

While making a preliminary survey of the literature concerning the diffusion of Western European science and civilization, I discovered a repeated pattern of events that I generalized in a model which describes how Western science was introduced into, and established in, Eastern Europe, North and South America, India, Australia, China, Japan, and Africa. The model, like the survey that produced it, is preliminary; it is a heuristic device useful in facilitating a discussion of a neglected topic in the history of science.

Three overlapping phases or stages constitute my proposed model. During "phase 1" the nonscientific society or nation provides a source for European science. The word *nonscientific* refers to the absence of modern Western science and not to a lack of ancient, indigenous scientific thought of the sort to be found in China or India; *European*, as used hereafter in this article, means "Western European." "Phase 2" is marked by a period of colonial science, and "phase 3" completes the process of transplantation with a struggle to achieve an independent scientific tradition (or culture).

These phases are conveniently represented by the three curves of Fig. 1. The shapes of the curves were not determined in any strict quantitative way, for qualitative as well as quantitative factors are to be included in the definition of scientific activity. In determining the height of a curve I am willing to consider quantifiable elements —number of scientific papers produced, manpower utilized, honors accorded —as well as the judgments of historians who evaluate, on a more subjective basis, the contributions of individual scientists. Furthermore, the curves describe a generalized process that must be modified to meet specific situations. Japan, for example, had an unusually long, and initially slow-growing, second phase because of the policy of political, commercial, and cultural isolation practiced by her rulers. This long interval quickly reached a peak after the Meiji Restoration (1868), when Japan was fully opened to Western influence.

Thus it should be clear that when I refer to the graph of Fig. 1, I will (i) be mainly concerned with the gross features of the curves and (ii) be using the curves to illustrate my discussion and not to bolster it with independent support from empirical sources (2).

The first phase of the transmission process is characterized by the European who visits the new land, sur- veys and collects its flora and fauna, studies its physical features, and then takes the results of his work back to Europe. Botany, zoology, and geology predominate during this phase, but astronomy, geophysics, and a cluster of geographical sciences—topography, cartography, hydrography, meteorology—sometimes rival them in importance. Anthropology, ethnology, and archeology, when they are present, clearly rank in a secondary position. These various scientific studies may be undertaken by the trained scientist or by the amateur who, in the role of explorer, traveler, missionary, diplomat, physician, merchant, military or naval man, artist, or adventurer, makes an early contact with the newly opened territory. Training and expertise in a science will increase the European observer's awareness of the value and novelty of his discoveries, but they are not the crucial factors. What is important is the fact that the observer is a product of a scientific culture that values the systematic exploration of nature.

Science during the initial phase is an extension of geographical exploration, and it includes the appraisal of natural resources. Whether the "New World" to be studied is North or South America, Africa, Antarctica, the moon, or a neighboring planet, it is first necessary to survey, classify, and appraise the organic and inorganic environment (3). If the territory under surveillance is to serve eventually as a settlement for European colonists, the observer will probably follow the advice Sir Francis Bacon offered 17th-century planters of colonies (4). First, he counseled, "look about [for] what kind of victual the country yields of itself" and then "consider . . . what commodities the soil . . . doth naturally yield, that they may some way help to defray the charge of the plantation." Botany, zoology, and geology have a direct relevance to this search for foodstuffs and exportable natural products.

Phase-1 science is not limited to the uncivilized country where European settlement is the object. It is also to be found in regions already occupied by ancient civilizations, some with indigenous scientific traditions. India and China, two nations in this category, fell under the scrutiny of European scientists when they came into continuous contact with the West. Although the possibilities for trade in exotic items partly explain European interest in the natural history of these countries, commerce did not supply the major impulse. Trade and the prospect of settlement both influence the European observer's investigation of a new land, but ultimately his work is to be related to the scientific culture he represents. He is the heir to the Scientific Revolution, that unique series of events that taught Western man the physical universe was to be understood and subdued not through unbridled speculation or mystical contemplation but through a direct, active confrontation of natural phenomena. The plants, animals, and landscape of Europe had revealed their secrets when subjected to this method of inquiry; why should not the flora, fauna, and geology of an exotic land reveal as much or more?

The historical record is filled with examples of European naturalists collecting and classifying the plant and animal life they find in remote jungles, deserts, mountains, and plains and then publishing the results for the illumination of the European scientific community. In the Americas we begin with Gonzalo Fernández de Oviedo, called the first naturalist of the New World, and his book delineating the natural history of the West Indies (1535). From Oviedo in the 16th century, through the 17th and 18th centuries, there is a constant stream of Spanish, French,

German, Dutch, Swedish, and English naturalists traveling on scientific expeditions to South America. In the early decades of the 19th century this movement culminates in the work of Alexander von Humboldt and Charles Darwin (5).

Thomas Harriot, a 16th-century traveler and writer on the natural products and natives of Virginia, is the progenitor of a North American group of collectors, geologists, and surveyors. During the 18th century American colonial naturalists joined their European-based

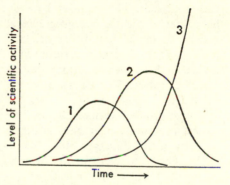

Fig. 1. Sequence of phases in the diffusion of Western science.

colleagues and continued the task of expanding European knowledge of the natural history of the northeastern and southeastern United States. Mark Catesby, John and William Bartram, Alexander Garden, Peter Kalm, and John Clayton are familiar names in this scientific enterprise. By 1800 the region east of the Mississippi River had been explored; now there was a shift of interest to the Western lands.

The wave of modern science had traveled from Europe across the Atlantic to the eastern and middle-western United States. During the 19th century science maintained its westward thrust as it was carried beyond the Mississippi by a series of government-supported and privately supported exploratory expeditions. From Lewis and Clark to the Colorado River venture of John Wesley Powell (1804–1870), the American West was the scene of phase-1 science. The sponsors of this science, however, did not reside in the older scientific capitals of Western Europe— London, Paris, Berlin—but lived in the eastern United States—in Boston, Philadelphia, and Washington, the emerging counterparts of the older capitals. This region, moving through the second into the third phase of the transmission process, was now in a position to act as a center for the diffusion of modern science. The time lag between the phases in the various geographical sections of the United States has had its effect on the current American scientific scene. The unequal distribution of scientific centers of excellence throughout the nation is due, *in part*, to the fact that some sections began the process of transplanting and nurturing science at a later date than others (6).

The Pacific Ocean was opened to European scientists by the three exploratory voyages undertaken by Captain James Cook between 1768 and 1780. Cook carried Sir Joseph Banks with him on his initial voyage, and it was the latter who uncovered the botanical, zoological, and ethnological treasures of the Australian continent. Botanist Robert Brown, spurred on by Banks's success, gathered some 3900 species of Australian plants and produced *Prodromus florae novae Hollandiae et insulae Van-Diemen* (1810), a classic in botanical literature. Later in the century Sir Joseph Dalton Hooker and Alfred Russell Wallace were to make significant contributions to science, based on their collecting ventures in, respectively, Antarctica (1839–43) and the Malay Archipelago (1856–62) (7).

China, India, and Japan posed new problems for the spread of Western science. Ancient and civilized peoples inhabited these nations, not the primitives encountered elsewhere. Nevertheless, the first Europeans who visited them began the surveying and collecting of plant and animal life that has consistently marked their early contract with new territory. Natural history was studied in Japan prior to the arrival of the Christian missionaries in the late 16th century, but this native endeavor was soon to be dominated by Europeans, with their superior classificatory systems. Two Germans, Andreas Cleyer and Engelbert Kaempfer, are noted for their botanical work in 17th-century Japan. In the succeeding century Carl Peter Thunberg and Philipp Franz von Siebold, two medical officers in the employ of the Dutch East India Company, made lasting contributions to the study of Japanese natural history (8).

China, once it was opened to Western ideas by the Jesuits in 1583, provided vast new opportunities for European scientific exploration. One customarily reads of the Jesuit missionaries as carriers of the new astronomy of Copernicus and Galileo to the learned men of China, but their correspondence and memoirs attest to their interest in the biological and geological sciences. The natural history studies of the first missionaries were soon to be expanded as hundreds of European scientists journeyed to China in the 17th, 18th, and 19th centuries. Botany alone caught the attention of so many of these Europeans that over 1000 pages in a two-volume history of European botanical discoveries in China (9) are devoted merely to a listing of their names and accomplishments!

The Portuguese, in pursuit of the spice trade, opened a sea route to India, bringing with them the first European science-collectors to that continent. When, in the 17th century,

England replaced Portugal as the major influence in Indian affairs, English missionaries and physicians assumed the task of investigating Indian natural history. In the 18th century the English became masters of Indian trade, and the men attached to the East India Company turned naturalists. They acquired extensive collections of flora and fauna and hired native artists to sketch the specimens in their proper colors and ecological setting. The Company formally acknowledged the economic importance of its servants' botanical labors by establishing the Botanic Gardens at Calcutta in 1787. The travels and writings of Sir Joseph Dalton Hooker, whose botanical expedition to the Himalayas was the basis for his *Flora Indica* (1855) (see *10*), are a reminder that professional scientists were also actively engaged in study of the natural history of India.

The western coastline of Africa was explored by 15th-century Portuguese navigators, but the easy availability of gold and slaves on the coast, and the natural barriers to the exploration of the interior, kept substantial European contact limited to the periphery of the continent until the late 19th century. The Cape area, however, serving as a way station for India-bound vessels, had a European settlement in 1652. South Africa, offering communities of European settlers and the advantages of a southerly location for telescopic observation, early attracted naturalists and astronomers, who came to observe its plants and animals, its geography and geology, and its heavens (*11*).

In the second half of the 18th century a small number of observers from France, England, Sweden, and Denmark began a more intensive investigation of the natural history of the continent of Africa. The most ambitious 18th-century scientific expedition was mounted in 1798 by Napoleon Bona-

parte as part of his military campaign in Egypt (1798–1801). Naturalist Geoffroy St. Hilaire, attached to the Napoleonic venture, collected Egyptian flora and fauna, paying special attention to the native fishes. His colleagues, including some eminent French scientists of the day, analyzed the soil and water of Egypt, made astronomical observations, and sketched and gathered Egyptian antiquities, thereby laying the foundations for modern Egyptology (*12, 13*).

One should not conclude from this swift survey of world history that phase-1 science is confined to the period beginning in the 16th and terminating in the mid-19th century. Late in the 19th century, when Germany became an imperial power by acquiring territory in Africa and the Pacific, she assessed her colonial wealth in *Das Deutsche Kolonialreich* (1909–10), a work that includes studies by zoologists, botanists, geologists, and geographers. In the first half of the 20th century the polar regions were the goals of the scientific explorer. The current need for natural history studies in underdeveloped regions (*14*) and the prospects of lunar and planetary exploration promise new tasks for the phase-1 scientist.

All of the plant, animal, and mineral specimens collected in the foreign lands, as well as the information amassed there, were returned to Europe (or, at a later date, to the United States) for the benefit of its scientists. Phase-1 science may be scattered around the globe, but only nations with a modern scientific culture can fully appreciate, evaluate, and utilize it.

As early as the 17th century it was realized that contact with new lands is certain to affect the development of science at home. Bishop Sprat, in his history of the Royal Society of London (1667) (*15*), wrote that maritime nations were "most properly seated, to bring home matter for new Sciences, and to make the same proportion of Discoveries . . . in the Intellectual Globe, as they have done in the Material" (see Fig. 2). The "matter" sent back by the collectors filled the zoological and botanical gardens, herbariums, and museums of Europe; made obsolete the classificatory systems devised for European flora and fauna; gave rise to the new studies of plant and animal geography; and decisively influenced the Darwinian theory of organic evolution (16).

The scientist who went out on an exploratory expedition often found that the experience gained from studying natural history in a foreign land modified his own scientific views. Michel Adanson, recalling his stay in Senegal (1749–54), commented (17): "Really, botany seems to change face entirely as soon as one leaves our temperate countries." And halfway across the earth in Australia, Sir James E. Smith (1793) concurred (18): "When a botanist first enters . . . so remote a country as New Holland, he finds himself . . . in a new world. He can scarcely meet with any fixed points from whence to draw his analogies." Thus European science, its practitioners forced to come to terms with exotic material at home and abroad, underwent a significant transformation while it was in the process of being diffused to a wider world.

Colonial Science

Colonial science (phase 2) begins later than phase-1 science but eventually reaches a higher level of scientific activity (Fig. 1) because a larger number of scientists are involved in the enterprise. Let me explain this use of the adjective colonial. First, as I use the term, colonial science is dependent science. At the phase-2 stage the scientific activity in the new land is based primarily upon institutions and traditions of a nation with an established scientific culture. Second, colonial science is not a pejorative term. It does not imply the existence of some sort of scientific imperialism whereby science in the non-European nation is suppressed or maintained in a servile state by an imperial power. Third, phase 2 can occur in situations where there is no actual colonial relationship. The dependent country may or may not be a colony of a European nation. This usage permits discussion of "colonial science" in Russia or Japan as well as in the United States or India (19).

Natural history and the sciences closely related to the exploration of new lands dominate phase 1. During the early years of phase 2, natural history is still the major scientific interest, with the first colonial scientists joining in the survey of the organic and inorganic environment conducted by the European observers. As colonial scientific activity increases, the range of the sciences studied is expanded and finally coincides with the spectrum of scientific endeavor in the nation, or nations, supporting the activity. There is a possibility that the colonial scientist will extend this spectrum, that he will open up wholly new fields of science, but this is unlikely, not because the colonial scientist is necessarily inferior to his European colleagues but because

Fig. 2 (right). The title page of Sir Francis Bacon's major contribution to the philosophy of science pictorially associated the acquisition of new knowledge with the travels of ships to the lands beyond Europe. [From F. Bacon, Instauratio Magna (London, 1620), reproduced with permission of the University of Texas Library]

he is dependent upon an external scientific culture and yet not a fully participating member of that culture.

Who is this colonial scientist? He may be a native or a transplanted European colonist or settler, but in any case the sources of his education, and his institutional attachments, are beyond the boundaries of the land in which he carries out his scientific work. This pattern is found in 18th- and 19th-century North and South America, Russia, and Japan; in 19th-century Australia and India; and in 20th-century China and Africa. If formally trained, the colonial scientist will have received some or all of his scientific education in a European institution; if informally trained, he will have studied the works of European scientists and will have purchased his books, laboratory equipment, and scientific instruments from European suppliers. This training will direct the colonial scientist's interest to the scientific fields and problems delineated by European scientists. Colonial scientific education is inadequate or nonexistent; the same can be said for colonial scientific organizations and journals. Therefore, the colonial scientist seeks the membership and honors of European scientific societies (20) and publishes his researches in European scientific journals.

Does the dependency of colonial science mean that it must be inferior to European science? Any answer to this question must consider the vigor of the scientific culture upon which the colonial science is dependent. Colonial science in Latin America, for example, advanced slowly as compared with developments in Western Europe. Several possible explanations of this lag may be proposed, but included among them must be the realization that modern science had not been extensively cultivated by Spain and Portugal, the colonizers of South America. A case

in point is Brazil. Brazilian science received its greatest impetus during the hiatus in Portuguese rule when the Dutch (1624–54) broke the old ties and brought the colony under the full influence of Western European culture (21).

Having mentioned the special case of Spain and Portugal, let me return to the general question of the inferiority of colonial science. As already noted, the colonial scientist works under handicaps at home and relies upon a scientific tradition located abroad. Although the group of men involved in the enterprise of colonial science is larger than that involved in phase-1 collecting, the number has not yet reached the critical size necessary for reciprocal intellectual stimulation and self-sustaining growth. The weakness, or lack, of colonial scientific institutions tends to cancel the advantages otherwise gained as the group approaches its critical size.

There is one final difficulty. Colonial scientists are oriented toward an established scientific culture but they cannot share in the informal scientific organizations of that culture. They cannot become part of the "Invisible Colleges" in which the latest ideas and news of the advancing frontiers of science are exchanged, nor can they benefit from the "continuing mutual education" provided by these informal groups of scientists (22). These are some of the disadvantages colonial scientists face even when they are in touch with the superior and vigorous scientific traditions of a France, Germany, Great Britain, or United States.

Colonial science has its drawbacks, but it is in the fortunate position of being able to utilize the resources of existing scientific traditions while it slowly develops a scientific tradition of its own. Although colonial science will rarely create great centers or schools of scientific research, open new fields of science, or completely dominate older areas of scientific inquiry, it does provide the proper milieu, through its contacts with the established scientific cultures, for a small number of gifted individuals whose scientific researches may challenge or surpass the work of European savants. These few men become the heroes of colonial science, and the debt they owe the older scientific traditions is often obscured, as is the fact that they are not representative of the state of colonial science. Benjamin Franklin is such a hero. He was a creative experimentalist and theorizer whose researches on electricity overshadowed the contributions of many of his European contemporaries. However, in praising Franklin we should remember that his intellectual and institutional home was London and Paris, not Philadelphia, and that his model was Sir Isaac Newton (23). The 18th-century chemist Mikhail V. Lomonosov holds a similar position in Russian colonial science, and, similarly, his intellectual base was outside of Russia, in Germany (24). Colonial science need not be inferior to European science, and in the hands of a scientific genius it might be superior, but its ultimate strength lies in the growing number of practicing scientists whose education and work are supported by an external scientific tradition.

The United States and Japan provide interesting illustrations of the course and nature of colonial science. The American colonial period of science extended beyond the nation's colonial political status. In 1847 Swiss-born Louis Agassiz criticized American deference to England in scientific matters (25), and as late as 1922 American physicists preferred to publish in the prestigious English journal *Philosophical Magazine* rather than in the American *Physical Review* (26). By the second half of the 19th century, Germany and France, not England, had come to hold the greatest attraction for American scientists. The young Josiah Willard Gibbs received his doctorate in science from Yale (1863) and immediately left for Europe to complete his scientific education in Paris and Berlin. Gibbs was not alone. Hundreds of American chemists, physicists, and biologists in the late 19th and early 20th century pursued graduate studies, or gained Ph.D.'s, at Berlin, Leipzig, Göttingen, Heidelberg, Munich, or Paris (27). In 1904 the president of the American Mathematical Society estimated that 10 percent of its members held Ph.D.'s from German universities, and at least 20 percent had studied mathematics there (28). American scientific institutions could not provide the training or experience these men needed to bring them to the forefront of scientific knowledge.

"Of all the wonders of the world the progress of Japan . . . seems to me about the most wonderful." So wrote Charles Darwin in 1879 to Edward S. Morse, the American zoologist who had introduced the theory of organic evolution into Japan (29). The rapid progress of Japanese science that impressed Darwin was of relatively recent origin. Prior to the Meiji restoration (1868) Japanese colonial science grew at a slow pace, thwarted by governmental prohibition, linguistic barriers, and cultural resistance. European science, carried to Japan by 16th-century Jesuit missionaries, was banned in 1636 when the government moved to halt the infiltration of Western religion and thought. This seclusionist policy was not relaxed until the first half of the 18th century, when Western ideas were permitted to enter in the form of Sino-Jesuit scientific treatises and Dutch books. The Dutch, having maintained

Fig. 3. The Tokugawa physician Hashimoto Sokichi (1763–1836) used a tall pine tree, instead of a kite, in an experiment confirming Benjamin Franklin's claim that lightning is identical with static electricity. [From Hashimoto Sokichi, *Erekiteru kyūri gen* (Osaka, 1811), reproduced with permission of Osaka Prefectural Library, Osaka, Japan]

limited commercial contacts during the period of isolation, provided the only direct channel of communication between Japan and Europe. Once the ban was removed, Japanese scholars took advantage of this channel by translating Dutch books summarizing Western science and learning. These books made available European knowledge of human anatomy and medicine, heliocentric astronomy, and developments in chemistry and physics. The Japanese translators went beyond their linguistic tasks and often repeated the experiments they learned about in their reading. Thus the physician Hashimoto Sokichi, while translating some Dutch books on electricity, decided to confirm their accuracy by repeating the electrical experiments of Benjamin Franklin (see Fig. 3) (30).

In the Tokugawa era (1600–1868) (see 31), especially in the later years, a growing number of Japanese savants were attempting to assimilate European science and technology. Nevertheless, Meiji science far surpassed the modest accomplishments of the previous period. After 1868 the Japanese government undertook a deliberate program of modernization, a program that paid special attention to the science of the West. The Japanese imported American, German, English, and Dutch scientists, engineers, and physicians to serve in native universities as teachers of aspiring scientists. Between 1868 and 1912 over 600 students were sent abroad for special training in the scientific and technological centers of America and Europe. Linguistic barriers were overcome by the translation of Western scientific textbooks and by the compilation of a dictionary of technical words (Japanese, English, French, and German). Insofar as her science was concerned, Japan was as dependent upon the Western scientific culture as any of those countries that are con-

ventionally classified as political colonies of the Western nations (32).

Colonial science begins when a small number of native workers or European settlers in the land recently opened to European science first participate in phase-1 exploration and then gradually shift their interest to a wider spectrum of scientific activity. All this takes place while the colonial scientist relies upon an external scientific tradition. The transition from phase 2 to phase 3 is more complex. Scientists in the third phase are struggling to create an independent scientific tradition; they are attempting to become self-reliant in scientific matters.

What spurs the colonial scientist to move from dependency to independency? Nationalism, both political and cultural, can sometimes be identified as the moving force. After the American Revolution there was nationalistic sentiment in the new nation which encouraged the building of an American science upon a native foundation (33). Similar sentiment appeared in the South American colonies after their break with Spain (34). In 1848 Andrés Bello, a Venezuelan thinker and educator, called for a South American science, bearing the stamp of its national origin, that would not "be condemned to repeat servilely the lessons of European science." "European science seeks data from us," he said. and then asked rhetorically, "shall we have not even enough zeal and application to gather it for them?" The answer was that data-gathering was not to be the only job of the Latin-American scientist, for the American republics had a "greater role to play in the progress of the sciences."

Nationalistic feelings may be significant in the transition from phase 2 to phase 3, but there are more fundamental forces working to bring about this change. Colonial science contains, in an embryonic form, some of the essential features of the next stage. Although the colonial scientist looks for external support, he does begin to create institutions and traditions which will eventually provide the basis for an independent scientific culture. A modest amount of scientific education will be undertaken by the colonial scientist, he will agitate for the creation of native scientific organizations, he may work for the establishment of a home-based scientific journal, and he begins to think of his work, and of the researches of his immediate colleagues, as being the product of his own nation. Colonial science has passed its peak when its practitioners begin a deliberate campaign to strengthen institutions at home and end their reliance upon the external scientific culture.

Independent Scientific Tradition

The struggle to establish an independent scientific tradition, which takes place during the third phase, is the least understood, appreciated, or studied aspect of the process of transference of modern science to the wider world. Historians and sociologists of science have failed to realize the difficulty of fully integrating science into a society that previously had little contact with Western science. The easy success of colonial science does not adequately prepare a country for the arduous task of creating and supporting native scientific institutions and fostering attitudes conducive to the rapid growth of science. Scientists working in phase 3, and historians who later attempt to plot the development of science during phases 2 and 3, often misunderstand the era of colonial science. In both cases they tend to praise the high level of scientific activity reached in the colonial era and forget that that level of attainment was made possible

through a reliance upon an older, established scientific tradition.

The colonial scientist, who was a member of a relatively small group of men oriented toward an external scientific culture, is to be replaced during the course of phase 3 by a scientist whose major ties are within the boundaries of the country in which he works. Ideally, he will (i) receive most of his training at home; (ii) gain some respect for his calling, or perhaps earn his living as a scientist, in his own country; (iii) find intellectual stimulation within his own expanding scientific community; (iv) be able to communicate easily his ideas to his fellow scientists at home and abroad; (v) have a better opportunity to open new fields of scientific endeavor; and (vi) look forward to the reward of national honors—bestowed by native scientific organizations or the government—when he has done superior work. These six elements are more in the nature of goals to be attained than common characteristics of phase-3 science. Since phase 3 is marked by a conscious struggle to reach an independent status, most scientists will not personally achieve all of these goals, but there will be general agreement that an overt effort should be made to realize them.

If a colonial, dependent scientific culture is to be exchanged for an independent one, many tasks must be completed. Some of the more important ones are as follows.

1) Resistance to science on the basis of philosophical and religious beliefs must be overcome and replaced by positive encouragement of scientific research. Such resistance might be ignored or circumvented by the colonial scientist, but it must be eradicated when science seeks a broad base of support at home.

The slow development of science in China can be explained, in large measure, by the inability of modern science to displace Confucianism as the prevailing philosophy. Confucian thought stressed the importance of moral principles and human relationships and discouraged systematic study of the natural world. The Confucian rejection of scientific knowledge is epitomized in a poem written in the early 19th century by a Chinese dignitary (*35*):

With a microscope you see the surface of things.
It magnifies them but does not show you reality.
It makes things seem higher and wider,
But do not suppose you are seeing the things in themselves.

Attitudes of this sort persisted in China until the end of the 19th century, at which time the Confucian ideals were decisively challenged and gradually replaced by value systems closer to the spirit of Western science (*36*).

2) The social role and place of the scientist need to be determined in order to insure society's approval of his labors. If science in general, or some aspect of the scientist's work, is considered suitable only for the socially inferior, the growth of science may be inhibited. When Louis Agassiz visited Brazil in 1865 he was surprised to find that the higher social classes held a strong prejudice against manual labor. This prejudice had its effect upon the development of science in Brazil. Agassiz noted (*37*) that as long as Brazilian "students of nature think it unbecoming a gentleman to handle his own specimens, to carry his own geological hammer, to make his own scientific preparation, he will remain a mere dilettante in investigation" (see Fig. 4). The Brazilian naturalists were thoroughly acquainted with "the bibliography of foreign science," but their social mores cut them off from "the wonderful fauna and flora with which they [were] surrounded." Prejudices so deeply rooted in the social structure are not likely to be removed easily, and science is retarded.

3) The relationship between science and government should be clarified so that, at most, science receives state financial aid and encouragement and, at least, government maintains a neutral position in scientific matters. The history of Japanese science affords examples of the several possibilities in a government's response to science. Western science was suppressed by the Japanese government in the 17th century, partially accepted in the 18th century, and then enthusiastically supported after 1868. At no time was the Japanese government reacting to the general will of its people.

In those nations where public opinion is more instrumental in the shaping of government policy, state aid to science will depend upon the citizen's evaluation of the significance of science. This was the case in Australia in the 1830's, when there was some hope for the establishment of a national geological survey. A Sydney newspaper, however, expressed the prevailing sentiment when it declared editorially (*38*): "Zoology, Mineralogy, and Astronomy, and Botany are all very good things, but we have no great opinion of an infantile people being taxed to support them. An infant colony cannot afford to become scientific for the benefit of mankind." Scientists seeking the help and recognition of the state have, until recently, found it difficult to justify the expenditure of public funds to promote scientific research.

4) The teaching of science should be introduced into all levels of the educational system, provided, of course, an adequate educational system already exists. This will entail the building, staffing, and equipping of schoolrooms and teaching laboratories; the training of science teachers and of instructors in supporting disciplines; the produc-

tion of science textbooks in an appropriate language; and the founding of libraries of science. Education in the sciences is not enough; a parallel program must be instituted to train the "foot soldiers of the scientific army"—the technicians, instrument makers, and their like. These changes can only be made if they are judged worth while by society, and if they are not too strongly opposed by conservative educators who are committed to other educational patterns. In view of the many possible sources of resistance to innovation in education, the creation of adequate programs in the teaching of science must necessarily be a long-term process. It is for this reason that American scientists were still seeking European scientific training after the United States had acquired many of the other features of an independent scientific tradition.

5) Native scientific organizations should be founded which are specifically dedicated to the promotion of science. These would include general professional associations, working for the advancement of the whole scientific profession; specialist societies, serving the particular needs of men engaged in research within a given field of science; and elite, honorific organizations, providing rewards for those who make the greatest contribution to the advancement of science. Scientific societies have always been closely associated with Western science; the foundation, in the 17th century, of the Accademia del Cimento, the Royal Society of London, and the Académie des Sciences is usually cited as one proof of the emergence of modern science in that era.

Napoleon Bonaparte acknowledged the importance of scientific societies when he founded the Institut d'Egypte, patterned after the major contemporary French scientific society, the Institut de France. Determined to bring the science of Western Europe to the ancient Near East, he attempted to recreate the Institut de France in Egypt in the hope that the new organization would play a part in the growth of Egyptian science as important as the part its progenitor had played in France. Military defeat (1801) ended Napoleon's plans, and it is doubtful whether the Institut alone could have carried the burden of introducing Western science into Egypt (13, 39). Nevertheless, Napoleon was correct in believing that scientific organizations were crucial to the establishment of modern science in a land hitherto untouched by Western influence.

6) Channels must be opened to facilitate formal national and international scientific communication. This can be accomplished by founding appropriate scientific journals and then gaining their widespread recognition. Many problems are likely to be encountered here (40). A scientific journal cannot flourish unless there are enough scientists and subscribers to fill its pages and pay its costs. Even if the requisite number of potential contributors exists, there remains the question of its prestige. The colonial scientist, who is accustomed to writing for established European scientific journals, may not wish to jeopardize his international reputation by reporting his work in an unknown native periodical. Will the 18th-century American scientist, or his counterparts in 19th-century India or Australia, whose contributions appear in the *Philosophical Transactions of the Royal Society of London*, be satisfied to write for a natively produced periodical with few readers and little influence?

Finally, there are the difficulties presented by language. Should national pride dictate that the contributions to the new journal be printed in the mother tongue when that language is not familiar to Western Europeans, or should some concession be made in order to gain European readers? This was the question faced by the founders of scientific periodicals in Japan, in China, and (in the case of Rumania) in Central Europe (41). Despite these problems, it is important that a country struggling to create an independent scientific tradition should publish journals of science filled with the researches of its own scientists.

7) A proper technological base should be made available for the growth of science. Western Europe had reached an advanced state of technical progress when modern science first made its appearance, and since that time it has been assumed that the two are fundamentally related. The exact nature of that relationship has not as yet been revealed by historians of science and technology.

Even without clear guidelines it is possible to indicate some of the links between science and technology that are significant for this discussion. A nation hoping to be self-sufficient in the realm of science certainly must maintain a level of technology that will produce the scientific instruments and apparatus needed for research and teaching. That this level is not to be reached without some difficulty is proved by the American example. European technology was transmitted to North America by the early settlers, but the colonies were slow to develop a craft tradition that specialized in the construction of scientific instruments for purposes other than navigation and surveying. Fine scientific instruments, to be used by American scientists in research, teaching, and exploration, were customarily purchased in England and France until the second half of the 19th century (42). If America found it necessary to rely on Europe, one can imagine that an African or Asian culture, existing beyond the influence of Western technology, would find it much more difficult to reach the desired technological level and make its own instruments.

Economic determinists, along with some historians of technology, argue that technology has more to offer science than a mere collection of scientific instruments. They say that technology poses the very problems that dominate a scientific field in a given era. For the most part, historians of science reject this external interpretation and concentrate on the internal, conceptual development of science. If technology does direct scientific inquiry, as the first group contends, then it will be the overriding factor in the establishment of an independent scientific culture; if it does not, then it should be reduced to its role of provider of gadgetry for the scientist.

These are the extreme positions, but there is the possibility of a compromise that calls for a recognition of the complexity of the relationship between science and technology and demands a more subtle analysis. A proponent of this compromise will ask that the following investigations be made. First, we should determine to what extent a lifelong familiarity with a variety of machines prepares and predisposes an individual or culture to accept and extend the predominantly mechanical view of the physical universe bequeathed to us by the founders of modern science. Second, we should study the products of technology not merely as mechanical contrivances designed to fulfill specific, limited purposes but as cultural complexes that carry with them the attitudes, skills, and ideas of the culture that produced them. The latter topic has been explored in a recent book on the introduction of steamboats on the river

Fig. 4. Nineteenth-century Brazilian naturalists, disdaining manual labor, assigned their Negroes the job of collecting and preparing specimens. [From D. P. Kidder, *Sketches of Residence and Travels in Brazil* (Philadelphia, 1845), vol. 1, p. 129, reproduced with permission of the University of Texas Library]

Ganges in the 1830's (43). These vessels provided far more than a rapid and effective means of transportation. They were vectors of Western civilization carrying Western science, medicine, and technical skills into the interior of India. In exploring these two topics we are likely to uncover the nature of the links between science and technology and learn more about the technological underpinnings of an independent scientific tradition.

Any one of the seven tasks listed above would present major problems for those who wished to gain an independent stronghold for modern science. Collectively, they present so severe a challenge that even a concerted effort on the part of the scientists will not soon bring noticeable results. Because of the difficulties involved in the completion of the tasks, I speak of a "struggle to establish an independent scientific tradition," and I illustrate it by the slowly rising curve of phase 3 (Fig. 1). Note, however, that, if the outcome of the struggle is successful, the curve rises abruptly, signifying the emergence of the nation among the leaders of world science (44).

If my analysis of phase 3 is correct, then we should find that the non-European nations, after a long period of preparation, have only recently approached the supremacy of Western Europe in science. The leadership achieved by Western Europe at the time of the Scientific Revolution was not challenged until the United States and Russia emerged as leading scientific nations in the period between world wars I and II. America first gained scientific eminence in the fields of genetics and big-telescope astronomy. In 1921 the English geneticist William Bateson, commenting upon recent American contributions to genetics, was moved to say in his address to the American Association for the Advancement of Science (45): "I come at this Christmas Season to lay my respectful homage before the stars that have arisen in the West." The stars were the American biologists who had finally attained European recognition with their work in a new field of science. Physics in America came of age within two decades of Bateson's speech. Recalling the state of American physics in 1929, and testifying to the beneficent influence of J. R. Oppenheimer upon its maturation, I. I. Rabi remarked (46): "When we first met in 1929, American physics was not really very much, certainly not consonant with the great size and wealth of the country. We were very much concerned with raising the level of American physics. We were sick and tired of going to Europe as learners. We wanted to be independent. I must say I think that our generation . . . did that job, and that ten years later we were at the top of the heap."

Contrary evaluations of Soviet science offered by friends and foes of the Communist ideology (47) have made it difficult to determine objectively the state of science in the U.S.S.R. In the 1940's, proponents of planned economy and planned science hailed Soviet scientific achievements, while opponents, pointing to the damaging influence of ideology on the biological sciences, held little hope for science in a totalitarian regime. Russia's advancement in weaponry and space technology during the next decade left no doubt that a strong program in basic science supported these technical feats. Critics might still complain of a bias toward applications in Soviet science, and point to the relatively small number of Russian scientists who have won the Nobel prize, but there is general agreement that the U.S.S.R. has taken her place as one of the leaders of world science (48).

After several centuries of contact with European science the United States and the U.S.S.R. finally reached, and in some cases surpassed, the science of the Western European nations. This cannot be said of any other land outside of Western Europe. Japan, Australia, and Canada have shown signs of vigorous scientific growth, but they definitely rank below these two nations. China, India, and perhaps some South American and African countries may be placed in a third grouping of nations with great potential for future scientific growth and with major obstacles to be overcome before they establish their independent scientific cultures.

Conclusion

There is no need to summarize the features of this simplified model, which describes the manner in which modern science was transmitted to the lands beyond Western Europe. The graph of Fig. 1 and the examples drawn from science in various lands should have made them clear. It may be in order, however, to reiterate that there is nothing about the phases of my model that is cosmically or metaphysically necessary. I am satisfied if my attempt will interest others to go beyond my crude analysis and make a systematic investigation of the diffusion of Western science throughout the world.

Such an investigation would include a comparative appraisal of the development of science in different national, cultural, and social settings and would mark the beginnings of truly comparative studies in the history and sociology of science. The present lack of comparative studies in these disciplines can be attributed to the widespread belief that science is strictly an international endeavor. In one sense this is true. As Sir Isaac Newton remarked in his *Principia* (49), "the descent of stones in Europe and in America" must both be explained by one set of physical laws. Yet, we cannot ignore the peculiar environment in which members of a national group of scientists are trained and carry on their research.

While I do not hold with the Nazi theorists that science is a direct reflection of the racial or national spirit (50), neither do I accept Chekhov's dictum (51) that "there is no national science just as there is no national multiplication table. . . ." In emphasizing the international nature of scientific inquiry we have forgotten that science exists in a local social setting. If that setting does not decisively mold the conceptual growth of science, it can at least affect the number and types of individuals who are free to participate in the internal development of science. Perhaps the effect is more profound; only future scholarship can determine the depth of its influence.

References and Notes

1. Since World War II the United States and Russia have been in a strong position to act as agents for the introduction of modern science to underdeveloped regions, but their examples do not break the line of transmission I have indicated. It is an easy matter to trace American and Russian scientific traditions back to the nations originally participating in the Scientific Revolution.
2. I. Bernard Cohen's "The New World as a source of science for Europe," *Actes du Neuvième Congrès International d'Histoire des Sciences* (Barcelona-Madrid, 1959), provided the inspiration for the model. Other works which influenced it included "Basic Research in the Navy," *Naval Res. Advisory Comm. Publ.* (1959); G. Holton, *Daedalus* 91, No. 2, 362 (1962); T. S. Kuhn, *The Structure of Scientific Revolutions* (Univ. of Chicago Press, Chicago, 1962); D. J. de Solla Price, *Little Science, Big Science* (Columbia Univ. Press, New York, 1963); and W. W. Rostow, *The Stages of Economic Growth* (Cambridge Univ. Press, Cambridge, 1960). Donald Fleming's "Science in Australia, Canada, and the United States," *Actes du Dixième Congrès International d'Histoire des Sciences* (Hermann, Paris, 1964), vol. 1, sharpened my analysis, but Fleming and I disagree on fundamental points. I thank Dr. Everett Mendelsohn, Harvard University, and Dr. David D. Van Tassel, University of Texas, for advice on matters relating to phase 3 of my model.
3. Donald Fleming [*Actes du Dixième Congrès International d'Histoire des Sciences* (Her-

mann, Paris, 1964)] speaks of the "reconnaissance of natural history" as a part of the Age of Discoveries. See also Robert Boyle's "General heads for a natural history of a countrey, great or small," *Phil. Trans. Roy. Soc. London* 1, 186 (1665); *ibid.* 2, 315 (1666); *ibid.*, p. 330. Boyle has written a guide for the European observer in a foreign land.

4. Sir Francis Bacon, *Collected Works*, B. Montague, Ed. (Hart, Carey & Hart, Philadelphia, 1852), vol. 1, p. 41.

5. G. Fernández de Oviedo, in *Natural History of the West Indies*, S. A. Stoudemire, Ed. (Univ. of North Carolina, Chapel Hill, 1959); A. R. Steele, *Flowers for the King: The Expedition of Ruiz and Pavon and the Flora of Peru* (Duke Univ., Durham, N.C., 1964); V. Wolfgang von Hagen, *South America Called Them* (Knopf, New York, 1945). I thank Susan Lane Shattuck, School of Library Science, University of Texas, for information she provided on botanical expeditions to colonial South America.

6. For the pre-1800 period, see T. Harriot, *A briefe and true report of the new found land of Virginia* (London, 1588) [facsimile edition with introduction by R. G. Adams (Edwards, Ann Arbor, 1931)]; W. Martin Smallwood, *Natural History and the American Mind* (Columbia Univ. Press, New York, 1941); W. Bartram, *Travels Through North & South Carolina, Georgia, East & West Florida*, Mark van Doren, Ed. (Dover, New York, 1928); T. Jefferson, *Notes on the State of Virginia*, T. P. Abernethy, Ed. (Harper, New York, new ed., 1964); E. Berkeley and D. S. Berkeley, *John Clayton: Pioneer of American Botany* (Univ. of North Carolina, Chapel Hill, 1963). For Western exploration in the 19th century, see H. N. Smith, *Southwest Rev.* 21, 97 (1935); W. H. Goetzmann, *Exploration and Empire* (Knopf, New York, 1966); S. W. Geiser, *Naturalists of the Frontier* (Southern Methodist Univ., Dallas, 1948).

7. B. Smith, *European Vision and the South Pacific: 1768–1850* (Oxford Univ. Press, London, 1960); F. W. Oliver, Ed., *Makers of British Botany* (Cambridge Univ. Press, Cambridge, 1913), pp. 108–125; L. Huxley, *Life and Letters of Sir Joseph Dalton Hooker* (Murray, London, 1918), vol. 1, pp. 54–167; A. R. Wallace, *My Life* (Dodd, Mead, New York, 1906), vol. 1, pp. 337–384. For early scientific collecting in other areas of the Pacific, see J. A. James, *The First Scientific Exploration of Russian America* (Northwestern Univ. Press, Evanston, 1942); S. P. Krasheninnikov, *The History of Kamtschatka* (Quadrangle, Chicago, 1962), pp. 57–167; P. Honig and F. Verdoorn, Eds., *Science and Scientists in the Netherland Indies* (Board for the Netherland Indies, New York, 1945), pp. 295–308; *Encyclopedia of the Philippines* (Philippine Education Company, Manila, 1936), vol. 7, pp. 52–107, 476–503.

8. Hideomi Tuge, *Historical Development of Science and Technology in Japan* (Kokusai Bunka Shinkokai, Tokyo, 1961), pp. 35–37, 76–77, 82–84; C. R. Boxer, *Jan Campagnie in Japan, 1600–1850* (Nijhoff, The Hague, 1950), pp. 50–52.

9. A. H. Rowbotham, *Missionary and Mandarin* (Univ. of California, Berkeley, 1942), pp. 271–274; P. M. D'Elia, *Galileo in China*, R. Suter and M. Sciascia, trans. (Harvard Univ. Press, Cambridge, Mass., 1960); E. Bretschneider, *History of European Botanical Discoveries in China* (Russian Academy of Sciences, St. Petersburg, 1898).

10. E. Hawks, *Pioneers of Plant Study* (Sheldon, London, 1928), pp. 151–156; H. J. C. Larwood, *J. Roy. Asiatic Soc.* 1962, 62 (1962); M. Archer, *Natural History Drawings in the India Office Library* (Her Majesty's Stationery Office, London, 1962); L. Huxley, *Life and Letters of Sir Joseph Dalton Hooker* (Murray, London, 1918), vol. 1, pp. 223–365.

11. E. A. Walker, Ed., *Cambridge History of the British Empire*: vol. 8, *South Africa, Rhodesia & the High Commission Territories* (Cambridge Univ. Press, Cambridge, 1963), pp. 905–914.

12. P. D. Curtin, *The Image of Africa* (Univ. of Wisconsin Press, Madison, 1964), pp. 3–27; A. A. Boahen, *Britain, the Sahara, and the Western Sudan: 1788–1861* (Oxford Univ. Press, London, 1964), pp. 1–28.

13. E. L. Schwartz, "The French Expedition to Egypt, 1798–1801: Science of a Military Expedition," senior thesis, Harvard University, 1962. I thank Dr. Thomas deGregori, University of Houston, for his advice on science in Africa.

14. For science in the new German colonies, see *Sci. Amer.* 111, 450 (1914). Proof that natural history studies are important to underdeveloped regions today can be found in J. P. M. Brenan, *Impact Sci. Soc.* 13, 121 (1963); C. F. Powell, in *The Science of Science*, M. Goldsmith and A. Mackay, Eds. (Souvenir, London, 1964), p. 82.

15. T. Sprat, *History of the Royal Society* (London, 1667), p. 86.

16. For the impact of specimens collected abroad upon European science, see W. Coleman, *Georges Cuvier, Zoologist* (Harvard Univ. Press, Cambridge, Mass., 1964), pp. 18–25; B. Smith, *European Vision and the South Pacific: 1768–1850* (Oxford Univ. Press, London, 1960), pp. 5–7, 121–125; W. George, *Biologist Philosopher: A Study of the Life and Writings of Alfred Russell Wallace* (Abelard, New York, 1964), pp. 122–155; L. Eiseley, *Darwin's Century* (Doubleday, New York, 1958), pp. 1–26.

17. See F. A. Stafleu, in *Adanson* (Hunt Botanical Library, Pittsburgh, 1963), vol. 1, p. 179.

18. See B. Smith, *European Vision and the South Pacific: 1768–1850* (Oxford Univ. Press, London, 1960), p. 6.

19. Compare this description of colonial science with the one found in D. Fleming, *Actes du Dixième Congrès International d'Histoire des Sciences* (Hermann, Paris, 1964), vol. 1, pp. 179–196, and in *Cahiers Hist. Mondiale* 8, 666 (1965).

20. As an example, consider the American colonial members of the Royal Society [R. P. Stearns, *Osiris* 8, 73 (1948)].

21. J. H. Elliott, *Imperial Spain: 1469–1716* (Arnold, London, 1963), pp. 291, 338, 362–364, 381; C. R. Boxer, *The Dutch in Brazil* (Oxford Univ. Press, Oxford, 1957), pp. 112–113, 150–155.

22. The importance of informal communication is discussed by D. J. de Solla Price, *Little Science, Big Science* (Columbia Univ. Press, New York, 1963), pp. 62–91, and L. K. Nash, *The Nature of the Natural Sciences* (Little, Brown, Boston, 1963), pp. 299–311.

23. See *Quart. Rev.* 10, 524 (Jan. 1814); I. B. Cohen, *Franklin and Newton* (American Philosophical Society, Philadelphia, 1956).

24. See B. N. Menshutkin, *Russia's Lomonosov*

(Princeton Univ. Press, Princeton, 1952), pp. 23–37; A. Vucinich, *Science in Russian Culture* (Stanford Univ. Press, Stanford, 1963), pp. 105–116.

25. E. C. Agassiz, *Louis Agassiz: His Life and Correspondence* (Houghton Mifflin, Boston, 1885), pp. 435–436.

26. J. H. Van Vleck, *Phys. Today* 17, 22 (1964).

27. L. P. Wheeler, *Josiah Willard Gibbs* (Yale Univ. Press, New Haven, Conn., 1952), pp. 32–45; J. M. Cattell, *Science* 24, 732 (1906).

28. D. E. Smith and J. Ginsburg, *A History of Mathematics in America Before 1900* (Open Court, Chicago, 1934), pp. 111–114.

29. F. Darwin, *More Letters of Charles Darwin* (Appleton, New York, 1903), vol. 1, pp. 383–384.

30. See Hideomi Tuge, *Historical Development of Science and Technology in Japan* (Kokusai Bunka Shinkokai, Tokyo, 1961), pp. 80–81.

31. See Yabuuti Koyosi, *Cahiers Hist. Mondiale* 9, 208 (1965); Shuntaro Ito, *Actes du Dixième Congrès International d'Histoire des Sciences* (Hermann, Paris, 1964), vol. 1, pp. 291–294; Nakayama Shigeru, *Sci. Papers Coll. Gen. Educ. Univ. Tokyo* 11, 163 (1961).

32. Watanabe Minoru, *Cahiers Hist. Mondiale* 9, 254 (1965); Nakamura Takeshi, *ibid.*, p. 294; Masao Watanabe, *Actes du Dixième Congrès International d'Histoire des Sciences* (Hermann, Paris, 1964), vol. 1, pp. 197–208. I call special attention to the work of Eri Yagi (Shizume) on the introduction of modern science into Japan: *Sci. Papers Coll. Gen. Educ. Univ. Tokyo* 9, 163 (1959); *Actes du Dixième Congrès International d'Histoire des Sciences* (Hermann, Paris, 1964), vol. 1, pp. 208–210. She specifically speaks of a colonial period in Japanese science, but limits it to the years 1870–1895, and draws a graph showing the production and education of native physicists in Japan during the period 1860–1960. I thank Dr. Nakayama Shigeru, University of Tokyo, and Dr. William R. Braisted, University of Texas, for their help on developments in Japanese science.

33. See B. Hindle, *The Pursuit of Science in Revolutionary America* (Univ. of North Carolina Press, Chapel Hill, 1956), pp. 380–385.

34. See L. Zea, *The Latin American Mind*, J. H. Abbott and L. Dunham, trans. (Univ. of Oklahoma, Norman, 1963), pp. 100–103.

35. Quoted from H. Bernard, *Yenching J. Social Studies* 3, 220 (1949).

36. For opposition to Western science, see Y. C. Wang, *Chinese Intellectuals and the West: 1872–1949* (Univ. of North Carolina Press, Chapel Hill, 1966), pp. 3–37; G. H. C. Wong, *Isis* 54, 29 (1963). Religious beliefs may act to spur on the acceptance and growth of science. Max Weber and others have attempted to link the initial appearance of modern science with the prevailing Protestant ethic. See R. K. Merton, *Osiris* 4, 359 (1938).

37. L. Agassiz, *A Journey in Brazil* (Houghton Mifflin, Boston, 1884), p. 499. Agassiz's remarks and the illustration of Fig. 4 were first brought together by T. B. Jones, *South America Rediscovered* (Univ. of Minnesota, Minneapolis, 1949), pp. 193–195.

38. A. Mozley, *J. and Proc. Roy. Soc. N. S. Wales* 98, 91 (1965). I thank Mrs. Mozley for information regarding the growth of science in Australia.

39. Y. Salah El-Din Kotb, *Science and Science Education in Egypt* (Columbia Univ. Press, New York, 1951), pp. 80–83.

40. B. Silliman's struggle to establish the *American Journal of Science* serves as a case study of the difficulties involved in the foundation of a new scientific journal [see J. F. Fulton and E. H. Thomson, *Benjamin Silliman, Pathfinder in American Science* (Schuman, New York, 1947), pp. 117–129].

41. For language problems and science in China and Japan, see, respectively, J. Needham, *Science and Civilization in China* (Cambridge Univ. Press, Cambridge, 1954), vol. 1, pp. 4–5, and Eri Yagi (Shizume), *Sci. Papers Coll. Gen. Educ. Univ. Tokyo* 9, 163 (1959). A French edition of the official organ of the Rumanian Academy of Science was published up until the year 1948 [see R. Florescu, *Ann. Sci.* 16, 46 (1960)].

42. D. J. de Solla Price, *Science Since Babylon* (Yale Univ. Press, New Haven, 1961), pp. 45–67; S. A. Bedini, *Early American Scientific Instruments* (Smithsonian Institution, Washington, 1964), pp. 3–13. The Wilkes Expedition (1838–42), America's first venture in government-sponsored maritime exploration, was outfitted with European scientific instruments [see D. E. Borthwick, *Proc. Amer. Phil. Soc.* 109, 159 (1965)].

43. H. T. Bernstein, *Steamboats on the Ganges* (Orient Longmans, Calcutta, 1960).

44. Certain factors affecting the acceptance or rejection of modern science have not been listed here because they are so fundamentally related to the culture within which the struggle for an independent scientific tradition takes place that the participants in the struggle are not in a position to alter them, even if they are aware of their existence. Furthermore, we know very little about these factors. The following are some examples. (i) *Language.* B. L. Whorf [*Language, Thought, and Reality* (M.I.T. Press, Cambridge, 1966), pp. 57–64, 207–219] has argued that a people's view of physical reality is conditioned by the structure of their language. Scientific concepts developed in one culture might be rejected, or misunderstood, in another. According to Whorf, the Hopi language embodies a metaphysics of space and time that is opposed to the classical Newtonian world view. (ii) *Child-rearing patterns.* A Japanese sociologist has suggested that "the introduction of modern science over the last century [has] been especially accelerated because Japanese culture values childhood curiosity and, unlike some other societies, does not attempt to repress it" [*Science* 143, 776 (1964)]. (iii) *Political nature of a society.* A. de Tocqueville [*Democracy in America*, P. Bradley, Ed. (Knopf, New York, new ed., 1948), vol. 2, pp. 35–47] believed that a democratic nation, fostering the individual's pursuit of profit and power, would necessarily excel in technology and applied science, while aristocratic societies would be predisposed to cultivate the theoretical aspects of science.

45. See *Science* 55, 55 (1922).

46. See *In the Matter of J. Robert Oppenheimer: Transcript of Hearing Before Personnel Security Board* (Government Printing Office, Washington, 1954), pp. 464–465. Remarks made by two other scientists on the late emergence of American science may be found in J. H. Van Vleck, *Phys. Today* 17, 21 (1964), and F. Seitz, *Science* 151, 1039 (1966). Many historians claim that American science achieved maturity at an earlier date, sometime in the 19th century. D. Fleming does

not think so [see *Cahiers Hist. Mondiale* **8**, 666 (1965)].

47. For the controversy over "free" and "planned" science in Great Britain, see N. Wood, *Communism and British Intellectuals* (Columbia Univ. Press, New York, 1959), pp. 121–151, 190–193.

48. For recent evaluations of Soviet science, see *Survey: A Journal of Soviet and East European Studies* **1964**, No. 52 (July 1964); J. Turkevich, *Foreign Affairs* **44**, 489 (1966).

49. I. Newton, *The Mathematical Principles of Natural Philosophy*, F. Cajori, Ed. (Univ. of California Press, Berkeley, 1934), p. 398.

50. See R. K. Merton in *The Sociology of Science*, B. Barber and W. Hirsch, Eds. (Free Press, Glencoe, Ill., 1962), pp. 19–22.

51. See *The Personal Papers of Anton Chekhov* (Lear, New York, 1948), p. 29.

2

On Visiting the 'Moving Metropolis': Reflections on the Architecture of Imperial Science

Roy MacLeod

The last decade has seen a growing interest in the role of science in the history of imperial expansion. In England this has mirrored a growing interest in the "imperial relations" of British science. In this country, as earlier in the United States and Canada, historians have begun to describe the ways in which national scientific traditions developed from imperial precedents, often modifying imperial structures in the process. The pioneering work of Ann Moyal and Michael Hoare has opened the field by mapping Australasian activity from the voyages of Banks and Cook to the emergence of an independent Australian scientific identity. Abroad, scholars in Canada and India have explored different models of colonial scientific development that appear within the experience of transplanted Britons. This work has revealed enormous gaps in our knowledge, particularly of those general features of innovation and consolidation that characterized the "heroic age" of "imperial science," whether in India, Africa, Asia, or the settler colonies. At this stage one is prompted to reflect on the nature of "metropolitan" and "peripheral" relations and on the wider architectural principles that gave British science, in its imperial setting, its special and enduring quality. In the experience of Swift's Lemuel Gulliver, prevailing views of court and metropolis assumed an intriguing perspective when seen from a distant point on the periphery; and from Gulliver's island, where that famous castaway found his bearings, familiar notions of the history of science and statecraft invite careful revision.[1]

I have borrowed my title from Professor W. K. Hancock, to whom I owe much.[2] With him, let me immediately deflect criticism for any misuse of the terms *empire* or *imperial, colonial* or *colonialism, capital* or *capitalism.* As Hancock reminds us, *imperialism* is no word for scholars; neither is the word *model,* and both rest especially uncomfortably upon historians of science.[3] This is because Western science has traditionally been regarded as benevolent, apolitical, and value neutral; its extension, a value-free aid to material progress and civilization. Western science, since the seventeenth century, has had, it is argued, little more than a contingent relationship to conquest. Trade follows the flag, and science may improve the prospects of trade, but this imposes no responsibility upon science. The civilizing, improving advantages of new knowledge, in moral and material progress, surely cannot be questioned. If the imperial idea is accepted, if the complex association of commercial, humanitarian, and ideological motives underlying empire is understood, then science has only an incidental function in its articulation.

Closer inspection, however, reveals certain flaws in this reasoning. The creation of a free market based on economic hegemony, the control of the seas, the provision of communication and the protection of transport, and the glorification of progress as a civilizing ideal, all raise questions in which new knowledge has quite specific application. The control of that knowledge became critical. The way that knowledge was controlled, the "metropolitan" forces to which it refers, may have moved and changed, but the bonds forged through science are indissolubly linked to political development. Through science comes a language—conveniently the language of the mother country; through this language, neatly conveying the instrumental rationality of Western knowledge, comes control—in the imperial context, control often without accountability to the people who are governed, and knowledge "marginalized"—directed to the limited purposes of government, in such a way that the great majority of people remain far from enjoying the "relief of man's estate." This condition of life, familiar to science educators and development economists, reveals the contradiction, familiar to all historians of empire, that improved means do not necessarily imply improved ends.

This fact raises a further question: How did the pursuit of natural knowledge become a part of statecraft, both directly as part of policy and indirectly as part of government-aided economic development? To this may be added the question, How did arguments alleged to have been derived from scientific views of the world and its purposiveness come to inform naturalistic models of economic and political development, and arguments for the introduction of techniques that have proved at best economically palliative, but far more often socially and economically divisive? Finally, what happens when imperial relations become so intertwined that the metropolis *depends* upon the periphery for both economic and intellectual resources. Can the Empire strike back?

Once these questions are asked, the central issue becomes no longer science *in* imperial history, but science *as* imperial history. "Imperial science" thus becomes an expression of a will and a purpose, a mission, a vocation, often inarticulate, but enormously powerful. At one point in *Britain's Imperial Century*, Ronald Hyam refers to the conventional wisdom that "England's writ ran no further than the range of her ship's guns."[4] In fact, her writ ran where English institutions survived, and of English imperial institutions, among the most durable and enduring were those of science. I have undertaken to understand this better, as part of what Laurens van der Post has called the "honest reappraisal of the meaning of the vanished British Empire . . . one of the most urgent historical tasks of our time."

In what follows, I want first to consider selected models of imperialism and science, in what they tell us both about the history of science and the outlook of historians, to illustrate some of the difficulties inherent in this form of analysis, to offer a slightly different framework within which old questions may acquire different emphasis, and, finally, to discuss some analytical implications and limitations of this and almost any other general framework that seeks to embrace the range and variety of experience now available to historians of colonial and postcolonial development.

Let me make one further apology for offering frameworks in preference to facts, systems instead of surgical analysis. Actually, there is little alternative. If the history of the British Empire has passed into an Alexandrian age, where criticism has overpowered creation, this has not yet applied to the history of the sciences and their role in the building and binding of empire. This is partly because there is so little agreement about the boundaries of the subject, or about the definition of its terms. Common words commonly acquire new layers of meaning, and the resultant definitions, such as they are, are porous in the extreme. For example, it is important not to confuse "colonial science," with its sense of structures, institutions, precepts and boundaries, with "scientific colonialism," a term that implies a process, even a deliberate policy, with objectives and means to achieve those objectives. To confuse is to conflate an interactive ideology with a particular historical form of its experience. Indeed, scientific—versus unscientific—colonialism may simply mean a version of colonial policy. Similarly, I take "imperial science" to be a set of structures, staff, and legal and corporate institutions, serving many areas of policy and embracing quite different philosophical and political principles at different times, while "scientific imperialism" describes a version of imperialism that flourished in the late nineteenth century and that in large measure reflected the "scientization" of social theory. Finally, there is the "imperialism of Western scientific ideas," a phrase that implies the incarnation of the Baconian program, a proposal to subject everything to the acceptance of scientific and technological development.

In practice imperial science and scientific imperialism are two sides of the same coin, but failure to keep them analytically distinct confuses historians of all persuasions. In the imperfect glossary that I shall use, *metropolitan science* means not just the science of Edinburgh or London, or Paris or Berlin, but a way of *doing* science, based on learned societies, small groups of cultivators, certain conventions of discourse, and certain theoretical priorities set in eighteenth-century Western Europe. The Transit of Venus expeditions were thus "metropolitan," not just because they were launched from London or Paris, but because they implied a set of intellectual structures and questions common to the metropolis.[5] Metropolitan science *was* science.

Colonial science, on the other hand, was, by definition, done at a remove from Europe. It was, to paraphrase Thornton, "imperial science seen from below."[6] It meant different things: to those at home, recognizing their dominion over palm and pine, it meant derivative science, done by lesser minds working on problems set by savants in Europe. It was, looked at from the metropolis, "low science," identified with fact gathering. The work of theoretical synthesis would take place elsewhere. This division of labor fitted epistemologically well with the requirements of natural history and astronomy and conceptually well with a philosophical climate predicated upon inductive discovery.

In the colonies, "colonial science" could mean something else—merely science as practiced in the colonies, for example. This could be intellectually derivative. It could also be "metropolitan," in Hancock's sense, with values confirming the rule of "Britannia in another world," looking to local or international mercantile interests in minerals and wheat, concerned as much with the generation of capital as with colonization. From this usage would grow the concept of imperial science, embodying intellectual and institutional rivalries that reflected political divisions.

Imperial science again took on a different coloration, when regarded from England, or from the periphery. From London, it embodied a "spirit of power and service" in science, expressed organically as a nervous system whose functional cerebrum reposed in Burlington House, the Athenaeum, or eventually in the Oxbridge-London triangle. From the perimeter, however, "imperial science" implied a cooperative spirit, in which the appropriate analogy was not that of a single organism, moving to instruction, but a family, coexisting in a common linguistic ecology, whose existence was necessary to maintain a balance of nature and culture.

In this language, our definitions suffer from historiographical confusion and neglect. The phrase "imperial science," like "imperialism" itself, gained currency in the 1870s and the 1880s as an expression of the wish to strengthen the links between Great Britain and the British Empire, through what Lord Rosebery later called a larger patriotism. Merely an implicit part of the expansion of Europe to Sir John Seeley and Goldwin Smith, science and technology were given a more definite place in imperialism by V. I. Lenin and J. A. Hobson, in describing the successive stages of capitalist development.[7] But when imperialism came to be understood principally as a shorthand for the development overseas of finance or monopoly capital, with the associated expansion and redivision of world markets and the growth of state intervention, militarism, and colonial annexation, the contribution of scientific activity was relegated to the status of a necessary but unproblematic given. Only with later elaborations of Marxist theory—often focused on colonial annexations and the search for markets, on stimuli to industrialization, and on the relations between industrial countries and the third world—has the importance of scientific activity, as instrument and ideology, become prominent again.[8] In this context, the history of science in European imperialism has acquired fresh significance.[9]

To illustrate the variety and assumptions of standard approaches to science and imperialism, let me consider four related models. The first, which I shall for convenience call instrumentalist, is embodied in Carlo Cipolla's *European Culture and Overseas Expansion*. Cipolla's method, in *Guns and Sails*, is to focus on *technique*, to explore the reasons Europeans gained better technology and why these achievements enabled Europe to make conquests overseas. Multiple social, economic, and technical factors are reflected in different periods: an early Age of Innovation is followed in the sixteenth century by an Age of Reconnaissance, when increased use of the compass and decreasing supplies of galley slaves prompted sailing and shipbuilding, which, with commercial impetus provided by new trade routes to the East, provided Europeans—especially the Portuguese and Spanish—with a competitive advantage. Reconnaissance was followed by religion, religion by riches. When Vasco da Gama dropped anchor at Calicut and was asked what the Portuguese were looking for in Asia, he replied: "Christians and Spices." Or, as Cipolla puts it, "Religion supplied the pretext and gold the motive. The technological progress accomplished by Atlantic Europe during the fourteenth and fifteenth centuries provided the means."[10]

The consequences, in Cipolla's terms, are later seen in a phase of maritime expansion overseas, and in the eighteenth century in the support of industrial revolution at home.[11] Cipolla, however, confines himself to technique; this is all important, he says, "while philosophy and social and human relations are degraded to the role of means."[12] Phases of imperial development are determined by the technologies needed to bring them about; the history of empire is also the history of technology.[13]

This instrumental approach has an interesting parallel with the cultural independence model fashionable among historians of

Reflections on the Architecture of Imperial Science 223

American science during the late 1950s and early 1960s. I. Bernard Cohen of Harvard referred in 1959 to the prevailing attitude of inferiority to European science until the Second World War, in a paper revealingly entitled "The New World as a Source of Science for Europe."[14] His model was bimodal: a long period of colonial science, extending "far into the mid-nineteenth century," slowly giving way, following the Civil War, to a view of university and industrial science, which, drawing on European, especially German, experience, eventually produced traditions identifiably American. Cohen was followed, in 1962, by Donald Fleming of Harvard, who drew Australia and Canada into an extended comparison, and subsequently added a third phase—the Flight of the Muses from Hitler during the 1930s.

Both Cohen and Fleming were concerned with two particular problems: the accuracy or inaccuracy of Tocqueville's prophecy that egalitarian countries could never—or could hardly ever—reproduce the "aristocratic," "high science" of metropolitan Europe, and the failure of the American public to patronize cultural activity for its own sake, and the special priority given "practical" science in America and the factors that impelled creative effort toward the fostering of an independent science-based technological tradition, as part of America's urge to national self-assertion. Reflecting their interest in American history, both Fleming and Cohen saw the principal intellectual dilemma of the colonies as one of *enforced* provincialism. This provincialism was highlighted by the emphasis, in the colonies, of the natural history tradition. This tradition was important to Europe for commercial and philosophical reasons, but was adopted willingly by colonists. First, because it served "a fundamental part of the quest for a national identity in societies where the cultural differentiation from Britain was insecure, and the sense of the land correspondingly important for self-awareness." Second, because it "coincided with the primary national purpose of mastering [the] environment and canvassing its economic potentialities."[15]

To both Cohen and Fleming, however, the natural history tradition was a two-edged sword; winning mastery over a new continent, but for whom? In fact, the process proved also to be an instrument of control. Colonial scientists in America were relegated to the status of mere collectors. European savants received their tribute from the ends of the earth and honored by eponymy their colonial servants. This model of "absentee leadership" placed colonists at a disadvantage; the "gatekeepers" in Europe determined the prizes, and the result was "intellectual colonialism," a "psychology of abdication," making over to Europeans "the highest responsibilities in science"—a view that ostensibly overcast American science for a hundred and fifty years.[16] Fleming and Cohen were both concerned with the alleged inferiority of American science and the connection between political and cultural independence. The accuracy of their interpretation, in American terms, has prompted much constructive criticism. Inadvertently, perhaps, Fleming and Cohen exposed a paradox. As Europeans moved abroad, as the Empire grew, cultural dependence was an unavoidable, even necessary consequence. One could maintain a place in metropolitan circles by accepting the role allotted by those circles. Colonists differed in the extent to which they found this role chafing; in America, "classification without recognition" too closely resembled "taxation without representation." Eventually the tables were turned, and colonial science would hold the metropolis in its debt. But within the surviving Empire, both black and white, any metropolitan recognition that this debt existed was long avoided, for reasons that I shall presently explore.

In 1967, these issues of dependency and dominion were subsumed into a diffusionist perspective, when George Basalla turned to the spread of Western science throughout the world. In an influential article in *Science*, Basalla proposed a three-phase model,[17] applying an evolutionary pattern of cultural progression to the diffusion of science. During phase one, what he calls the nonscientific society, be it China, India, or pre-Columbian America, provides, borrowing Cohen's phrase, "the source for European science"—nonscientific, in his terms, meaning non-Western. In this phase of exploration by travelers or diplomats, flora and fauna are described and classified. Observers, all from Europe, settle and report their findings. In this model, the duration of phase one varies from region to region: consider the Spanish and the Portuguese in the Americas in the sixteenth century, the British in America in the seventeenth century, the French and British in India and the Pacific in the eighteenth century; both in Africa in the nineteenth century, and the Germans in the Pacific in the twentieth century. In phase one the scientific interests are those of the mother country, invariably a maritime power. As Thomas Sprat wrote in his *History of the Royal Society*, it was the maritime nations that were "most properly seated, to bring home matter for new sciences, and to make the same proportion of Discoveries . . . in the Intellectual Globe, as they have done in the Material."[18]

In his new philosophy, with commercial interests closely at issue, this matter of science was the stuff of which more than dreams were made. Eventually, this phase, argued Basalla, gave rise to a second phase, which he calls colonial, or dependent, science—not a pejorative phrase, he adds, nor one implying a relation of servility. Colonial science is essentially the same, he continues, whether it be within the Spanish sphere of influence or the British. It is inferior in a technical sense; it is subcritical in size; it lacks unity; colonial scientists cannot share in the "invisible college" of Europe or of twentieth-century America. Its strength lies in producing facts and field-workers. Its speed of development can be accelerated by favorable circumstances, as in America, Canada, and Australia, or retarded by an unfavorable environment, as in Africa and Latin America. Ultimately, says Basalla, when certain conditions are reached, a sense of nationalism pervades the colonial community; national institutions are created, and absolute reliance upon the external scientific culture is ended. This leads to phase three, of "independent science," in which a country's scientists are trained at home, rewarded at home, for work done at home and overseas, and published in national and international journals.

Basalla goes on to describe a set of barriers that must be overcome before phase two can give way to phase three: (1) resistances to science, especially religious or philosophical, must be overcome (China being a notable case); (2) the social status of scientists must be clarified and raised—that is, science must be seen as socially prestigious; (3) state aid to science must be forthcoming; (4) science education must be advanced; (5) scientific organizations must be founded and journals established; and (6) a "proper technological base" should be made available, with adequate scientific instrumentation as vectors of technical skill.

This model presents a program for scientific development familiar to students of bilateral and international aid policies in the 1970s. Basalla is careful to say it is not "necessarily causal," but the program has strong necessitarian overtones. In fact, let us examine its difficulties. Perhaps the greatest of these are:

1. It generalizes all societies, regardless of cultural context, into a single scheme.

2. The scheme is linear and homogeneous, assuming that there is a single Western scientific ideology which is disseminated uniformly. It does not take into account "south-south," or intercolonial movement, or movement between the colonies of one country and other European countries.

3. It aludes to, but does not explain, the political and economic dynamics within a "colony" that make for change and that occupy a shaded area between phases one and two or between two and three.

4. It fails to account for the relations among technological, social, and economic developments and the part played by science in bestowing legitimacy on political forces that may arrest development in other spheres.

5. It does not take into account the cultural dependence that lingers long after formal colonial political ties have been thinned or cut.

6. It does not take into account the wider economic interdependencies that have, since empire, contributed to the plight of the third world, for which science alone scarcely offers consolation.

Indeed, Basalla's model conveys a sense of economic unreality. Regarding with impatience this liberal, ostensibly value-free picture, the Argentine economist Francisco Sagasti rejected its implicit belief in an "invisible hand" guiding the responsible to independence. He sees in cultural imperialism instead a series of phases leading to economic control by Europe, the United States, and the multinationals and producing a marginalization of research effort and the erosion of democratic development.[19] In his "countermodel," there was a colonial, or preindustrial, stage of metropolitan science from the eighteenth century to the early nineteenth century, followed by a stage of Western science from the 1850s to the 1930s, during which dependent economies were manipulated to increase colonial integration through world markets and in which the extension of knowledge, through education, remains dependent on the metropolis. This gave way to a slow progress of independent industrialization, after World War II, by means of the substitution of imports—a process which, since the 1960s, has been overtaken by the concerted economic strategies of Western governments and multinationals, rendering dependent economies vulnerable to wider patterns of international trade. From Sagasti's perspective, one form of dependency, based upon the import of manufactured goods, has merely been replaced by another, more powerful, dependency, based upon the import of capital, machinery, and technical knowledge. Either system denies the illusion of independence. The image of the West diffusing science for the greater glory of the human spirit diminishes, even disappears, when thus closely examined.[20]

Finally, the Basalla model—almost inescapably, given its context—fails to account for the *political* character of science within this process of "intellectual colonization." Even if consideration is limited to the British Empire, at least four questions immediately arise:

1. Why is there no *analysis* of the proposition that knowledge is controlled or manipulated by the mother country? If there is an independence movement, when and how are alternative institutions established, and what extrascientific factors bring them about? What are the agents of change between phases? Is there an indissoluble affinity between political and cultural dependence, or independence, which it may be in the interest of both parties to preserve? In India, science was arguably an instrument of control, to which Indians were denied access.[21] What were the implications of this policy for India in the postcolonial world?

2. What use is made of colonial science, precisely, by the mother country? Possessions, notably India and Ireland, were consciously used as "social laboratories" for metropolitan policies.[22] New information, drawn from the colonies, was used to support European theoretical positions, whether concerning race, the structure of the earth, or the movement of the heavens. Colonial science, forcing open held positions to the incontestable evidence of the senses, may paradoxically hold a vital, not a subordinate position in institutions at home.

3. What features characterized the "scientific colonists"? Basalla's model is too broad to articulate with any precision the particular influences at work upon individuals within *different* settings. To explain imperialism in science as an irradiation of barbarism by civilization can be to offer an explanation so general as to be distorting. At the same time, it can neglect the traditions of different *corps d'élite*—"generalists" and geologists, astronomers and engineers—of which the stuff of history is made. Just as history based exclu-

sively on "explorers" neglects the wider social and political implications of discovery, so history without individuals neglects the importance of anomaly, and makes men mere mannequins in the
fashions of political theory.

4. Finally, what connection, if any, can be found between patterns
of economic and political evolution and patterns of intellectual development in the various sciences? While it would be too sweeping
to suggest that the conceptual content of specific fields was *determined* by the fact of imperial expansion, it would not be unreasonable to explore the dynamic interaction occurring between the two.

So far, this discussion may have provoked the recollection of many
long and contentious debates about the utility of historical models—debates that no historian since Marx or Toynbee has been able
to ignore or resolve. There are many models of imperial development: *sociological models*, dwelling on the relationships of culture
and distinctions between center and periphery; *economic* models,
dealing in labor supply and capital investment; and *diplomatic-
administrative* models, based on international relations, and the
"right to rule." Each poses difficulties which any description of imperial science, or of imperialism in scientific ideas and institutions,
tends to highlight.

Among social historians, the use of models is often confusing and
imprecise. We commonly confuse explanatory models, for example,
with predictive or heuristic models. Historical blades seem at times
too dull for philosophical chopping blocks. Since Collingwood's cor-
rective, and the arid debates of the 1930s on the nature of historical
causation, we have often delegated "cause" to the philosophers, and
have got on with the job. But at the same time, we may have lost
sight of the damage this delegation can do to our own analytical
purposes. In particular, we commonly let our language confuse the
ordinary act of imposing structure upon chronology or events for the
purpose of explanation and interpretation with the more unusual
act of identifying "natural processes" abstracted from particular
contexts or periods. The latter tendency inclines us toward a kind
of naturalistic fallacy, in which social systems are interpreted as reflecting regularities observable in the natural world. There follows
from this a tendency to assume that what is highly valued is natural,
rational, and therefore unproblematic. This is the difficulty with
Basalla's model. In fact, this kind of model seems to acquire a som-

nambulist historicism, which not only can do inadvertent injustice to the density of contextual variation, but also can lend itself to misleading uses.

In this case, and for the purpose of my argument, it is necessary to recast Basalla's pioneering effort, perhaps considering in a different light some of the important evidence he assembled. Of course, creating new categories is no virtue in itself. But any improved model should reflect, rather than remove, the importance of controversy and conflict and should allow for the possibility that stages of underdevelopment are not necessarily transitional or intermediate, awaiting some eventual, revolutionary call to independence.

It is obviously impossible to reduce easily into a simple scheme the diversity of the experience that reflected different versions of imperial development in different parts of different European empires. It is all the more difficult to superimpose upon the history of empire this history of the natural sciences and of technologies that served different functions at different times and that underwent quite distinct patterns of development. Nonetheless, some attempt at a wider synthesis may be helpful, if only to focus criticism and to encourage the cultivation of counterexamples.

Accordingly, I would like to offer an impressionistic taxonomy to describe some characteristics of the main phases of British imperial science between c.1780 and 1939 and to outline in passing some of the structural relations which, whether necessary or contingent, appear to have strengthened the connection between political, economic, and technical developments. Examples will be selected principally from the experience of Australia, although comparisons with other parts of the British Empire may well be relevant and worth pursuing. In this speculative blueprint there are five phases or "passages" (see table 1).

Phase One: Metropolitan Science

The first period, extending from 1780 until the mid 1820s, might be described as the Banksian era or, just as well, the Laplacian or Cuvierian era. In this period the selection of problems, the ordering of nature, was dictated from the Royal Society—or the Académie des Sciences.[23] This policy continued the European tradition of discov-

Table 1. *Passages in British Imperial Science*

Aspect of scientific practice	Metropolitan	Colonial	Federative	Efficient imperial	Empire or commonwealth
Institutional ethos	Explorative; Banksian; internationalist; systematist; centrist; individualist	Envelopment by metropolis; degagement by periphery; autochthonous societies; individual research; scientific services	Cooperative, imperial research; university development and professional legitimation; extended scientific services	Expert, official, public; codified science; specialization of disciplines; expansion of tertiary education;	Metropolitan trusteeship; coordinated fundamental research; delegated research responsibility from London
Social and political characteristics	Monarchist; centripedal	Colonial ascendancy; intercolonial rivalry; responsible government	Intercolonial and interimperial association	Optimistic liberalism; defensive imperialism; application of scientific methods to government	Imperial unity; self-determination
Economic and technological functions	Expansion of maritime trade; discovery of raw materials and new markets	Primary products; pioneer, adaptive technology; local markets	Improved technology (communications, agriculture); extended participation in world markets	Management of land, resources, industry; early government regulation of means of mode of production	State encouragement of applied science; early growth of secondary industry

ery and explanation, in part with the hope of completing a world view determined by Europeans: geographically, to settle for all time questions concerning the shape and texture of the earth; botanically and zoologically, to confirm systematic views of the continuity, linearity, and continuous gradation of species; astronomically, to complete the Newtonian world picture—to "fix the frame of the world." Thus, the Transit of Venus expedition of 1769 was to determine the "astronomical unit," the "celestial meter stick." During this period there was a clearly internationalist ethos in science, given force by instructions from the admiralty against interfering. So, too, were there indignant protests against the confinement of Matthew Flinders in Mauritius by the French.[24]

With the spirit of common endeavor came a vigorous sense of cultural competition. Even amid the stresses of war, France and England had enjoyed an almost uninterrupted flow of scientific and philosophical influences. After Waterloo military rivalries were replaced by commercial and scientific competition. If fears of French invasion had died, the specter of French domination in cultural and material progress remained. Anxiety and caution, suffused with national pride, resounded through the pages of the "heavy quarterlies" and informed the reform movements in English science and education. This invocation of domestic motives in imperial maneuvers became a standard practice, neglected by historians of science today at their peril. To an earlier French historian of empire Britain was explicable only as a country in which "l'esprit commercial s'allie curieusement à l'esprit de découverte . . . et les appétits du sport."[25]

After 1780, the end of Britain's first empire and the consolidation of her second did not interrupt this process of cultural expansion. Economically, the metropolis at first exported little and invested little. But by the late eighteenth century Britain was seeking new sources of raw materials and the development of new markets. Politically and commercially, activity was directed from London through chartered companies in Hudson's Bay, India, and the East Indies and through plans to explore the commercial utility of newly discovered products. In all this activity strategic considerations were never far distant. As Geoffrey Blainey points out, the Royal Navy surveyed the possibility of cultivating flax for sails and pines for masts on Norfolk Island well before permanent settlements were envisaged. No astute observer could ignore the importance of exploration to the prestige of learned societies of London and Edinburgh. New reports of discoveries created new intellectual capital and strengthened the sterling of English science.

Phase Two: Colonial Science

After the loss of the American colonies, the greatest imperial investments, in science as in capital, were in India. But, around the 1830s, metropolitan science, consolidating its position in Calcutta and Bombay, began to move beyond India. During this period, and for about thirty-five years, is seen the first permanent extension of the metropolis, at once enlarging and ensuring the domain of what became known as colonial science. Cosmopolitanism among metropolitan peers was an indulgence to be enjoyed from a position of strength. Hence the pressure to occupy greater intellectual space, from Herschel's explicit efforts to annex the Southern Skies from his observatory at the Cape of Good Hope to Sir Thomas Brisbane's zeal for astronomy in New South Wales; so, too, Sir Edward Sabine's proposed ring of magnetic stations from Bangalore to Baffin Bay.[26]

So, also, the importance of Kew—botanical specimens, cinchona, rubber—all sought for wider imperial purposes of political and economic expansion.[27] So, finally, the need for fresh voyages of discovery. The search for the Northwest passage, long a fascination of maritime nations, became by the 1830s important to the security of Britain's trade routes.[28] Hydrographic surveys and the voyages of HMS *Beagle* and HMS *Rattlesnake* drew their impulse from this simple fact of geopolitics. The navy's surveyors and surgeons, and often its regular officers as well, were, as before, the handmaidens of science.

Where there was trade, there was the navy, and where the navy sailed, or the army rested, the natural sciences benefited.[29] But so did the newer, more specialist and metropolitan scientific societies, which, in Banks's memorable phrase, threatened to dismantle the Royal Society, not leaving "the old lady a rag to cover her."[30] Against this fragmenting pressure of new knowledge, the imperial epicenters of metropolitan science fought to buttress themselves. In 1833, Vernon Harcourt used the same imperialist metaphor at the British Association, when he warned of the dangers of specialization, as colony after colony separated itself from the declining Empire of the Royal Society.[31] The politics of science were embedded in the politics of the wider Empire. If, by degrees, the commonwealth of science was under threat in the colonies there was also danger of imperial fragmentation, with local interests becoming paramount. Many of these interests were vital to Britain—from the minerals and forests of Canada to India and Ceylon and their markets for textiles and teas, from the plantation products of the West Indies to the agriculture and livestock of Australia and New Zealand.

In the event, traditional British institutions, pressed at home by economic recession and demands for constitutional reform, adapted to these portending breezes of change by assuming a wider vision of empire and creating a new conceptual framework for colonial science. To London, this represented a convenient "political envelopment"; in the colonies, among transplanted Britons, the same impulse produced a mythology of devolved responsibility, even a division of labor, which seemed equitable enough.

In this conceptual structure there were two principal, and sometimes contradictory, tenets, both reflected in Fleming's account of colonial American science. First, there was an emphasis on practical versus theoretical knowledge. Thus, Kathleen Fitzpatrick comments on Sir John Franklin's innovations in Tasmania:

Bushlife demands the virtues of action—initiative, hardihood, quickness in decision and improvisation. The most blessed word in the colonial vocabulary is 'practical' as the need for the virtues appropriate to pioneering conditions passes away, the tradition is tenacious. A contemptuous tolerance is the best that the scholar, the artist and the pure research scientist can . . . hope for.[32]

This emphasis was accompanied by a spirit of deference to the metropolis, a spirit that reinforced the colonial mentality decried by imperial historians today. This fact-gathering, derivative mentality was not, one would think, a source of pride. But, pace Fleming, it glorified the character of colonial science. From the Asiatic Society of Bengal to the Philosophical Society of Australasia, colonial scientists saw their task as one of ascertaining "the natural state, capabilities, productions and resources of [theirs] and the adjacent regions . . . for the purpose of publishing from time to time such information as may be likely to benefit the world at large."[33] Thus, information arising from P. D. King's maritime geography was processed by John Grey at the British Museum.[34] In the colonies, the fact of intellectual dependence underscored the practical realities of frontier life. As the *Sydney Morning Herald* editorialized in 1830, "Zoology, Mineralogy, Astronomy and Botany are all very good things, but we have no great opinion on an infantile people being taxed to support them. An infant colony cannot afford to become scientific for the benefit of mankind."[35]

Unavoidably, these two colonial characteristics—the practical and the deferential—obscured deeper currents. In fact, in North America, India, and Australasia, colonial science could be highly theoretical and highly dispositive, especially in the Humboldtian sciences of natural history, geology, astronomy, and meteorology. Exploration in Africa and the tropics revealed features that bore directly on central debates and important reputations in geology and zoology. Michael Adanson, visiting Senegal during the 1750s, recalled that "botany seems to change face entirely as soon as one leaves our temperate countries."[36] Australia, especially, caught the metropolis off guard. Sir James Smith agreed that "When a botanist first enters . . . so remote a country as New Holland, he finds himself . . . in a new world. He can scarcely meet with any fixed points from whence to draw his analogies."[37] As John Oxley wrote in 1821, referring to continental theorists, "Nature has led us through a mazy dance of intellectual speculation, only to laugh at us . . . on this fifth continent."[38] More than providing mere exceptions to European systematics, Australia was the "land of contrarieties," a strange place, wrote Barron Field, "where the laws of Nature seem reversed: her zoology can only be studied and unravelled on the spot, and that too only by a profound philosopher."[39] In botany, Robert Lawrence, collecting for W. J. Hooker, found evidence for external proofs of the new "natural system" of Jussieu, which was ultimately to question the system of Linnaeus. In astronomy, as Sir Thomas Brisbane recognized, the skies were no limit. "Avec un ciel vierge," he wrote the Colonial Office, "what may not be achieved."[40]

It was perhaps inevitable that, as the metropolis moved, the same controversies would march in step. The same beliefs in the wisdom of God read through the Book of Nature; the same debates between idealists and associationists, and the same zeal to find evidence confirming, rather than disputing, the received view of creation.[41]

Reflections on the Architecture of Imperial Science   235

That all these would migrate to the colonies, transmitting a "carrier conservatism" in the knapsacks of the fossicking frontiersman, is not surprising. But to dismiss colonial scientists as blinkered conservatives misses a wider reality. In this connection, three separate questions arise: whether the Empire was important to metropolitan science; whether colonial scientists appreciated their importance; and if so, whether they did anything about it. How did the center actually deal with the new insights available only from the periphery?

By the 1820s, there was already wide recognition of the central role that colonial science would play in metropolitan debates. Robert Knox, the Edinburgh anatomist, admitted to Sir Thomas Brisbane that Australian specimens revealed "the most wonderful deviations from the usual types of forms which nature employed in the formulation of the animal kingdom."[42] Certainly, in the tradition of Cuvierian comparative morphology, these "deviations" from a "European standard" were of first importance. In the organization of English science, they bore directly upon the prestige of that handful of men whose fortunes rested upon the tenets of catastrophism, Neptunism, and *Naturphilosophie*.

But the threat was swiftly contained. This rush to maintain metropolitan primacy is reflected spectacularly in the expedition of Matthew Friend, who arrived in Sydney in April 1830 bearing a combined commission to find correspondents for the Royal Society, the Zoological Society, the Geological Society, the Medico-Botanical Society, and the British Museum (Natural History). As he rather patronizingly told John Henderson's remarkable Scientific Society in Van Diemen's land:

Your country is still a land of mystery, supposed to abound with anomalies, which, if verified and ably described, would tend much to illustrate many of the most abstruse and important questions in the history of organic life. The transition forms—the animals intermediate betwixt different orders where the diagnostic marks are mixed with each other, are of the utmost consequence in physiology.[43]

The colonists, he advised, had a duty to collect placental organs and crania and ship them home, where there were "greater experience [and] more numerous and better fitted appliances." The mother country and they, he added, would "divide the honours" between them.

The political implications of this were lost neither on the colonists—though their protests were muted—nor on London, where the power brokers of metropolitan science rushed to assimilate the new revelations from Australian discoveries, just as the Royal Society had done for the American colonies and India a century before. These were very numerous in the middle decades of the nineteenth century; indeed, they accounted for about two thirds of the articles in the *Annual Magazine of Natural History* in the 1850s and 1860s. This process of manipulation, and its implications, are easy to trace. As William Hooker was to botany and George Airy to astronomy, so Richard Owen (at the Royal College of Surgeons, 1826, and the British Museum [Natural History], 1856–84) was to zoology and morphology. Owen had succeeded Banks as the Czar of English natural history in the colonies. During the 1840s, as we know from Ann Moyal's pioneering work, he moved particularly quickly, in Banksian manner, to seize the results of new discoveries, particularly associated with marsupials, recognized as the key exception to most governing principles in the "great chain of being."[44]

Owen, following the idealist tradition in Cuvier and Oken, had fashioned a theory of a unitary archetype, to which all animal creation approximated and from which all animal creation may have drawn, in the mind of the Creator, its governing plan. The existence of this archetype was supported by interpretations of analogy of function and homology of structure that connected all sections of the animal kingdom with each other, but which required continuous and separate creations. The archetype required consistent interpretations, which required a confident grasp of periods and processes of creation and an ability to overlook, or dismiss as uncertain, discordant evidence. But fossil deviances, and the analysis of organ and reproductive structure among living animals of Australia, threatened this position. In 1827, Peter Cunningham returned from two years in New South Wales to announce that "The dissimilarity of the animal and vegetable diluvial remains [in Australia] to what we see in a state of living existence, proves that all the products of the earth were quite different to what they are now."[45] And when, in 1829, the Wellington Cave Fossils were taken as evidence of Huttonian principles, soon to be elevated to a broader position of uniformitarianism by Lyell's *Geology* in 1830–33, it was clear that new and unbeatable forces were massing against him. Normally, new ideas do not gain ground by the logic of their advocates but by the death of their opponents. In this instance it was different. From the 1830s Owen was forced into a slow, bitter retreat before the advancing forces of scientific naturalism. His defeat, anticipated in 1884 by William Caldwell's discovery of the oviparous nature of the platypus, was a crisis in a drama that touched every corner of Britain's cultural empire.

From the 1840s to the 1870s, this spirit had been anticipated by a steady flowering of colonial scientific enterprise, celebrated in the expansion of learned societies and museums and in scientific surveys from India to British North America.[46] The colonial scientific movement was not without its martyrs. Thus, Edmund Kennedy, the young surveyor of the York Penninsula, fell to Aboriginal arrows in 1846, "a sacrifice," as recorded in St. James's, Sydney, "to the cause of science, the advancement of the colony and the interests of humanity." John Gilbert, the ornithologist, and a casualty of the Leichhardt expedition, was similarly commemorated in marble above Sydney's leading congregation, with the revealing Horatian paraphrase: *Dulce et decorum est pro scientia mori.* Coinciding with anti-imperialist sentiment in England and with the policies associated with Aberdeen, Russell, and Derby and interrupted only by Palmerston, this "colonial ascendancy" in science was not resisted by London through the 1860s, especially since the administrative importance of colonial science for imperial rule could not be denied. As Sir William Denison told Admiral Beaufort in 1849, an astronomer in a colony was a guarantee that a certain amount of science was there at the disposal of the government.[47]

Eventually, this spirit suffused the new universities at Sydney, Melbourne, and Cape Town and kept alive, under difficult circumstances, learned societies from New South Wales, Victoria, and New Zealand to the Cape Colony, Ontario, and India. Still, however, the twin principles of intellectual deference and practical service operated to sustain dependence upon the metropolis.

Phase Three: Federation

In 1875, in order to study the tropical diseases, Patrick Manson had, typically, to return to England to "drink at the fountain of science."[48] But these artesian sources were not to be confined to England indefinitely. By the early 1880s, accompanying the arrival of new political factors in the government of metropolitan science, a "federative" language begins to replace the language of colonialism in science. In 1884, Seeley's *Expansion of England* led to a belief in the merits of encouraging a "greater Britain" in cultural and political affairs. In part, this was accompanied by the victory of T. H. Huxley and his allies, many of them reflecting sympathies and experience in the colonies.[49] In London, new men were succeeding to the czardom of English science. In natural history, the "Winter Palace" moved its court from Kew, the Linnaean Society, and the Natural History Museum to Cambridge, Rothampstead, and the Imperial Institute; in astronomy, Greenwich shared influence with the Solar Physics Observatory at South Kensington. Facing increasing competition from Germany and the United States, arguments for containing "by federation" the skills of Britons overseas needed little justification. Thus, the British Association, the "Parliament of Science," met in Montreal in 1884, in the first steps toward what would become a virtual beating of the bounds of Empire, reminding the colonies of their status in respect to the Mother of Parliaments.[50] In 1885, Huxley, as president of the Royal Society, urged all colonial learned societies to "associate" with each other, through the Royal. This federative strategy was not immediately successful, but it established a clear precedent. It is with the late 1880s, moreover, that imperial science also became an explicit political program, accompanying Disraeli's vision of empire and the opportunism of Chamberlain's Unionists.[51] As always, there was Ireland, and Home Rule contributed to both the division of the Liberal Party and the political separation of scientific friends along imperial lines.[52] In many ways, just beginning to be explored, federation arose as a solution to such fissiparous tendencies that seemed both neutral and attainable. All shades of political interest could be united, with economic science and public sentiment sustained by "scientific" social Darwinism and given force by voluntary interimperial cooperation.[53]

Regarded from scientific London, federation was a policy of promoting Britain as primus inter pares. Within the Royal Society, as in government, a species of institutional condescension ran in counterpoint to expressed desires for cooperation. From India to Canada, the passing of "colonial science" saw the reinforcement of "imperial science," in the reassertion of imperial interests in geology, botany, meteorology, astronomy, agriculture, and forestry, all now staffed by a new army of "scientific soldiers."[54] As the tribulations of Manson and Ross in India revealed, "constructive imperialism" was a policy of containment. The font of honors remained securely unchallenged in Burlington House and in Whitehall.

But the prospect of federation was seen differently at the periphery. It was local pride that prompted the government astronomer, H. C. Russell, F.R.S., to tell the Royal Society of New South Wales in 1888 that "there were many objects for investigation which men coming from the civilised world took the honour and credit of studying what might otherwise belong to the colony."[55] To support that contention, the same year saw the creation of the Australasian Association of the Advancement of Science. Michael Hoare argues that the establishment of this daughter association (ANZAAS, of today) was the first concrete step toward political federation. Indeed, Sir James Hector told the association as much in 1891.[56] Certainly, the movement to federate local societies on a colonial level—and colonial societies on an imperial level—provided a tantalizing precedent. In fact, by federation the colonies strengthened their intellectual position and their loyalty to British science in the same stroke. The *Sydney Morning Herald* in August 1888 welcomed the first meeting of the Australasian Association for the Advancement of Science, in Huxleyan metaphor, as presaging a new imperial scientific army marching together under the Southern Cross. But make no mistake, England had accommodated, assimilated, and kept control. The Southern Cross was still quartered by the Union Jack.

Phase Four: "Efficient" Imperialism

By the turn of the century, the institutions of imperial science, in common with most British institutions, were badly shaken by the Boer War. In the aftermath, the directorates of Kew, South Kensington, Bloomsbury, and Burlington House found allies in Liberal Imperialism and Conservative Unionism. The Empire was an important trust and resource. Its efficient administration was central to the idea of national efficiency. Under Churchill at the Colonial Office, that quarter of the globe covered red would, as W. S. Blunt put it, be kept "in part by concession, in part by force, and in part by the constant intervention of new scientific forces to deal with the growing difficulties of imperial rule."[57]

If imperial unity was the desired end, scientific unity was the one universally acceptable means. In Britain, the equinoctial symbol of efficiency was found in the British Science Guild (BSG), founded in 1905 by Sir Norman Lockyer, editor of *Nature*. The BSG welded the ambitions of science and the purposes of politics, through the rational use of scientific method.[58] The universal applicability of scientific method to domestic politics, reasoned both the Fabians and the BSG, had equally universalist application to the Empire. Men of science agreed, as William Ramsay put it, "The best way of fitting your men for the manifold requirements of Empire is to give them the power of advancing knowledge."[59] The exaltation of scientific method served to bring fresh attention to the prevention of epidemic disease, whether plague in Sydney or cholera in India. As Chamberlain said at a luncheon to raise funds for a proposed school for tropical hygiene in 1898,

The man who shall successfully grapple with this foe of humanity and find the cure for malaria, for the fevers desolating our colonies and dependencies in many tropical countries, and shall make the tropics liveable for white men . . . will do more for the world, more for the British Empire, than the man who adds a new province to the wide Dominions of the Queen.[60]

From this to the spirit that sanctioned the Imperial Universities Conference in 1903 was a short step. The encouragement of the universities would in practice buttress empire. Indeed, if Lord Rosebery had had his way, the University of London would have become the center of that empire. At the same time, the enshrinement of science in the universities of the Empire would make the world safe for English liberal values. Science would also, it was alleged, in time improve the management of agriculture in India, Africa, and the West Indies and the success of manufacturing industry in India and the Crown Colonies. Indeed, scientific method would, it was argued, unite empire in unity of truth, of tradition, and of leadership, from Curzon's India and Lorne's Canada to Smuts's South Africa. In its identification of the rule of law with scientific method, this policy was pleasingly nonpartisan. Science was the balm of Gilead; so the British Association preached when it visited Pretoria and Johannesburg in 1905 to heal the wounds of war. Imperial science was the route to a wider patriotism that transcended party, national, and even imperial politics.

This implicit political meaning of imperial science was voiced in 1907, when Alfred Deakin, then Prime Minister of Australia, told the BSG and the British Empire League that the most urgent task of empire was "the scientific conquest of its physical, and shall we not be bold to say, ultimately its political problems."[61] Deakin, in 1910, welcomed the prospect of a British Association meeting in Australia, which came to pass in 1914, as securing the country in the "brotherhood of nations . . . visibly and before the eyes of the world [bringing] us into notice as a portion of Europe . . . united by intellectual ties as well as those of patriotism and blood . . . an added step towards Imperial unity . . . and one likely to be of great value to the Commonwealth."[62]

Until the First World War, imperial bonds between Britain, India, and the white settler colonies stressed this image of imperial unity. For Lord Milner and Lord Amery, imperial communication and research were the twin keys to imperial development. In this development, Britain was intended to retain leadership. As Tom Mboya remarked, "Efficiency is the last refuge of the imperialist."[63] Wider social programs involving holistic, preventive models, or the improvement of living standards, as proposed by Ronald Ross for West Africa, were not easily accepted, or even understood, by the Colonial Office. Throughout the Empire, at least until 1914, the application of technical knowledge was principally limited to the purposes of government. The direction of science for metropolitan self-interest continued well into the new century. The idea of a neat division of labor—cultivating mines and forests in the colonies and theoretical physics in the metropolis—was threatened from the day Ernest Rutherford won a scholarship to Cambridge. But it sustained a spirit of cooperation in the market of scientific ideas within the Empire, transacted by the scientific "city," with the colonies providing more and more of the merchant capital. As we know, this proved to be of decisive benefit to Britain in 1914 and beyond.

Phase Five: Empire and Commonwealth

Efficiency might be considered ironical, given the waste of the Great War. In the event, the fellow suffering of the war saw the mechanistic language of efficiency give way before the organic language of coordination. A new phase emerged in imperial science, one in which London was regarded as the "honorary secretary" of a voluntary association, the "home" of the imperial "family." *Deference* was, if anything, now defined as *loyalty*. The Empire paid embassy to Britain in science and confirmed, after all was said, the idea of imperial unity that Banks had assumed as natural and inevitable a century earlier. As A. G. Butler, writing of the Australian wartime medical effort, put it, the organization of science witnessed the same "uncertainties, compromise, cooperation without compulsion, the union that is organic rather than formal, which characterises the relation between the various parts of the Empire."[64] In fact, imperial cooperation in science provided an exemplary model for allied and imperial cooperation in other directions. In the process, debts were imposed on all sides. Arguably, British recognition of Indian independence began not with 1947, but with the first meeting in Calcutta of the Indian Science Congress in 1914.

In this coordinative phase, continuing from the First World War until well after the Second, intellectual leadership in British science was increasingly shared with the dominions. Indeed, in many fields—such as agriculture, entomology, and nutrition—the leadership of British science was in fact no longer in Britain. In the postwar decades, models of the British Department of Scientific and Industrial Research (DSIR), transmitted throughout the Empire, contained the residual seeds of centralism.[65] But the architecture of "imperial science" altered to incorporate a timely sense of cooperation, especially in economic policy. As *Nature* put it, in 1924, at the time of the Empire Exhibition, there was "a by no means imaginary connection between the spirit of science and the political ideals of Empire."[66]

During the interwar years, the spirit of science was redefined to suit these political ideals. In the circumstances of the 1920s, that meant cooperation, not metropolitanism. This was exemplified particularly well in the new pattern of scientific cooperation between Australia, New Zealand, and Canada and was preached widely throughout East Asia and South Africa. Imperial self-sufficiency through science was the goal of which the Imperial Bureaux, the Empire Marketing Board, the Colonial Research Committee, and the Imperial Economic Conferences were the collective symbols.[67]

As a political strategy, it had difficulties. But the scientific model survived.[68] By 1930–31, following the Ottawa conference, coordination gave way to a species of delegation in which metropolitan scientific research was conceived as an aid to local economic development and self-determination, particularly in Africa, Malaya, and the West Indies. One consequence was the slow but steady encouragement of "indigenous" scientific activity, often, as it transpired, as a prelude to political independence. That dependence was, of course, to prove illusory, as the old Empire began, with the aging metropolis, to suffer the new imperialism of the superpowers, the international agencies, and the multinational corporations. The passages of imperial science reached an end, perhaps sometime in the 1950s, and a beginning, as a new set of dependencies replaced the old, with Britain no longer at the center. In a psychological sense, "dependency" would remain a characteristic of science as practiced in the Empire for many years. But in many ways, by then the spirit of innovation, long resident at the metropolis, had moved to the periphery, and the fixed certainties of power and competition were replaced by fresh tests of partnership and commonwealth.

Conclusion

In this essay I have not proposed to examine the complex effects of empire on the development of individual disciplines; this is too large a universe for a single exploration. I have suggested, however, that certain mentalities do operate in the relations of science and empire, which may affect the conduct of those disciplines, if at one remove. Indeed, if it is possible at all to distill a generalized conception of science and empire, it is certain that this must be as much concerned with political as with technical issues. I use the word *political* in two senses. First, the changing connotations of what I have described as metropolitan science, colonial science, and imperial science reflect and mediate the changing perceptions of vested interests, both in Britain and in the colonies. By observation, it is clear that imperial science, looked at from the center, was an integral part of the changing policies of colonial development, that problems chosen as important were determined by the interests of the imperial power, and that the practice of science in the Empire was itself influenced by changing ideologies of empire. Changing patterns of trade, incentives to development, all had direct effects on scientific activity, and that activity was more and more to shape the direction of policy well outside the laboratory and the learned society. At the periphery, the particular relations distinguishable between science and politics in any country—contrast the differences, for example, between the elite, mock-metropolitan institutions of Canada, torn between America and Britain with the more egalitarian, isolated scientific societies of Australasia—do vary, as did the corresponding histories of scientific development and political leadership. There are also obvious differences in the requirements of official science in various places, and thus in the overall complexion of imperial science in the political configuration of the settler colonies, India, the "occupied" empire of Africa and the West Indies, and the informal empire of Latin America. Of course, the *precise* political dimension of science in any particular context remains to be revealed by national comparisons. But it is clear that in its most general political usage, science became a convenient metaphor for empire itself—or, more exactly, for what the Empire might become. The ethos, methods, and organizational strategies of science were all used by imperial spokesmen in the discussion of federation, of coordination, and of cooperation. The British Association, the universities, and the machinery of economic policy gradually replaced the metropolitan learned societies in fostering the sense of an imperial mission, but the universal appeal of this mission was never a phantom. We have only to recall the eagerness of colonial governments and societies to copy and preserve metropolitan models and the testimony of those hosts of imperial and colonial botanists, surveyors, astronomers, zoologists, and geologists who, in serving science and empire, helped expose the problems and opportunities that political independence would bring.

"Science and empire" is also a political expression in cultural terms. Unquestionably, there were vital issues of cultural and economic domination involved in the pursuit of natural knowledge. What *is* striking is that so few colonials were aware of the influence they enjoyed over the center. That famous telegram sent in 1884 by William Caldwell from the Burnet River to Archibald Liversidge, relayed to the British Association in Montreal: "Monotremes oviparous, ovum meroblastic," signaled the beginning of a revolution against the czardom of Owen. It was to the scientific world as a signal from the battleship *Aurora*, giving fresh support to the anti-Owenite sentiment gathering in Cambridge and South Kensington. It remains to us to discover more instances in which the institutions and leadership of Britain were *dependent* upon colonial discovery and enterprise. Ironically, ex-colonials—American, Australian, Canadian, and perhaps South African—may have been looking at the metropolis upside down and cosseting unnecessarily defensive and deferential attitudes toward the diffusion of metropolitan science.[69]

Finally, I have suggested that a dynamic conception of imperial science gives a fresh outlook to the study of imperial history. There is no static or linear extrapolation of ideas; there are multiple autochthonous developments that have reverberating effects. I have suggested, following Hancock, that the idea of a fixed metropolis, radiating light from a single point source, is inadequate. There is instead a moving metropolis—a *function* of empire, selecting, cultivating intellectual and economic frontiers. In retrospect, it was the peculiar genius of the British Empire to assimilate ideas from the periphery, to stimulate loyalty within the imperial community without sacrificing either its leadership or its following.

This flexible formulation of imperial science may also afford a new perspective on the study of underdevelopment in the postcolonial world. V. G. Kiernan once remarked upon the tendency today to ascribe to British rule a far less forceful effect, for good or ill, than used to be supposed by friends and foes alike. When the history of imperial science is written, it may well demonstrate how pervasive, yet how unobtrusive, that influence could be.

This essay, previously published in *Historical Records of Australian Science* 5, no. 3 (1982), was given originally as a lecture, delivered, in different versions, at the Australian National University in August 1980 and at the University of Melbourne in May 1981. The author is grateful to the Research School of Social Sciences of the Australian National University, Canberra, for generous support of the work from which it is derived. For helpful comments he is particularly grateful to Oliver MacDonagh, Rod Home, Lloyd Evans, Pat Moran, and Ann Moyal.

Since this essay was published, a number of studies have appeared which bear on the subject of "imperial science," particularly within Australian and Canadian contexts. These are to be found in the *Historical Records of Australian Science* and in the proceedings of the Kingston (Ontario) Conferences. Qualifications and applications of the interpretation advanced in this essay form the basis of two major studies currently underway in Sydney.

1. According to Swift, Gulliver was driven to shore at 32° 2'S, northwest of Van Diemen's Land—a position that might have placed him on the Sydney side of the Murray River.

2. Keith Hancock, "The Moving Metropolis," in *The New World Looks at History*, ed. A. R. Lewis and T. F. McGann (Austin: University of Texas Press, 1963), pp. 135–41.

3. For a discussion of historical models in imperial history see J. M. S. Careless, "Frontiers, Metropolitanism, and Canadian History," *Canadian Historical Review* 35 (1954): 1–21.

4. Ronald Hyam, *Britain's Imperial Century, 1815–1914: A Study of Empire and Expansion* (London: Batsford, 1976), p. 23.

5. Harry Woolf, *The Transits of Venus: A Study of Eighteenth Century Science* (Princeton: Princeton University Press, 1959).

6. A. P. Thornton, *The Imperial Idea and Its Enemies: A Study of British Power* (London: Macmillan, 1959).

7. See J. A. Hobson, *Imperialism: A Study* (London: Nisbet, 1902); and V. I. Lenin, *Imperialism, the Highest Stage of Capitalism* (Moscow: Foreign Language Publishing House, 1974).

8. Standard accounts, which vary widely in their treatment of science and technology, include M. Barratt-Brown, *After Imperialism* (London: Heinemann, 1963); A. P. Thornton, *Doctrines of Imperialism* (London: John Wiley, 1965); R. Owen and B. Sutcliffe, eds., *Studies in the Theory of Imperialism* (London: Longman, 1972); P. D. Curtin, *Imperialism* (London: Macmillan, 1972); see also Peter Worsley, *The Third World* (London: Weidenfeld & Nicholson, 1968).

9. Cf. Anis Alam, "Imperialism and Science," *Race and Class* 19, no. 3 (1978): 1–13; Deepak Kumar, "Patterns of Colonial Science in India," *Indian Journal of History of Science* 15 (May 1980), pp. 104–13; and "Racial Discrimination and Science in Nineteenth-Century India," *Indian Economic and Social History Review* 19 (1982): 63–82.

10. Carlo Cipolla, *European Culture and Overseas Expansion* (Harmondsworth: Penguin Books, 1970), part 1, "Guns and Sails," p. 100.

11. See Eric Hobsbawm, *Industry and Empire* (London: Weidenfeld & Nicholson, 1968).

12. Cipolla, *European Culture*, p. 108.

13. J. Allen, "The Technology of Colonial Expansion," *Industrial Archaeology* 4 (1967): 111–37; François Crouzet, "Trade and Empire: The British Experience from the Establishment of Free Trade until the First World War," in *Great Britain and Her World, 1750–1914: Essays in Honour of W. O. Henderson*, ed. Barrie M. Ratcliffe (Manchester: Manchester University Press, 1975).

14. I. B. Cohen, "The New World as a Source of Science for Europe," *Actes du IXe Congrès International d'Histoire des Sciences*, Madrid, 1–7 September 1959, pp. 96–130; cf. R. P. Stearns, *Science in the British Colonies of America* (Urbana: University of Illinois Press, 1970).

15. Donald Fleming, "Science in Australia, Canada, and the United States: Some Comparative Remarks," *Proceedings of the 10th International Congress of the History of Science* 18 (1962): 180–96; and "Emigré Physicists and the Biological Revolution," *Perspectives in American History* 2 (1968): 152–89.

Reflections on the Architecture of Imperial Science 247

16. Cohen, "New World as a Source"; Fleming, "Science in Australia," p. 181.

17. George Basalla, "The Spread of Western Science," *Science* 156 (5 May 1967): 611–22.

18. Thomas Sprat, *History of the Royal Society of London* (London, 1667), p. 86.

19. F. Sagasti and M. Guerno, *El desarrollo científico y technológico en America Latina* (Buenos Aires: Instituto para la Integración de America Latina, 1974).

20. Cf. T. W. Keeble, *Commercial Relations between British Overseas Territories and South America, 1806–1914* (London: Athlone, 1970).

21. R. MacLeod and R. Dionne, "Science and Policy in British India, 1858–1914: Perspectives on a Persisting Belief," *Proceedings of the Sixth European Conference on Modern South Asian Studies*, Colloques Internationaux du CNRS, Asie du Sud: Traditions et Changements (Paris: CNRS, 1979).

22. W. L. Burn, "Free Trade in Land: An Aspect of the Irish Question;" *Transactions of the Royal Historical Society*, 4th ser., 31 (1949): 61–74.

23. The most recent life of Banks is by Charles Lyte, *Sir Joseph Banks: Eighteenth Century Explorer, Botanist, and Entrepreneur* (London: David & Charles, 1981).

24. Cf. Hunter Dupree, "Nationalism and Science: Sir Joseph Banks and the Wars with France," in *A Festschrift for Frederick B. Artz*, ed. D. H. Pinckney and Theodore Ropp, (Durham, N.C.: Duke University Press, 1964).

25. F. de Langle, *La Tragique Expedition de la Pérouse et de Langle* (Paris: Hachette, 1954), p. 16; cf. C. W. MacFarlane and L. A. Triebel, eds., *French Explorers in Tasmania and the Southern Seas* (Sydney: Australasian Publishing Company, 1937).

26. David S. Evans and others, *Herschel at the Cape: Diaries and Correspondence of Sir John Herschel, 1834–1838* (Austin: University of Texas Press, 1969). European astronomy had, of course, a well-established political pedigree. Matthew Turner, radical lecturer in physics, compared the discovery of Uranus by Herschel's father in 1781 to an intellectual conquest. "It is true we had lost the *terra firma* of the thirteen colonies in America, but we ought to be satisfied with having gained in return by the generalship of Dr. Herschel a *terra incognita* of much greater extent *in nubibus*"; J. T. Rutt, ed., *The Theological and Miscellaneous Works of Joseph Priestley* (London, 1817), pp. i, 76.

27. Lucile Brockway, *Science and Colonial Expansion: The Role of the Royal Botanic Gardens* (New York and London: Academic Press, 1980).

28. Louis Becke and Walter Jeffrey, *The Naval Pioneers of Australia* (London: John Murray, 1899).

29. See G. F. Lamb, *Franklin: Happy Voyager* (London: Ernest Benn, 1956), chaps. 3 and 4.

30. Quoted in Hector Charles Cameron, *Sir Joseph Banks* (London: Batchworth Press, 1952).

31. William Vernon Harcourt, Objects and Plans of the Association, *Report of the First and Second Meetings of the British Association for the Advancement of Science, held at Cambridge in 1831, and at Oxford in 1832* (London: John Murray 1833), p. 28.

32. Kathleen Fitzpatrick, *Sir John Franklin in Tasmania, 1837–1843* (Melbourne: Melbourne University Press, 1849), p. 51.

33. *Minutes of the Philosophical Society of Australasia*, 4 July 1821.

34. On P. D. King, see Michael Hoare, "Science and Scientific Associations in Eastern Australia, 1820–1890" (Ph.D. dissertation, Australian National University, 1974), p. 27 and passim. I am indebted to Hoare's work for several Australian examples used in this essay.

35. Quoted in Ann Mozley Moyal, "Sir Richard Owen and His Influence in Australian Zoological and Palaeontological Science," *Australian Academy of Science* 3 (November 1975): 41–56.

36. F. A. Stafleu, in *Adanson: The Bicentennial of Michel Adanson's "Fawiller des Plantes,"* ed. George H. M. Lawrence (Pittsburgh: Hunt Botanical Library, 1963), vol. 1, p. 179, quoted in Basalla, "Spread of Western Science," p. 613.

37. B. Smith, *European Vision and the South Pacific, 1768–1850* (London: Oxford University Press, 1960), p. 6.

38. J. Oxley, quoted in Hoare, "Science and Scientific Associations," p. 8.

39. B. Field, *Geographical Memoirs* (London, 1825), p. viii.

40. Brisbane to Bruce, 28 March 1822, *Brisbane Papers*, National Library of Australia; see also Sir Thomas Brisbane, *Reminiscences of General Sir Thomas Mac-Dougall Brisbane* (Edinburgh: Constable, 1860).

41. Cf. Moyal, "Sir Richard Owen."

42. Quoted in Hoare, "Science and Scientific Associations," p. 37.

43. Matthew Friend, quoted ibid., pp. 72–73.

44. Moyal, "Sir Richard Owen," pp. 45f.

45. Peter Cunningham, *Two Years in New South Wales*, 4 vols (London, 1827), quoted in Hoare, "Science and Scientific Associations," p. 50.

46. Cf. Ronald Strahan, *Rare and Curious Species: An Illustrated History of the Australian Museum, 1827–1929* (Sydney: The Australian Museum, 1979); S. C. Ghosh, "The Utilitarianism of Dalhousie and the Material Improvement of India," *Modern Asian Studies* 12 (1978): 97–110.

47. Sir W. T. Denison, *Varieties of Vice-Regal Life*, 2 vols. (London, 1870), p. 107; see also Stephen G. Foster, *Colonial Improver: Edward Deas Thomson, 1800–1879* (Melbourne: Melbourne University Press, 1978); and Frederick M. Johnston, *Knights and Theodolites: A Saga of Surveyors* (Sydney; Edwards and Shaw, 1962).

48. Quoted in M. Worboys, "The Emergence of Tropical Medicine," in *Perspectives on the Emergence of Scientific Disciplines*, ed. G. Lemaine and others (The Hague: Mouton, 1976), p. 81.

49. In this context, the Royal Gardens at Kew, the India Office and the Colonial Office deserve reappraisal; see Brockway, *Science and Colonial Expansion*. For the intellectual circle of Huxley and Booker, see R. MacLeod, "The X-Club; A Scientific Network in Late-Victorian England," *Notes and Records of the Royal Society* 24 (1970); 305–22.

50. Cf. R. MacLeod, "On the Advancement of Science," in *The Parliament of Science: Essays in Honour of the British Association for the Advancement of Science*, ed. R. MacLeod and P. Collins (London: Science Reviews, 1981).

51. Cf. M. Worboys, "Science and Colonial Imperialism in the Development of the Colonial Empire, 1895–1940" (D. Phil. dissertation, University of Sussex, 1979); V. de Vecchi, "Science and Government in Nineteenth Century Canada" (Ph.D. dissertation, University of Toronto, 1978).

52. On the conflict between John Tyndall, Huxley, and others in the X-Club, see A. S. Eve and C. H. Creasey, *The Life and Work of John Tyndall* (London: Macmillan, 1945).

53. B. Semmel, *Imperialism and Social Reform* (London: George Allen & Unwin, 1960).

54. Cf. R. MacLeod, "Scientific Advice for British India: Imperial Perceptions and Administrative Goals, 1898–1923," *Modern Asian Studies* 9 (1974); 343–84.

55. H. C. Russell, F.R.S., Government Astronomer, *Minutes of the Australasian*

Association for the Advancement of Science, 12 April 1888, MSS 988/1, Mitchell Library, Sydney.

56. Sir James Hector, F.R.S., Presidential Address, Australasian Association for the Advancement of Science, Christchurch, 1891.

57. Winfred Scawen Blunt, *My Diaries* (1909), vol. 2, pp. 287–95, quoted in Ronald Hyem, *Elgin and Churchill at the Colonial Office, 1905–1908: The Watershed of the Empire-Commonwealth* (London: Macmillan, 1968), p. 506. During the 1890s, departments of botany and agriculture were created in the West Indies and in the British possessions of Africa; for the development of the colonial scientific service, see G. B. Masefield, *A History of the Colonial Agricultural Service* (Oxford: Oxford University Press, 1972), and C. J. Jeffries, *The Colonial Empire and Its Civil Service* (Cambridge: Cambridge University Press, 1938).

58. For the British Science Guild, see W. H. G. Armytage, *Sir Richard Gregory: His Life and Work* (London: Macmillan, 1957), chaps. 6–11.

59. Sir William Ramsay, *Essays, Biographical and Chemical* (London: Constable, 1908), p. 239.

60. Quoted in R. V. Kubicek, *The Administration of Imperialism* (Durham, N.C.: Duke University Press, 1972), p. 143.

61. Report of speech by Alfred Deakin, "Science and Empire," *Nature* 76 (9 May 1907): 37.

62. Federal Parliament, *Hansard* 55 (1910): 1266–67.

63. Quoted in Robin Winks, "On Decolonization and Informal Empire," *American Historical Review* 81 (1976): 540; cf. G. Jones, *The Role of Science and Technology in Developing Countries* (Oxford: Oxford University Press, 1971).

64. See A. G. Butler, *The Australian Army Medical Service in the War of 1914–18* (Canberra: Australian War Memorial, 1943) vol. 1, p. vii.

65. R. MacLeod and K. Andrews, "The Origins of the DSIR: Reflections on Ideas and Men," *Public Administration* 48 (1970): 23–48.

66. C. W. Hume, "The British Empire Exhibition," *Nature* 113 (1924): 863.

67. G. Currie and J. Graham, "Growth of Scientific Research in Australia: The Council for Scientific and Industrial Research and the Empire Marketing Board," *Records of the Australian Academy of Science* 1 (November 1968): 25–35.

68. R. MacLeod and K. Andrews, "The Committee of Civil Research: Scientific Advice for Economic Development, 1925–1930," *Minerva* 7 (1969): 680–705; A. G. Church, *East Africa: A New Dominion* (London: Wetherby, 1927).

69. For alternative models, see Careless, "Frontiers, Metropolitanism, and Canadian History."

3
Viajes, comisiones y expediciones científicas españolas a ultramar durante el siglo XVIII

Francisco de Solano

El siglo XVIII ha sido definido con muchas calificaciones, todas ellas correctas y atinadas: se le ha denominado la centuria del estilo neoclásico, el tiempo de la revolución burguesa, la época del Despotismo Ilustrado. Le viene bien, además, el de siglo de las expediciones científicas, por ser el propiciador de numerosos viajes, comisiones y expediciones científicas al ultramar español. En efecto, durante el Setecientos se efectuó un crecido número de ellos, impulsados por diversos objetivos e intencionalidades. Y sostenidos todos ellos por los esfuerzos de un Estado convencido de que la más completa definición que se hiciese de su imperio le llegaba de la mejor investigación científica.

Sin embargo, este esfuerzo de promoción científica no fue ni exclusivo, ni original del siglo XVIII. América suponía una permanente tarea de investigación científica para el Estado y los españoles desde su descubrimiento, y el afán por ampliar los conocimientos geográficos y culturales, unido a directrices geopolíticas y socioeconómicas, así como por motivaciones coyunturales, fueron empresas continuadas en América durante los cuatrocientos años coloniales. Pero, nadie puede arrebatarle al siglo XVIII su papel programador y de ser el fomentador de numerosos viajes científicos, abarcadores de varias ciencias: complemento de la preocupación que por ellas se tenía en España y en Europa.

No obstante este interés expedicionario tuvo una vigencia temporal bastante corta: se mantuvo vitalmente muy creador durante medio siglo largo, devaluándose bruscamente a partir de 1820 y la independencia de Hispanoamérica. Y apenas reverdecido en un par de ocasiones del siglo XIX. Aquel esplendor y este rápido silencio han sido los culpables del escaso conocimiento que se tiene de los viajes científicos, apenas sabido alguno de ellos por el tesón erudito de algún especialista. Esta situación de desamparo ha empezado a corregirse con motivo de las coyunturas favorables de haberse desarrollado recientemente una preocupacion por el papel de las ciencias y de los científicos en América, en donde tienen los viajes tan clave relieve. La oportunidad del bicentenario de la muerte de Carlos III, en cuyo reinado se procedieron gran número de expediciones, ha hecho multiplicar —muy justificadamente— los homenajes en los que la Ciencia ocupa un lugar de avanzada.

El número de estos viajes científicos alcanza a unos sesenta,[1] la mayor parte de ellos

---

[1] *Sesenta y tres cuantifica Angel Guirao en «Clasificación de las expediciones españolas a América durante el siglo XVIII, según su finalidad y disciplina científica», en* La Real Expedición Botánica a Nueva España, 1781/1803, *Real Jardín Botánico, CSIC, 1987, pp. 17-24.*

147

tuvieron un desarrollo muy meritorio, alcanzando sus objetivos. Fueron promovidos todos ellos por razones políticas, sostenidos en programas de potenciación socioeconómica para zonas subdesarrolladas o semidespobladas. Pero lo político multiplicó la urgencia del Estado en solucionar viejos problemas tenidos por insolubles en otros tiempos —corrección y delimitación de zonas de soberanía española y los territorios de otras potencias, definición de los conocimientos hidrográficos y náuticos de las rutas marítimas, etc.— a los que se suma el empeño triple de cartografiar América con mapas y planos lo más científicamente fiables, y de llegar al mejor conocimiento botánico y geológico, lo mismo que hidrográfico en Hispanoamérica e Hispanoasia.

Estos empeños se llevan a cabo por un crecido número de viajes científicos (expediciones, comisiones, misiones), en un tiempo muy corto y sobre un área geográfica muy amplia: casi como una *conquista* científica, remedando (o imitando) la rapidez de la conquista española por Iberoamérica durante el siglo XVI y su extraordinario y único proceso de fundación de núcleos urbanos. Pero esta destacada actividad científica está muy desigualmente conocida: una neblina de imprecisión rodea a estos viajes, ignorándose, incluso, su número exacto, lo mismo que el de los expedicionarios que tomaron parte en ellos. Para unos, las expediciones son más de sesenta, mientras para otros no llegan a treinta las que alcanzan este carácter, siendo apenas viajes científicos los restantes.[2]

Tipología de los viajes

1. *Por su forma*

Esta imprecisión en el número de las expediciones dieciochescas tiene su nacimiento en la propia definición de los viajes. Se acostumbra a denominar expedición a cualquier viaje, desarrollando con ello un indudable exceso de generosidad. Entiendo que expedición científica debe contar, para serlo, con un importante número de especialistas y con destacados materiales (instrumental, enseres, barcos, ayudantes, etc.), dejando a los restantes viajes —que cuentan con escaso o mínimo personal y medios— el carácter de *misión* o de *comisión científica*.

Esto en modo alguno supone rebajar el alcance científico de estas misiones y comisiones, pero sí coloca en su exacto lugar a los esfuerzos e intencionalidades estatales y de algunos promotores particulares (Consulado de La Habana, Compañía de Filipinas, etc.). La financiación de un par de científicos, y sus criados, a algún lugar de América o del Pacífico, así como la preparación de sus empeños, resulta menos dificultosa y costosa que los de una expedición, en la que entran bastantes (a veces muchos) científicos, artistas, personal colaborador que se dirigen a regiones diferentes, implicando varias administraciones coloniales. La expedición tiene un jefe, con precisas instrucciones para alcanzar el objetivo político considerado de alto interés y que con la ayuda

[2] Francisco de Solano, «Expediciones científicas a América durante el siglo XVIII», en Expedición Malaspina, 1789/1794. Viaje a América y Oceanía de las corbetas «Descubierta» y «Atrevida», *Madrid, Ministerio de Cultura, pp. XXXII-XLII, 1984.*

148

de los científicos conseguirá lograrse aquel fin deseado. Aquellos objetivos son, obviamente, de elevada política: lo que justifica los numerosos medios puestos al alcance de los expertos. Expediciones son, por este concepto, escasas: las que definen límites (con Portugal, por la anchísima frontera de Brasil con Venezuela, Nueva Granada, el virreinato del Perú y el Río de la Plata; en el noroeste de Nueva España, etc.), las que dibujan hidrográficamente las costas de las Antillas, de Malvinas y Patagonia, de Magallanes y Chiloé; algunas botánicas (a Nueva Granada, a Perú, a Nueva España y sus ramificaciones, ya viajes científicos a América Central y Cuba). Por su lado, las misiones y comisiones son encargos de importantes trabajos científicos desarrollados por un equipo mínimo de personal —a veces una sola persona—.

Los objetivos, los resultados y los empeños también son diferentes en estos viajes. Todos ellos pueden medirse por su propia estatura: los alcances de las misiones y comisiones llevan como temática de su propósito una investigación concreta, a veces de una única ciencia; las expediciones, por el contrario, contienen una variada gama de intencionalidades y están compuestas por un personal multidisciplinario.

Pero estos viajes menores (comisiones, misiones) científicos son acometidos durante todo el tiempo colonial, no siendo monopolio del siglo XVIII, sino característico de todas las centurias. Francisco Hernández, toledano de Puebla de Montalbán, médico de Felipe II, puede presentarse como el prototipo del viajero con misión específica, de gran relieve durante el siglo XVI y paradigma durante todo el tiempo restante. El carmelita Antonio Vázquez de Espinosa ofrecería el puesto del papel que alcanza la iniciativa privada, aunque asimismo contara con cierta protección oficial a través del Regio Patronato, y ejemplo del siglo XVII. Su obra *Compendio y descripción de las Indias Occidentales* es una historia urbana y regional de la Hispanoamérica de 1620, fruto de investigación directa. También existen, obviamente, viajeros de estos tenores durante el siglo XVIII. Me atrevo a incluir en este apartado a Cuéllar (1785), Parra (1790), a los hermanos Heuland (1795) —viajeros a Filipinas, Cuba y Chile, respectivamente—, lo mismo que incluir en este riquísimo apartado a muchos que, ganados por el desarrollo de la curiosidad científica, se interesan por la astronomía, la historia natural, física, historia antigua, también matemáticas, que se llegan a regiones americanas describiéndolas después con variado resultado: como Antonio de Ulloa y su viaje a México, descrito en su *Relación de Nueva España* [3] y Pedro Alonso O'Crowley y su *Idea del Reino de la Nueva España* (1774), pero también los extranjeros, como los franceses Charles Plumier (1646/1704), Louis Feuillée (1660/1732), Amédée Frezier (1682/1773), Fréderic Moreau de Saint-Mary (1746), el inglés William Betagh (1728), etc. Todos ellos eclipsados por la personalidad y la riqueza documental ofrecida por Alejandro de Humboldt y por Aimé Bonpland. Y todos ellos, viajeros científicos, no corporeizados en expediciones.

Estos y otros viajeros —comerciantes, diplomáticos, espías, políticos, etc.— publican sus impresiones, produciendo una rica literatura, exponente asimismo de una importante faceta, aprovechada por la Ilustración para el mejor conocimiento de los pue-

---

[3] *Publicada por Francisco de Solano en su obra* Antonio de Ulloa y la Nueva España, *México, UNAM, 1979, pp. 1-119.*

149

blos. Conocida es la afición de la Ilustración por el libro de viajes, porque cada viaje es una experiencia para el lector, pues le aproxima a las costumbres y a la particularidad de otros pueblos. Cúmulo de utilidades, al libro de viajes se le define como un «diccionario razonado que pone en orden un conjunto de conocimientos teóricos y geográficos».[4] Jean Pierre Duviols ha estudiado a los viajeros franceses a las colonias españolas y portuguesas[5] contabilizando 140 libros de viajes que cataloga, según los objetivos de los mismos, en descubridores y colonizadores, en contrabandistas, espías, filibusteros y negreros, concluyendo con la literatura producida por los viajeros científicos y políticos. El apartado más rico es el dedicado a los contrabandistas: lo que da cierto tono a los autores, que vertieron en libros las experiencias de sus ilegalidades. Veintiocho de esos autores ocupan el siglo XVIII. Entre ellos algunos son técnicos o formaron parte de misiones pseudocientíficas que entran en Hispanoamérica con los permisos oportunos del Consejo de Indias, pero que en realidad ocultan verdaderas misiones de auténtico espionaje: así los viajes de Bauchene-Gouin y los ingenieros de marina Delabat y Duplessis, de 1699/1702: justo cuando en España se procedía al cambio dinástico, que investigan el cabo de Hornos y las Malvinas. Pero también es contabilizado en este apartado de las misiones de espionaje el viaje realizado por Amédée François Frezier, que publica en 1716 su *Relation du voyage de la Mer du Sud aux côtes du Chili et de Perou*, obra dedicada al duque de Orleans, el Regente de Francia.

Lo importante de estas observaciones es que viajes tan arteramente parciales han sido catalogados por algunos como expediciones científicas, encuadrados como acciones bilaterales hispanofrancesas, cuando sólo fueron viajeros enviados por sus gobiernos con el fin de obtener dolosamente informaciones geográficas, comerciales o de otra índole.

El mismo Duviols cataloga los viajes y viajeros científicos franceses a Hispanoamérica. En el apartado de su obra, correspondiente al siglo XVIII, aparecen Charles Plumier (1646/1704), Louis Feuillée (1660/1732), Courte de la Blanchardière (1745), Nicolás Louis de la Caille (1763), Philibert de Commerson (1727/1773), Pierre Marie de Pagès (1776) y muchos otros que se aventuran aisladamente por América para verificar en ella sus investigaciones científicas. Junto a estos viajeros solitarios se hallan los científicos que componen las expediciones bilaterales hispanofrancesas: Charles Marie de la Condamine (1735), Pierre Bouger (1747), Louis Godin (1747), Jean Chappe d'Auteroche (1772). Y, por último, dentro de esta clasificación, Duviols incluye al botánico Nicolás Thiery de Menonville, que publicó en París en 1787 un *Traité de la culture du nopal et de l'éducation de la cochenille dans les colonies françaises de l'Amérique*. Precedía a este estudio una descripción de su viaje por Oaxaca en donde, simplemente, procedió a un espionaje industrial, conociendo la forma mexicana de elaboración de la púrpura y de la plantación del añil para intentar, más tarde, la adaptación del nopal y del xiquilite en las islas antillanas de Francia. Antonio de Ulloa, que estaba en Veracruz en 1777, comunicaba al virrey Antonio de Bucareli la presencia de este sabio y de sus trabajos: porque, obviamente, para la entrada de cualquier extranjero, y más

[4] *Michèle Duchet*, Antropología e historia en el Siglo de las Luces, *Siglo XXI Editores, p. 61, México, 1971.*

[5] Voyageurs français en Amérique (Colonies espagnoles et portuguaises), *París, 1978.*

150

para hacer experimentos en Hispanoamérica, se requerían los correspondientes permisos o visados del Consejo de Indias.

El botánico Mr. Thiery desea que le conceda vuestra merced el permiso de pasar a esa ciudad [México] por término de un mes, para el reconocimiento de plantas nuevas. No le he reconocido otra ocupación, ni cuidado, desde que está aquí que correr los campos con incansable tesón para buscar plantas. Y en este corto distrito Veracruz ha numerado más de cuarenta, de que faltaba conocimiento en los catálogos. La *xalapa* es muy común aquí y monstruosa de grande: la tiene por mejor de la que se saca de Xalapa, a causa del terreno y del temperamento. Se pueden cargar navíos de ella.

Y no se excusa a que le acompañe algún aplicado del país para que se instruya y pueda seguir, después, a los descubrimientos en esta facultad. Todo esto digo a vuestra merced por desvanecer cualquier escrúpulo que pueda haber de su venida con otro fin.[6]

El virrey de Nueva España no participaba tan confiadamente en los razonamientos de su paisano Ulloa:

Me habla vuestra merced del extranjero botánico, y yo desconfío siempre de esta especie de gentes, que vienen siempre con ideas torcidas. Las leyes y órdenes resisten su admisión y es menester mucho examen de la persona, porque hay incógnitos mandados, aseguran.[7]

Estas advertencias de Bucareli hacen ser precavido y pesquisidor a Ulloa, y su juicio después de vigilancia y conversaciones con Thiery lo refleja en otra carta al virrey:

El botánico, hasta aquí, no se le ha visto hacer otra cosa que correr el campo, sin reserva del sol y cargarse de hierbas, que le cuesta mucha dificultad disecarlas por causa del temperamento. No es entrometido, ni se le oye tratar de otro asunto que el de las plantas. Lo interior, no podemos juzgar.

Bien considerado estar prohibido por leyes la introducción de extranjeros y muy encargado por reales órdenes, y así se lo he dado a entender desde que se me presentó, trayéndome recomendación de La Habana para atenderlo. Y es cuanto puedo decir a vuestra merced de él: como que su ánimo era pasar herborizando hasta México y restituirse inmediatamente, para volverse en el correo inmediato o en la primera embarcación que saliese.[8]

Las reservas de Bucareli le dieron la razón. Las investigaciones de Thiery de Menonville en Oaxaca permitieron que saliera de México con la cochinilla suficiente para adaptarla en nopales en las colonias francesas. Y con la materia colorante obtenida de estos insectos hemípteros se tiñó de púrpura un vestido de Napoleón, entonces cónsul.[9]

2. *Por sus ámbitos*

Uno de los modos de adentrarse en la atmósfera científica del siglo XVIII es verificar aproximaciones clasificatorias para hacer más comprensible el fenómeno científico y político del siglo XVIII, capaz de generar —y haber generado— tanta expedición y tanto

---

[6] *Carta de Ulloa al virrey Bucareli, Veracruz, 16 de abril de 1777. En «Correspondencia privada entre Antonio María Bucareli, virrey de la Nueva España, y Antonio de Ulloa de la Torre-Guiral, jefe de la Flota de Indias, 1776/1779», en Francisco de Solano,* Antonio de Ulloa y la Nueva España, *UNAM, México, 1979, p. 259.*

[7] *Carta de Bucareli a Ulloa, México, 23 de abril, 1777. En* ídem, ibídem, *p. 260.*

[8] *Carta de Ulloa a Bucareli, Veracruz, 30 de abril, 1777. En* ídem, ibídem, *p. 266.*

[9] Ídem, ibídem, *p. 259.*

151

viaje científicos. Y obteniendo entre todos ellos muy elevados resultados. No obstante, no todos los viajes fueron provechosos, porque cuando podían haberse potenciado sus resultados, los movimientos de independencia coartaron sus aplicaciones. Esta falta de aprovechamiento en bastantes aspectos, se une a los silencios que cayeron sobre muchos viajes, dispersándose esfuerzos e importantes hallazgos y añadiéndose el que, en ocasiones, los científicos padecieran injustamente el abandono, el olvido o el desdén por su trabajo, la falta de reconocimiento y de comprensión por sus afanes. Estos lados negativos y deplorables apagan el brillo de una centuria brillante que se había empeñado en administrar y colonizar el ultramar español apoyándose en soportes científicos.

Los ámbitos abarcados por los viajes científicos quedan definidos por sus propósitos y las necesidades que los impulsaron: algunos de ellos tocan aspectos que alcanzan varias científicas y a una multivariada intencionalidad política; otros, son casi monográficos. En general la expedición es una empresa sostenido con subvención pública para llevar a cabo investigaciones científicas que pueden ser de valioso (o imprescindible) apoyo a diversos propósitos:

— desde reclamaciones territoriales a repoblación de áreas despobladas: en dónde hay que marcar la situación astronómica de la zona y fijarla cartográficamente (expediciones de límites);

— hasta la búsqueda de materiales botánicos, zoológicos y mineralógicos y empresas mineras e hidrográficas; así como de apertura o consolidación de rutas náuticas (expediciones botánicas, hidrográficas, mineralógicas).

Las misiones y comisiones, por su lado, son más monográficas: bastantes veces son viajes desgajados de las expediciones —por ejemplo, los viajes de José Longinos Martínez y José Mariano Mociño a Guatemala (1794) y de Martin de Sessé a Cuba (1797) dentro de la Real Expedición Botánica a Nueva España (1787/1803)—. Pero todas estas empresas son inventos del siglo XVIII y suponen, en conjunto y en su realización, así como aisladamente, un formidable empeño promotor que resulta insólito que exista tan pobre conocimiento de él.[10]

Lo verdaderamente destacable es señalar que el fenómeno de los viajes y expediciones científicas se realiza en un momento histórico breve: de 1735 a 1810; repetido sesenta años más tarde en un par de ocasiones. Y que a la vez, se está produciendo coyunturalmente un profundo cambio ideológico y político en España y su mundo. Estas exploraciones se hacen a la vez que se cuida geopolíticamente al mundo colonial y se atiende, en los mismos enunciados, a España: en donde se procede a la definición geográfica e hidrográfica de la península y se continúa con la misma preocupación por el mundo de las comunicaciones. Porque cuanto mejor cuidados estuvieran los caminos

---

[10] *Es muy desigual la bibliografía que estudia estos viajes: para unos, es muy crecida (expedición hispanofrancesa para la medición del meridiano del ecuador, al reino de Quito, por ejemplo) siendo muy escasa para los restantes. Tampoco son numerosos los estudios en conjunto. La oportunidad de celebrar algunas efemérides históricas de estos viajes ha permitido que el reconocimiento hacia ellos salga de los límites académicos en que se hallaban constreñidos: Exposición Malaspina 1789/1794 (Madrid, 1984), Exposición 250 aniversario de la medición del arco del meridiano y la forma de la tierra, 1736 (Madrid, 1986); Exposición sobre la Real expedición botánica a Nueva España, 1787/1803 (Madrid, 1987); Astronomía y cartografía de los siglos XVIII y XIX (Madrid, 1987).*

152

—trazados idóneos, firmes consolidados, curvas peraltadas, puentes, etc.— más rápidamente se agilizarían el comercio y la noticia, y mejor se procedería a la administración y la defensa.

La repoblación de ciertas áreas fue una constante en la política ilustrada: comenzando por España (Sierra Morena) y ampliando la preocupación a Florida y Luisiana, norte del virreinato de México, Antillas, Río de la Plata, Patagonia, etc. que tiene en el caso hispanoamericano, además, el cariz político de la defensa de las fronteras. Las áreas fronterizas con territorios limítrofes con los dominios de Portugal, Gran Bretaña y Francia, a la expedición científica que fue enviada para situar límites y asegurar soberanías, siguió la fundación de núcleos urbanos que promocionaran tanto tierras baldías como fijación de espacios hispánicos.[11]

El ámbito científico de los viajes y expediciones es muy variado. Son monográficos la mayor parte —medición de un meridiano, fijación de una frontera, etc— pero resultan multidisciplinarios por añadirse a la expedición algún científico especialista de otra disciplina, o miembros de ella abarcan trabajos de diversa índole. En 1754, por ejemplo, se incorpora a la expedición dirigida por Iturriaga, que tiene como objetivo la definición de la frontera norte entre los dominios españoles y portugueses —por Venezuela y Brasil—, el botánico sueco Peter Loëfling, que permanece dos años en el sur de Venezuela, realizando una destacada labor de clasificación botánica y zoológica. Pero la presencia de este sabio no matiza como botánica a la expedición, ni puede contabilizarse como viajero solitario a aquel alumno de Linneo.

Pero existen, asimismo, expediciones en donde el objetivo principal no es el meramente político, sino búsqueda de materiales botánicos, mineralógicos, zoológicos, cristalográficos y arqueológicos. Conforman un importante grupo dentro de los viajes científicos (Ruiz y Pavón al virreinato del Perú, 1777/1787; Mutis al Nuevo Reino de Granada, 1783/1810; Sessé y Mociño al virreinato de la Nueva España, 1787/1803) que se unen a los viajes de descubrimiento y afianzamiento de nuevas derrotas náuticas, como alternativa de rutas marítimas comerciales ultramarinas: resaltando el papel del océano Pacífico, proyectando una comunicación directa entre Cádiz y Filipinas, a través del cabo de Buena Esperanza (viajes de Cassens y Lángara, 1765/1767 y 1772/1774; Guinal, 1769; Bonaechea, 1772; Sarabia, 1774) y no dependiente únicamente de la intercomunicación filipina con México a través de la nao de Acapulco.[12]

3. *Por el destino de los viajes*

El viaje científico es programado de acuerdo a urgencias o necesidades geopolíticas o económicas. El destino de las expediciones está, obviamente, allá donde hiciere falta asegurar soberanías, fortalecer rutas marítimas, consolidar fronteras lo mismo que perfeccionar la cartografía o medir las profundidades del paisaje submarino de las costas

[11] *Francisco de Solano, «Ville et geoestrategie espagnole en Amérique au cours du XVIII' siècle», en* L'Amérique Espagnole à l'epoque des Lumières, *CNRS, pp. 31-44, París, 1987.*

[12] *Salvador Bernabeu, «Ciencia ilustrada y nuevas rutas: las expediciones de Juan de Lángara al Pacífico (1765-1773)» en* Revista de Indias, *n.° 180, Madrid, 1987.*

153

hispánicas; también ayudando a rellenar los vacíos poblacionales, a catalogar especies botánicas con positivo recurso farmacológico, alimenticio, ornamental, etc. Y urgencias de esta naturaleza se encuentran, desde mediados del siglo XVIII, en todo el mundo hispánico. Viajes y expediciones se dirigen a todos los lugares ultramarinos, no faltando ni una única región que no contara con la visita —más o menos prolongada— de una expedición. Y bastantes de esas provincias reciben varios viajes científicos. Así el virreinato del Perú [13] y el de Nueva España [14] a Venezuela [15] y las Antillas, con preferencia a Cuba [16] se dirigen tantos viajes como a Nueva Granada [17] y al Río de la Plata, Paraguay y la Patagonia,[18] así como a diversas islas y archipiélagos españoles del Pacífico (Tahití, Pascua, Filipinas)[19] para destacar, por último, la gran expedición dirigida por Alejandro Malaspina (1789/1794) alrededor del mundo hispánico (Canarias, Río de la Plata, Chile, Perú y reino de Quito, Panamá, Nueva España y su noroeste hasta Nutka, islas Marianas y Filipinas), que representa el más alto nivel científico y emprendedor alcanzado por la política española.

4. *Por los expedicionarios*

Los viajes y los viajeros son, masivamente, españoles. Tan sólo en un par de ocasiones se realizan dos expediciones bilaterales con Francia: colaboración casi sin precisión de explicación tratándose del siglo XVIII y con Borbones en Madrid y París: promocionadas ambas por la Real Academia de Ciencias de París, para verificar mediciones astronómicas en el reino de Quito y en la Baja California, en las que participan los españoles Jorge Juan y Antonio de Ulloa (1735) en la primera y el criollo Joaquín Velázquez de León (1768) en la segunda. La colaboración entre peninsulares y criollos se estrechará en todos los viajes científicos: aunque la proporción numérica de los viajeros sea mayoritariamente favorable a los peninsulares.

Los viajes son preparados y realizados en España y de ella salen en su mayoría, rumbo a ultramar, sabios, colaboradores, artistas, marineros y criados. Pero también hay expediciones y viajes que se preparan, realizan y salen de la misma América: Mutis y los

---

[13] *1735, hispanofrancesa al mando de La Condamine y los españoles Jorge Juan y Antonio de Ulloa; 1777, Pavón y Ruiz; 1786, Moraleda; 1795, los Heuland.*

[14] *La comisión hispanofrancesa dirigida por Chappe d'Auteroche de 1768, le siguen el importante capítulo de los viajes al noroeste (1770, Fagues; 1774, Pérez; 1775, Heceta; 1779, Bodega; 1788, Longinos Martínez y de 1790 de Fidalgo, Quimper y Bodega de 1792, y otro de Eliza del año siguiente) y la expedición de Sessé y Mociño, de 1787/1803; incluyendo los viajes hidrográficos de Ceballos de 1801 y el arqueológico dirigido por Dupaix en 1805.*

[15] *1754, la expedición medidora de límites dirigida por Iturriaga y José de Solano; siguen los viajes hidrográficos de Alvear/Mazarredo (1773) y de Fidalgo (1792).*

[16] *1788, Barcáztegui; 1790, Parra; 1792, Rigada; 1792, Churruca; 1796, Mopox y 1801, del Río.*

[17] *Mutis, 1783.*

[18] *Expediciones de límites (1753, Valdelirios; 1781, Azara) e hidrográficas (1785, Córdoba; 1788, Córdoba; 1788, Churruca; 1789, Clairac; 1790, Elizalde; 1792, Moraleda; 1794, Gutiérrez Concha) con aquellas que pretenden la fundación y arraigo poblacional en Patagonia (1767, Perler; 1768, Pando; 1778, Piedra; 1780, Viedma).*

[19] *1765, Casens y Lángara; 1769, Guinal; 1770, Córdoba; 1771, Mendizábal; 1772 y 1774, Lángara; 1792, Caamaño; 1794, Meléndez, viajes hidrográficos todos; botánico, el de Cuéllar en 1785.*

154

numerosos viajes por el noroeste del virreinato de la Nueva España, así como los que salen del puerto de Callao para adentrarse en el Pacífico. En el primer caso los viajeros son casi todos ellos nacidos en España; en los viajes criollos, el número de éstos compone altamente la proporción de las expediciones. Pero la jefatura de una expedición está monopolizada por peninsulares: salvo en las expediciones de Bodega Quadra, el marqués de Valdelirios y José Mociño.

A pesar de este masivo carácter de componentes españoles —peninsulares y criollos—, los viajes se ayudan, en ocasiones, de especialistas de otras nacionalidades: de Suecia (Peter Löeffling), de Checoslovaquia (Tadeo Hanke), de Francia (Louis Née, N. Dombey), de Italia (Brambila, Malaspina) que vierten sus saberes hacia disciplinas botánicas y mineralógicas. Muchos alemanes expertos ingenieros de la Escuela de Friburgo pasan a Chile y al Alto Perú, una vez, conformando una comisión mineralógica (hermanos Heuland) y otra componiendo una atípica y numerosa expedición dirigida por el sueco barón Timoteo de Nordenflycht para aplicar a las minas la nueva tecnología europea.

Las expediciones, en fin, estuvieron todas ellas dirigidas por científicos españoles, menos en el caso del parmesano Alejandro Malaspina, aunque marino español, formado en la Real Escuela de Guardiamarinas de Cádiz y oficial de la armada desde 1776.

5. *Por reinados y gobiernos*

Entre los 75 años que median entre 1735 (expedición hispanofrancesa al reino de Quito) y 1810 se realizan los sesenta y tantos viajes científicos españoles, favorecidos sin reservas por todos los gobiernos de los reinados de cuatro monarcas: de Felipe V a Carlos IV. El volumen y esfuerzo —aún sin cuantificar, ni medir— realizado por el Estado en estas empresas, durante este breve espacio de tiempo, se agiganta si se analiza el número de estas iniciativas sostenidas por cada uno de estos reyes de la Casa de Borbón.

Durante Felipe V se realizan dos expediciones: la comandada por La Condamine a Quito y la de P. Quiroga a Patagonia (1745). Número que se repite durante el reinado de Fernando VI (expediciones para delimitar las fronteras con los dominios portugueses: marqués de Valdelirios, 1753; Iturriaga/Solano, 1754/1760). Pero el ritmo representado por la política científica de los gobiernos de Carlos III (Jerónimo Grimaldi, Floridablanca) y de Carlos IV (Floridablanca, Godoy, Aranda, Pedro Cevallos) es, realmente, muy elevado.

Durante el reinado de Carlos III la secretaría de Indias y Marina (ministros Julián Arriaga, 1765/1776 y José de Gálvez, 1776/1786) se desarrollan treinta y dos viajes científicos. Es decir, que se atiende a esta promoción como otra de las directrices reformadoras implementadas durante el Despotismo Ilustrado: tan necesaria e importante, a ojos de los políticos, como las visitas de inspección a los virreinatos de Nueva España (José de Gálvez, 1765/1772) y de Perú (José Antonio Areche, 1777/1782 y Jorge Escobedo, 1782/1789) y las intendencias. Durante este tiempo se siguen atendiendo las fronteras, enviándose a ellas a numerosas expediciones (cuatro, al noroeste de México; una a Paraguay), lo mismo que se envían siete para reforzar los espacios desprotegidos de América del Sur ante la amenaza de ocupación por otras potencias y dieciséis viajes hidrográficos. Motivos geopolíticos todos, porque la geopolítica se pensaba que podía resolverse, también, científicamente. Del mismo modo es tratada la definición botánica y mineralógica de ultramar, como parte de la política reformista, para un mejor y mayor conocimiento de los territorios (cuatro expediciones botánicas: Ruiz / Pavón, 1777; Mutis, 1783; Cuéllar, 1785; Sessé / Mociño, 1787).

Por su lado, durante el reinado de Carlos IV se realizan veinticinco viajes científicos, que siguen los mismos enunciados políticos y científicos del reinado anterior; diez expediciones hidrográficas: dos de límites (noroeste de México, Florida), cinco viajes al noroeste de la Nueva España; uno, botánico (Parra, 1790) y dos mineralógicos (Heuland, Nordensflycht), continuando con la promoción de los espacios abandonados (dos a Patagonia, uno a Cuba) y concluyendo con la expedición Alejandro Malaspina, como expresión del más alto rango alcanzado por esta consistente política científica.

Conviene resaltar que las coyunturas adversas no detienen, ni aplazan, estos viajes científicos. Y así, mientras éstos se llevan a cabo, hay cuatro guerras contra Inglaterra (1739/1748, 1756/1763, 1779/1783, 1796/1799), dos directamente contra Portugal (1777/1778 y 1801), una contra Francia (1793/1795) y se verifican dos expediciones militares contra Argel (1775 y 1783).

6. *Por los resultados*

Los resultados del gran esfuerzo renovador de las expediciones científicas al ultramar español no estuvieron muy acordes con los objetivos que habían proyectado sus organizadores. El gran causante del freno de estos empeños fue, sencillamente, la independencia de los países por los que se habían realizado aquellos viajes. Las perspectivas mineralógicas, botánicas, historia antigua y arqueología, renovación de técnica minera no procedieron, aunque quedaran como huellas de su paso algunas importantes instituciones científicas (Tribunal de Minería de México, Jardines Botánicos de México y Guatemala, Observatorio Astronómico de Santa Fe de Bogotá, etc.). Los estudios derivados de estas expediciones fueron recogidos y traídos a España, donde se dispersaron por diferentes entidades (Real Jardín Botánico, Museo de Ciencias Naturales, Museo Naval). Bastantes de estos trabajos han sido poco utilizados (informes etnográficos, colecciones botánicas y zoológicas, etc.), porque fueron entorpecidas su difusión y su publicación, por mil y una dificultades.

Pero, asimismo, las expediciones alcanzaron grandes logros:

— Se fijan definitivamente las fronteras con Portugal —de cuya mejor expresión es el Mapa de América del Sur, debido a Juan de la Cruz Cano y Olmedilla— y en el noroeste de Nueva España.

— Otras fronteras se consolidan, con el desarrollo de una política fundacional y poblacional, repetición durante el siglo XVIII del gran auge poblador español del siglo XVI.

— Se llega a adquirir un alto conocimiento hidrográfico de las rutas marítimas (Caribe, Seno Mexicano, Atlántico Sur, Pacífico americano y asiático), a la par que se crea el Depósito Hidrográfico, que comenzaría desde principios del siglo XIX

156

a la impresión de cartas náuticas genuinamente españolas, desterrando la dependencia de las cartas impresas fuera de España, por no existir durante bastante tiempo el organismo competente, ni los trabajos científicos en los que apoyarse.

— Los viajes y expediciones científicas, en fin, contribuyen de modo decisivo a la mejora de las comunicaciones, patentizándose en una cartografía muy perfeccionada.

Consideraciones finales

El siglo de las expediciones científicas merece mejor suerte de la que le ha cabido. El gran esfuerzo estatal por definir científicamente a América, para mejor dirigirla, ha tenido una muy pobre atención, aventándose los resultados y hundiéndose los propios científicos en la indiferencia más dolorosa. Pero por esta labor ejercida por sesenta viajes científicos, a lo largo de setenta y cinco años, América se halla interconexionada con la política española y nunca antes las Indias aparecen dirigidas por una política tan coordinada.

Expediciones y viajes traen a España informes directos y rápidos de la realidad americana, a la vez que en Indias se crean las Intendencias —una mayor presión fiscal y un control de los poderes regionales— y se procede a la remodelación de la distribución de la tierra.

La respuesta criolla a estos viajes y políticas que le llegan masivamente desde España es muy favorable: tanto que gracias a estas intencionalidades reformistas y científicas del Despotismo Ilustrado se aceleran las actitudes y posturas favorables a la independencia.

Los numerosos informes científicos elaborados por estos viajes están siendo hoy día estudiados y publicados. Es el mejor homenaje, sin duda, a los monarcas que propiciaron las expediciones y al tiempo ilustrado, que se obstinó en lograr reformas y mejoras en muchos campos, invirtiendo en ello a los mejores talentos y grandes sumas.

4
Science for Political Purposes: European Explorations of the Pacific Ocean, 1764–1806

Alan Frost

IT is now a commonplace that the period 1764–1806 constitutes a second great age of European exploration. The explorers of that era—Byron, Wallis and Carteret, Bougainville, Cook, Surville, La Pérouse, Phillip, Malaspina, Vancouver, d'Entrecasteaux, Baudin, and Flinders—vastly extended European knowledge of the world's oceans and islands, of the coastlines of the continents shaping the Pacific Ocean, and of the peoples inhabiting them. These expeditions form one of the bases of our present science. For the most part well-equipped for scientific investigation, they gave rise to immense natural history and ethnographic collections, which scientists at home then examined, classified, and used in the development of the modern disciplines.

The historiography of these voyages is now immense.[1] In their attention to the great scientific achievements, however, historians have often overlooked the extent to which these expeditions also had distinct political purposes that gave a global dimension to the European nations' continental and imperial rivalry. Each commander sailed with the intention of obtaining detailed information about the resources and defenses of rivals' existing empires, of acquiring knowledge of unknown coasts and harbors, and of obtaining possession of new territories promising strategic or commercial advantage. The rivalry expressed by the competing scientific expeditions was intense; and there are some good grounds for finding their underlying political impulse more important than the scientific one.

The origins of this rivalry lie in the development of the modern European states and in their overseas expansion during the Renaissance; but we may conveniently take George Anson's famous circumnavigation of 1740–1744 as a starting point. Anson sailed with the immediate purposes of raiding the Spanish settlements on the western coasts of America and capturing the annual treasure galleon; but in the longer term, he sought to encourage rebellion in the Spanish dominions, which might lead to the British gaining access to rich new markets. When he returned, he did so not only with treasure, but also with well-developed ideas of how best to promote the "important purposes of navigation, commerce, and national interest."[2]

Anson's scheme involved establishing a way station to the Pacific where ships could refresh and refit, and he saw the Falkland Islands as being well-situated for this purpose. In 1749, at his urging, the British Admiralty set about equipping two ships to sail to these islands and then to proceed into the Pacific, but the Lords Commissioners put off this scheme "for discovery of New Countries & Islands in the American Seas" in the face of Spanish resentment. A dozen years later the British revived it in another guise when they sent an expedition to capture Manila from the Spanish as a first step to opening trade with the Pacific region at large. While the expedition succeeded, the government at home failed to gain the hoped-for advantage because news of the result did not reach Europe in time to influence the peace settlement.[3]

The British Admiralty then reverted to Anson's scheme. Pretending they were intended for the East Indies, the Lords Commissioners fitted out two ships for a lengthy voyage. They told the commander, Captain John Byron, that his immediate task was to survey the Falkland Islands and locate a suitable site for a base; afterwards he was to examine the coast of New Albion for Juan de Fuca's Strait and to return via the strait if found.[4]

That the accomplishment of these specific purposes was a prelude to the more general and grander one of acquiring empire in the southern hemisphere the Lords Commissioners showed when they began their secret instructions with the rubric developed by predecessors over the previous two hundred years:

Whereas nothing can redound more to the honor of this Nation as a Maritime Power, to the dignity of the Crown of Great Britain, and to the advancement of the Trade and Navigation thereof, than to make Discoveries of Countries hitherto unknown, and to attain a perfect Knowledge of the distant Parts of the British Empire, which though formerly discovered by His Majesty's Subjects have been as yet but imperfectly explored. . . .[5]

Byron sailed in June 1764. After searching unsuccessfully in the South Atlantic for Pepys's Island (thought to be an outlier of the southern continent), he surveyed the Falklands and decided that Port Egmont on the western island was suitable for a base. Byron relayed this information via a storeship, and the British sent a small party to settle it. Byron proceeded through the Straits of Magellan into the Pacific. Once there, however, he made no attempt to look for the Straits of Anian. His idea was instead "to make a NW Course til we get the true Trade wind, and then to shape a Course to the W^t ward in hopes of falling in with Solomons Islands if there are such, or else to make some new Discovery."[6] This route would have been along the coast of Terra Australis as depicted by Ortelius, the Mercators, and their successors, but Byron found neither the southern continent nor the Islands of Solomon. Taking his course at 23°S, he crossed too far north to run among the great atoll clusters of the central Pacific. He reached the Ladrones at the end of July 1765 and then proceeded home by way of Batavia.

Unknown to the British, the French, who also considered the Falklands the "key" to the Pacific, had anticipated them, for Louis de Bougainville had placed a colony on East Falkland early in 1764.[7] On learning of these settlements, the Spanish protested to both Britain and France that the islands belonged to them. The issue was not simply about possession of these small specks bounded by a bleak ocean. Spain claimed the exclusive right both to hold South America apart from Brazil and to navigate the southern Atlantic Ocean and the entire Pacific. The claim was based on the "Law of the Americas," the Papal Bulls of 1493 and the Spanish and Portuguese practice based upon them; and on the guarantee to respect the status quo in Spanish America given by the other European nations in the Treaty of Utrecht in 1713. Accordingly, the Spanish envoy told the British that their penetration of the Southern oceans gave his nation "occasion to . . . Suspect a War."[8]

The British considered Spain's claim that its American possessions "included the A[merican] and S[outh] Seas" preposterous
and said that they would not shrink from war if Spain "insisted on
reviving such a vague & strange pretension, long since wore out,
as the exclusive right of [navigation in] those Seas."[9] But Britain
was nonetheless worried that Spain might be able to enforce the
claim and therefore hastened to take advantage of the new settlement on the Falklands to discover Terra Australis about which
Europeans had for so long held such rich expectations. In June
and July 1766 the Admiralty fitted out the *Dolphin* and the *Tamar*
for another voyage of exploration and gave the command to Captain Samuel Wallis. The Lords Commissioners told Wallis to begin
looking for the southern continent, which they supposed to lie
between "Cape Horn and New Zealand" directly west of the
Straits of Magellan. If following its coast took him a good distance
northwards, he was to return via the East Indies. Otherwise, he
should return by way of Cape Horn and the Falklands. He was to
cultivate friendships with any peoples not previously visited by
Europeans whom he should discover, and, with their permission,
"take Possession of convenient Situations in the Country." If uninhabited, he was to take possession of it "for His Majesty, by setting up proper Marks and Inscriptions as first Discoverers and
Possessors." If, "contrary to Expectation," he did not find the continent, he should proceed across the Pacific to China or the East
Indies, seeking out islands on the way.[10]

In a later note, the First Lord of the Admiralty sketched the context of the voyage:

> After the Return of Commadore Biron from the Expedition . . .
> and his discovery of Falklands Islands, together with other Islands
> in his Track thro yᵉ Pacifick Ocean; Upon Representation . . . to
> the King, that the Knowledge of the Ports in Falklands Islands, & of
> the Streights of Magellan would greatly facilitate farther discoveries
> in yᵉ Pacifick Ocean, South of the Line, if pursued, before a War
> with France or Spain, or the Jealousy of those two Powers should
> oblige Great Britain to part with yᵉ Possession of Falklands Islands,
> or otherwise Interrupt yᵉ attempts of Great Britain in that Part of yᵉ
> World, His Majesty was graciously pleased to Authorize this second
> Expedition to be undertaken, in hopes of finding a Continent of
> Great Extent never yet Explored or seen between the Streights of
> Magellan and New Zeeland.[11]

To assist in these tasks, the Admiralty recruited a Mr. Harrison, the purser of a sixty-gun ship, who, having "a very Mathematical Turn," was sent to calculate longitude according to Maskelyne's method.[12]

Wallis sailed through the Tuamotus to Tahiti, which he claimed for the King. Near this island, he and his men thought that they saw the coastline of the mysterious southern continent, "but afterwards thought [it] most prudent . . . not to take Notice that they had Ever seen it at all."[13] They discovered other islands as they continued across the Pacific; and on their return in May 1768, Wallis gave all Harrison's observations, "together with Plans, Views & Charts of the whole Voyage" to the Admiralty, reporting secretly on the discovery of Terra Australis and on the many islands offering safe anchorage and refreshment—which were, in Wallis's words, "a Happiness to be greatly esteemed for the Benefit of future Adventures, & may be the Means of making them usefull Settlements hereafter."[14]

Wallis's expedition marked the beginning of the scientific exploration of the Pacific. Even as he sailed, another navigator, Bougainville, began his circumnavigation in November 1766. Its immediate occasion was formally to hand over the East Falkland settlement to Spain, whose claim France had conceded, but its larger purpose was to lay a basis for imperial expansion in the Pacific such as envisaged by Charles de Brosses.[15] The ships' complement included the naturalist Philibert Commerson and the astronomer Pierre Véron (also there to solve the problem of determining longitude at sea). Bougainville too came through the Tuamotu archipelago to Tahiti, then west through the Samoan islands and the New Hebrides (Vanuatu) to the coral fringe of Australia, before turning north for the East Indies. The scientific importance of the voyage proved to be less than expected, for Bougainville's published charts lacked details, and Commerson died at Mauritius before he was able to write up his notes and organize his collections. Nonetheless, in the location and charting of the western Pacific islands, there were distinct results; and Bougainville also brought back up-to-date information concerning navigation to and the state of such European outposts as the river Plate settlements, Rio de Janeiro, and Batavia.[16]

Immediately, French adventurers sought to build on the results of these voyages. At the Cape of Good Hope, some of Wallis's men had been "so enthusiastic" about their discovery of Tahiti that they were "unable to stop themselves from gossiping," from which came a garbled story of a very rich island settled by Jews. Considering the adventure worth attempting and that its success "could become too important for our nation for me not to be in honour bound to sacrifice everything to make it succeed," Jean-Baptiste Chevalier sent Jean de Surville "to take possession of this island."[17] Then in 1770 Marion du Fresne began planning his voyage, making the return of the Tahitian Bougainville had brought to France the occasion of discovering Terra Australis and providing a basis for an imperial resurgence in the East.[18]

Nor were the British behindhand. In 1768 Captain James Cook began the first of his three voyages. This was intended as an explicitly scientific voyage. Cook himself was skilled in survey and astronomical observation, and the *Endeavour* carried besides the astronomer Charles Green and Joseph Banks's party, which included the naturalists Daniel Solander and Herman Spöring, and the draughtsmen Sydney Parkinson and Alexander Buchan.[19] An English correspondent told Linnaeus that "no people ever went to sea better fitted out for the purpose of Natural History, nor more elegantly"; and, as is well-known, the scientific results were stunning, the explorers returning in 1770 with a large number of specimens from South America, the Pacific Islands, New Zealand, and Australia, many of which were entirely new to science. Linnaeus was moved to speak of a "matchless and truly astonishing collection, such as has never been seen before, nor may ever be seen again."[20]

The voyage of the *Endeavour* was a great feat of science. Nonetheless, while its scientific purposes provided its occasion, they do not represent its most important impulse. Of profounder import was that purpose which the Lords Commissioners of the Admiralty conveyed to Cook in their secret instructions:

Whereas the making Discoverys of Countries hitherto unknown, and the attaining a Knowledge of distant Parts which though formerly discover'd have yet been but imperfectly explored, will redound greatly to the Honour of this nation as a Maritime Power, as well as to the Dignity of the Crown of Great Britain, and may tend greatly to the advancement of the Trade and Navigation thereof; and Whereas there is reason to imagine that a Continent or

Land of great extent, may be found to the Southward of the Tract lately made by Captⁿ Wallis in His Majesty's Ship the Dolphin . . . or of the Tract of any former Navigators in Pursuits of the like kind; You are therefore in Pursuance of His Majesty's Pleasure hereby requir'd and directed to put to Sea with the Bark you Command so soon as the Observation of the Transit of the Planet Venus shall be finished and observe the following Instructions.[21]

Cook was further instructed to:

- carefully observe the location of the coast of any land discovered and chart it accurately;
- carefully observe the "Nature of the Soil, and the Products thereof";
- observe "the Genuis, Temper, Disposition and Number of the Natives," and cultivate friendships with them;
- with the consent of the inhabitants take possession of "Convenient Situations in the Country in the Name of the King of Great Britain; or, if you find the Country uninhabited take Possession for His Majesty by setting up Proper Marks and Inscriptions, as first discoverers and possessors";
- accurately observe "the Situation of such Islands as you may discover in the Course of your Voyage that have not hitherto been discover'd by any Europeans, and take possession for His Majesty and make Surveys and Draughts of such of them as may appear to be of Consequence, without Suffering yourself however to be thereby diverted from the Object which you are always to have in View, the Discovery of the Southern Continent so often Mentioned."[22]

Careful commander that he was, Cook followed these injunctions diligently. He rather disingenuously professed himself surprised at the viceroy of Brazil's wariness; but while the Marquis of Lavradio was wrong to suspect a smuggling venture, he was not wrong to consider that the expedition comprehended more than its announced scientific purpose. Its fundamental purpose was— no more and no less, as the above quotations indicate—to ensure that the British reached Terra Australis before their European rivals, and, by this discovery or by others, to give themselves the means to a rich Pacific trade. As they proceeded, Cook and his

34   ALAN FROST

companions charted islands, coastlines, and harbors; they noted
local resources; and they established preliminary rights of possession. And although they effectively abolished the southern continent so beloved of theoretical geographers, they established Tahiti
as a focus for future voyaging in the Pacific. They decided that, if
the colonization of New Zealand should become an object, then
either the river Thames estuary or the Bay of Islands would be
suitable locations, both of which offered "the advantage of a good
harbour and by means of the former an easy communication
would be had and settlements might be extended into the inland
parts of the Country."[23] And they claimed all of eastern Australia
(New South Wales) for the British Crown, also with the idea that
parts of it might be suitable for settlement.

Cook returned to England with a precise scheme for finally
settling the question of Terra Australis and for making further discoveries:

> the most feasable Method of making further discoveries in the South
> Sea is to enter it by the way of New Zeland, first touching and
> refreshing at the Cape of Good Hope, from thence proceed to the
> Southward of New Holland for Queen Charlottes Sound where
> again refresh Wood and Water, takeing care to be ready to leave that
> place by the latter end of September or beginning of October at far-
> thest, when you would have the whole summer before you and after
> geting through the Straight might, with the prevailing Westerly
> winds, run to the Eastward in as high a Latitude as you please and,
> if you met with no lands, would have time enough to get round
> Cape Horne before the summer was too far spent, but if after meet-
> ing with no Continent & you had other Objects in View, than haul
> to the northward and after visiting some of the Islands already dis-
> cover'd, after which proceed with the trade wind back to the
> Westward in search of those before Mintioned thus the discoveries
> in the South Sea would be compleat.[24]

This was the scheme which Cook pursued with such relentless
vigor on his great second voyage, in two ships carrying, again,
astronomers and naturalists. The collections from this voyage
were as extensive as those from the first, with the addition of
Johann Reinhold Forster's pioneering attempt toward a world cli-
matology. Yet political considerations loomed as large as scientific
ones, with the explorers charting, drawing, observing, and hy-

European Explorations of the Pacific Ocean 35

pothesizing as assiduously as before. Like Cook and Banks before him, J. R. Forster thought that a settlement might profitably be made in the North Island of New Zealand, partly to take advantage of its naval materials; and the subsequent discovery of New Caledonia and Norfolk Island, with their stands of striking trees, added to the sense of the Pacific's potential as a convenient source of naval materials and offered further incentive for colonization.[25]

On his third voyage, Cook turned his attention to the northern Pacific, seeking (among other things) the entrance of a northwest passage above 65°N. As before, his exploring and charting were impressive, and the collecting of his scientifically minded colleagues extensive. However, his scientific complement was much slighter than on his previous voyages. This might be a sign of the lessening importance of the scientific motive, and an increase of that of the political and commercial ones. In any case, he and his companions observed with a political eye, finding that the Hawaiian Islands might admirably play the role that Tahiti had in the southern Pacific; and gathering information about the Russian settlements in northern Asia.[26]

The American War of Independence, which in 1778 became in effect a global conflict, put a temporary halt to further European exploration and to any expansion based upon it. But no sooner was the war concluded (1783) than the maritime nations turned again to scientific expeditions designed to promote their abiding quest for trade, empire, and strategic advantage. During the first half of 1785 the French mounted La Pérouse's voyage. The most lavishly equipped French scientific expedition to this time, it carried a retinue of scientists, who received fulsome instructions concerning matters of interest in the fields of geography, geometry, astronomy, mechanics, physics, chemistry, anatomy, zoology, mineralogy, botany, medicine, and ethnology.[27]

Though secret instructions of the sort issued to Cook are lacking, the French—both those who sent the expedition and those who went on it—well knew that it might also have important political and commercial consequences. Indeed, the earliest schemes stress these above likely scientific ones.[28] In his public instructions La Pérouse was told to observe and report on the forces in and trade of the colonies he visited, on the commercial potential of the products of the lands in and about the Pacific, and on the purpose of any settlement the British may have formed in the southern half of the Pacific. The navigator and his companions followed these instructions assiduously, recording strategic details of the settlements at Teneriffe, Trinidada, Santa Catarina, Conception, Monterey, Manila, and Formosa. And when he learned in Kamchatka of the British settlement of Botany Bay in New South Wales, he sailed there to investigate it.[29]

As La Pérouse was preparing to leave France, the British heard a rumor that he was taking along sixty convicts to found a ship-building colony in New Zealand. The idea certainly was believable. Cook's voyages had shown the potential; and such a move would have significantly affected the balance of power in the East, where the European nations often had difficulty refitting their ships. The forestalling of the move was a powerful motive in the British decision to colonize Botany Bay.[30] As Evan Nepean, under secretary at the Home Office and the official most concerned with colonization, said on one occasion, the venture would be "a means of preventing the emigration of Our European Neighbours to that Quarter, which might be attended with infinite prejudice to the [East India] Company's Affairs." And, apart from "the removal of a dreadful Banditti" from Britain, the principal advantages to be expected were supplies of masts "which the Fleet employed occasionally in the East Indies frequently stand[s] in need of," and the cultivation of the New Zealand flax plant for cordage and canvas. Accordingly, Captain Arthur Phillip, the founding governor, was instructed to "send a small Establishment [to Norfolk Island] to secure [it] to Us, and prevent its being occupied by the Subjects of any other European Power."[31]

Earl Howe, the First Lord of the Admiralty, described the Botany Bay venture as a "Voyage of discovery & Settlement";[32] and while it was not fundamentally scientific in orientation, a scientific component was originally planned for it, which rather foundered when the botanist Francis Masson, then collecting at the Cape of Good Hope, decided that he did not wish to go to New South Wales. Nonetheless, there were men in the First Fleet who knew enough of botany and zoology to know what would interest the learned in Europe, and they sent back specimens in large numbers, together with ethnographic details. It was as a consequence of this data, added to that earlier obtained by Banks and Solander, that scientists in England began to understand how much Australia was scientifically a "new world." As Linnean Society founder J. E. Smith remarked in 1793:

When a botanist first enters on the investigation of so remote a country as New Holland, he finds himself as it were in a new world. He can scarcely meet with any fixed points from whence to draw his analogies; and even those that appear most promising, are frequently in danger of misleading, instead of informing him. The whole tribes of plants, which at first sight seem familiar to his acquaintance, as occupying links in Nature's chain . . . prove, on a nearer examination, total strangers, with other configurations, other economy, and other qualities; not only the species themselves are new, but most of the genera, and even natural orders.[33]

In the manner by now well-established, this scientific activity went hand in hand with political and strategic ones. By their settlement of New South Wales, the British gained an advantage in the Pacific not only over the French, but also over the Spanish. In 1788, one Spanish commentator observed: "The endeavours of [the] energetic [Cook], his perseverance and labours, besides enriching the sciences of geography and Hydrography by new discoveries, have placed his Nation in a position to compensate itself for the loss of North America by the acquisition of a country almost as vast, and with possibilities for becoming one of the most flourishing and advantageous on account of its position." After describing how a settlement in New Holland offered advantages in navigation to China and created a threat to Spanish trade in the Pacific, he continued: "These possessions will have a Navy of their own, obtaining from the southern region everything necessary to create it, and when they have it ready formed they will be able to invade our neighbouring possessions with expeditions less costly & surer than from the ports of England, & it will not be difficult to foretell even now, which will be their first conquests."[34]

Nor was this an uninformed or idiosyncratic speculation, as the British choice of Arthur Phillip as founding governor of the colony shows. One of Phillip's qualifications was that he was a "discreet" officer who had previously collected information concerning South American coastlines and the Spanish settlements about the river Plate, and spied in France. On his way to New South Wales, he gathered more information about the forces at Montevideo and Buenos Aires;[35] and once there, he saw the settlement as capable of being a way station to the west coasts of America. So, too, did his counterparts in the Spanish dominions. In December 1788, one viceroy of Mexico reported that "the Russian projects and those which the English may make from Botany Bay . . . already menace us"; and in 1790, when the Nootka Sound crisis had made that menace actual, another wrote: "[There are] not enough forces in our South Sea and the Department of San Blas to counteract those which the English have at their Botany Bay, and I think therefore we should withdraw those we have in the pretended establishment at Nootka so that, instead of exposing them to be readily made prisoner, they can fall back to redouble the defences of our older and established possessions."[36]

The Nootka Sound crisis wove these various threads tightly together. By the late 1780s, British traders had begun to frequent the southern Atlantic and the Pacific in search of the whales and seals whose numbers Cook had so tellingly described. The presence of British whalers off the South American coasts and British fur traders at Nootka Sound mightily disturbed the Spanish, who continued to believe that they had an exclusive right to the trade and navigation of these areas, and who therefore protested to Britain. The Spanish did more than protest, though. In 1788 the Spanish court accepted Alejandro Malaspina's proposal for a voyage of scientific discovery to outshine Cook's. It was hoped that this would bring "new discoveries, careful cartographic surveys, important geodesic experiments in gravity and magnetism, botanical collections, and descriptions of each region's geography, mineral resources, commercial possibilities, political status, native peoples, and customs." But behind these scientific purposes lurked the usual political ones, for planners were aware of how much the voyage might do "to explore, examine, and knit together Madrid's far-flung empire, report on problems and possible reforms, and counter the efforts of rivals to obtain colonial possessions at Spain's expense."[37]

Inevitably, the northwest coast of America was on Malaspina's agenda, but as his grand expedition was being mounted, the viceroy at Mexico City sent a small expedition to Nootka Sound to assert Spain's priority there and to expel the interlopers. Commodore Martinez's seizure of the British traders' ships and his detention of their crews led to a diplomatic crisis. The Pitt Administration's first response, in February and March 1790, was to propose an expedition to "lay the foundation of an establishment for the assistance of His Majesty's subjects in the prosecution of the Fur trade from the North West Coast of America," which should sail via New South Wales so as to take on convict artificers.[38] In April

European Explorations of the Pacific Ocean   39

the British put off this expedition in favor of forcing the Spanish to retract their claims. With the issue settled in Europe, the British returned to the idea of an expedition, which then sailed under George Vancouver's command.

Vancouver's voyage, like the others, is famous for its contribution to geographical and oceanic knowledge, but it carried only one person who can be considered a scientist, and its political significance can scarcely be exaggerated. Indeed, the idea of the voyage had emerged from the dispute over the right to navigate in, trade with, and possess territory in and about the Pacific. The British developed the idea conscious of the need to counteract the likely political and commercial effects of Malaspina's voyage; and a central purpose of the proposed scientific activity was to be the securing of all of what is now western Canada for Britain:

> [It being his Majesty's intention] that an Establishment should be formed at one of those ports or places, [of which His Subjects have been dispossessed] or in such other situation as shall appear to be more advantageous with a view to the opening a Commercial intercourse with the Natives, as also for establishing a line of communication across the Continent of America, and thereby to prevent any future intrusion, by securing to this Country the possession of those parts which lye at the back of Canada and Hudson's Bay, as well as the Navigation by such Lakes as are already known or may hereafter be discovered.[39]

Among the consequences of Vancouver's voyage were that the Spanish effectively relinquished their centuries-old claim to enjoying the Pacific as their "lake," and Britain forestalled an American territorial claim to what is now British Columbia.

But if Britain settled its imperial rivalry in the Pacific with Spain by the Nootka Sound crisis and Vancouver's voyage, that with France continued unabated. In 1791 the French National Assembly authorized d'Entrecasteaux's expedition. The immediate occasion was the need, if possible, to succor the missing La Pérouse expedition. Like its predecessors, this was an explicitly scientific voyage. Again, however, it had important political consequences, for d'Entrecasteaux charted the southwestern corner of Australia and the southeastern corner of Tasmania, enabling France to claim an interest in the continent Britain was settling, even if war and the fact that British authorities retained the records of the voyage delayed any realization of this interest for some years.[40]

Napoléon took the matter up even before the Peace of Amiens (1802) when he mounted Nicolas Baudin's expedition. Like that of La Pérouse, this was intended as an exemplar of modern science. It sailed with a specialist complement; and it returned with very extensive collections:

> Apart from a multitude of cases of minerals, dried plants, shells, fishes, reptiles, and zoophytes preserved in alcohol, of quadrupeds and birds stuffed or dissected, we still had seventy great cases full of plants in their natural state, comprising nearly two hundred different species of useful plants, approximately six hundred types of seeds contained in several thousand small bags, and finally, about a hundred living animals, rare or absolutely new.[41]

And Antoine Laurent de Jussieu, professor of botany at the Muséum d'Histoire Naturelle, considered this the greatest collection to be brought from different lands to France.[42] Nonetheless, the voyage was also intended to achieve a distinct political purpose —the reconnaissance of the western coasts of New Holland. This would allow the entire coastline of "this great south land" to be known and therefore provide for a French presence, for though it was "situated not far from the countries of *Asia* where, for three centuries, Europeans have been forming settlements, [it] seemed until recently to [have been] condemned to a sort of oblivion."[43] Baudin and his officers reflected this purpose in naming the area of which Adelaide is now the center "Terre Napoléon" and in their loose talk at Sydney of intentions to form one or more settlements in the Bass Strait region.

Alarmed by these rumors, Governor Philip Gidley King immediately dispatched an officer to ask an explanation of the French, whom he found at King Island in Bass Strait. There, the much inferior British party insisted on hoisting the Union Jack above the French camp. While Baudin accepted this charade in a good-natured way, he pointed out that Tasman was the discoverer of Van Diemen's Land, and that the British party had found him only several days after the French had "left in prominent parts of the island . . . proofs of the period at which we visited it." (With studied generosity he also announced that he would nonetheless name the island after the governor.) King sent another party to form a settlement at Storm Bay, near D'Entrecasteaux Channel (Hobart); and, simultaneously, the equally anxious home government sent a much larger expedition to settle Port Phillip (Melbourne), so as to forestall the French and ensure control of Bass Strait.[44]

The British made another countermove at this time, too. In keeping with his generosity of outlook and his sense that science overrode nationalism, Sir Joseph Banks had assisted Baudin's expedition. However, with the French threat apparent, he also contributed massively to that which the British mounted in opposition, commanded by Matthew Flinders. During his three-and-a-half-year survey of the Australian coastline, Flinders and his party of natural historians, draughtsmen, and mineralogists made extensive and important collections. Robert Brown's, for example, numbered thirty-four hundred items, of which approximately two thousand were new. The political results of the voyage were equally important, for it established Britain's interest in the whole continent, an interest that would be substantiated twenty years later by additional settlements (Melville Island, King George's Sound, Swan River) after the French again made their presence felt by such striking scientific voyages as those of Louis de Freycinet and Jules Dumont d'Urville.

That his voyage should so much have helped to establish Britain's control of the real southern continent, and that his narrative of his arduous work should have given this continent its modern name, could have been of little comfort to Matthew Flinders, who —legend has it—died with the first copy of his *Voyage* in his hand.[45] The privations of the years at sea joined to the anxieties of the confinement at Mauritius had exhausted him. There, he was no ordinary prisoner of war. As a principal in imperial rivalries he was a state prisoner whom the governor could not exchange without explicit approval from France. This approval was years in coming, for while Banks organized his scientific acquaintances in France to intercede on his protégé's behalf, political considerations proved stronger. In Flinders's sad fate we see reflected the fundamental reality of the great age of scientific exploration as a whole —that imperial interests ultimately had precedence over scientific ones.

42   ALAN FROST

Notes

1. The relevant scholarship makes for a very long list. Particularly noteworthy are J. C. Beaglehole's editions of Cook's and Banks's journals (cited below); Bernard Smith, *European Vision and the South Pacific, 1768–1850,* 2d ed. (Sydney: Harper and Row, [1985]); Bernard Smith and Rudiger Joppien, *The Descriptive Cataloque of the Art and the Charts and Views of Captain James Cook's Voyages of Discovery to the South Pacific,* 2 vols. (Melbourne: Oxford University Press, 1985). See also the various essays in *Captain Cook: Navigator & Scientist,* ed. G. M. Badger (Canberra: Australian National University Press, 1970); *Employ'd as a Discoverer,* ed. J. V. S. Megaw (Sydney: A. H. and A. W. Reed, 1971); *Captain James Cook and His Times,* ed. Robin Fisher and Hugh Johnson (Vancouver: Douglas and McIntyre, 1979); *Captain Cook and the South Pacific* (Canberra: Australian National University Press, 1979); and *Sydney Parkinson,* ed. D. J. Carr (Canberra: Australian National University Press in association with the British Museum [Natural History], 1983). Other works include John Dunmore, *French Explorers in the Pacific,* 2 vols. (1965; Oxford: Oxford University Press, 1969); John Dunmore and M. R. de Brossard, *Le Voyage de Lapérouse,* 2 vols. (Paris: Imprimerie Nationale, 1985); M. Dolores Higueras Rodriguez, *Catalogo Critico de los Documentos de la Expedicion Malaspina (1789–1794) del Museo Naval* (Madrid: Museo Naval, 1985); *La Expedicion Malaspina 1789–1794* ([Madrid]: Ministerio de Cultura, 1984); David Mackay, *In the Wake of Cook: Exploration, Science & Empire, 1780–1801* (Wellington: Victoria University Press, 1985); J. E. Martin-Allanic, *Bougainville,* 2 vols. (Paris: Presses Universitaires de France, 1964); Étienne Taillemite, ed., *Bougainville et ses companions autour de monde, 1766–1769,* 2 vols. (Paris: Imprimerie Nationale, 1977).

2. See Glyndwr Williams, ed., *A Voyage round the World* (London: Oxford University Press, 1974), 9, for quotation; *Documents Relating to Anson's Voyage round the World, 1740–1744* (London: Navy Records Society, 1967).

3. Synopsis of Admiralty Correspondence, and Lenox to Shelburne, 17 September 1766, Shelburne Papers, vol. 75: 321–325, 331–332, William L. Clements Library, Ann Arbor, Michigan; and N. P. Cushner, ed., *Documents Relating to the Fall of Manila* (London: The Royal Historical Society, 1971).

4. Lords Commissioners of the Admiralty, Secret Instructions to Byron, 17 June 1764, in *Byron's Journal of His Circumnavigation, 1764–1766,* ed. R. E. Gallagher (Cambridge: At the University Press for the Hakluyt Society, 1964), 3–8.

5. Ibid., 3. These instructions were modeled on earlier ones to Sir John Narborough (1669).

6. Ibid., 89.

7. For an account of the settlements, see Julius Goebel, *The Struggle for the Falkland Islands* (1927; New Haven: Yale University Press, 1982), 221–270.

8. "Notes on a Conversation with Prince Masserano," 26 September 1766, Shelburne Papers, vol. 166, item 7.

9. Ibid.

10. Helen Wallis, ed., *Carteret's Voyage round the World,* 2 vols. (Cambridge: At the University Press for the Hakluyt Society, 1965). Includes the Lords Commissioners' Secret Instructions to Wallis, 16 August 1766, vol. 2:302–306.

11. Egmont, Notes on the Voyage, undated but probably June–December 1768, in ibid., 2:311–312.

12. Wallis to Egmont, 19 May 1768, Shelburne Papers, vol. 75:435–445.

13. Egmont, Notes on the Voyage, 2:312 (quotation); George Robertson, *The Discovery of Tahiti,* ed. Hugh Carrington (London: The Hakluyt Society, 1948), 189, 233.

14. Wallis to Egmont, 19 May 1768, Shelburne Papers, vol. 75:435–445.

15. Charles de Brosses, *Histoire des navigations aux terres Australes* (1756; Amsterdam: N. Israel, 1967), 1:1–81.

16. Louis de Bougainville, *A Voyage round the World,* trans. J. R. Forster (1772; Amsterdam: N. Israel, 1967).

17. Quoted in John Dunmore, ed., "Introduction," in *The Expedition of the 'St Jean-Baptiste' to the Pacific, 1769–1770* (London: The Hakluyt Society, 1981), 21–23.

18. See John Dunmore, *French Explorers in the Pacific* (Oxford: Clarendon Press, 1965–1969), 1:166–168.

19. See J. C. Beaglehole, ed., *The Journals of Captain James Cook,* vol. 1: *The Voyage of the 'Endeavour,' 1768–1771* (1955; Cambridge: Cambridge University Press for the Hakluyt Society, 1968).

20. Quoted in J. C. Beaglehole, ed., "Introduction," to *The 'Endeavour' Journal of Joseph Banks,* 2d ed. (Sydney: Public Library of New South Wales in association with Angus and Robertson, 1963), 1:30, 70.

21. Beaglehole, *Journals of Captain Cook* 1:cclxxxii.

22. Ibid., cclxxxii–cclxxxiii.

23. Ibid., 278.

24. Ibid., 479.

25. Michael Hoare, ed., *The "Resolution" Journal of Johann Reinhold Forster, 1772–1775* (London: The Hakluyt Society, 1982), 3:429; J. C. Beaglehole, ed., *The Journals of Captain James Cook,* vol. 2: *The Voyage of the "Resolution" and "Adventure"* (1961; Cambridge: Cambridge University Press for the Hakluyt Society, 1969), 527–561, 565–568, 868–869.

26. J. C. Beaglehole, ed., *The Journals of Captain James Cook,* vol. 3: *The Voyage of the "Resolution" and "Discovery,"* 2 vols. (Cambridge: Cambridge University Press for the Hakluyt Society, 1967).

27. See L. A. Milet-Mureau, ed., *A Voyage round the World* (London: G. G. and J. Robinson, 1799), 1:1–255.

28. See Catherine Gaziello, *L'Expédition de Lapérouse, 1785–1788* (Paris: C. T. H. S., 1984), 52–54. I am grateful to Madame Carpine-Lancre for referring me to this work.

29. La Pérouse, "Subjects Relating to Politics and Commerce," in Milet-Mureau, *A Voyage round the World* 1:24–32; Monneron, "Observations on different places," in ibid., 2:391–404; La Pérouse, "Account of Manila and Formosa," in ibid., 2:405–411; La Pérouse to Fleurieu, 28 September 1787 and 7 February 1788, in ibid., 2:499–500, 501–508.

30. See Alan Frost, *Convicts and Empire: A Naval Question, 1776–1811* (Melbourne: Oxford University Press, 1980).

31. [Nepean/Sydney] to Chairmen of the East India Company, 15 September 1786, India Office Records, E/1/79:187; Nepean to Sackville Hamilton, 24 October 1786 (draft), Public Record Office, HO 100/18:369–372; George III, Instructions to Phillip, 25 April 1787, PRO, CO 202/5:35.

32. Howe to Blankett, 19 August 1786 (draft), National Maritime Museum, HOW 3.

33. Quoted in Smith, *European Vision,* 5.

34. Francisco Munoz y San Clemente, "Discurso politico sobre los establicimientos Ingleses de la Nueva-Holanda" [20 September 1788], English version in the British Library, Add. MS. 19264.

35. See Frost, *Convicts and Empire,* 133; and Phillip to Nepean, 2 September 1787, *Historical Records of New South Wales* (Sydney: Government Printer, 1892–1901), 1:ii, 114.

36. Quoted in Robert King, "The Territorial Boundaries of New South Wales in 1788," *The Great Circle* 3 (1981): 74, and in Warren L. Cook, *Flood Tide of Empire: Spain and the Pacific Northwest, 1543–1819* (New Haven: Yale University Press, 1973), 300–301.

37. Cook, *Flood Tide,* 118; see also chapter 5 for a detailed account of events at Nootka Sound.

38. See Frost, *Convicts and Empire,* 154–157.

39. [Nepean] to Lords Commissioners of the Admiralty, December 1790 (draft), PRO, HO 28/7:392–399.

40. See Dunmore, *French Explorers* 1:283–341, and Hélène Richard, "L'Expédition de d'Entrecasteaux (1791–1794) et les origines de l'implantation anglaise en Tasmanie," *Revue française d'histoire d'outre-mer* 69 (1982): 289–306.

41. Péron, quoted in Dunmore, *French Explorers* 2:37–38.

42. Jussieu is quoted in Christine Cornell, *Questions Relating to ˉNicolas Baudin's Australian Expedition, 1800–1804* (Adelaide: Libraries Board of South Australia, 1965), 83.

43. Christine Cornell, trans. and ed., *The Journal of Post Captain Nicolas Baudin* (Adelaide: Libraries Board of South Australia, 1974), 1.

44. Baudin to King, [23 December 1802], *Historical Records of New South Wales* 4:1008–1010; Frost, *Convicts and Empire,* 166–167.

45. Matthew Flinders, *A Voyage to Terra Australis,* 2 vols. (1814; Adelaide: Libraries Board of South Australia, 1966).

5
Seapower and Science: The Motives for Pacific Exploration

Daniel A. Baugh

Among the principal expanses of ocean there were three whose geography remained substantially unknown to Europeans at the beginning of the eighteenth century: the Arctic, the Antarctic, and the Pacific. The Pacific, still generally called the South Seas (Mer du Sud, Mar del Sur), was the prime focus of curiosity. Its uncharted regions were suspected of containing not only many more tropical islands but also considerable landmasses in temperate latitudes. Eighteenth-century explorers investigated the Arctic and Antarctic mainly to facilitate development of Pacific routes: Their object was either to find a short passage via the Arctic or to discover and secure places suitable for refreshing ships' crews along the two lengthy cape routes, both of which skirted the Antarctic.

European curiosity about the Pacific Ocean intensified suddenly at the end of the 1690s. Soon thereafter Daniel Defoe and Jonathan Swift, to name only the most famous of early eighteenth-century English authors, put the grow-

2   DANIEL A. BAUGH

ing curiosity about the unknown ocean to various literary and loosely philosophical purposes. Granted, the plots of *Robinson Crusoe* and *Gulliver's Travels* both required some sort of "men from Mars," and in those days the Pacific seemed to provide the most plausible source and setting. But there also arose at this time a quasi-scientific curiosity about the South Seas. This was enhanced enormously by William Dampier's charming yet incisive and faithful accounts of his voyages. His first account was published in 1697.[1] Moreover, there was a firm popular belief, especially in England, that the commercial and strategic potential of the South Seas was enormous.[2]

All these infatuations spread remarkably during the first two decades of the century, and if nothing more than curiosity and enthusiasm were needed to launch expeditions, a flurry of exploratory activity in the Pacific, led by the English, should certainly have commenced by about 1720. Nothing of the sort occurred. The years 1697 to 1760 saw only four significant voyages of exploration in the Pacific, that is, voyages properly equipped and primarily intended for exploratory purposes: one by an Englishman, Dampier; two by a Dane, Vitus Bering, who was hired by the tsar of Russia; the other by a Dutchman, Jacob Roggeveen. Thus, notwithstanding the heightened curiosity early in the century, the major powers of Western Europe mounted only two exploratory voyages—Dampier's and Roggeveen's—before the 1760s.

This eighteenth-century period of delay was really the latter portion of a longer period, roughly 120 years, in which very little effort was made by Europeans to unlock the secrets of the great ocean. This period, stretching from the 1640s to the 1760s, separates two great ages of Pacific exploration. The first age was long and drawn out; it lasted from about 1510 to the 1640s. Then came the 120-year period of fallow. The second age, signaled by the voyages of Bougainville and Cook, ran from the 1760s to about 1800; exploratory voyages in the Pacific did not thereupon cease, but all the main cartographical outlines were filled in by 1800.

Two questions are raised by these chronological facts, and they constitute the main concerns of this essay: Why was there a 120-year lapse of exploratory effort? And in what ways, if any, did the leading motives of the 1760s and 1770s differ from those of earlier times? As to the first question, some historians would not agree that there was a 120-year lapse. It will be necessary, therefore, both to establish the limiting dates clearly and to offer an explanation of why the lapse occurred. The second question, regarding differing motives, lies at the heart of my interpretive theme.

Perhaps the most famous person to comment on the question of differing motives was the great Polish-English writer Joseph Conrad. He judged that the era of Cook's voyages marked a fundamental change:

> The voyages of the early explorers were prompted by an acquisitive spirit, the idea of lucre in some form, the desire of trade or the desire of loot, disguised in more or less fine words. But Cook's three voyages are free from any taint of that sort. His aims needed no disguise. They were scientific. His deeds speak for themselves with the masterly simplicity of a hard-won success. In that respect he seems to belong to the single-minded explorers of the nineteenth century, the late fathers of militant geography whose only object was the search for truth.[3]

Conrad appears to be focusing here on personal motives, but he would not have denied the influence of culture in shaping personal motives. He is, in fact, contrasting modern, disinterested, scientific exploration with the exploratory venturing of the bad old days of blatant acquisitiveness. (The passage is suffused with esteem for nineteenth-century liberal virtue.) As we shall see, this historical contrast is broadly valid, but not so starkly as Conrad implied. One need only recall from the earlier period the conduct of Columbus, Verrazano, Torres, the Nodal brothers, or Hudson to be reminded that there were men of those times whose desire to be honored for sedulous

4   DANIEL A. BAUGH

and dangerous navigation seems to have matched, and possibly exceeded, their desire for material gain. And if Captain James Cook's motives were "free from any taint" of "the desire of trade or . . . loot," that was partly because as an officer of the Royal Navy he belonged to a well-established and respected professional corps. Within that institution he could look forward to material and social advancement as well as honor, if he did his job well.[4] Very few explorers of the sixteenth or seventeenth centuries were in anything like that position. The institutions of their times were less solidly established.

In this essay, however, we are concerned not with the personal motives of the explorers but rather with the motives that underlay decisions to finance the voyages. To put the matter bluntly, Cook's voyages were expensive and obviously he did not pay their costs. The expenditures for his three voyages were authorized by the British government within a framework of objectives that could be expected to stand up to taxpayer scrutiny. Similarly, Dampier was expected to pursue objects that "may tend to the advantage of the Nation." Lord Keynes's remark, "For only individuals are good, and all nations are dishonorable, cruel and designing," although perhaps unduly bitter, has a bearing here.[5] In short, it is one thing to say that an explorer's motives were purely scientific and professional and quite another to say that the motives underlying the decision to finance his voyages were equally of the same character.[6] Even in our own time, when the pursuit or maintenance of scientific preeminence is generally acknowledged to be a motive sufficient unto itself, considerations of national power and prosperity set limits on public appropriation of funds for exploratory research.

Our theme therefore requires us to step back from the voyages themselves in order to examine the kinds of motives that got the explorers their authorization and funding. We shall find that throughout the whole period from 1500 to 1800 one consideration never ceased to be of primary importance: great-power politics. But we shall also discover that the geopolitical perspective of ministers of state did begin to change in the 1760s and 1770s.

In the end we shall see that the surge of exploration in the Pacific during those decades was carried forward by a convergence of three broad motivating forces. One of them had operated powerfully from the sixteenth century onward and never ceased to operate: the inclination of the European powers to parcel out the world and its resources— *le partage du monde,* as Fernand Braudel has spoken of it—in which process the Treaty of Tordesillas (1494) between Portugal and Spain stands as one of the earliest and greatest landmarks.[7] Although traces of the second motivating force might be seen in the sixteenth century, it did not crystallize as a powerful force in Western Europe's policy-making until the later part of the seventeenth: this was the development of a widespread public appreciation of the role and importance of seapower. (The focus on seapower was not the same thing as *le partage du monde;* its rationale and policy implications were considerably different.) The third was a force whose promise was first announced by Francis Bacon in the 1620s; however, it did not attain the power to open large purses until the middle of the eighteenth century: a new conception of the role of science. This conception held that knowledge of the natural world should be pursued not only for the glory of God and man but also because such knowledge translates to prosperity and power. In this view, any society whose capacity for acquiring knowledge is inferior or merely derivative must therefore expect to hold an inferior and derivative role in global affairs.

The impact of the second and third of these motivating forces, seapower and science, forms the concluding theme of this essay. More immediately our task is to place all three forces in the long historical context of exploration in the Pacific, taking notice not only of their influence, stage by stage, but also the conditions and developments that at certain times overrode them and thus inhibited exploration.

6   DANIEL A. BAUGH

THE FIRST AGE OF PACIFIC
EXPLORATION (CA. 1510–1640s)

The European exploration of the world's largest ocean
may be said to have begun either with the penetration of
Indonesian waters by the Portuguese in the decade after
1510 or with the circumnavigation by Ferdinand Magellan's
ship (1519–1522). Whichever beginning is preferred, it
must be granted that the "year 1519 was indeed a year of
destiny for the Pacific. A month before Magellan sailed
from San Lucar, the city of Panama had been founded."[8]
The first age of exploration may be divided into two phases.
The initial phase was dominated by the Iberians and lasted
about a century. The Spanish played by far the dominant
role—largely because after about 1520 the Portuguese
concentrated their energies on integrating a trading system based on the Indian Ocean.

What were the Spanish trying to achieve in the Pacific?
This question raises the larger question of the motives of
Spanish imperialism. The familiar historical answer is that
offered by the conquistadors: to seek gold and to serve
God. Certainly these goals were approved by Ferdinand
and Isabella and their successors. Yet Columbus himself
repeatedly sought and was expected by his backers to find
an alternate passage to the Indies, so that Spain might enjoy the same profits of trade in spices that Portugal seemed
to have within its grasp. Just five years after the conquest
of Mexico, Cortés was urged by dispatches from the Spanish court to launch exploratory expeditions in the Pacific
(from the west coast of New Spain). The Philippine Islands
were finally reached from America in 1543. It took another thirty years for the Spanish to work out a practicable
return route, and until the correct method was found (by
sailing in more northerly latitudes where the winds were
favorable) dreadful losses were incurred from lack of water
and shipboard diseases. Hence it was not until the 1560s
that "the Manila galleon" could be instituted; Spanish trad-

ing with the Indies became an accomplished fact seventy years after Columbus's first voyage.[9]

Clearly this exploratory thrust across the Pacific had an ambitious yet narrow purpose: to reach the islands discovered by Magellan, to establish a trading center there, and to learn how to get back. Along the way other islands were inevitably discovered, most notably the Marianas (Guam was settled for a watering and refreshment station), but once the correct routes were known most voyages adhered closely to them. The exceptions were the voyages of Mendaña and Quiros, in pursuit of gentlemanly and religious goals, and the voyage of Torres (an experienced pilot of Portuguese extraction and low birth), the first great explorer of the waters around New Guinea.

The voyages of Quiros (1606) and Torres (1610) marked the end of Spanish transpacific probing. Thereafter the policy of the Spanish Empire reflected an awareness of inadequate and declining resources. The result was a defensive posture marked by an almost paranoid attitude toward foreign intrusion, particularly in the Pacific Ocean.

The preceding sketch represents the less familiar, oceanic side of Spain's thrust in its first and greatest century of overseas expansion. It ignores what are generally regarded as the key developments: the impact of silver, the *encomiendas*, the Christian missions, the conquest of Peru, and so on. But it reminds us that the Spanish crown did not abandon the original purpose of Columbus's voyages. Although the large expedition (seventeen ships) that comprised his second voyage might seem to have reflected a change of priorities, it really reflected only a change of plan. Hispaniola was to be settled with Spaniards and sprinkled with cattle chiefly that it might serve as a marshaling point for further exploratory attempts to find a sea route to the true Indies. In the meantime, the aim was to enable the colony to support itself by gold discoveries and plantation products, following models established principally by the Portuguese at Madeira and other Atlantic islands.[10] To be sure, when silver was discovered on the mainland in great quantities, development of territory proceeded apace. But before then development of territory was by no means the clear-cut primary goal of the crown. In the early decades Castilian authorities were undecided as to the course of empire, and there were strong pressures in favor of continuing to seek out a path to the Indies.[11] Of course the Spaniards who migrated generally cared nothing about this, and it was they, plus the discovery of silver, that set the dominant style of Spain overseas.

The amazing energy and persistence of Spanish expansion in the sixteenth century, fully exemplified by not only the conquistadors but also Mendaña, Quiros, and Torres, was blanketed in the early seventeenth century by a protective conservatism that proved to be profound and enduring. In this regard the influence of the crown, whose concerns were primarily centered on Europe, was decisive. The cost of maintaining Spain's European dominions, though diminished in the seventeenth century by a less ambitious policy, remained heavy. From Madrid's viewpoint, therefore, nothing was more important than the continuance of plentiful bullion supplies from America. There were even moments when the crown considered abandoning the Manila galleon. Since Manila was essentially an entrepôt at which Oriental luxury goods destined for New Spain were traded for silver, Manila appeared to be diverting the all-important silver flow away from the mother country.

This protective conservatism had a pervasive effect on the general pattern of Pacific exploration. It not only curtailed Spanish exploratory activity but also constrained the initiative of other nations. As thinking in Seville, Cadiz, and Madrid became increasingly preoccupied with the narrow aims of shielding the monopoly of Spanish-American trade and the bullion lifeline, a lifeline that traversed a small corner of the Pacific Ocean, the possibility that the Pacific might be better known or "opened up" could only be regarded with foreboding. In fact, a major reason why the crown could never bring itself to abandon the Manila trade altogether was the strong probability that some other nation might eagerly fill the role. That nation would not only break the trade monopoly but also seek to dominate the Pacific coast of the American empire and thereby command the fate of the indispensable silver shipments from Peru to Panama. Because the seventeenth-century Spanish Empire was usually destitute of means to police its Pacific shores and sailing routes, it saw its best hope in preserving their inaccessibility. The obvious policy was to discourage anyone, even Spaniards, from finding out anything that might entice other Europeans into establishing a foothold nearby. Accordingly, the achievement of Torres was virtually suppressed,[12] and the first circumnavigation of Tierra del Fuego by the Nodal brothers—an impressive voyage which exhibited effective command, navigational skill, and seamanship—was largely obscured.[13]

From a legalistic viewpoint the government of Spain had long regarded the entire ocean from the Philippines to the New World as an exclusive Spanish preserve. During the seventeenth century, and most of the eighteenth as well, Spain treated its vast claim to the Pacific as would a manufacturing company that has obtained a patent in order to suppress its use. The Manila trade, which was the culmination, however disappointing, of the initial excitement about westward access to Eastern riches, was the sole and rather reluctantly pursued exception.[14]

The first age of Pacific exploration was not yet at an end, however. In the decades after 1600 the Dutch converted a prolonged struggle for independence into an aggressive global maritime war against the Iberian powers; they did not hesitate to ignore Spanish claims. By 1625 the Dutch East India Company had effectively expelled the English from the Indonesian archipelago and pushed the Portuguese to the perimeter. In the 1620s the worldwide expansive energy of the Dutch was at its peak, and no other nation was better positioned to embark on further probing of the Pacific. Yet the Dutch exploratory effort was initially delayed, and after it did begin it was quickly aborted. Although the governors-general and councillors at Batavia in the 1620s and 1630s were, according to their successors, "seriously inclined to send out expeditions for the discovery of the unknown regions," they had wound up giving other matters priority.[15] At last in the 1640s, while Anthony Van Diemen was governor-general, two voyages for this purpose were sent out in quick succession. Their main objectives were, first, to learn more about the "Southland" (Australia), whose coasts and adjacent sea passages were only slightly known; second, to find and claim for the States General any unknown lands which might lie east of the Southland; and, third, to be "better assured of any eventual passage from the Indian Ocean into the South Sea, and to prepare the way for ultimately discovering a better and shorter route from there to Chili" (shorter because of the favorable prevailing wind in southerly latitutdes).

Upon examining the details of the instructions one is struck by the businesslike and practical outlook. The chance of running into civilized peoples was deemed to be slim; the objectives were realistic (Tasman by his two voyages did in fact validate many of the key expectations); and it was even recognized that trading to Chile might, at least initially, be forbidden by authorities in Amsterdam because Chile lay within the West India Company's sphere.[16] Tasman carried out his instructions competently, but no more than that. His main accomplishments were to establish the existence of the southernmost route from the Indian Ocean to the Pacific and to reckon the approximate size from north to south of the Australian continent. A report sent from the officials at Batavia to the company directors at the end of 1644 presented a calmly balanced assessment of the possibilities, problems, and requirements of dealing with the Australian landmass. The assessment was guardedly optimistic, but the task, they said, could not be hurried. They admitted that "investigating lands is not everybody's work," while adding: "God grant but one rich silver and gold mine, . . . to the solace of the general shareholders and honour of the finder."[17]

But the directors were not interested. In 1645, respond-
ing to a preliminary report from Batavia, they wrote a
letter that effectively terminated all further exploration of
both the Australian landmass and the South Pacific. As for
attempting to investigate the southern landmass in hopes
of discovering precious metals, the directors wrote:

We do not think it part of our task to seek out gold- and silvermines for
the Company, and having found such, to try to derive profit from the
same; such things involve a good deal more, demanding excessive expenditure and large numbers of hands; it is clearly seen in the West Indies [i.e., New Spain], what numbers of persons and quantities of neces-
saries are required to work the King's mines, so that gold and silver are
not extracted from the earth without excessive outlay, as some would
seem to imagine. These plans of Your Worships somewhat aim beyond
our mark. The gold- and silver-mines that will best serve the Company's
turn, have already been found, which we deem to be our trade over the
whole of India, and especially in Taijouan and Japan, if only God be
graciously pleased to continue the same to us.[18]

It was a sound, conservative, business decision. A century later Charles de Brosses remarked that the driving
spirit of business was to make timely profits. When big
commercial companies undertook voyages of discovery, he
noted, they tended to focus on particular prospects of
profit; upon encountering great expense or obstacles, they
tended quickly to revert to their customary modes of commerce.[19] Certainly this describes the Dutch East India Company's policy in the 1640s. The company's success had
been founded on ships, efficient commercial operations,
shoreline establishments, and control of small enclaves
and islands. Soldiers were expensive and the company
tried to keep their use to a minimum. Investigation of Australia's interior therefore would have constituted a marked
departure from the hitherto successful line of Dutch East
Indian enterprise. The directors' refusal to undertake
such exploration was consistent and understandable.

It is, rather, their refusal to countenance maritime exploration in the unknown parts of the Pacific that constituted
a departure. They ruled out the possibility of a transpacific
trade with Chile because that coast lay within the West In-

dia Company's preserve. Hence exploration of the seas to the eastward was useless. And, in the same vein as the Spanish imperial authorities, the directors hoped that the unknown land would remain unknown, "so as not to tell foreigners the way to the Company's overthrow."[20] Hitherto the directors had often been willing to assent to bold proposals from abroad, even where commercial prospects were distant or uncertain. In the mid-1640s, however, their policy changed.[21]

The change of policy was undoubtedly a reflection of the general pressure, especially financial, on the Dutch republic that began to take the wind out of its maritime expansion. The Dutch West India Company, whose objectives proved beyond its means, had begun to impose heavy demands on the taxpayers that appeared to have no limits. By the 1650s—in fact from then on—the Dutch were on the defensive: the English attacked their commerce and Atlantic settlements by sea, and the French, in the 1670s, put pressure on their home borders by land. Although the directors of the East India Company were overly optimistic when they presumed that Japan and Taiwan would remain part of the eastern network, their commercial decision to stick to the profitable spice trade proved to be wise.[22] But as a result the Dutch East India Company, like the Spanish Empire, retained yet refused to exploit a diffuse monopolistic claim to the vast expanses of the Pacific.

DIVERSIONS AND DETERRENTS
(CA. 1640s–1760s)

Exploration is planned discovery. Discoveries may be made casually or accidentally, but those are not part of our subject. We have thus far traced the manner in which planned exploration of the Pacific came to an end by the 1640s. Our task now is to explain why the lapse persisted for 120 years. Basically there are two avenues of interpretation. One would emphasize diversions—other concerns, other priorities. The other would emphasize deterrents—most of which related directly to the geographic and political situation in or near the Pacific basin. In some respects the two interacted, of course, but on the whole they remained separate.

Certainly there is a powerful case for stressing exogenous diversions. Key points would include the conservatism which enveloped Spanish and Dutch policy, concentration of English and French resources on colonial development in North America and the West Indies, and the task of improving trading opportunities in India. Perhaps the most important diversion of all was the peculiarly unsettled condition of seventeenth-century European politics, marked by an intensive yet highly unstable process of state building in the two emerging maritime powers, England and France; for this reason those countries were strongly inclined toward short-term goals. Furthermore, throughout the first half of the eighteenth century all European governments tended to concentrate on the immediate requirements of European rivalry and the balance of power.

Turning to the factors indigenous to the Pacific basin that tended to deter exploration, the most obvious was geographic—the Pacific Ocean's size, distance, and difficulty of access from Europe. Nevertheless, the monopolistic claims of the Spanish Empire and the Dutch East India Company did in fact play a powerful role in discouraging exploratory activity after the 1640s.

At first glance a historian would be tempted to deny this. Everyone knows that Spain's bold claim to the whole of North America was freely ignored by the English, Dutch, and French with impunity. Although seventeenth-century Spain made an effort to police its vital core of American waters in the Caribbean and near the isthmus,[23] practically nothing was done to guard the periphery. Similarly, the Dutch East India Company did not attempt to police any regions east of the Spice Islands. Thus, though trespassers were warned, the ocean between the Moluccas and the South American coast appears to have been wide open.

But in reality it was not. By themselves the inflated monopolistic claims were undeniably frail. But when taken in combination with circumstances of geography, the limited range of commercial opportunity, and the vicissitudes of European diplomacy, the claims wound up having a powerful influence on the history of exploration.

We begin by examining the ways in which the combination of these circumstances and the monopolistic claims tended to deter serious exploration. Then we will take up the influence of Atlantic and European diversions.

The size of the Pacific and its distance from Europe were of course unchanging factors, but however great the toll on ships and crews, these obstacles obviously did not deter exploratory efforts prior to the 1640s. There was, however, a third geographical factor: Ships could reach the Pacific only by the two southerly approaches, both of which—unless the voyage was very fortunate—entailed the hazards of human and material exhaustion. The fact that within a century of Magellan's voyage the two routes of access had come to be dominated strategically by the Spanish Empire and the Dutch East India Company constituted a considerable hindrance to other nations. These two powers might contrive to interdict the approaches, of course, but mainly they rendered the nearby shores hostile and hence substantially increased the risks of passage.

Let us first consider the South Atlantic approach. The discovery of the route around Cape Horn by Jacob Le Maire made it theoretically far more difficult for the Spanish to interdict this approach. But because the Spanish could scarcely afford the resources to guard either the straits or the cape route on a regular basis during the seventeenth century, Le Maire's discovery did not in reality make much difference.[24] The key problem was wear and tear on ships and crews. Both routes were arduous; voyages completing the passage often needed repairs and refreshment. The austere, rockbound coast of the far south, though unoccupied, was hardly suitable. Because of the pattern of wind belts it was prudent (necessary really) to

head north for quite a distance before striking out westward. Along this path there existed one useful point of relief, 600 miles off the coast and not occupied by the Spaniards: the island of Juan Fernández (Robinson Crusoe's
island), where ships could find fresh water, fruits, and
greens. It became a well-known refuge for early eighteenth-
century English adventurers.[25] But because no accurate
method of ascertaining longitude at sea existed before the
1760s, there was considerable risk of not finding the island. For instance, in 1741 Commodore George Anson,
upon reaching the island's known latitude, mistakenly estimated that he was west rather than east of it and therefore
began his search by sailing away from it; the consequent
delay cruelly amplified the deaths from scurvy. As a result
of Anson's use of the island, the Spanish undertook at long
last to occupy and fortify it.[26] Since in 1741 Britain and
Spain were at war, Anson's voyage was an expedition of
war. In peacetime a foreign vessel in dire distress might
venture to call at a South American port, but it was taking
a chance, for the Spaniards assumed—almost always correctly—that foreign vessels in those waters were up to
no good.

The importance of this inhibition to Pacific voyaging is
further illustrated by the repeated efforts, made especially
by the English, to find a Northwest Passage; these efforts
were motivated by a desire to find not only a shorter route
to the Far East but also a route which was well clear of
Spanish power. As well, the flurry of excitement over the
Falkland (or Malvinas) Islands in 1770, a feature of the
second age of Pacific exploration, was founded on a British urge to possess a base for refreshing crews en route to
and from the Pacific via Cape Horn.

On the other side of the Pacific there were, after Tasman's discovery of the passage south of Australia, two
known approaches. The southernmost route was favorable only for eastbound voyages because of the prevailing
winds. Access north of Australia passed through the Dutch
preserve. Again, it was the need for a safe place to recu-

perate that mattered most. Two illustrations of the difficulties encountered by explorers because of the Dutch East India Company's attitude toward trespassing will suffice.

When William Dampier made his second voyage to the western Pacific, a planned voyage of exploration sponsored by the English government, he found his ship to be much in need of water and sought assistance at Dutch Timor. He sent his clerk ashore to tell the governor the nature of his voyage, and

> that we were *English* Men: and in the *King's* ship. . . . But the Governour replied, that he had Orders not to supply any Ships but their own *East-India Company;* neither must they allow any *Europeans* to come the Way that we came; and wondred how we durst come near their Fort. My clerk answered him, that had we been Enemies, we must have come ashore among them for Water: But, said the Governour, you are come to inspect into our Trade and Strength; and I will have you therefore be gone with all Speed. My Clerk answered him, that I had no such Design.

Agreeing to keep a distance from the fort, Dampier got the water.[27] This occurred in 1699, in the reign of William III. It was probably not a coincidence that Dampier's voyage of exploration to regions near the Dutch East Indies was authorized at a time when the English and Dutch heads of state were, to say the least, on good terms, being the same person. Even so, the Dutch reception of Dampier at Timor exuded hostility and suspicion.

The voyage of Jacob Roggeveen, who set sail from the Texel in August 1721 with two ships, provides our second illustration. It was also a genuine voyage of exploration, undertaken by arrangement with the Dutch West India Company. Roggeveen's aim was to try to find *terra australis incognita*, the great continent rumored to exist in the south central Pacific. He had some goods with him for trading with the new customers. After an extensive voyage, with provisions running low, he was forced to find relief at Batavia. Roggeveen had been worried about this eventuality and had written ahead requesting permission to put in there for supplies. To no avail. When he reached

Batavia ships, crews, and cargoes were detained. He had to return home in an East India Company vessel.[28]

To sum up the account at this point, we have seen that neither the Spanish Empire nor the Dutch East India Company was willing after the 1640s to undertake serious exploration. Although they were incapable of closing the Pacific to foreign intrusion, they were able to make repeated intrusions hazardous and thus to call into question the future usefulness of exploratory findings. Outsiders had to calculate that substantial and expensive force would eventually be required. The deterring consideration was not so much the hazard of the single exploratory voyage as the degree of commitment faced by sponsoring governments, syndicates, or companies if they wished to assure themselves of future returns. It is small wonder that most ventures in this period pursued quick profits rather than long-term goals. But of course serious, planned exploration generally presumes long-term goals; it is ordinarily a kind of preliminary research in which the benefit, if any, is to come from subsequent and repeated journeys.

There is no doubt that in some spheres quick profits could indeed be got, and this brings us to the question of commercial opportunities. At the outset, a negative point should be noted. Because the Pacific Ocean was distant and relatively inaccessible from Europe, its islands were not economically suitable for "plantation" products except for those which would not flourish in Atlantic regions. Similarly, its fisheries were too far away for the catch to be sold competitively in European markets (during the eighteenth century). These constraints ruled out two inducements that had played major roles in opening up the Atlantic and Caribbean.

The commercial opportunities that did exist in the Pacific during this 120-year period may be divided into five categories. First, the real and attainable but not glitteringly attractive: furs, skins, walrus ivory, whale oil, and minerals. Second, the real and attractive but probably unattainable: chiefly trade with Japan, which the Japanese kept closed off except for a tiny window open to the Dutch; trade with the Spice Islands, tightly monopolized by the Dutch; direct trade to South America, about which more will be said in a moment; and a transpacific carrying trade between China and South America, which only the Spanish were in an immediate position to conduct through their entrepôt at Manila. Third, the real and probably attainable but essentially irrelevant to discovery of the unknown parts of the Pacific: chiefly trading between China and India. The fourth category does not perhaps deserve to be classed as commercial opportunity: the real though unknown and problematic. For instance, an exploratory voyage, if conducted assiduously, could hope to discover "rare commodities"—pharmacopoeial, culinary, or otherwise. If the plants that produced them could be made to grow on islands or shores nearer Europe, the eventual returns could be sizable. The search for valuable and exotic commodities was a commonly stated object of later eighteenth-century European exploration in the Pacific, even before Sir Joseph Banks applied his enthusiasm, wealth, and influence to the quest.[29] But clearly this sort of goal—not at all foolish—tends much more toward basic research than commercial viability. The fifth and last category of opportunities is impossible to ignore though it may appear strange on the list: the unknown and unreal. It cannot be ignored because it played a role in the resumption of European exploratory activity after 1760. Our concern here, however, is with the first three categories—the known and calculable opportunities.

It was the first category that led the Russians into the North Pacific in the eighteenth century. In the nineteenth century these commodities (especially those derived from sea mammals) became an important foundation of Western European and American commerce in the Pacific, but their value-to-bulk ratio was not generally high and therefore the profit margins did not seem attractive in the early eighteenth century—except to the Russians. But the Russian situation was unique. In the seventeenth century the

Russian Empire had extended itself across all of Siberia and was probing Kamchatka. The drive had been fueled mainly by profits from furs and to a lesser extent by *iasak*, a tax payable in furs levied upon subjugated aborigines. The furs were chiefly sold by Russian entrepreneurs to China, and the tsar's treasury took 10 percent of the gross. By the early eighteenth century Siberian sources were showing signs of becoming depleted, but entrepreneurs, taking to the sea, were finding plentiful supplies in the Aleutian Islands. Thus Russian expansion into the "Eastern Ocean" was economically self-sustaining, indeed highly practical. The product could be conveniently sold in Asia, and a handsome income flowed to the tsar's treasury, which grew ever more needful of it as Peter the Great and his successors pursued militarily expensive ambitions in Europe. In fact, there is a strong case, contrary to the traditional view, for thinking that the primary purpose of the government's sponsorship of Bering's voyages, even his first voyage, was not to settle a geographical question but to lay a foundation for eastward expansion of the Russian Empire.[30] Obviously, in this period such commercial attractions could apply only to Russia.

Western Europeans when they eyed the Pacific were left to contemplate, among the known commercial opportunities, only the very faint hope that either Japan or the Dutch Spice Islands would be opened to them and the extreme unlikelihood of being able to mount a successful transpacific carrying trade. In the latter regard the most likely Asian country was China; it became gradually more accessible to the British in the eighteenth century. But the British East India Company stood in the way. China lay within its monopoly sphere, and in the later eighteenth century the growing trade between China and India was seen as essential to the company's financial viability. With the whole imperial position in India at stake, there was no chance that parliament or cabinet would allow a transpacific sideshow unless the company wanted to undertake it, however much free-traders might rail against the allegedly constraining effects of the company's monopoly. The overall effect on British policy was to attach China to concerns in India rather than to new possibilities in the Pacific.[31] The French government, on the other hand, was from time to time prepared to close its eyes to the monopoly claims of its India company if there was money in it for a hard-pressed treasury to tax or borrow.[32] In the first two decades of the eighteenth century French trading vessels made more than a half-dozen voyages carrying Chinese goods to South America. These voyages fitted the description of a carrying trade, but they were in reality only a small adjunct to a much larger commercial enterprise of the time whose focus was South America—by far the most enticing of the opportunities on our list. To the South American opportunities we now turn.

In 1669, amid a burst of enthusiasm at court for distant commerce, two English naval vessels under the command of Captain John Narborough were dispatched to the nether part of South America "to make a Discovery both of the Seas and Coasts of that part of the World, and if possible to lay the foundation of a Trade there." The plan entailed charting, recording navigational data, and inventorying flora, fauna, and minerals. Perhaps most important of all, Narborough, while taking care to avoid contact with the Spaniards, was to "mark the temper and inclinations of the Indian Inhabitants" in hopes of making friends and preparing the way for trade.[33] The idea was far from new. Though such schemes repeatedly failed, the Protestant powers could not bring themselves to give up the hope that friendly natives, annoyed with Spanish rule, might provide access to the wealth of Peru. (Hendrick Brouwer had led a similar venture in the 1640s on behalf of the Dutch West India Company; he used force, and it ended in disaster.)[34] The English probe of 1669 ended in disappointment and minor losses. The mission and its results illustrated two key points: the tremendous allure of Peruvian treasure (chiefly the silver from Potosí) and the futility of English attempts to find a peaceful method of trading for it.

Narborough's voyage is properly classed as one of exploration. It was designed to gain geographical knowledge and to smooth the way for future developments, and he did succeed in obtaining data for some high-quality charts. As it happened, the English wound up devoting their navigational research to predatory rather than commercial purposes. There was further navigational "research" of a more casual sort: Bartholomew Sharp, during a piratical expedition upon the Pacific in 1680, managed to take from a Spanish ship her secret book of charts and sailing directions and bring it back to England. He reported: "The Spaniards cryed when I gott the book (farewell South sea now)."[35] One may well doubt that this cry was really voiced, but the point is easy enough to grasp: the era in which the Spanish could rely on the assistance of navigational ignorance to protect the west coast of America from foreigners had come to an end.[36] William Dampier's career illustrates the importance of buccaneering to the English. He began his nautical career in the South Seas as a buccaneer—in the same expedition as Bartholomew Sharp—and ended it in a similar manner with two privateering voyages during the latter part of the 1702–1713 war. Another English privateer of the period, Edward Cooke, wrote in the dedication of his published account: "I present a Voyage round the World, principally intended to reap the Advantages of the South-Sea Trade, whereof your Lordship is the Patron, and which prov'd successful in the plundering the Town of Guayaquil, on the Coast of Peru, and the taking of a rich Ship bound from Manila to Acapulco."[37] Cooke's manner of using the word "trade" is interesting. It neatly sums up the overall character of English enterprise on the west coast of South America at this time.

On the whole, the various English efforts to tap the wealth of that coast must be counted a failure—though punctuated here and there by some dazzling successes. Buccaneering in the reign of Charles II did not yield much success. The Darien scheme (1697–1700), aimed at siphoning Peruvian wealth at the isthmus, was wiped out by Spanish arms. The War of the Spanish Succession (1702–1713),

which many enthusiasts hoped and believed would have
the effect of securing direct English access to the west
coast, yielded instead the *Asiento* privilege, whose stipula-
tions explicitly forbade such trade. (In the treaty negotiations Spain obdurately refused the English request for a
port of call on the coastline.) Even Anson's voyage during
the war of 1739–1748 became a material success only by
the lucky stroke of his running into a well-laden galleon
near the Philippines. There had been so much noisy English enthusiasm, over so long a period of time, yet so little
to show for it.[38]

Until about 1700 the French had no better access to the
region than the English. After that the story was quite different. In 1698 a reconnaissance voyage by Beauchesne
wound up paving the way for a new era. For by the time he
returned home in 1701 France and Spain were united by
a strong dynastic tie—the dying king of Spain had bequeathed the throne to Louis XIV's grandson—and a war
to defend that inheritance was fast brewing. The Spanish
navy at this point was moribund, so the task of defending
the silver lifeline and the trading monopoly in wartime
had to be given over—though Madrid did so with the
greatest reluctance and misgiving—to the French. Because
the approved imperial channels of trade to Peru had been
cut off for almost a decade, the west coast was sitting on a
great pile of silver and starved for European goods. At the
end of the war of 1689–1697 the Compagnie de la Chine
and the Compagnie de la Mer Pacifique (or Mer du Sud)
had been allowed to form in order to provide employment
for privateering crews and ships, especially those of Saint-
Malo, upon which the monarchy had come to rely heavily
for carrying on maritime warfare.[39] When war recom-
menced in 1702 the moment had come for direct French
trade to the west coast. Wartime circumstances, extraordinary influence at the court of Madrid, and subterfuge at
Versailles, as steady as it was shameless, produced a bo-
nanza for the adventurers of Saint-Malo, La Rochelle, and
other ports. Between 1695 and 1726 the figures show 168

French vessels venturing to the South Seas, of which 117 returned (26 were sold in America, 12 wrecked, 13 captured). More than half a dozen are known to have crossed the Pacific.[40] The Spanish were given to understand that it was all occurring without French governmental approval. After granting permission to some merchants of Saint-Malo to trade in the South Seas in August 1705, the king's minister, Chamillart, wrote to the minister of marine: "Since the king does not wish to give any public title or personal authorization to their enterprise, it is necessary for the passports to state some other purpose, such as going to our American islands, or going on exploration, or some other pretext." To the French ambassador at Madrid, who was raising questions, he wrote: "You may assure the Spaniards that the king has not given and will not give any permission to his subjects to go and trade in the American territories ruled by the king of Spain. All that have been issued are some permits given in the normal way for the French islands in America and for going on explorations."[41] The returns were enormous, and largely in the form of bullion.

On the one hand, this surge of lucrative trade actually tended, at least in an immediate sense, to deflect interest away from exploration of the unknown parts of the ocean. The many French voyages tracked along known coasts and routes, and although the government took steps to gather accurate navigational knowledge of the South American littoral, the character of the voyages was almost wholly commercial. On the other hand, these voyages demonstrated to the European nations the feasibility of regular sailings around Cape Horn (at least when the nearby shores were not guarded in a hostile manner).

Thus by about 1710 the Pacific Ocean seemed open. Ordinary merchantmen were sailing there, and the breach of the Spanish monopoly seemed irreparable. Yet, as it happened, there was only one serious exploratory effort in the epoch that followed—by Roggeveen, the Hollander, in 1722. Neither Britain nor France essayed a serious voyage of Pacific exploration for the next forty years. And by the mid-1720s trade to the west coast was again closed to outsiders.

Both Britain and France deliberately allowed the Spanish monopoly to be restored. To explain why they did this is also to explain why the British and French governments did not encourage peacetime expeditions of any kind to the Pacific during the next forty years. The explanation is to be found partly in the Atlantic but mostly in Europe. Hence the last 40 years of the 120-year period of fallow are to be explained primarily by the influence of exogenous diversions.

Notwithstanding the attractiveness of Peruvian wealth, Britain and France had higher priorities. The final outcome of the treaty negotiations of 1713 made this clear: Both nations agreed to forgo direct trade with the west coast. In each case the policy was prompted by caution and therefore acceptance of the status quo ante, and during the next two decades this disposition suited well the inclinations of the leading ministers of state, Sir Robert Walpole and Cardinal Fleury. The calculations were nicely balanced. Britain feared that French influence at the court of Madrid, enhanced by the Bourbon connection, might secure to French merchants a continuing privilege of direct trade. The French feared that if their own direct trade to the west coast persisted, the burgeoning power of the British navy would be brought to bear in support of British contraband traders on that coast. It was for this reason that the French court decided it could no longer wink at the direct trading.[42] The two newly risen giants of maritime enterprise, warily eying one another, thus kept their distance from the Pacific except when Britain was formally at war with Spain.

France's general inclination to cultivate Spanish allegiance is a commonplace of eighteenth-century diplomacy. It is Britain's posture that requires explanation. Although Britain went to war with Spain three times between 1714 and 1750, British interests on the whole were well served by the policy of trying to maintain peaceful relations with Spain. Of course, the proponents of aggressive maritime expansion did not agree; the popular cause—popular in London anyhow—mustered enough political support to bring on a major war with Spain in 1739. (On the other two occasions armed conflict arose more from Spanish than from British impetus.) Popular clamorings for war, however, were offset by British statesmen's concern not to put the export trade with southern Europe to hazard. During the fifty years after 1714 this trade was very important.[43] Within its orbit the Iberian peninsula played a major role both as a market itself and as a conduit for goods reexported to South America via Cádiz and Lisbon. Moreover, both Spain and Portugal bought large quantities of the most politically sensitive English export product: wool cloth. (Portugal was practically the only market in the world where English cloth exports expanded during the eighteenth century.) Finally, the trade balance with Iberia was strongly favorable to England, and the difference was made good in precious metals and coin. In fact, a prime reason for the expansion of Anglo-Portuguese trade in the decades prior to 1760 was the discovery of gold in Brazil in the 1690s.[44]

Over many centuries England had little difficulty in maintaining close ties with Portugal, both for strategic and for commercial reasons. Relations between England and Spain, on the other hand, were continually plagued by basic problems. Aside from the popular English enthusiasm for aggression in Spanish America, there were the potentially hostile Bourbon connection, the English wish to retain Gibraltar and Minorca (for strategic positioning against French seapower), incidents arising from contraband trading in the Caribbean, and other frictions. In view of these issues and the actual eruptions of war, it is all too easy to forget that during the half-century that followed 1714 British diplomacy generally tried to steer its way through the difficulties. It did this out of concern not only for the balance of power in Europe but also the substantial commercial advantages of the trade with Old Spain. In 1750 a commercial treaty, highly beneficial to English trade with Old Spain, was concluded under auspicious circumstances, and Anglo-Spanish relations remained friendly until Ferdinand VI died in 1759.

Summing up the situation down to 1759, we may say that both Britain and France avoided the Pacific in time of peace in order to avoid offending Spanish sensibilities. In 1749, for example, the British cabinet canceled a projected voyage to the Falkland Islands and South Seas because Madrid learned of it and objected—this occurring at a moment when promising negotiations were under way concerning the commercial treaty signed in 1750.[45] But after 1759 British policy toward Spain underwent a significant change.

The seeds of change lay in the new Spanish monarch's mistrust of the British. By 1761 William Pitt, who had formerly valued Spanish neutrality (and the lucrative trading that went with it), believed that Spain was preparing for war and urged his cabinet colleagues to commence hostilities immediately. They refused and he resigned. But Pitt had read the drift of Spanish policy correctly: French counsels were prevailing at the court of Charles III and the following year Britain found itself at war with Spain anyway. For Spain had made a decision unequivocally, willfully—and disastrously as it turned out—to join France in the Seven Years' War.

This decision transformed the extended outlook for Anglo-Spanish relations, because it happened at a time when English politicians of an older generation—Walpoles and Pelhams—who had nursed relations with Old Spain as best they could for half a century were retiring from the political stage. The new men fretted far less about European ties than had their predecessors. Moreover, the trend of trade statistics in the 1760s showed that the relative importance of Iberian trade was declining rapidly.[46] Spanish goodwill seemed scarcely worth an effort. When peace returned to Europe in 1763, an altered British attitude toward Spain soon became obvious. Hence the somewhat nebulous opportunities and concerns of the Pacific no longer had to be weighed against a concrete and compelling European case for not giving offense to Spain.

THE COMMENCEMENT OF THE
SECOND AGE OF EXPLORATION

Initially, we saw how the Spanish Empire and Dutch East India Company turned conservative and thus inclined toward keeping others and even themselves ignorant of the Pacific Ocean's geography. In the preceding section we noted that reliable access to the ocean was circumscribed by Spanish and Dutch monopolistic claims; that French and English activity on the west coast of South America between about 1700 and 1720 had much to do with immediate acquisition of wealth but little to do with exploration; and that during the period from 1713 to 1760 diplomatic and commercial considerations in Europe inhibited both Britain (when not at war with Spain) and France—the emergent maritime powers—from undertaking Pacific ventures because the Spanish so disliked them. Finally, we observed that in the early 1760s the third point lost most of its force as far as the British were concerned.

It is important to notice the kinds of deterrents and diversions that are being excluded. My inclination is to share Spate's doubts about the applicability to the history of the Pacific of long waves of economic expansion and contraction ("phase A" and "phase B") which some modern French scholars have put forward with skill and subtlety.[47] Moreover, Braudel's accent on the diversionary effect of the effort put into "building America" ("it was necessary to build America, which was Europe's task, in the *long term*") is not detectable in the policies of the various European powers. His idea appears to be based on the energies and efforts of colonists, but the logic of a diversion-of-effort argument must rest on what mother countries do, not what colonists do.[48]

But the most notable proponent of the diversion-of-effort thesis was Vincent Harlow, who stated it as follows:

> The seamen and geographers of the Renaissance had devised the novel and daring expedient of establishing a means of communication with the Eastern World by sailing west across the unknown ocean of the Atlantic, but the unexpected discovery of the American barrier between Europe and Asia had caused a complete diversion of this outward movement. The Europeans who used the sea-routes opened by Cabot, Columbus, and other navigators of the time were not merchants on their way to the court of the Great Khan or the bazaars of Ophir, but *conquistadors*, sugar and tobacco planters, settlers, and *coureurs de bois*. For a century and a half the Europeans devoted their energies to the consolidation of the American inheritance, interspersing their activities with fierce quarrels among themselves. . . .
>
> By the middle of the 18th century the Europeans were on the move again.[49]

Down to about 1700 this thesis has some validity. Undeniably, the "consolidation of the American inheritance" was the main preoccupation in the seventeenth century (though one should not forget the activities of the Dutch and English East India companies). After 1700, however, there was ample energy and eagerness available for the Pacific in London (and Saint-Malo too). We have seen that the British and French governments were unwilling to unleash it in peacetime. Moreover, when these governments did show interest in the Pacific in the 1760s, the "fierce quarrels among themselves" were by no means considered to be things of the past.[50] All in all, the diversion-of-effort thesis cannot surmount two historical obstacles: why the Spanish and Dutch ventured in the Pacific and East Indies before the 1640s and why the British and French did not do so from about 1720 to 1760.

Harlow's diversion thesis laid the groundwork for the main objective of his study, which was to show that British imperial policy underwent a profound reorientation after

1763. The new orientation was marked by two features: a preference for trade over territorial dominion and a "swing to the East," where the new trading opportunities were to be sought. ("The Second Empire began to take shape in the 1760's as a system of Far Eastern trade.") The "First" British Empire had got itself entangled with colonies of settlement, plantations, and the like, and these, he argued, entailed vexing political problems which came to a head in the 1760s and provoked a search for different methods in a different place. Britain's interest in the Pacific Ocean, signaled by the surge of exploratory voyages, heralded the change.[51]

This is no place for a comprehensive critique of Harlow's schema. But the terms of the debate "on the questions of motivation and direction" of British imperial policy after 1763 have been set by him,[52] and he interpreted the commencement of British exploration in the Pacific during the 1760s as a leading indicator of "the swing to the East" and the new preference for commerce over dominion. Since our purpose here is to ascertain the motives and reasons for the timing of the second age of Pacific exploration— and in so doing to show that concerns over seapower as well as a new way of thinking about scientific research were paramount (and commerce was not)—it is necessary to confront Harlow's interpretation.

The basic flaw is that both of Harlow's key propositions are largely chimerical. The "swing to the East" cannot be substantiated by evidence of any type.[53] The other proposition, that British policy moved toward a preference for trade over dominion after 1763, is to be doubted on three counts.[54]

First, it is a profound error to suppose that the quest for dominion had ever been the mainspring of English imperial policy before 1763. Recently a very strange reinterpretation of the British Empire has been elaborated on the basis of a similar idea.[55] To accept it one has to perceive the empire throughout its earlier history as mainly a matrix of tributary arrangements designed to satisfy the patronage needs and military predilections of a portion of the English governing class. Undeniably such a matrix formed a subplot and appeared dominant on some occasions and in some places, but it is beyond question that trade, plunder, and the defense of trade had always been the primary motive forces of English overseas policy before 1763.[56]

Second, there is the problem of Indian imperialism. If any imperial situation did accord with the idea that the main concerns were tribute, patronage, and dominion, it was the situation in India *after* about 1760. From then on the East India Company behaved more like a tax-collecting governing body than a trading establishment. The scope of its dominion expanded. In fact, the idea of a commercial "swing to the East," to the extent that it has any genuine substance (trade to China and Southeast Asia), tends to clash with the idea that dominion was shunned, because the urgent quest for these new avenues of trade was spurred by the need to find an economically viable method of supporting dominion in India within the framework of a private company.[57]

The third count is that in the 1760s British policymakers were still at least a half-century away from putting their faith in free trade. Rightly or wrongly, commerce was still seen as something that had to be husbanded and therefore carried on under conditions controlled by the mother country. In other words, trade continued to be conceived of as an "imperial" matter.[58] One may fairly say that Harlow was not denying this. His argument did not directly address the question of free trade but centered rather on a preference for trade over dominion—in the same manner, one might say, that the Dutch East India Company had preferred trade to dominion in the seventeenth century. The eventual development of British commerce under "informal empire" (that is, relying on economic rather than political sinews) appears to lend substance and plausibility to the argument. Still, Harlow's discourse at times verges near the authentic language of free trade. The British Empire was, he says, moving toward a commercial system "beneficent and profitable, imposing no restrictions and incurring no burdens." He envisions a "network of commercial exchange extending through the Pacific and Indian Oceans. By opening up vast new markets in these regions, a diversity of exotic commodities, earned by home production, would flow back into British ports." This was what the architects of the "Second British Empire" were looking for: "The hope and intention was to find a vent for the widening range of British manufactures" by creating such a network.[59] The puzzle is that if finding a vent for the widening range of British manufactures was the main object, why was it desirable to search for the solution in distant and unknown seas while a booming trade with North America was admirably serving the purpose? Harlow does not address this point. Alexander Dalrymple, however, clearly did, and because Harlow derives a good deal of inspiration from him, Dalrymple's views on this question, published in 1770, are worth examining.

Dalrymple saw nothing but danger in the North American trade. His reason was unusual and highly relevant to our purpose. It was not the familiar objection that North America did not fit into the Old Colonial System but rather that the North American market was *too* successful in receiving British manufactured goods. The American colonists were thus in a position to put pressure on the imperial government; the mother country was too dependent upon them as buyers. "Discovery of new lands" and thereby new markets for British goods, he wrote, would diminish the "decisive importance" of the American colonies to the empire.[60] In other words, a new trading region and system were needed to keep the imperial-commercial system from becoming too dependent upon one region—particularly a region that, at the time Dalrymple was drafting these ideas, had become notably obstreperous about obeying the decrees of the imperial legislature.

The key point here is that Dalrymple's reasons for exploring new commercial realms do not accord with Harlow's. For Dalrymple's argument is essentially defensive in character: he insisted that Britain must seek to develop a controllable and counterbalancing alternative system. To be sure, he spoke of "discoveries in the South Sea" leading to "an amicable intercourse for mutual benefit," but these benign and optimistic phrases must be evaluated in the general context of his imperial objective.[61] Whereas Harlow sees the thrust into the Pacific as something born of confidence,[62] Dalrymple saw it as an antidote to potential imperial disaster.

Upon turning to the true motives, we may begin by observing that the motives behind the British thrust to the Pacific in the 1760s and 1770s involved both moods: confidence and anxiety. There was in the early 1760s (as there had been for forty years) great pride and confidence in Britain's standing as the world's leading naval power. There was also a deep concern to do everything necessary to retain that position of naval preeminence. It is not a trivial fact that the British voyages of discovery were all organized by the Admiralty (with cabinet approval) and in each instance—John Byron, Samuel Wallis, Philip Carteret, and James Cook—the ships were commanded by officers of the Royal Navy. The primary objectives, both short-term and long-term, were directly concerned with seapower.

The initial strategic aim was to secure claim to the Falkland Islands, an independent way station for assisting ships on the Cape Horn passage; their possession, as Lord Anson had remarked, would make the British "masters of those seas." Anson was First Lord of the Admiralty and was thinking mainly of the problem of supporting naval expeditions to the Pacific in time of war, though he also spoke of the potential advantages of gaining a commercial foothold in Chile. The Earl of Egmont, the First Lord who presided over the dispatching of Byron's expedition, was thinking along identical lines. A secondary objective of the 1760s was to see whether any islands or continents existed in the Pacific which might be made to serve naval or commercial ends. But the immediate concern was a base in the Falkland Islands.[63] The Admiralty had pursued a policy of establishing permanent overseas bases since the 1720s; the interest in the Falklands harmonized with this trend.

But the secondary objective may have weighed just as heavily on the minds of those who looked to the future of British seapower. Their concern was to maintain a continued preponderance of the two main underpinnings of naval strength at that time: merchant shipping and skilled seamen. The Navigation Acts had been chiefly addressed to these ends; they were designed to facilitate a national merchant marine and thus to provide early training and subsequent employment for skilled British seamen who could be enlisted or impressed into the navy in wartime. The trouble with the vibrant, growing, industrially beneficial transatlantic trade with America was that it was being carried on increasingly in ships of the Thirteen Colonies, many of which never got near British ports. Moreover, impressment of "American" seamen (it was often a nice question what "American" meant in this regard) had been running into serious political and practical barriers. The seamen in the transatlantic trade thus appeared to be largely unavailable to the Royal Navy in case of need. This problem was plainly visible by 1763—well before American independence.

To those concerned for the future of the navy, therefore, the development of new arenas for British shipping seemed highly desirable.[64] And it was even more important to prevent the French from doing the same thing. Thus the British Admiralty was, in effect, buying insurance. The cost of all the British exploratory voyages of the 1760s was probably less than the cost of one ship of the line fully fitted—a reasonable insurance premium. The lords of the Admiralty did not need to suppose that possibilities of commerce were of much immediate importance; nor did they have to seriously believe that large, well-populated, undiscovered continents or islands existed. They only had to make sure the French would not be able to claim such places first.[65]

The question of underlying British motives in the Pacific, it might be noted, has given rise to an interesting debate on the decision to colonize New South Wales. In this debate the revisionists argue that the government had something more in mind than a place to dump convicts when it chose Australia. The subject lies in the 1780s, beyond the bounds of this essay, but the theme is highly relevant. All in all, the case for a naval role is rather strong, but it does not nullify the importance of finding a suitable spot for the convicts. The case for a commercial role, however, seems to be rather feeble.[66]

In sum, then, the financial sponsorship of British exploration in the 1760s was motivated by a *protective maritime imperialism*. (One witnesses here an early instance of that phenomenon which became so characteristic of modern British imperialism and so exasperating in its apparent hypocrisy to Britain's rivals: expansion for defensive purposes.) The voyages to the Pacific were part of the ongoing global struggle between Britain and France. The key ingredients were national defense, rivalry, and pride. The voyages were undertaken not in a spirit of fulsome self-confidence but in the mood that purchases insurance. If prospects of commerce proved to be unreal or remote, the premium would nevertheless have been wisely paid.

Seapower also played an important role in the French effort, but allowance must be made for the differing commercial and naval situations of the two nations. It is well known that Charles de Brosses, whose work inspired Louis Antoine de Bougainville to go out to the Pacific, was an Enlightenment figure of some note, a savant fascinated by geography who like Dalrymple believed the "scientific" case for the existence of *terra australis incognita* to be very strong. De Brosses was also a fervent patriot convinced that France's future lay in maritime commerce and naval strength. The trouble was, he wrote in the preface to his *Histoire des Navigations aux terres australes*, that Britain ("a neighboring power") had appropriated to itself "la monarchie universelle de la mer," without consideration or care for any other nation. It was that fact, he said, which gave birth to the book.[67] Inspired by reading de Brosses's book, Bougainville set out first to claim and establish a base on the Falkland Islands. He arrived there before Byron, whose mission was practically the same. In the instructions for his second voyage, however, the famous circumnavigation of 1766–1769, one may detect a more specific commercial accent than one finds in the instructions of Wallis, Carteret, or Cook. The French hoped that Bougainville might help to lay new foundations for a revival of French maritime power, whereas the British were mainly concerned to hold onto their advantage.[68]

There remains the question of why the surge of activity occurred in this particular decade. In the first half of the eighteenth century statesmen in Britain and France had turned away from conjectural and distant prospects. Yet it cannot be disputed that the potential importance of the Pacific to seapower was pointed out by maritime expansionists at that time. Captain George Shelvocke wrote in 1726 that anything which would contribute to the improvement of British "Navigation, tho' in never so small a degree," ought to be considered acceptable to the people of a maritime power like Britain.[69] In 1740 and 1741 De Lozier Bouvet used a traditional blend of mercantilist arguments, including the bullionist theme, when seeking sponsorship for an exploratory voyage to the South Pacific. He also used the naval argument: "It is no longer permissible that France should neglect this means of increasing her own power. Nothing but a great commerce can support a great navy."[70] Yet nothing was done until the 1760s—when a great deal was done.

Why the 1760s? The answer has two aspects: One involves politics; the other concerns the role of science and involves deeper currents of cultural history. In the political aspect there is considerable continuity with past motives. In the second aspect there is a rapidly unfolding, profoundly interesting discontinuity.

We have already laid much of the groundwork for the political aspect of the answer. Admiral George (first baron) Anson, who became head of the Board of Admiralty not long after completing his voyage across the Pacific, naturally had his eye on that ocean as a possible theater of war and therefore wished to secure for Britain the assured use of the Falkland Islands as a way station. The voyage the Admiralty was putting into preparation in 1749 for this purpose was canceled because commercial and diplomatic relations with Old Spain held priority. After 1762, however, concern for Spanish goodwill evaporated; the cabinets of the period of peace after 1763 generally cared less than their predecessors had cared about relations with Europe, and in fact these cabinets were quite attuned to maritime concerns.

There was in addition a personal ingredient. The First Lord of the Admiralty from 1763 to 1766, the second earl of Egmont, was a fervent advocate of a more forward policy and was especially inclined toward the Pacific. Egmont's main concern, like Anson's, was strategic, and his attention was fixed on possible future operations against the Spanish Empire. When, in 1766, a planned expedition (under Wallis) ran into high-level opposition—certain cabinet members were apprehensive as to French and Spanish repercussions—he managed to execute a modified plan as a last act before resigning his office.[71]

But there was more to the new orientation of British policy than Lord Egmont's enthusiasm. A year and half later, when the Royal Society asked the government to sponsor and prepare a scientific expedition to the South Seas, the proposal was approved and a suitable vessel purchased in only seven weeks by a different Board of Admiralty. A. C. Taylor has commented: "Such haste, which might almost be described as indecent, might well suggest that the Authorities regarded the Royal Society's request as a heaven-sent pretext to allow them to carry on the series of voyages designed to forestall the French in general and Bougainville in particular."[72] "Heaven-sent" is exactly right; the result was Cook's first voyage, which went out ostensibly to carry observers to an optimum location for recording one of the rare transits of Venus. It is easy, however, to detect the continuity of naval motives—motives which were able to find expression in the 1760s because of significant changes in British political leadership and Anglo-Spanish relations.

Turning briefly to the French political causes, we may

observe that there is probably no period of French history in which maritime concerns played a greater role in French policy than the period delimited by the rise of Choiseul and the demise of Vergennes (roughly 1763–1783). In the 1760s, however, the French were more careful than the British to stay in the good graces of the Spanish. Hence they quickly handed over their claim to the Falklands to Spain and sought new commercial opportunities farther westward.

As a postscript we may note that activity bred activity. The intensified rivalry of the British and French in the distant ocean, combined with the ambitious probes of the Russian Empire across the North Pacific in the 1760s, even woke up the Spanish. The missionary establishments and settlements in Alta California during the 1770s were aimed at solidifying the claim and keeping the Russians at a distance. The viceroy of Peru, with Madrid's approval, even sent an expedition westward in 1770 to make sure there was no large and alluring island nearby.[73]

From the foregoing it would appear that scientific curiosity merely provided a convenient cover for moves in a maritime cold war. It did. But upon examining science's role at this moment in history one realizes that it was in fact genuine and pervasive.

Public sponsorship of science was not a new phenomenon in the 1760s, any more than concern for the foundations of seapower was new. From Louis XIV's reign onward the court of France had supported scientific research rather handsomely, particularly with respect to establishing a correct geography of the world. Admittedly the English government had not been lavish in this regard. According to a (possibly biased) English opinion, given in 1694, the other leading maritime nations made it a practice to send technical observers and recorders on voyages:

'Tis to be lamented, that the English Nation have not sent along with their Navigators some skilful Painters, Naturalists, and Mechanists, under Publick stipends and Encouragement, as the Dutch and French have done, and still practice daily, much to their Honour as well as Advantage. . . . We are apt to imitate a certain Prince in every thing, except in the most glorious and best part of him, viz. The Encouragement and Rewarding great Men in all Professions, and the promoting Arts and Sciences with his Treasure: A Secret which some Ministers think not fit to practise, or perhaps may be insensible of, for want of penetration. This makes a great Figure in the present and future Ages, covers many Spots and Deformities, and secures the best Heads, and Hands to carry on, and effect great Designs.

Whether this opinion (put forward by the "Printers to the Royal Society") accurately reported the practices of the Dutch and French is not so interesting as the manner in which the quotation captures the essence of attitudes prevalent seventy years later.[74]

The charge that English royal government was backward about giving broad support to science was valid.[75] This, however, should not be allowed to obscure the intimate and long-standing connection in England of science and navigation (in both the sense of the word "navigation" today and the broader sense familiar in the Early Modern period)— a connection reinforced by the growing belief in the seventeenth and eighteenth centuries that human progress and maritime-commercial progress were interdependent. Moreover, in the century that dates from the founding of the Royal Observatory at Greenwich in 1675, the main object of which was to develop means of ascertaining longitude at sea, the government showed itself willing to pay lavishly in order to encourage the progress of navigational science. Parliament's establishment in 1714 of the Board of Longitude and its £20,000 prize is a notable further instance.[76] Finally, for reasons I have not been able to unearth—perhaps because the relevant statesmen's papers are not extant—a few voyages primarily of a scientific character were authorized (prepared and paid for by the navy) during the brief period of peace toward the end of William III's reign. Edmond Halley's voyages to the South Atlantic (1698–1700) were chiefly aimed at learning more about the southern skies and compass variation. The case for thinking that Dampier's voyage begun in 1698 was mainly scientific in character is also quite strong.[77] These were certainly the only English voyages of the century from 1660 to 1760 whose primary aims were scientific—and quite probably the only primarily scientific voyages authorized by any European power in that period.[78]

The modern tendency to suppose that scientific curiosity, pure and simple, motivated the voyages of the 1760s is understandable. That Cook's first voyage was occasioned by the broad international effort made to observe a transit of Venus is well known. As well, speculative geography certainly played a role in determining areas to be searched. Most important of all, Bougainville and Cook, each in his own way, put a personal imprint on the voyages that imparted a scientific as well as heroic character to them: Bougainville was an educated, insightful, articulate observer; Cook was as meticulous as he was relentless. All this is true, but the voyages of the 1760s would have gone forth to the Pacific regardless of the wishes of scientists and scholars. In that decade science was only marginally the motivating force.[79]

But its role became increasingly evident in the ensuing decades. The British government's willingness to support voyages to assist the observation of the transits of Venus (1761 and 1769) foreshadowed the change. One indicator of the shifting attitude in the 1770s was the preamble of the statute of 1775 which extended the £20,000 reward for finding a Northwest Passage that Parliament had originally established in 1745. As Beaglehole has observed: "The 1745 act was all trade—'of great benefit and advantage to the trade of this Kingdom'; it was now, in 1775, possible to bring science before a British parliament, and the bill was aimed at the 'many advantages both to commerce and science' that were promised by the discovery."[80] By the 1780s the Admiralty was routinely allowing scientists to accompany pioneering voyages.[81] Although the European world had not yet entered the era of "militant geography whose only object was the search for truth,"—remembering Conrad's words—its foot was on that threshold.

40   DANIEL A. BAUGH

Concomitant with this change came a shift in the character and class of public support in Britain for voyages of
discovery. Elite groups—the Royal Society, for instance—
were successfully enlisting in the cause a considerable con-
stituency. This enlargement of the "scientific" public occurred notably in France as well as Britain; its growth was
of course a symptom of the Enlightenment and occurred in
some degree throughout Europe.[82] The primary themes of
the earlier part of the century—commerce, naval strength,
and national defense (whose noisiest adherents were the
partisans of aggressive mercantile expansion)—were not
abandoned, but after 1750 the combined themes of far-
seeing scientific progress and imperial destiny imparted a
new accent. The new themes were of course more conge-
nial to the polite, educated persons who now took up the
cause.

Some of these new supporters of exploration and expansion undoubtedly disdained the social character and
some of the leading shibboleths of the old.[83] But one should
not push this idea too far. Just as scientists in former times
had willingly linked many of their concerns with those
of mariners and traders, so the geographical savants of
the later eighteenth century commonly subscribed to the
precepts of commercial and imperial power. Sir Joseph
Banks—a natural-resource imperialist if there ever was
one—could write as follows in the later 1790s: "As increased Riches still increase the wants of the Possessors,
and as Our Manufacturers are able to supply them, is not
this prospect, of at once attaching to this country the whole
of the Interior Trade now possessed by the Moors, with
the chance of incalculable future increase, worth some
exertion and some expense to a Trading Nation?"[84] One
point, however, is clear. The new supporters of exploration were quite fond of high-minded motives, whether scientific or imperial.

The public sphere quickly felt the effects. Support of
scientific discovery became a matter not only of royal honor
but also of national honor.[85] Exploratory voyages were con-

sidered in the later eighteenth century to be under international inspection; the conduct of scientists, explorers, and governments that supported them was watched with critical interest. As the Royal Society commented, it was desirable to satisfy "the universal Expectations of the World in this respect."[86]

We noted a moment ago that the personal qualities and conduct of Cook and Bougainville gave the voyages of this epoch a scientific character. But we should not overlook the role of technology in this same regard. To consider Cook's case in particular, we must take note that his habitual persistence and exactitude paid unprecedented cartographical dividends because he had the advantage of new precision instruments for ascertaining his geographical position (most notably, quadrant, sextant, and chronometer). Above all, *two* valid techniques for ascertaining longitude at sea—the age-old problem—came to fruition in the 1760s (by chronometer and by observation of lunar distances) in time for Cook to make the best use of them.[87] To appreciate the scientific value of the voyages it was sufficient to note the quality of the charts that they yielded.

Certain general cultural factors also served to elevate the influence of science and long-term perspectives at this time. There was not only the rise of anthropological curiosity (which made the Tahitians "Exhibit A" for all sorts of theories) but also, and perhaps more important, the full flowering by the 1760s of the idea of a stage-by-stage development of human society. This notion was accompanied by the idea that advanced societies (in the "commercial stage") bore prime responsibility for further human progress. Few doubted that Europe had moved forward into higher ground and that scientific achievement was the main reason for thinking so. Furthermore, at this same historical moment romantic ideals were claiming attention. Enthusiasm, though hardly back in fashion, was no longer condemned in all spheres. The passionate, single-minded vision, however dubious the practicality of its objects, now seemed acceptable, even laudable. One result was a greater patience regarding profits and dividends. Long-term possibilities of commerce and strategic advantage seemed worth considering. A final point: One of the greatest figures of the British Enlightenment, Adam Smith, published in *The Wealth of Nations* (1776) an argument that not only made a strong case in the economic sphere for a gradual, developmental view of progress but also—this is particularly relevant—belittled the role of precious metals, which had so dazzled the proponents of maritime aggressiveness in earlier times.

To end this essay on the subject of science and its relation to intellectual culture would perhaps be a mistake. History best remembers beginnings—achievements that are new and pointed toward the present. The new, strong scientific tone of the voyages of the later 1760s and 1770s clearly suits this disposition. If these voyages, especially Cook's, strike a responsive chord in us today, it is mainly because we recognize their scientific and technological modernity (dramatized by the exemplary conduct of the two great explorers of the age) and are fascinated by its infant freshness. But we must not forget that in those decades, though science provided a further motive of exploration, it did not replace the traditional motives. Seapower remained at the center of governmental concern. In fact, long-term projection of seapower's requirements was a notable feature of eighteenth-century strategic thinking. The world chiefly remembers the voyages of Bougainville and Cook for the heroic quality of the scientific endeavor. But the voyages also stand as testimony to the geopolitical hopes and fears of a bygone age.

NOTES

1. Regarding the publication of the various collected and foreign-language editions of Dampier's voyages see Joseph C. Shipman, *William Dampier: Seaman-Scientist* (Lawrence, Kansas, 1962), pp. 2–4. Dampier's influence on Defoe is readily traceable; see Oskar H. K. Spate, *The Pacific Since Magellan*, Vol. II: *Monopolists and Freebooters* (Minneapolis, 1983), pp. 156–158: "No fewer than eight of Defoe's narratives are in-

debted to Dampier, on whom he relies more than any other travel writer" (p. 157). Spate's fine work (the first two volumes, now published, carry the story down to the mid-eighteenth century) is the best introduction to the political history of the Pacific.

2. See generally Glyndwr Williams, "'The Inexhaustible Fountain of Gold': English Projects and Ventures in the South Seas, 1670–1750," in John E. Flint and G. Williams, eds., *Perspectives of Empire: Essays Presented to Gerald S. Graham* (London, 1973), pp. 27–53.

3. Joseph Conrad, "Geography and Some Explorers," in *Last Essays*, ed. Richard Curle (London, 1926), p. 10.

4. To understand Cook's conception of how he would be rewarded, one must understand the process of advancement in the Royal Navy. It was difficult for an officer to gain promotion in peacetime unless he had good connections and good luck. When Cook returned from his first voyage he was raised in rank to commander. After the second voyage he was made captain of a ship of the line which was about to be decommissioned, so the appointment was clearly contrived by the Admiralty for the purpose of giving him post, i.e., captain's rank. Almost simultaneously he was made a captain of Greenwich Hospital, a billet for deserving retired officers which paid a nice pension, but Cook took it on the clear understanding that he had not retired. See J. C. Beaglehole, *The Life of Captain James Cook* (Stanford, 1974), pp. 275–276, 444.

5. On Dampier's instructions see note 77 below. The quotation from John Maynard Keynes is found in *Essays in Persuasion* (London, 1931), p. 62. Keynes wrote this in 1921 when he was most disgusted and despairing over the conduct of the allied nations.

6. These underlying motives are shaped in any particular epoch by society's conception of the uses of exploration. A list of goals might include national or monarchical prestige; religious mission; science (pure lust for knowledge); commercially useful information; development of opportunities for commercial poaching, predatory expeditions of war, or human exploitation; and lucre (by seizure or mining). This list would pertain as readily to private as to public ventures. The main public or governmental concern would center on national self-preservation through various means—for instance, enhanced treasury revenue, increased prosperity (and hence taxable and loanable funds), enhancement of strategic knowledge or skills useful in combat (such as seamanship) among the populace, or enlargement of the nation's affiliated population through colonization. Additional benefits, of course, could include augmented pools of patronage and kindred opportunities for politicians.

7. Fernand Braudel, "The Expansion of Europe and the 'Longue Durée,'" in H. L. Wesseling, *Expansion and Reaction* (Leiden, 1978), pp. 17–27.

8. Oskar H. K. Spate, *The Pacific Since Magellan*, Vol. I: *The Spanish*

Lake (Minneapolis, 1979), p. 58. There was a certain continuity. Although Magellan's voyage was in the service of Spain, he was Portuguese and had participated in the conquest of Malacca (ibid., p. 34).

9. The geographical and economic nature of things dictated that this Indies trade which centered on Manila, though it proved to be of some value to New Spain and was not without impact on commerce in the Pacific basin, could scarcely have any effect on the economy of Old Spain.

10. See generally T. Bentley Duncan, *Atlantic Islands: Madeira, the Azores and the Cape Verdes in Seventeenth-Century Commerce and Navigation* (Chicago, 1972), especially chap. 2.

11. See J. H. Parry, *The Discovery of the Sea* (Berkeley and Los Angeles, 1981), pp. 243, 253–257.

12. See Brett Hilder, *The Voyage of Torres* (St. Lucia, Queensland, 1980), p. 135: "As the discoveries made by Torres were thought to have a possible value to the enemies of Spain, his letter to the king was filed away out of sight. To historians seeking to tie the voyage of Torres into the wider perspectives of European expansion and world politics, there are no dividends. Nor were the results of the voyage of any help to exploration, colonization, trade, or navigation at the time. Torres's only reward was the belated naming of the strait after him, a well-deserved honour, as he was the first man to pass through it and no one was to follow him until Cook in 1770."

13. Spate, *Monopolists*, pp. 25–26. Bartolomé and Gonzalo Garcia de Nodal were Galicians who had amply demonstrated their abilities in the Spanish navy. Spate remarks that the conduct of this voyage of exploration "was a model of decision and efficiency." It is perhaps symbolic that they subsequently served in the Atlantic silver convoys (where they lost their lives in a hurricane).

14. Reluctantly from Madrid's point of view; Spanish Americans had a different perspective. A brief summation of the extent of the initial enthusiasm may be found in G. V. Scammell, *The World Encompassed: The First European Maritime Empires, c. 800–1650* (Berkeley and Los Angeles, 1981), pp. 320, 328–329. For a brief sketch of the eighteenth-century history of the Manila galleon, see Spate, *Monopolists*, pp. 281–283.

15. From the preamble of the instructions given to Tasman, 13 August 1642, printed in J. E. Heeres, "His Life and Labours," in *Abel Janszoon Tasman's Journal* (Amsterdam, 1898), p. 128. See also the resolution taken by the officials at Batavia on 1 August (p. 131). On the probing voyages that the company did undertake in the 1620s and 1630s, see pp. 88–104, 147–148.

16. From the letter of 12 December 1742 from Batavia to Amsterdam explaining the purposes of the voyages (ibid., pp. 137–139). See also Andrew Sharp, *The Voyages of Abel Janszoon Tasman* (Oxford, 1968), pp. 30–39. At this time the Dutch called Australia the Southland; within

a generation they would call it New Holland. It was still called New Holland in the time of Captain Cook.

17. Report from Batavia to the directors at Amsterdam dated 23 December 1644. I have preferred Sharp's translation here (ibid., p. 317).

18. Heeres, "His Life," p. 115, n. 4.

19. Charles de Brosses, *Histoire des navigations aux terres australes* (1756; reprinted Amsterdam and New York, 1967), Vol. I, pp. 8–9: "Si elle [une riche compagnie] agit, c'est avec des vûes particulières: c'est dans l'esperance d'un grand profit facile à faire. Si les premières tentatives n'ont aucun fruit, bientôt rebutée par la dépense & par les obstacles, elle se renferme dans les branches de son commerce accoutumé" (p. 9).

20. J. C. Beaglehole, *The Exploration of the Pacific*, 3rd ed. (London, 1966), p. 162.

21. The views at Batavia and Amsterdam were sharply divergent in the 1640s. The governor and councillors at Batavia wrote (12 December 1642): "We are sadly deficient in what would be required [proper ships] for the discovery of unknown countries and for the seeking of fresh trade-markets, on both which points, as aforesaid, a great deal more might be done" (Heeres, "His Life," p. 138). The directors wrote (9 September 1645): "The Company has now made a sufficient number of discoveries for maintaining its trade, provided the latter be carried on with success" (ibid., p. 115, n. 4).

22. The Dutch had high hopes in 1640 of replacing the Portuguese in Japan, but within a year or two all Dutch merchants in Japan were forcibly confined to a tiny island in Nagasaki harbor where they were able to conduct only a very limited trade. The Japanese policy of seclusion had already been implemented when the directors wrote their "wet blanket" letter to Batavia in 1645; it would appear that they did not yet know the true facts. Taiwan was lost to Chinese forces in 1662. See Spate, *Monopolists*, pp. 73–84.

23. See, generally, Kenneth R. Andrews, *The Spanish Caribbean: Trade and Plunder 1530–1630* (New Haven, 1978).

24. In the sixteenth century the danger of meeting a Spanish patrol was greater. Apparently Sir Francis Drake chose to return to England by circumnavigation in 1578 because, having plundered Spanish vessels in the Pacific, he dared not try to leave the ocean by returning southward and through the Strait of Magellan; so he sought a Northwest Passage and, failing to find anything promising, set his course westward across the ocean. See Kenneth R. Andrews, "Drake and South America," in Norman J. W. Thrower, ed., *Sir Francis Drake and the Famous Voyage, 1577–1580* (Berkeley and Los Angeles, 1984), p. 51.

25. For the discovery and use of the island of Juan Fernández, see Spate, *Spanish Lake*, pp. 117–119.

26. Anson realized his mistake upon sighting the coast of Chile, which he dared not touch despite the desperate state of health of his

crews; so he reversed course and eventually reached the island. For the Spanish occupation, see Spate, *Spanish Lake,* p. 119.

27. William Dampier, *A Voyage to New Holland,* edited by James A. Williamson (London, 1939), pp. 136–137. For Dampier's wariness of the Dutch during his first voyage to the area (as a buccaneer), see Christopher Lloyd, *William Dampier* (London, 1966), pp. 54–62.

28. Afterward the East India Company directors were forced by litigation to make restitution. See Andrew Sharp, *The Journal of Jacob Roggeveen* (Oxford, 1970), pp. 166–177. The governor-general and council at Batavia, when they ruled that his voyage constituted an encroachment upon the company's monopoly, had recourse to the precedents established when Jacob Le Maire's ships and goods were similarly arrested in 1615. The two cases, however, were quite different. Le Maire had intended to break the company's monopoly by exploiting a possible loophole in its charter. The company had been granted exclusive rights *in waters west of the Strait of Magellan;* Le Maire reasoned that if he reached the East Indies by a different route—he was the first to sail round Cape Horn—he could legitimately trade. His claim to be seeking new lands was not false, but neither was it the main point, and the seizure of his ships and goods when he began to trade in the East Indies was not entirely without justification. Nevertheless, upon suit by Le Maire's father in an Amsterdam court, the company was required to give compensation.

29. On Sir Joseph Banks and botanical projects, see David Mackay, "A Presiding Genius of Exploration: Banks, Cook, and Empire, 1767–1805," in Robin Fisher and Hugh Johnston, eds., *Captain Cook and His Times* (Seattle, 1979), pp. 21–39, especially p. 28.

30. On the commercial and imperial motives, see Raymond H. Fisher, *Bering's Voyages: Whither and Why* (Seattle, 1977), chap. 7; see also Raisa V. Makarova, *Russians on the Pacific, 1743–1799,* translated and edited by Richard A. Pierce and Alton S. Donnelly (Kingston, Ont., 1975). The question of the scientific objective of Bering's first voyage is discussed in note 78 below.

31. It seemed possible in the early 1760s to expand trade with China by establishing a company entrepôt on an island in the Sulu Sea (off the northeast point of Borneo). The scheme was launched by Alexander Dalrymple. The idea was to encourage Chinese merchants to come there as they did to Manila. Whatever its merits, it failed under the mismanagement of another person. See Howard T. Fry, *Alexander Dalrymple (1737–1808) and the Expansion of British Trade* (London, 1970), pp. 36–93. In the following decades the main concern of the company was to establish a reliable and efficient gateway to the South China Sea by means of a defensible place that would give shelter and aid to the company's vessels and perhaps also serve as an entrepôt. The island of Rhio (Riau) near the Malacca Straits was most coveted, but the Dutch would

not give it up. Eventually Singapore filled the bill. See John Ehrman, *The Younger Pitt: The Years of Acclaim* (London, 1969), chap. 14.

32. John Dunmore, *French Explorers in the Pacific*, Vol. 1: *The Eighteenth Century* (Oxford, 1965), p. 13.

33. *An Account of the Several Voyages to the South and North . . . By Sir John Narborough . . .* [et al.] (1694; reprinted Amsterdam and New York, 1969), pp. 10–11.

34. Spate, *Monopolists*, pp. 51–53. In the long run, Chile did prove to be a chink in the imperial-commercial armor. See T. W. Keeble, *Commercial Relations Between British Overseas Territories and South America, 1806–1914* (London, 1970), especially p. 1, n. 2.

35. Quoted by J. H. Parry, *Trade and Dominion: The European Overseas Empires in the Eighteenth Century* (New York, 1971), p. 20. Sharp was rewarded with a Royal Navy captain's commission by Charles II, though officially his voyage had been completely illicit.

36. Actually, Dutch threats in the earlier seventeenth century had moved the viceroyalty of Peru to take defensive measures; see Peter T. Bradley, "The Defence of Peru (1600–1648)," *Ibero-Amerikanisches Archiv* 2 (2) (1976): 79–111.

37. Captain Edward Cooke, *A Voyage to the South Sea, and Round the World . . . 1708, 9, 10, 11* (1712; reprinted New York, 1969), p. 3 of dedication (to Robert Harley, Earl of Oxford, lord high treasurer). This was a competing account of Woodes Rogers' voyage.

38. On English propaganda and enterprise concerning the South Seas in this period, see Williams, "'Inexhaustible Fountain.'"

39. Geoffrey J. Walker, *Spanish Politics and Imperial Trade 1700–1789* (Bloomington, 1979), p. 22; Spate, *Monopolists*, pp. 180–182.

40. Spate, *Monopolists*, pp. 189–194. Everyone has relied on the table and descriptive lists of M. E. W. Dahlgren, "Voyages Français à destination de la Mer du Sud avant Bougainville," *Nouvelles Archives des Missions Scientifiques et Litteraires* 14 (1907): 446–551. It does not appear that every sailing actually reached the Pacific.

41. Henry Kamen, *The War of Succession in Spain, 1700–15* (Bloomington, 1969), pp. 149–150. As Kamen comments: "Such deception was so transparent that it is difficult to see whom the French government was trying to delude."

42. Rejecting the pleas of the merchants of Saint-Malo, the French government undertook the painful task of squelching it.

43. Its statistical importance is displayed by a table in Stetson Conn, *Gibraltar in British Diplomacy in the Eighteenth Century* (New Haven, 1942), p. 267. See also Ralph Davis, "English Foreign Trade, 1700–1774," in W. E. Minchinton, ed., *The Growth of English Overseas Trade in the Seventeenth and Eighteenth Centuries* (London, 1969), p. 119.

44. Jean O. McLachlan (Lindsay), *Trade and Peace with Old Spain, 1667–1750* (Cambridge, 1940), p. 18: "The trade to Old Spain pro-

vided a supply of vitally necessary bullion, a market for the staple English products, a source both of valuable raw materials and of cheap popular luxuries, and, moreover, was not monopolised by any company." On Portugal, see H. E. S. Fisher, *The Portugal Trade: A Study of Anglo-Portuguese Commerce 1700–1770* (London, 1971).

45. On the cancellation of the projected voyage of 1749, see Robert E. Gallagher, ed., *Byron's Journal of His Circumnavigation 1764–1766* (Cambridge, 1964), pp. xxxvii–viii.

46. There are some figures on Spanish trade and its decline in Conn, *Gibraltar*, p. 267. On the decline of Portuguese trade, which was absolute in this period, see Fisher, *Portugal Trade*, chap. 2.

47. Spate, *Monopolists*, pp. 110–111. As he remarks, "There seems to be some tendency to take things both ways."

48. Braudel, "Expansion of Europe," p. 18. He was speaking of the *longue durée*, but his ideas clearly apply here to the period from 1500 to 1800. Only sixteenth-century Spain and seventeenth-century England provide any support for his argument and even there the support is only partial. The French consistently gave more effort overseas to trade and fishing; the Dutch "building" effort in America was almost nil. As for the English in the seventeenth century, it should be remembered that the East India Company was launched about the same time as the Virginia Company and that the English traders were evicted from the Spice Islands in the 1620s by the Dutch. Dutch expansion hardly suits Braudel's formula at all, though he contrived to make it seem so by reference to the abortive Dutch effort in Brazil. Finally, the period from 1714 to about 1760 has been rightly termed the period of "salutory neglect" in British North America.

49. Vincent T. Harlow, *The Founding of the Second British Empire, 1763–1793*, Vol. I: *Discovery and Revolution* (London, 1952), pp. 59–60.

50. Harlow presented his point somewhat differently in another passage. Before 1763, he wrote, "the energies of the British were heavily engaged in defending their positions against the French in Europe, America and India. Until that issue was decided, further ambitions were beyond the horizon" (ibid., p. 17). Once again one must ask whether statesmen really believed that on all three of these continents the "issue was decided" by 1763. On this matter see also Glyndwr Williams, *The Expansion of Europe in the Eighteenth Century: Overseas Rivalry, Discovery and Exploitation* (London, 1966), pp. 96–97. (Chapter 7 of his book provides a good, brief introduction to the opening of the Pacific.)

51. The interpretive framework is set forth in Harlow's first two chapters. Chapter 3 is entitled "The Swing to the East." The quotation is on pp. 10–11.

52. D. L. Mackay, "Direction and Purpose in British Imperial Policy, 1783–1801," *Historical Journal* 17 (1974): 487.

53. See especially Peter Marshall, "The First and Second British Empires: A Question of Demarcation," *History* 49 (Feb. 1964): 13–23. Marshall answered the case statistically and by a survey of policy decisions. David Mackay has concluded that the whole notion of a conscious directional shift of policy is mistaken: "There was not within the governmental bodies . . . [any locus] capable of sustained conceptualization that Harlow's themes imply or necessitate. . . . The machinery of colonial administration was such that no new philosophy of empire, no coherent, forward-looking policy emerged. . . . [T]he government had no clear ideas as to overall direction and purpose in imperial policy. This is not to suggest that a pattern is not discernible; but the pattern reveals itself only to the historian. It was not deliberately planned." See "Direction and Purpose," pp. 500–501; see also Mackay's earlier study, "British Interest in the Southern Oceans, 1782–1794," *New Zealand Journal of History* 3 (1969): 142. I should add here that I feel the same admiration which other scholars have expressed for the range and depth of Harlow's contribution.

54. I shall leave aside the intricate question of why the British, by treaty, gave back Havana and Manila (commerce) and kept or accepted Canada and Florida (dominion).

55. See Stephen Saunders Webb, *The Governors-General: The English Army and the Definition of the Empire, 1569–1681* (Chapel Hill, 1979).

56. My view is based on what moved the English taxpayer to open his purse. In the long run that was decisive. I therefore focus upon the mother country's declared interest (declared by government and by public debate): to nurture and defend maritime capacity and commerce. For that there was public support; for defending or extending overseas dominion per se, almost never. Webb should be given credit for calling attention to the semi-hidden agenda, but I cannot agree that it should be given primacy. T. R. Reese's comment has a bearing here: "The cry that 'we prefer trade to dominion' is significant, but the two activities are not easily dissociated. From the very beginning British maritime activity had nourished both trade and colonization, the one being the complement of the other." See Trevor Richard Reese, "The Origins of Colonial American and New South Wales: An Essay on British Imperial Policy in the Eighteenth Century," *Australian Journal of Politics and History* 7 (Nov. 1961): 195.

57. Harlow could not ignore the fact that Indian dominion expanded after 1760. In fact, Alexander Dalrymple (whom he often cites) observed the trend at the time: "But the East-India Company are too much engaged in *territorial dominion* to think of commerce and discovery" (p. xxvi of the introduction to Dalrymple, *An Historical Collection of the Several Voyages and Discoveries in the South Pacific Ocean* [1770; reprinted Amsterdam and New York, 1967]). Harlow explained this fact

50   DANIEL A. BAUGH

away by saying that it arose from the need to keep the French from getting the upper hand in the subcontinent. He did not raise the further question of why this was considered a necessity, nor did he give much attention to the growing influence of those in Britain who were prepared to see the question of Eastern trade mainly in the light of maintaining dominion in India. (The China trade provided a solution to the problem of making adequate returns to English shareholders back home without impoverishing Bengal by exporting hard money from there.) See Ehrman, *Younger Pitt*, chaps. 14 and 15. See also Alan Frost, "Botany Bay: A Further Comment," *Australian Economic History Review* 17 (1977): 64–77. On trade to Southeast Asia, see generally D. K. Bassett, *British Trade Policy in Indonesia and Malaysia in the Late Eighteenth Century* (Hull, 1971), especially chap. 1.

58. See Marshall, "First and Second," p. 23.

59. Harlow, *Founding*, I, 3–4, 37.

60. On American absorption of "the widening range" of British manufactured goods at this time, see Davis, "English Foreign Trade, 1700–1774," pp. 105–117. Dalrymple's argument here is sophisticated. It lays out a scenario wherein American colonial interests, during a trade depression, would be able to put pressure on Parliament through the clamorous "distress of the industrious manufacturer" of Great Britain; see p. xxvii of Dalrymple, *Historical Collection*.

61. Dalrymple, *Historical Collection*, p. xxviii.

62. Harlow, *Founding*, I, 3: "Scientific and industrial development at home, and the possession of decisive superiority at sea, naturally led a self-confident island people to search the oceans for new markets."

63. Byron's instructions did not specify that he should go in search of new lands to the westward; he did that on his own. He was ordered to go first to the Falklands, which he did, then to search for a northwest passage from the Pacific side, which he did not do. Evidently, the reason he did not was rather "Byronic." See Gallagher, *Byron's Journal*, pp. xliii–lviii. He was in fact the poet's grandfather. On Anson's views see ibid., p. xxxvii; on Egmont's, see pp. xxxix–xl, 160–163.

64. The best evidence of the continued importance of the Navigation Acts to British policy in this period was the government's pertinacious retention of them in the British West Indies after American independence, where they faced practically insurmountable difficulties.

65. By accenting the positive commercial prospects that came to a degree of fruition in the nineteenth century Harlow's interpretation obscured the pressing concerns of eighteenth-century statesmen that were the main motivating force behind the exploratory thrust. Harlow recognized that seapower considerations were among the motivations, but he placed his emphasis on commercial reorientation. General historians have tended to remain under his influence, but quite a few specialized studies have strongly dissented.

J. H. Parry's general study followed Harlow only halfway. Parry offered the outline of Harlow's account, yet elsewhere he laid stress on the noncommercial flavor of the voyages. The latter point Parry hammered home by remarking that "even after Cook's second voyage had shown that the Pacific had relatively little to offer in the way of commercial advantage, there was no immediate slackening of interest" (*Trade and Dominion*, pp. 244, 256).

Dalrymple too might have disagreed with Harlow's emphasis, but it is not easy to ascertain Dalrymple's position; his expansive views did not deign to put objectives in rank order. Still, one notes that the last paragraph of Dalrymple's introduction deals with seapower. Britain, he said, could not afford to let any "competitors . . . gain the superiority at sea. . . . [I]f other nations are negligently permitted to extend their navigation to remote parts," and to gain thereby "commerce and power," it would certainly reveal the "worthlessness of ministers" who allowed it to happen (*Historical Collection*, p. xxx).

66. Alan Frost, in an appendix to *Convicts and Empire: A Naval Question, 1776–1811* (Oxford, 1980), has set forth a comprehensive case against commercial motivation (pp. 185–195) in which he pays special attention to the monopoly rights of the British East India and South Sea companies. The aim of the book is to emphasize the role of naval power in the decision. Although I believe this aim is broadly correct, I doubt whether so much stress should be laid on the hope that New South Wales (and nearby Norfolk Island) could provide naval stores for refitting ships that operated in the Indian Ocean.

There can be no doubt that the British government in the mid-1780s was searching for more than just a place to dump convicts, though the disposition of the convicts was indisputably an urgent problem; the initial idea was to have them settle a way station near the Cape of Good Hope, but no suitable spot could be found. As well, the idea that a base in New South Wales might prove useful to the navy notwithstanding its apparently useless location was probably in the minds of those who made the decision. For its greatest strategic importance related to a contingency which was better left unstated by officialdom even in confidential memoranda—namely the possibility that the Dutch East Indies would fall under French control. Since this did not happen—Pitt's administration took strong measures to thwart French ambitions in the Netherlands in the 1780s—the contingency now seems a bit unreal. But it was real enough then. On these points see Frost, *Convicts and Empire*, chaps. 6, 7, and 8; Mackay, "British Interest," pp. 126–134. We may note that James Matra did not shy away from stating that the place had its uses against the Dutch East Indies, Manila, or Spanish America, "if we were at war with Holland or Spain" (Reese, "Origins," p. 193). As for naval stores, it should be realized that a base was first a reliable place for water, shelter, and "refreshment" (capable of supplying fresh food so that crews could recover their health) and second a place for performing ship repairs—in that order. The history of overseas bases generally bears this out. The essential point was to have a friendly population ashore, in a defensible location, which could grow or stock the necessary fresh provisions. A means of obtaining cordage, canvas, or spars from local resources was an attractive bonus but rarely decisive.

67. De Brosses, *Histoire*, pp. iii–iv.

68. For a brief discussion of De Brosses and Bougainville see A. Carey Taylor, "Charles de Brosses, the Man Behind Cook," in *The Opening of the Pacific: Image and Reality*, National Maritime Museum Monographs, no. 2 (1971). Bougainville's first voyage was financed by a syndicate of merchants from Saint-Malo plus his personal funds. The cost was reimbursed by the courts of France and Spain after the French gave over their claim to the Falklands to the Spanish. The second voyage was financed by the French government; its instructions mentioned precious metals and spices and the hope that he would find "some island close to the Chinese coast, which could be used as a commercial centre for the Compagnie des Indes for trade with China." See Dunmore, *French Explorers*, I, 63–64, 67. For further information on Bougainville's role in trying to secure East Indian spices, see Helen Wallis, ed., *Carteret's Voyage Round the World, 1766–1769* (Cambridge, 1965), I, 96.

Commercial motives were central to the next French Pacific venture, commanded by Jean de Surville (1769–1770); it was backed by a syndicate hoping to exploit opportunities arising from the collapse of the Compagnie des Indes. Surville wished to discover important islands in the Pacific before the British claimed them. See Dunmore, *French Explorers*, I, 114–126; see also Dunmore, ed., *The Expedition of the St. Jean-Baptiste to the Pacific* (Cambridge, 1981), pp. 15–29.

69. Captain George Shelvocke, *A Voyage Round the World by the Way of the Great South Sea, Perform'd in the Years 1719, 20, 21, 22 . . .* (1726; reprinted Amsterdam and New York, 1971), p. ii.

70. See O. H. K. Spate, "De Lozier Bouvet and Mercantilist Expansion in the Pacific in 1740," in John Parker, ed., *Merchants and Scholars* (Minneapolis, 1965), especially pp. 238–240. Bouvet's proposals were addressed to the minister of marine and the Compagnie des Indes. He never got sponsorship for this voyage. His voyage of 1737 had been in search of a way station near one of the cape routes.

71. See Wallis, *Carteret's Voyage*, I, 4–18, II, 298, 322.

72. Taylor, "Charles de Brosses," p. 13. Taylor notes that Spanish pressure had inhibited Egmont in 1766.

73. Warren L. Cook, *Flood Tide of Empire: Spain and the Pacific Northwest, 1543–1819* (New Haven, 1973), pp. 47–54; Donald D. Brand, "Geographical Exploration by the Spaniards," in Herman R. Friis, *The Pacific Basin* (New York, 1967), pp. 138–139; Williams, *Expansion of Europe*, pp. 172–173.

74. The quotation is the last paragraph of the "Booksellers Preface of Introduction" (p. xxix) to *An Account of the Several Voyages to the South and North* . . . , cited in note 33 above. The printers were Samuel Smith and Benjamin Walford. I have omitted the copious italics of the original.

75. The Royal Society's efforts to encourage oceanographic research date almost from its foundation. But it had to rely on voluntary experiments and reports of ships' officers and issued standing instructions to them for guidance. Regarding these *Directions*, issued to guide seamen (masters, pilots, and "other fit persons") in the endeavor, see Margaret Deacon, *Scientists and the Sea, 1650–1900: A Study of Marine Science* (London, 1971), chap. 4.

76. The Board of Longitude was also authorized to give grants in aid of promising research on this problem to anyone who qualified, regardless of nationality, and did so.

77. There can be no controversy about the character of Halley's voyages. See Norman J. W. Thrower, ed., *The Three Voyages of Edmond Halley in the "Paramore," 1698–1701* (Cambridge, 1981), pp. 29–49. As for Dampier's, of course there was the usual hope that he might find spices and other valuable commodities, but the case for science rests on two strong points: (1) his proven reputation as a scientific observer and reporter, which seems to be what gained him sponsorship in the first place; (2) the latitude of his instructions. Dampier had asked for a free hand as to what areas he should probe, and essentially he got it. The Admiralty's instructions mentioned that since the king was "at great charge" in fitting out the expedition, he should try to discover things that "may tend to the advantage of the Nation"—not at all confining. See John Masefield, ed., *Captain William Dampier: Dampier's Voyages* (Edinburgh and New York, 1906), II, 335. On the first point see Shipman, *William Dampier*, p. 8, and Deacon, *Scientists and the Sea*, p. 171; both emphasize the high quality of Dampier's "Discourse of Winds, Breezes, Storms, Tides and Currents," which must have been seen by the Admiralty or other influential persons before its publication in 1699.

78. Although Roggeveen's voyage sought *terra australis incognita*, it is obvious that commerce was the chief object and its backing was commercial. There is no question that Bering's second voyage (1741) was undertaken for the purpose of imperial and commercial expansion, but until fairly recently his first voyage (1728), through the Bering Strait, was accounted a voyage of scientific-geographical inspiration. Taking his cue from certain Soviet scholars, Raymond Fisher has called the traditional interpretation into question. One must read the whole book to gather in the full force of a convincing argument; its central hinge is that Bering learned in Siberia, probably at Yakutsk, geographical information not known at St. Petersburg when his instructions were drawn

up; consequently he sailed northward from Kamchatka toward America instead of eastward. It suited the imperial government's interests to let the scientific interpretation of the voyage's motives enjoy credence. One result of the misinterpretation was that many historians were led to consider the instructions for the second voyage "a mistake" because they were not properly designed to settle the geographical question of the true configuration of the Arctic Ocean in that region—whereas, if Fisher is right, the instructions for the *first* voyage had been faulty and the second voyage was designed to redress the fault (*Bering's Voyages*, especially pp. 73–80, 144–146, 151).

79. See Glyndwr Williams, "Seamen and Philosophers in the South Seas in the Age of Captain Cook," *Mariner's Mirror* 65 (1979): 4: "The motives for the Pacific expeditions after 1763 were not simply, or even primarily, scientific." A large proportion of the scientific equipment (other than that provided for the astronomers) which went on Cook's first voyage was paid for privately by Sir Joseph Banks, though, as Beaglehole observes, certainly not at a cost of £10,000. On the second voyage Banks overdid it and overestimated his influence too; there was a quarrel, the Admiralty at length stood firm, and he did not embark. See Harry Woolf, *The Transits of Venus* (Princeton, 1959), p. 168; Beaglehole, *Life of Cook*, pp. 146–147, 293–297, 303.

80. Beaglehole, *Life of Cook*, p. 484.

81. Mackay, "A Presiding Genius," especially pp. 23, 30.

82. Jean Mayer's comment is apt: "Les expéditions sont donc portées par tout un courant des opinions publiques savantes: l'Europe éclairée approuve chaudement le but fixé: 'parvenir à la parfaite connaissance du globe.' . . . Le mot de 'science' est devenu l'une des clefs de l'Europe." See Mayer, "Le Contexte des grands voyages d'exploration du XVIIIᵉ siècle," in *L'Importance de l'exploration maritime au siècle des lumières: table ronde*, edited by M. Mollat and E. Taillemite (Paris, 1982), p. 38.

83. De Brosses and Dalrymple are interesting in this connection. Both needed the concern for enlarged commerce and maritime power to sustain their advocacy (and seem to have sincerely sought those goals), yet both disliked commercial views. The commercial views they claimed to dislike, however, were the narrow ones of the countinghouse and the careful calculation of profits. Against these they set the bold, the imaginative, and the honorable—"militant geography" joined to militant commerce.

84. Quoted by Mackay, "A Presiding Genius," p. 30. According to Mackay, Sir Joseph favored occupying "the whole coast of Africa from Arguin to Sierra Leone."

85. The British compound of motives during this decade of transition is captured nicely by the preambles to the secret instructions which were given by the Admiralty to the commanders of the expeditions of the 1760s. Any one of these will suffice; the same components are set

down, though in permutated order, in all of them. The opening lines of Cook's secret instructions, dated 30 July 1768, were: "Whereas the making Discoverys of Countries hitherto unknown, and Attaining a Knowledge of distant Parts which though formerly discover'd have yet been but imperfectly explored, will redound greatly to the Honour of this Nation as a Maritime Power, as well as the Dignity of the Crown of Great Britain, and may tend greatly to the advancement of the Trade and Navigation thereof" (Beaglehole, *Life of Cook,* p. 148). The next line directed him to look for *terra australis incognita.* (Cook's overt instructions dealt of course with the transit of Venus.) Byron's secret instructions may be compared; see Gallagher, *Byron's Journal,* p. 3.

The high-sounding formula was dropped in the instructions for Cook's second and third voyages. Their preambles were brief and businesslike, indeed almost nonexistent. Was the merit of exploration now considered self-evident? The instructions of 25 June 1772 began, "Whereas several important Discoveries have been made in the Southern Hemisphere [by specified preceding British voyages]" and then went straight to the point. Printed in J. C. Beaglehole, *The Journals of Captain James Cook on His Voyages of Discovery* (Cambridge, 1961), Vol. II, p. clxvii. For the instructions of 6 July 1776, see Vol. III (1967), p. ccxx.

86. Woolf, *Transits,* p. 83. When the Royal Society, realizing that its budget would not enable it to do what was needed, approached the government concerning the transit of 1761, the earl of Macclesfield wrote a letter of support which stressed national reputation: "And it might afford too just ground to Foreigners for reproaching this Nation in general," if the project were not supported. Macclesfield went on to make an interesting reflection on public versus private sponsorship of science: "But were the Royal Society in a much more affluent State, it would surely tend more to the honour of his Majesty and of the Nation in general, that an Expense of this sort, designed to promote Science and to answer the general Expectation of the World, should not be born by any particular Set of Private Persons" (ibid.). For the 1769 transit the society's memorial to the king said: "It would cast Dishonour upon them [the British nation] should they neglect to have correct observations made of this Important Phenomenon" (Royal Society Council Minutes, vol. 5, fol. 293, 15 February 1768).

87. A succinct account of Cook's navigational and other equipment may be found in J. C. Beaglehole, "Eighteenth Century Science and the Voyages of Discovery," *New Zealand Journal of History* 3 (1969): 115–118.

6
Anthropological Analysis of Exploration Texts: Cultural Discourse and the Ethnological Import of Fray Marcos de Niza's Journey to Cibola

Daniel T. Reff

THE FIRST EUROPEANS TO OBSERVE NATIVE LIFE in many areas of the New World were explorers, individuals who were commissioned by the regents of Europe to discover and claim the riches of the Americas. Upon completion of their missions, the explorers drafted reports and maps, and in the case of many Spaniards, appeared before a judge *(juez de residencia)* to answer questions regarding their exploits. Although the explorers' comments on native peoples whom they encountered often are highly impressionistic, particularly regarding native sociopolitical and religious systems (Sturtevant 1983), the explorers did comment on population numbers, settlement and subsistence systems, trade, warfare, and other more visible aspects of aboriginal culture. There is good reason to believe that Old World diseases accompanied or soon followed many explorers, undermining aboriginal culture before other Europeans were in a position to record more details of native life (Crosby 1972; Dobyns 1966, 1976, 1983; Hudson 1976:102ff.; Jennings 1976:15ff.; Milner 1980; Ramenofsky 1987; Reff 1981, 1987a, 1991).[1] Thus, the exploration chronicles often provide our only glimpse of native life under truly aboriginal conditions.

Despite their potential usefulness, the exploration chronicles often have been ignored or rejected by archeologists, ethnohistorians, and others interested in the period A.D. 1492–1700 and the dynamics of culture change and contact. This neglect is due in part to uncertainty surrounding the explorers' travel routes, and thus the identity of native peoples and settlements described by the explorers (e.g., Hedrick 1978; Hudson 1987). Nowhere is the problem of the explorers' itineraries more apparent than in the Greater Southwest (northwestern Mexico and the American Southwest). For over a century, scholars from a variety of disciplines have debated the routes of explorers such as Diego de Guzmán (1533), Alvar Núñez Cabeza de Vaca (1535–36), Fray Marcos de Niza (1539), Francisco Vásquez de Coronado (1540–42), and Francisco de Ibarra (1564–65) (e.g., Bancroft 1886; Bolton 1949; Di Peso 1974; Reff 1981; Riley 1976; Sauer 1932; Undreiner 1947; Winship 1896). Significantly, native settlements or "kingdoms" such as Corazones, Oera, Señora, and Totonteac, which figure prominently in these explorers' accounts, were rarely if ever mentioned by later missionaries who retraced the explorers' footsteps beginning in the early 1600s.[2] Although recent research indicates that this lack of correspondence between the explorers' and missionaries' reports partly reflects profound, disease-induced changes (Dobyns 1988; Reff 1981, 1987b, 1991; Upham 1982), many have assumed that the explorers exaggerated or lied about the size and complexity of aboriginal cultures (e.g., McGuire and Villalpando 1989:170; Mecham 1927:157). Southwesternists are not alone in this regard, as researchers in other areas of the Americas often have questioned the veracity of the explorers' accounts, particularly observations on the size and complexity of native cultures (Borah 1976:14; Denevan 1976:8; Dobyns 1966:398).

This article focuses on Fray Marcos de Niza's account of his journey to Cibola in 1539, a journey of over 1,000 miles from the frontier settlement of San Miguel de Culiacán in western Mexico to what were seven Zuni settlements in present-day New Mexico (see Figure 1). As is the case with many exploration chronicles, the ethnological import of Marcos's *relación* has never been fully realized. The problem is not simply one of uncertainty surrounding Marcos's travel route. Marcos's critics, and anthropologists, in particular, have been lulled into a false sense of security with respect to the "accuracy" of modern ethnographic texts. Mistrust of pre-anthropology or pre-scientific texts (Thomas 1989) has led many to ignore or reject Marcos's *relación* and other exploration chronicles. This mistrust is evident in previous analyses of Marcos's *relación*, which often have focused largely on whether the friar was a credible witness. Only recently have researchers begun to analyze Marcos's *relación* as narrative discourse (e.g., Ahern 1990), and thus clarify Marcos's motives and audience as well as the many constraints (e.g., literary, philosophical, historical, political) that influenced the form and content of his report (Genette 1980; Pastor 1983).

Marcos's *relación* and other explanation chronicles also have been ignored or rejected for theoretical reasons, specifically the unwitting acceptance of what Jennings (1976) has called the "civilization-savagery" myth. Many researchers have assumed, often implicitly, that Spanish or mission ways of life were superior to their Indian counterpart. The Jesuits, who enjoyed remarkable success in northwestern Mexico between 1591 and 1767 (Alegre 1956–60; Pérez de Ribas 1944; Polzer 1976; Spicer 1962), traditionally have been cast in a role analogous to modern extension agents. Through a variety of innovations (e.g., wheat, plows) the Black Robes are said to have made possible native settlement in towns, regular surpluses, craft specialization, trade, and more complex sociopolitical organizations (see Bannon 1945:194–195; Bolton 1917; Spicer 1962, 1980). The widespread acceptance of this model, which is not supported by data from the 17th century, has predisposed researchers to question the veracity of explorers, such as Marcos, who reported permanent villages, regular surpluses, and other advances that have been attributed to the missionaries.

In the discussion that follows I first review the events surrounding Marcos's journey to Cibola. I then examine the major criticisms that have been leveled at the friar, which I contend reflect important methodological and theoretical presuppositions. The goal is not to defend the friar, but to place his *relación* in its appropriate historical and cultural context. With contextual knowledge, we can assess the substantive value of Marcos's report. Of course, like all forms of cultural discourse, Marcos's comments reflect varying degrees of "reality." Some of his more specific comments regarding native life, when juxtaposed with the archeological record, suggest a continuation into the historic period of the Hohokam and Trincheras cultures, which generally are thought to have collapsed a century before Marcos's *entrada*. I conclude that the friar's *relación*, despite its brevity and shortcomings, is an invaluable window on the protohistoric period (A.D. 1450–1700).

Marcos's *Entrada*

In the summer of 1536, Cabeza de Vaca and three fellow survivors of the ill-fated Narváez expedition to Florida arrived in Mexico City, completing a remarkable eight-year

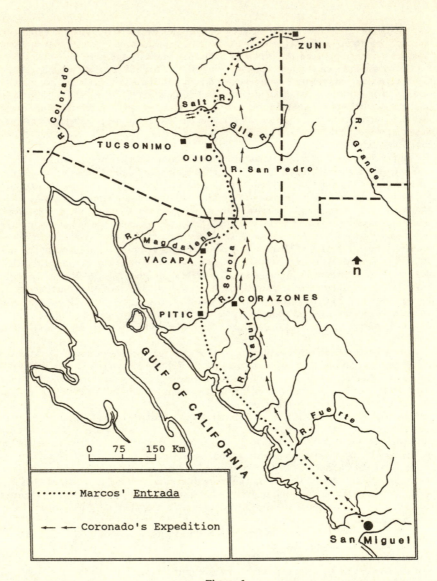

Figure 1
Map showing route of Fray Marcos de Niza's journey to Cibola in 1539 and Coronado's expedition in 1540–42.

trek across the North American continent (Cabeza de Vaca 1986; Hedrick and Riley 1974). The three Spaniards and a Black slave, Esteban, told of fertile and populous lands where turquoise, bison hides, and gold and other metals were seen or spoken of by the natives. The stories gave credence to myths and legends regarding fabulously wealthy cities far to the north. Among those who were stirred to action was the recently appointed Viceroy of New Spain, Antonio de Mendoza. Mendoza proposed to Cabeza de Vaca and his companions that they conduct a further reconnaissance of the lands beyond Nueva Galicia. The three Spaniards all declined the viceroy's offer, although one of the three, Dorantes, volunteered the services of his slave, Esteban, who was perhaps the most knowledgeable survivor of the Narváez expedition with respect to native languages and travel routes in the northern frontier (Cabeza de Vaca 1986:122).

A year or so after Mendoza secured the services of Esteban, Bishop Juan de Zumárraga introduced the viceroy to Marcos de Niza, a Franciscan friar who was experienced in navigation and cosmography, and who had traveled extensively in central America and Peru (Hammond and Rey 1940:61). At the viceroy's request, Fray Marcos agreed to take Esteban and investigate the reports of Cabeza de Vaca and his companions. On March 7, 1539, Fray Marcos, Fray Onorato (a fellow Franciscan), Esteban, and an Indian escort set out from the frontier settlement of San Miguel de Culiacán, along the western coast of Mexico (see Figure 1). Shortly after they departed, Fray Onorato became ill and was forced to return to San Miguel. Marcos and Esteban continued on, and some three months later, Fray Marcos returned without Esteban. In a brief *relación*, the friar reported seeing from a distance a kingdom called Cibola that was larger than Mexico City, and which Indian informants described as wealthy beyond belief. Marcos was prevented from visiting Cibola by the death of Esteban, who had been sent ahead by the friar and was killed at Cibola after he ignored Zuni demands to turn back (Hallenbeck 1987; Hammond and Rey 1940:63ff.).

The information regarding Cibola that was brought back by Fray Marcos followed closely on the heels of the discovery of gold in Peru, and led many in Mexico to believe that Fray Marcos had discovered yet another source of great wealth. Viceroy Mendoza promptly directed the governor of Nueva Galicia, Francisco Vásquez de Coronado, to assemble a full-scale expedition to Cibola. As is well known, Coronado's expedition in 1540–42 found little gold or other riches at Cibola or in other native provinces. To make matters worse, western Mexico was rocked by a native uprising in 1541, while Coronado and many Spaniards from the region were absent in the north. The Mixton War left many Spaniards dead and Spanish property throughout Nueva Galicia destroyed. The revolt as well as the subsequent discovery of silver in and around Zacatecas brought to a close a decade of exploration and discovery (Bancroft 1886:490–514; Brand 1971; Hammond and Rey 1940).

Marcos's *Relación* and Its Interpretation

Although Weber (1987:xxvi) has suggested that anthropologists have been eager to utilize the ethnographic data contained in Marcos's *relación*, few scholars actually have done so. The notable exceptions are Di Peso (1974) and Riley (1982), each of whom has advanced different interpretations of Marcos's travel route. Among historians, those who have accepted Marcos's veracity largely have discussed his journey as an event, as one of several early Spanish explorations of the American Southwest (e.g., Faulk 1968; Perrigo 1971). In point of fact, the ethnohistorical and ethnological import of the friar's *relación* has not been fully pursued. This neglect is attributable to doubts about Marcos's veracity that were raised many years ago by a number of prominent researchers (e.g., Hallenbeck 1987; Sauer 1932; Wagner 1934) who concluded that Marcos lied or exaggerated (see Weber 1987). The doubts persist to the present day. I contend that many if not most of the charges leveled at the friar reflect: (1) an ignorance of exploration discourse and discovery texts, (2) a misreading of Marcos's travel route, and (3) incorrect presuppositions about aboriginal culture.

Marcos's Relación *and Discovery Texts*

One of the most frequent charges leveled against Marcos was that his *relación* lacked specifics and failed to provide information as specified in Viceroy Mendoza's letter of instructions (e.g., Hallenbeck 1987:84ff.; Sauer 1932; Wagner 1934). A related charge is

640   AMERICAN ANTHROPOLOGIST   [93, 1991

that Marcos frequently cited native informants and infrequently wrote in the first person (Hallenbeck 1987:86). Hallenbeck and Sauer argued that the friar could not write in the first person and had to cite native informants because Marcos never traveled as far as he claimed, that is, to Cibola.[3]

Those who have attacked Marcos for the brevity of his report have ignored the fact that, early in his narrative, Marcos explicitly referred to "another paper" in which he recorded more details of his journey, such as the names of islands and settlements he visited or heard about from native informants (Hallenbeck 1987:lviii). Toward the end of his narrative, Marcos again commented "I do not record here many particulars" (Hallenbeck 1987:lxix), implying that he did record them elsewhere, presumably in the "paper" earlier mentioned. This "paper," which has never been found, may well have been in the form of a map, as both the *carta* and the *mapa* were integral parts of discovery texts (Mignolo 1982:60). Although critics may question whether Marcos ever drafted his missing "paper," note that many explorers drafted papers and maps that have never come to light (see Bolton 1949:472ff.). Importantly, Marcos never was accused by the viceroy or his superior (Fray Antonio de Ciudad-Rodrigo) of failing to provide sufficient and/or appropriate information. Indeed, Ciudad-Rodrigo and Mendoza not only approved the friar's report, but both men were instrumental in Marcos's promotion to provincial or head of the Franciscan order in New Spain (Bolton 1949:52; Chavez 1968; Hallenbeck 1987:93).

The accusation that Marcos quoted native informants, rather than writing "I saw," because the friar never reached Cibola also reflects an ignorance of exploration discourse and text formation processes. As Ahern (1990:311) has pointed out, Marcos, unlike other explorers, lacked a notary or *escribano* who could certify the friar's observations. Presumably, Fray Onorato, who was left behind at Petatlán after becoming seriously ill, accompanied Marcos, in part, to affirm Marcos's findings. Fray Onorato's premature return and Esteban's death left no eyewitnesses to certify Marcos's comments. This may help explain why Marcos frequently wrote as if he were a witness, emphasizing what he was told, rather than what he saw.[4] This was particularly true with respect to Cibola, which by Marcos's own statement he never visited.

It should be noted that such influential writers as Sauer (1932, 1940) and Hallenbeck (1987) suggested that Viceroy Mendoza either conspired with Marcos or condoned the friar's "exaggeration" of the wealth of Cibola to secure crown approval for Coronado's expedition. As evidence of this conspiracy, Hallenbeck (1987:90) drew attention to the *legalización* that accompanies Marcos's *relación*, which was certified by two notaries of the Royal *Audiencia*. Hallenbeck argued that the *legalización* states that the notaries were commanded by the viceroy to attest to the truthfulness of the *relación*. However, a careful reading of the *legalización* (see Hallenbeck 1987:lxix–lxx) indicates that the notaries did not attest to the truthfulness of Marcos's report but, rather, acted as witnesses to the formal submission and acceptance of the report. There is nothing sinister or unusual about such proceedings. Indeed, they were characteristic of Spanish colonial government in the Americas (Clonard 1885–1932).

Marcos's Travel Route and Its Interpretation

Many of the charges that have been leveled against the friar are due to a misreading of Marcos's travel route. The friar's critics have assumed that he retraced Cabeza de Vaca's footsteps through the foothills of northern Sinaloa and Sonora. This assumption has been based in part on the erroneous belief that Esteban, who was with Cabeza de Vaca, acted as Marcos's sole or principal guide. Although Esteban accompanied and at times may have advised Fray Marcos, the friar testified that he followed Indian guides (Hammond and Rey 1940:82, n. 19). Still others have assumed that Coronado's expedition followed the same trails as Fray Marcos. Both historical and archeological data indicate that Coronado's expedition did in fact travel up through the Rio Sonora Valley (Reff 1981).

While the majority of researchers have inferred that Marcos traveled well inland, the case also has been made that Marcos traveled near the coast (Oblasser 1939; Riley 1982; Undreiner 1947), as suggested by early observers such as Father Eusebio Kino (Burrus 1971:106). There are several arguments that support this minority view of a coastal route, which have not been made or fully developed in the past. Specifically, it is apparent that Viceroy Mendoza began planning a major expedition to Cibola before Marcos's *entrada*, hoping to forestall or preempt expeditions by Cortés and de Soto (Aiton 1927:120; Bolton 1949:16; Hammond and Rey 1940:3). In drawing up his plans, Mendoza was aware that his principal rival, Cortés, held a patent to explore the coast of western Mexico. Two months before Viceroy Mendoza forwarded his instructions to Fray Marcos, in September 1538, Cortés wrote the Council of the Indies that he had nine ships ready to explore in the north (Bolton 1949:45). The following year, two of the ships, commanded by Francisco de Ulloa, actually set sail to explore the Gulf of California; Viceroy Mendoza seized the other seven ships and blocked Ulloa's progress up the coast (Bancroft 1886:424ff.).

Thus, Mendoza's plan for a major expedition, of which Fray Marcos's *entrada* was but a reconnaissance, called for both land and sea operations. When the plan was implemented in 1540, Coronado led the land forces and Hernando de Alarcon commanded three ships that simultaneously followed the coast northward. Because Mendoza had learned from Cabeza de Vaca and his companions about inland travel, but knew little about the coast, he specifically instructed Fray Marcos to gather information about the seacoast (Hammond and Rey 1940:60).[5] Marcos, himself, commented in his *relación* that "my instructions were not to go away from it [the coast]" (Undreiner 1947:433, n. 60). Coronado also noted in one of his letters to the king that Fray Marcos was sent to explore the coast of New Spain (Hammond and Rey 1940:46). Castañeda, who accompanied Coronado, also implied that Fray Marcos followed the coast when he noted that Coronado initially thought his army would have to travel along the coast to reach Cibola (Hammond and Rey 1940:202). Still other contemporaries of Marcos, such as Motolinía, wrote that Marcos followed the coast (Sauer 1932:21).

Finally, nowhere in his *relación* did Marcos either state or imply that he retraced Cabeza de Vaca's footsteps. Along these lines, the friar made no mention of Corazones or other settlements in the "land of permanent houses," where just three years earlier Esteban and the other survivors of the Narváez expedition were given a warm welcome. Esteban and the three Spaniards were hailed by the Ópata as "sons of the sun"—emissaries of god—and were showered with gifts of food and otherwise treated with reverence (Cabeza de Vaca 1986:118–121; Hedrick and Riley 1974:60–63). As discussed below, Marcos reported encountering Indians "who had not heard of Christians" (Hallenbeck 1987:lvi, see also lx).

The fact that most researchers have assumed that Marcos journeyed inland through the Rio Sonora or Bavispe Valley, rather than near the coast, necessarily has led to "inconsistencies." For instance, Sauer (1932:26) and Hallenbeck (1987) accused Marcos of lying when he reported that some 80 leagues north of Petatlán he encountered Indians who knew nothing of Christians. Sauer argued that Marcos fabricated this lie to support Viceroy Mendoza's claim to lands that previously had been penetrated (and thus claimed) by Nuño de Guzmán. However, if as suggested, Marcos traveled near the coast, then the friar might well have met Indians (Seri) near the lower Rio Sonora who had never seen or heard about Christians. At the time, the coastal region to the north of the Rio Yaqui had not been explored (and thus claimed) by Nuño de Guzmán or his lieutenants. In 1533, an expedition led by Guzmán's nephew, Diego de Guzmán, reached the Rio Yaqui, but subsequently was unsuccessful in finding a route northward along the coast and around the Bacatete Mountains (Hedrick and Riley 1976:49–50).

Many other charges leveled against the friar become spurious once it is acknowledged that Marcos traveled near the coast as far as the Rio Matape, at which point the friar turned slightly northward toward Pitic (Hermosillo), subsequently ascending the Rio Zanjón and the Rio Magdalena, and then turning inland to Cibola (Undreiner 1947). It

642   AMERICAN ANTHROPOLOGIST   [93, 1991

is possible, for instance, to explain how Marcos could have learned about a change in the direction of the seacoast, something that Bolton argued would have been impossible, again, assuming that Marcos traveled inland through the middle and upper Sonora Valley (Bolton 1949:30). Similarly, the fact that Marcos had difficulty guiding Coronado the following year makes sense, given that Marcos's initial route followed the coast, whereas Coronado traveled inland.[6]

Presuppositions about Aboriginal Culture

A significant number of charges that have been leveled against Marcos reflect presuppositions about aboriginal culture that are not supported by data. For instance, Hallenbeck, who was perhaps Marcos's most ardent critic, commented that Marcos's observation that he was escorted by 30 *principales* from one native village "is manifestly absurd," because the largest Ópata town could not have mustered that many shamans (Hallenbeck 1987:81). Yet Marcos neither stated nor implied that these *principales* were shamans. The term as Marcos used it referred to men with political influence (Corominas 1980:IV:650) who were probably heads of local descent groups.[7]

Hallenbeck also rejected as false Marcos's account of the circumstances surrounding Esteban's death. The friar reported that he learned from native informants that Esteban had sent a native with a decorated gourd ahead to announce his impending arrival at Cibola, whereupon the Zuni dashed the gourd to the ground and sent word to Esteban that he and his native entourage should stop and go back, otherwise all would be killed. Hallenbeck (1987:79) insisted that this behavior was European, not Indian. Yet we know that five years earlier, during Diego de Guzmán's *entrada*, a Yaqui chief drew a line on the ground and threatened to kill the Spaniards if they crossed it (Hedrick and Riley 1976:47–48). The Hopi did the same in 1540–41, when a detachment of cavalry from Coronado's expedition penetrated the province of Tusayán (Hammond and Rey 1940:214). It should be noted that the Yaqui, and later the Zuni and the Hopi, undoubtedly were aware of the destruction wrought by the Spaniards in central Mexico and in southern and central Sinaloa. Word traveled quickly (see Hammond and Rey 1940:145). Thus, Marcos's comments regarding the Zuni's treatment of Esteban are entirely consistent with native reactions to European invasion.

Perhaps the most serious charge made against Marcos is that he lied about the size and wealth of Cibola. At issue is not only what the friar reported in his *relación*, but comments that were attributed to the friar by contemporaries. For instance, Fray Gerónimo Ximénez wrote to his provincial in Spain that Marcos personally had told him of temples with idols whose walls, both inside and out, were covered with precious stones ("I believe he [Fray Marcos] told me emeralds"). We have only Ximénez's word, however, that Marcos made such a statement. Significantly, Ximénez's comments were made in a letter that ostensibly was a request that more missionaries be sent to Mexico, an investment that Ximénez implicitly argued would yield riches, not just souls (Icazbalceta 1941:187–188).

Fray Gerónimo Ximénez is one of a number of individuals who claimed to have spoken with or who overheard Fray Marcos describe Cibola as a land of great wealth. As Bolton (1949:30) argued, few if any of these individuals constitute credible witnesses. Other contemporaries of Marcos, such as Bishop Zumárraga (Icazbalceta 1886:283) and Motolinía (Sauer 1932:20), who most certainly spoke with Marcos, neither mentioned nor alluded to the friar having discovered a fabulously wealthy kingdom. The argument can and has been made that it was not Fray Marcos, but restless Spaniards inflamed with gold fever who seized upon a centuries-old myth of seven golden cities (Chavez 1968:11–12; Udall 1987:64). Still other contemporaries of Marcos, such as Las Casas (O'Gorman 1967:I:281, II:183), appear to have embellished the friar's report, to make a point about the complexity and worth of native life and culture (Elliott 1989:54–55).

Contrary to what has been asserted (McGuire and Villalpando 1989:170), Marcos never reported cities of gold. The most provocative statement in Marcos's *relación* was his observation that Cibola had a larger population than the city of Mexico (Hammond and Rey 1940:79).[8] This statement is not as provocative, however, as it first appears to be. Bandelier (1981:100), in particular, pointed out that Marcos had never seen or known the Mexica city of Tenochtitlán. Accordingly, when the friar spoke of Mexico, he probably referred to the colonial settlement of Mexico, which in 1539 had a population that even Marcos's critics acknowledged may have numbered in the thousands—not tens of thousands (Hallenbeck 1987:69–70). Note also that Marcos prefaced his comment regarding the size of Cibola with the admission that he viewed the city and its houses from a distance. It is instructive to cite Coronado's letter to the king, in which he described what he found upon reaching Cibola in 1540, a year after Marcos first saw it. Coronado reported that Cibola consisted of seven "little" villages in a radius of 16 kilometers: one village was said to have 500 hearths; another was even larger (500 +); another was the same size (500 + hearths); and the other four were "somewhat smaller" (450 hearths?). Coronado implied that each "village" included a multi-storied pueblo enclosed by a compound wall, and outside the wall were apparently several hundred hearths distributed among a like number of what were apparently single-storied structures (Hammond and Rey 1940:170–171).

Coronado's comments suggest that the largest Zuni settlement—presumably the same upon which Marcos focused, albeit from a distance—had a population of between 2,500 and 3,000 (assuming 5 or 6 individuals per hearth/house). Nearby, were other "villages" or multi-storied pueblos that were surrounded by upward of 100 or 200 single-storied structures that may have come within Marcos's view (Bandelier 1981:92ff.). If so, then it is perhaps understandable that the friar compared Cibola to Mexico.[9]

The Devaluation of Exploration Texts

The intention here is not to suggest that Marcos's travel route is readily inferable or that Marcos's *relación* provides a complete and accurate picture of native life. No brief account of a journey of over 2,000 miles (round-trip) into unknown territory, and among unknown peoples, with whom communication is through interpreters, could be complete and precise. Note that Marcos himself alluded to the difficulty of gathering information when he noted in his *relación* that he tried "by all possible means" (Hallenbeck 1987:lvi), presumably through interpreters, through sign language, and by illustration (on paper or in the sand) to learn about populous and advanced native cultures. Elsewhere, Marcos mentioned that he brought various metals with him, which he showed native peoples in an effort to learn about the metals that existed in areas through which he passed (Hammond and Rey 1940:65). The dangers inherent in this and other forms of indirect communication are apparent from the friar's experience along the lower Rio Sonora, where he was told, or inferred, that the natives farther upstream, the Ópata of the middle Sonora Valley, had pendants and vessels of gold. The reality, as revealed by archeological research (Pailes 1978, 1981), is that the Ópata added crushed mica to their potters' clay, which does have the appearance of gold, and fashioned pendants from sheets of mica.[10]

Marcos's *relación*, like all interpretations and descriptions of another culture, necessarily was constrained by the limitations of time, language, and the cultural categories and perceptions of both Marcos and his informants (White 1978). It is unreasonable to expect Marcos's report or the accounts of other explorers, which were written some 400 years ago, to address all the issues that researchers today deem important. This is true, for instance, of the explorers' itineraries, about which the explorers frequently said relatively little. Implicitly, many have assumed that it was desirable or necessary for the explorers to record details about their travel routes. As Marcos testified (Hammond and Rey 1940:82, n. 19), the explorers relied on Indian guides, who knew which trails to take during which seasons and where food and water could be obtained at different times of the year, and who had other information (e.g., current wars) that was crucial to travel in unfamiliar regions, particularly arid regions such as the Greater Southwest (see also Di

644   AMERICAN ANTHROPOLOGIST   [93, 1991

Peso 1974:37; Riley 1971). No explorer contemplated leading an expedition without Indian guides. Accordingly, Marcos was neither expected (see Mendoza's letter of instructions [Hammond and Rey 1940:58ff.]) nor did he consider it practical or necessary to detail the precise route he followed. Note also that there was stiff competition among Spaniards as well as between Spaniards and other Europeans, particularly the Portuguese, to discover America's riches (Bolton 1949:40ff.). Accordingly, explorers and their financial backers may have preferred reports that were vague about the explorers' routes, to prevent competitors from making use of this information.

In sum, placing Marcos's report in its proper historical and cultural context sheds light on how and why the friar addressed some issues and not others. In the past, researchers instead have focused largely on one inappropriately framed question: Did Marcos tell the truth? As noted at the outset, Marcos is not the only explorer who has been held suspect— many early explorers have been accused of misrepresenting the facts. The argument continues to be made that the explorers were not social scientists, and accordingly, their accounts often are conflicting and vague, filtered through a European ethnocentrism, and/or were composed for ulterior motives, to defame or defend the explorers' actions (see McGuire and Villalpando 1989:170).

Clearly, explorers such as Marcos were not social scientists. However, formal social science education does not render observers free of bias, ethnocentrism, imprecision, and ulterior motives. For many years anthropologists have assumed that only trained anthropologists can interpret another culture correctly; explorers and the like have been denigrated as pre-scientific amateurs (Thomas 1989:22ff., 69ff.). Fortunately, more and more anthropologists, historians, and other social scientists have begun to critically analyze their own research (e.g., Brown 1987; Clifford 1988; Clifford and Marcus 1986; Geertz 1990; Hodder 1986; Thomas 1989), acknowledging that their observations and textual production necessarily are filtered through a Euro-American ethnocentrism. In practical terms, anthropological texts or ethnographies are much like exploration texts in that they often are (1) based on relatively brief exposure to native peoples, (2) the product of interviews with a relatively small number of informants, usually males, particularly senior males, and (3) are committed to paper several months or even years after the fieldwork itself. Phenomenologists also would point to the dominant-submissive relationship inherent in both the ethnographer's and the explorer's interaction with non-Western people.

It also is apparent that modern research has suffered from ideological and theoretical biases that have filtered or otherwise distorted "reality." Is there a significant difference between Marcos, who saw a city where there was a group of Zuni villages, and a modern ethnographer such as Benedict, who, encumbered by prevailing theoretical currents, lost sight of Zuni history and the complexity of Zuni culture, subsuming it in an Apollonian stereotype (Benedict 1930, 1934)? More contemporary research has suffered as well from theoretical presuppositions every bit as "blinding" as those that clouded the friar's vision. Historians and anthropologists long have assumed that Jesuit innovations, such as plows, cattle, and wheat, revolutionized native life in northwestern Mexico and southern Arizona, making possible native settlement in towns, crop surpluses, craft specialization, trade, and more complex sociopolitical organization (see Bannon 1945:194–195; Bolton 1917; Doyel 1989:144ff.; Fontana 1976:50–51; Sheridan 1988; Spicer 1962, 1980). Although many Jesuit innovations, in time, did come to play an important part in native life, both archeological (Di Peso 1953:238, 275) and historical data (de Faria 1657; Pérez de Ribas 1638; Hackett 1937:95ff.) indicate that many innovations were of little consequence during the early historic period. The Jesuit materials indicate that, rather than "revolutionizing" native life through European innovations (Spicer 1980:32, 86), the Jesuits effectively *reconstituted* native productive and organizational strategies that faltered or collapsed in the wake of Old World diseases (Dobyns 1983; Reff 1987b, 1991). Epidemics of smallpox, measles, typhus, and other maladies occurred throughout the Jesuits' tenure in northwestern New Spain (1591–1767), affecting such groups as the Pima Alto after

Marcos's *entrada* and before the founding of the first permanent mission among the Pima Alto in the late 1600s. In this regard, the fact that Marcos's comments regarding Pima culture are seemingly at odds with the later views of missionaries such as Kino reflects disease and its consequences, not Marcos's presumed predilection to lie or exaggerate.

The evidence regarding disease and the inconsequential nature of Jesuit innovations during the 16th and 17th centuries frequently has been overlooked by Southwesternists, many of whom have been "blinded" by presuppositions about the dynamics of Jesuit and Indian relations. To acknowledge that anthropological texts are encumbered by theoretical and methodological presuppositions or constraints is not to suggest, however, that the texts should be ignored or rejected in their entirety. As Thomas (1989:79) has noted with respect to the functionalist literature, functionalist premises do not animate or permeate the entire fabric of a functionalist ethnography. Similarly, the fact that Benedict employed psychological types, or that Bolton and Spicer consistently overlooked historical evidence of disease and its profound consequences, does not negate their otherwise insightful research.[11] The ambiguity surrounding Marcos's comments regarding the size and greatness of Cibola, is, likewise, insufficient ground for ignoring or rejecting the friar's *relación*.

Marcos's *Relación* and Its Anthropological Import

If we approach Marcos's *relación* with the same concerns that we ordinarily bring to the analysis of modern texts, acknowledging the evidence that the friar did not willfully lie, then we are at once provided with a window on the protohistoric period. Because of the brevity of Marcos's *relación* and the fact that it was written for reasons quite different from those that motivate a modern ethnographer, the friar's account provides only a glimpse of native life. Still, the view is of immeasurable importance for archeologists and ethnohistorians.

For almost a century now, archeologists have postulated that warfare, floods, or other natural or man-made disasters were responsible for the demise or collapse around A.D. 1400–1450 of the Trincheras and Hohokam cultures of northwestern Mexico and southern Arizona. The remnants of these once-populous and advanced cultures are equated with the Pima Alto—the historic inhabitants of northwestern Sonora and southern Arizona (Ezell 1963; Fontana 1983; Gumerman and Haury 1979; Haury 1976). Despite considerable research in the past two decades, particularly in southern Arizona, both the dating and causes of the collapse remain problematic (Braniff 1985; Doelle and Wallace 1989; Doyel 1989:142ff.; Eighmy and McGuire 1988; LeBlanc 1986; McGuire and Villalpando 1989).[12] When and why the vast majority of Hohokam and Trincheras settlements were abandoned remains unclear, although it is apparent that some and perhaps many were forsaken during the late prehistoric period. Surprisingly, archeologists have not made use of Marcos's *relación* to address issues pertaining to the "collapse" (e.g., Doelle 1981; Doyel 1989; Gumerman and Haury 1979; McGuire and Villalpando 1989:171).

The friar's comments, in fact, suggest that the Hohokam and Trincheras cultures persisted into the historic period. The fact that Fray Marcos reported only two uninhabited areas *(despoblados)*[13] during his entire journey from the lower Rio Sonora to Zuni suggests that northwestern Sonora and southern Arizona retained a sizable population in 1539. Most anthropologists have assumed that the entire Pima Alto population numbered between 20,000 and 30,000, aboriginally. This estimate is based on reports from circa A.D. 1700, and does not reflect population losses from disease, which probably exceeded 50%. Losses of greater magnitude (80%) during the period prior to A.D. 1700 have been documented for the Pima Alto's kin, the Pima Bajo—as well as for neighboring groups, such as the Ópata, Pueblos, and Yaqui (Gerhard 1982; Reff 1991; Upham 1982).

Sixteenth-century Spaniards and other Europeans were quite conscious of settlement-size distinctions, for both legal and ideological reasons (Nader 1990; Pagden 1982:97–98; Vassberg 1984). It is significant, therefore, that Marcos mentioned "good lodging" and

646 *AMERICAN ANTHROPOLOGIST* [93, 1991

"good size" settlements such as Vacapa and referred to *villas* or pueblos, as opposed to *ranchos* or *aldeas* (see Gibson 1964:32). The friar's comments support the idea that a significant number of Pima were still residing in permanent villages in 1539, as opposed to small *rancherías* (70 to 120 persons) with single-unit structures of poles and mats or brush (Doelle 1981; Franklin and Masse 1976; Masse 1981). During his journey northward, Fray Marcos commented on at least several occasions about native use of irrigation and Pima surpluses of food and cotton. That the Pima were able to exceed subsistence needs is apparent from the friar's numerous references to trade in turquoise and what apparently were bison robes. Marcos also mentioned traveling along a wide and much-used road that was lined at intervals with "old huts, and many signs of dead fires, made by the people who travelled the road to Cibola" (Hallenbeck 1987:lxiv). At what apparently was the pueblo of Ojio (Undreiner 1947:449), Fray Marcos saw what he described as "very pretty bowls" *(xícaras muy lindas)* (Hallenbeck 1987:lx). The friar's use of the term *xícaras* is suggestive of Gila Polychrome, one of several decorated pottery types that archeologists once thought were no longer made after A.D. 1450, but which are now known to have been made well into the historic period (Di Peso 1976).[14] Marcos also mentioned or alluded to native elites or individuals with differential access to goods and services, as when he commented on the ruler of Ojio and his two brothers being "very well dressed in cotton, adorned, and each wearing a turquoise necklace" (Hallenbeck 1987:lx).

Although Fray Marcos did not visit the Hohokam heartland along the lower Gila and Salt rivers, the information he received from native informants regarding the "kingdom" of Totonteac suggests that at least some of the "Great Houses" survived into the early historic period. Note that an error in Hammond and Rey's (1940) widely used translation of Marcos's account (see Undreiner 1947:462, n. 131) as well as unfounded assumptions (e.g., Hallenbeck 1987:40) have led many researchers to wrongly equate Totonteac with the Pueblos of the Rio Grande drainage. Fray Marcos explicitly was told by the inhabitants of the Salt River Valley that Totonteac was "toward the west" (Undreiner 1947:462, n. 131). Moreover, Fray Marcos repeatedly was told that the Totonteacs wore clothing of a wool-like material *(paño de laña)* that was taken from an animal the size of a Castellan greyhound (Hallenbeck 1987:lxi). Captain Juan Manje reported in 1697 a large number of wild-sheep horns (more than 100,000 antlers) at Tucsonimo, a short distance downstream from the Classic period ruins of Casa Grande—in the former Hohokam heartland (Burrus 1971:209).[15] Of particular significance is that Marcos was told on more than one occasion by natives of different villages that the houses of Totonteac were like those in Cibola (single- and multi-storied structures), but greater in number, and "better" (e.g., Hallenbeck 1987:lxi). Marcos also was told that the Totonteacs had complex sociopolitical and ideological systems *(gente de mucha pulicía)*,[16] quite different from other native peoples. The Totonteacs also were described as the most populous and wealthiest of native groups (Hallenbeck 1987:lix–lxiii, lxviii; Hammond and Rey 1940:71–72, 78–79). These summary statements are consistent with conventional archeological descriptions of the Classic period (A.D. 1250–1450) Hohokam.

Much of what Marcos was told about Totonteac was volunteered by natives of the Salt River Valley, in the lower Tonto Basin. On the basis of archeological evidence, we know that the Salado of the lower Tonto Basin were living in small villages as well as multi-storied pueblos a century before Marcos's *entrada*. The remains of some of the largest and architecturally more complex pueblos ("mound sites") occur at fairly regular intervals below the juncture of Pinto Creek and the Salt River, and are associated with a substantial number of water-control features (e.g., check dams, linear terraces), including canals (Jewett 1989:377ff.). In recent years, some archeologists have suggested that the Salado were part of the Classic period Hohokam interaction sphere (LeBlanc 1986:126; Wood and McAllister 1982). Continued Salado-Hohokam interaction would explain why the Salado were so knowledgeable about and talked so favorably of Totonteac (Classic period Hohokam).

Nevertheless, the possibility that the Salado persisted into the historic period has not been fully considered (Doyel and Haury 1976; Wood and McAllister 1982). Although Gila Polychrome, which is known to have been made during the 16th century, has been found at more than half the "mound sites" in the lower Tonto Basin (Jewett 1989:379), archeologists have inferred that the Salado of the lower Tonto Basin disappeared or abandoned the region at roughly the same time the Classic period Hohokam disappeared or collapsed (A.D. 1400–1450). This interpretation clearly is at odds with Marcos's brief but telling comments about the inhabitants of the Salt River Valley. The friar spent over a week in the Valley, passing through the lower Tonto Basin (Hammond and Rey 1940:71–73; Undreiner 1947:455ff.). According to Marcos, the Valley was very well populated, and "all irrigated like a flower garden," with pueblos every one or two kilometers (Hallenbeck 1987:lxii).[17] Fray Marcos further commented that the natives had abundant food and what apparently was cotton. The natives also spoke highly and at great length of Totonteac and Cibola (Hallenbeck 1987:lxiii; Hammond and Rey 1940:71–73). Marcos was told that some natives went to work at Cibola to acquire turquoise and bison hides, of which they had an abundance.[18] Again, these comments are entirely consistent with archeological interpretations of the "prehistoric" Salado.

There are numerous other observations regarding native life that can be gleaned from Marcos's *relación*. The friar's comments challenge a number of our assumptions regarding aboriginal culture and our interpretations of both the archeological and historical records. Specifically, Marcos's *relación* suggests that we have misconstrued the protohistoric period (A.D. 1450–1700) in the Greater Southwest, equating the failure of some and perhaps many communities with the wholesale collapse of cultures such as the Hohokam and Trincheras.

Conclusions

Over a century before archeologists began working in the Greater Southwest, Jesuit missionaries and historians (e.g., de Albieuri 1633; Nentvig 1980; Pfefferkorn 1949) began fabricating a variant of what Jennings (1976) has termed the "civilization-savagery" myth. Modern historians and anthropologists have unintentionally reified the myth, particularly the notion that Jesuit innovations played a dynamic role in acculturative processes during the early historic period. To accommodate both the archeological evidence of large and sophisticated cultures and the notion that the missionaries revolutionized native life, archeologists posited a collapse centuries before the arrival of the Jesuits. The idea of a collapse and the idea that Jesuit innovations revolutionized aboriginal culture, in turn, have predisposed researchers to question or ignore exploration texts, such as Marcos's *relación*, which contradict both postulates.

As previously discussed, the exploration chronicles also have been viewed as pre-scientific and, therefore, unreliable texts. This negative view of nonanthropological discourse is a reflection of an early yet persistent concern with distinguishing anthropology as a science (Hudson 1987). In the process, anthropologists often have lost sight of the value of historical descriptions of "the other." The recent debate about whether members of one society or culture can interpret and speak for another has helped to correct this situation. It is hoped that this discussion will encourage more research with early texts such as the exploration chronicles. As is the case with Fray Marcos's brief report, the chronicles often provide an invaluable glimpse of the early historic period—arguably the most significant of all periods with respect to our understanding of native America. Our knowledge of contemporary native American culture—be it native languages, kinship systems, or religion—necessarily hinges on a better understanding of what we know or suspect were profound changes during the two centuries following Columbus's fateful "discovery." Some understanding of these changes is a prerequisite for accurately interpreting the archeological record of prehistory as well, particularly given our extensive use of ethnographic analogies, which generally are assumed to reflect or roughly approximate aboriginal conditions.

648   *AMERICAN ANTHROPOLOGIST*   [93, 1991

In short, the 16th and 17th centuries are too important a period for us to ignore or dismiss the exploration chronicles, particularly on the basis of rudimentary textual analysis. As others have demonstrated or suggested (e.g., Ahern 1990; Galloway 1990; Mignolo 1982; Molloy 1987), critical, contextual analysis of the exploration chronicles can shed invaluable light on both the European and Indian participants in the early contact drama.

Notes

Acknowledgments. I wish to thank Nancy Ettlinger, Maureen Ahern, and William Dancey for reading and commenting on one or more drafts of this article. The anonymous *AA* reviewers also offered a number of very helpful suggestions, for which I am grateful.

[1]There also is evidence that Old World diseases preceded European explorers in some areas (e.g., Cieza de Leon 1959:52; Craine and Reindrop 1970:65–68).

[2]The "Señora Valley" is a notable exception. Pérez de Ribas (1944:II:186) and the anonymous author of the *Estado de la Provincia de Sonora* (Anonymous 1730:625) both equated the "Señora Valley" with the present-day Rio Sonora Valley (Reff 1981).

[3]Castañeda, who accompanied Coronado's expedition in 1540–42, was the first to accuse Marcos of not reaching Cibola (Hammond and Rey 1940:199). Scholars long have questioned Castañeda's objectivity (see Bolton 1949). As an example, Castañeda erred or lied when he implied that one or more Franciscans were with Marcos when the latter received word of Esteban's death.

[4]The literature of 16th-century Spain includes innumerable histories, "relations," epic poems, and other works on the Indies that confused fact and fiction, and exploited sensational elements to engage the reader's attention (Adorno 1986). Writers who sought to emphasize the truth of a statement invariably noted that it was based on firsthand observation (Mignolo 1982:57ff.). This may further explain Marcos's concern with distinguishing what he observed and what he was told by the Indians.

[5]Cabeza de Vaca (1986:122) and his companions (Hedrick and Riley 1976:63) learned at Corazones, upriver from modern Ures, that the region along the coast to the north was well populated, and the natives lived in large houses that were well supplied with food, cotton, and turquoise. Presumably, this information was shared with Viceroy Mendoza, providing him with additional reason to have Fray Marcos travel near the coast.

[6]Prior to Coronado's departure for Cibola, the Viceroy sent Melchior Diaz and a small detachment of cavalry northward from the Villa of San Miguel to reconnoiter and to affirm Marcos's report. The onset of winter prevented the reconnaissance from reaching Cibola, although Diaz did learn from native peoples en route about Cibola and Totonteac. Much of what he was told is consistent with what Marcos reported (Hammond and Rey 1940:156ff.).

[7]Pérez de Ribas, who was one of the first Jesuits to work among the Cahita, noted that each Yaqui *ranchería* contained groups of kinsmen who were led by certain *"principales,"* reportedly "those who had sons among them" (Pérez de Ribas 1617). Pérez de Ribas (1944:I:132, II:227) noted that it was primarily the *principales* and *cabezas* who enjoyed the benefits of polygamy and that having more than one wife meant having more children, which was the basis of political power (Reff 1991).

[8]Critics also have taken Marcos to task for commenting that Cibola *appeared* (emphasis mine) to be the greatest and best of all the lands that had been discovered. Again, Marcos explicitly acknowledged that he never saw Cibola close-up, and that his comments were based on what he was told by native informants. It must be kept in mind that Marcos's *relación* was written first and foremost to his superior. From the perspective of evangelization, the friar had reason to characterize the northern frontier as the greatest and best of all the lands that had been discovered. Native groups in the Greater Southwest appeared to lack idols, human sacrifice, and extensive polygamy (see Icazbalceta 1886:283), all of which were major obstacles to religious conversion in Mesoamerica (Ricard 1966).

[9]Archeologists disagree about which settlements were occupied, as well as the population of individual pueblos and the entire "Cibola area" in A.D. 1540 (Ferguson and Mills 1982; Kintigh 1990; Upham 1982).

[10]Marcos was not the only European who inferred that the Ópata made pottery with gold. Father Joseph Och, who worked among the Ópata prior to the Jesuit expulsion (1767), also incorrectly reported that the Ópata made pottery with thousands of gold "scales" (Och 1965:112–113).

[11]Both Bolton and Spicer made extensive use of Jesuit materials, such as the *anuas* and the works of Pérez de Ribas (1896, 1944), which abound in references to disease and epidemics.

[12]The dating of the collapse or the abandonment of Classic period sites has been particularly problematic. Although hundreds of archeomagnetic dates have been secured in recent years from sites in southern Arizona, published site reports are available for only a fraction of the dated samples. A recent analysis of reported dates concluded that there was insufficient data to determine when the Civano, El Polvoron, or other local phases in the Hohokam area came to an end, although the date was sometime after A.D. 1425 or 1450 (Eighmy and McGuire 1988:48; see also Dobyns 1988, 1990; Eighmy and Doyel 1987: Table 2, 339).

[13]The term *despoblado* had a precise, legal meaning in 16th-century Spain, and referred to "Any municipality deserted or too small to maintain a functioning council" (Nader 1990:228). Presumably, Fray Marcos used the term as a referent for an area that was wholly or largely uninhabited or that lacked permanent settlements.

[14]*Xícara* or *jícara* is from the Nahuatl *xícalli* and was used in Mexico and Central America originally as a referent for a hemispherical bowl with a large mouth that was carved from the *jícara* plant, and which was used by the Mexica and other groups for drinking a beverage made from *cacao*. Apparently the bowls frequently were decorated using one or more techniques, including the application of various colors (polychrome), engraving, polishing, and smudging. The term *xícara* or *jícara* also was used in a more general sense as a referent for any hemispherical bowl with a large mouth (Santamaria 1974:633–634). Along these lines, the most common form of Gila Polychrome is apparently a hemispherical bowl, some of which had smudged interiors (Di Peso 1976:59; McGregor 1965:369–370).

[15]Although Manje mentions or alludes to the sheep being utilized for food, presumably the Hohokam/Pima also used the animal's wool for some items of clothing, as did other prehistoric people (Kent 1983:26).

[16]Although *mucha pulicía* has been translated as "very orderly" (Hammond and Rey 1940:72) or "much culture" (Hallenbeck 1987:26), the term *pulicía* implied much more to Spaniards and other Europeans in the 16th century. People who had *pulicía* or lived in *politia* necessarily were town or city dwellers and were "civilized," having among other things, "true" government, with rulers and elites (see Corominas 1980:IV:598; Pagden 1982:98ff.).

[17]Marcos used the term *barrios* and then *pueblos* to refer to the same settlements. The friar may have perceived that each pueblo was inhabited by distinct kin group(s), which prompted his use of the term *barrios* (see Beals 1932:118–119; Boyd-Bowman 1974:115; Burrus 1971:378; Pérez de Ribas 1617).

[18]In what may have been a veiled reference to "Salado" sites in southwestern New Mexico (Le Blanc 1986:125–126), the natives told Marcos of another "kingdom" called Marata, "which used to have many and very large settlements, and that all of them had these stone houses and terraces." Because of warfare with Cibola, Marata had been greatly reduced, "although it is still independent and at war with the others" (Hammond and Rey 1940:72).

References Cited

Adorno, Rolena
    1986   Literary Production and Suppression: Reading and Writing about the Amerindians in Colonial Spanish America. Dispositio (Revista Hispanica de Semiótica Literaria 11(28–29):1–25.
Ahern, Maureen
    1990   The Certification of Cibola: Discursive Strategies in *La Relación Del Descubrimiento De Las Siete Cuidades* by Fray Marcos de Niza (1539). Dispositio (Revista Hispánica de Semiótica Literaria) 14(36–38):303–313.
Aiton, Arthur S.
    1927   Antonio de Mendoza, First Viceroy of New Spain. Durham, NC: Duke University Press.
Alegre, Francisco Javier, S. J.
    1956–60   Historia de la Províñcia de la Compañía de Jesús de Nueva España. 4 vols. E. J. Burrus and F. Zubillaga, eds. Rome: Jesuit Historical Institute.
Anonymous
    1730   Estado de la Provincia de Sonora, con el catalogo de sus pueblos, iglesias, lenguas diversas. . . . Anonymous Jesuit Missionary, July, 1730. Documentos para la Historia de Mexico, Cuarta Serie, Tomo III, Mexico (1857).
Bancroft, Hubert H.
    1886   The Works of Hubert Howe Bancroft, Volume 10: History of Mexico. Volume 2:1521–1600. San Francisco: A. L. Bancroft.

650   *AMERICAN ANTHROPOLOGIST*   [93, 1991

Bandelier, Adolph F.
    1981   The Discovery of New Mexico. M. T. Rodack, trans. Tucson: University of Arizona
        Press.
Bannon, John Francis, S. J.
    1945   Pioneer Jesuit Missionaries on the Pacific Slope of New Spain. *In* Greater America: Essays
        in Honor of Herbert Eugene Bolton. Pp. 181–197. Berkeley: University of California Press.
Beals, Ralph
    1932   The Comparative Ethnology of Northern Mexico before 1750. Ibero-Americana, 2.
        Berkeley: University of California Press.
Benedict, Ruth
    1930   Psychological Types in the Cultures of the Southwest. Proceedings of the 23rd Interna-
        tional Congress of Americanists. Pp. 572–581. New York.
    1934   Patterns of Culture. New York: Houghton Mifflin.
Bolton, Herbert E.
    1917   The Mission as a Frontier Institution in the Spanish-American Colonies. American His-
        torical Review 23:42–61.
    1949   Coronado, Knight of Pueblos and Plains. Albuquerque: University of New Mexico Press.
Borah, Woodrow
    1976   The Historical Demography of Aboriginal and Colonial America: An Attempt at Per-
        spective. *In* The Native Population of the Americas in 1492. William Denevan, ed. Pp. 13–34.
        Madison: University of Wisconsin Press.
Boyd-Bowman, Peter
    1974   Lexico Hispanoamericano del Siglo XVI. London: Tamesis Books.
Brand, Donald B.
    1971   Ethnohistoric Synthesis of Western Mexico. *In* Handbook of Middle American Indians,
        Volume 11: Archaeology of Northern Mesoamerica, Part 2. Gordon F. Ekholm and I. Bernal,
        eds. Pp. 632–656. Austin: University of Texas Press.
Braniff, Beatriz C.
    1985   La frontera protohistorica Pima-Ópata en Sonora, Mexico: Proposiciones arqueologicas
        preliminares. Ph.D. dissertation, Department of Anthropology, Universidad Nacional Auton-
        oma de Mexico.
Brown, Harvey
    1987   Positivism, Relativism, and Narrative in the Logic of Historical Sciences. American His-
        torical Review 92:908–920.
Burrus, Ernest J., S. J.
    1971   Kino and Manje, Explorers of Sonora and Arizona. Sources and Studies for the History
        of the Americas, 10. Rome: Jesuit Historical Institute.
Cabeza de Vaca, Alvar Nuñez
    1986   La relación o naufragios de Alvar Núñez Cabeza de Vaca. Martin A. Favata and Jose B.
        Fernandez, eds. Potomac, MD: Scripta Humanistica.
Chavez, O. F. M., Fray Angelico
    1968   Coronado's Friars. Washington, DC: Academy of American Franciscan History.
Cieza de Leon, Pedro
    1959   The Incas. H. de Onis, trans., V. W. von Hagen, ed. Norman: University of Oklahoma
        Press.
Clifford, James
    1988   The Predicament of Culture. Cambridge, MA: Harvard University Press.
Clifford, James, and George Marcus, eds.
    1986   Writing Culture: The Poetics and Politics of Ethnography. Berkeley: University of Cali-
        fornia Press.
Clonard, Serafin Maria de Soto, Conde de
    1885–1932   Colección de documentos inéditos relativos al descubrimiento, conquista y organ-
        izacion de las antiguas posesiones españolas de ultramar. 25 vols. Segunda serie. Madrid: Real
        Academia de la Historia.
Corominas, Joan
    1980   Diccionario crítico etimológico Castellano e Hispánico. 5 vols. Madrid: Editorial Gredos.
Craine, Eugene R., and R. C. Reindrop, trans. and eds.
    1970   The Chronicles of Michoacan. Norman: University of Oklahoma Press.

Crosby, Alfred
  1972   The Columbian Exchange: Biocultural Consequences of 1492. Westport, CT: Greenwood Press.
de Albieuri, Juan
  1633   Historia de las missiones apostolicas, que los clerigos regulares de la Compañía de Jesús an echo en las Indias Occidentales del reyno de la Nueva Vizcaya. Mexican Manuscript 7. Hubert H. Bancroft Collection, Bancroft Library, University of California, Berkeley.
de Faria, Francisco Xavier
  1657   Historia 316. Apologetico defensorio y puntual manifesto que los Padres de la Compañía de Jesús, missioneros de las Provincias de Sinaloa y Sonora. Archivo General de la Nación, Mexico City.
Denevan, William M.
  1976   Estimating the Unknown. *In* The Native Population of the Americas in 1492. W. M. Denevan, ed. Pp. 1–12. Madison: University of Wisconsin Press.
Di Peso, Charles C.
  1953   The Sobaipuri Indians of the Upper San Pedro River Valley, Southeastern Arizona. Dragoon, AZ: Amerind Foundation.
  1974   History. *In* Casas Grandes, A Fallen Trading Center of the Gran Chichimeca, Volume 4. C. Di Peso, J. B. Rinaldo, and G. Fenner, eds. Pp. 37–120. Flagstaff, AZ: Northland Press.
  1976   Gila Polychrome in the Casas Grandes Region. Kiva 42(1):57–64.
Dobyns, Henry F.
  1966   An Appraisal of Techniques with a New Hemispheric Estimate. Current Anthropology 7:395–449.
  1976   Native American Historical Demography. Bloomington: Indiana University Press.
  1983   Their Number Become Thinned. Knoxville: University of Tennessee Press.
  1988   Piman Indian Historic Agave Cultivation. Desert Plants 9(2):49–53.
  1990   Comments, Prehistoric to Historic Transitions: Chronological Considerations. *In* Perspectives on Southwestern Prehistory. P. E. Minnis and C. L. Redman, eds. Pp. 301–307. Boulder, CO: Westview Press.
Doelle, William H.
  1981   The Gila Pima in the Late Seventeenth Century. *In* The Protohistoric Period in the North American Southwest, AD 1450–1700. D. R. Wilcox and W. B. Masse, eds. Pp. 57–70. Tempe: Arizona State University Anthropological Research Papers, 24.
Doelle, William H., and Henry W. Wallace
  1989   The Transition to History in Pimeria Alta. *In* Perspectives on Southwestern Prehistory. P. E. Minnis and C. L. Redman, eds. Pp. 239–258. Boulder, CO: Westview Press.
Doyel, David E.
  1989   The Transition to History in Northern Pimeria Alta. *In* Columbian Consequences, Volume 1: Archaeological and Historical Perspectives on the Spanish Borderlands West. D. H. Thomas, ed. Pp. 139–159. Washington, DC: Smithsonian Institution Press.
Doyel, David E., and Emil Haury, eds.
  1976   The 1976 Salado Conference. Kiva 42(1).
Eighmy, Jeffrey L., and David E. Doyel
  1987   A Reanalysis of First Reported Archaeomagnetic Dates from the Hohokam Area, Southern Arizona. Journal of Field Archaeology 14(3):331–352.
Eighmy, Jeffrey L., and Randall H. McGuire
  1988   Archaeomagnetic Dates and the Hohokam Phase Sequence. Technical Series, No. 3. Fort Collins: Colorado State University Archaeometric Lab.
Elliott, J. H.
  1989   Spain and Its World. New Haven, CT: Yale University Press.
Ezell, Paul H.
  1963   Is There a Hohokam-Pima Culture Continuum? American Antiquity 29:61–66.
Faulk, Odie B.
  1968   Land of Many Frontiers: A History of the American Southwest. New York: Oxford University Press.
Ferguson, T. J., and Barbara Mills
  1982   Archaeological Investigations at Zuni Pueblo, New Mexico, 1977–1980. Zuni, NM: Zuni Archaeology Program, Pueblo of Zuni Report 183.

652   AMERICAN ANTHROPOLOGIST   [93, 1991

Fontana, B. L.
    1976   The Faces and Forces of Pimeria Alta. *In* Voices from the Southwest, A Gathering in Honor of Lawrence Clark Powell. D. C. Dickinson, ed. Pp. 45–54. Flagstaff, AZ: Northland Press.
    1983   Pima and Papago: Introduction. *In* Handbook of North American Indians, Volume 10: Southwest. Alfonso Ortiz, ed. Pp. 125–136. Washington, DC: Smithsonian Institution.
Franklin, Hayward H., and W. B. Masse
    1976   The San Pedro Salado: A Case of Prehistoric Migration. Kiva 42(1):47–56.
Galloway, Patricia
    1990   The Archaeology of the Ethnohistorical Text. Paper presented at the annual meeting of the Society for American Archaeology, Las Vegas.
Geertz, Clifford
    1990   Works and Lives: The Anthropologist as Author. Palo Alto, CA: Stanford University Press.
Genette, Gerard
    1980   Narrative Discourse: An Essay in Method. J. Lewis, trans. Ithaca, NY: Cornell University Press.
Gerhard, Peter
    1982   The North Frontier of New Spain. Princeton, NJ: Princeton University Press.
Gibson, Charles
    1964   The Aztecs under Spanish Rule. Stanford, CA: Stanford University Press.
Gumerman, George J., and Emil W. Haury
    1979   Prehistory: Hohokam. *In* Handbook of North American Indians, Volume 9: Southwest. Alfonso Ortiz, ed. Pp. 75–90. Washington, DC: Smithsonian Institution.
Hackett, Charles Wilson
    1937   Historical Documents Relating to New Mexico, Nueva Vizcaya and Approaches Thereto, to 1773, Volume 2. Adolph F. Bandelier and Fanny R. Bandelier, eds. Washington, DC: Carnegie Institution of Washington.
Hallenbeck, Cleve
    1987[1949]   The Journey of Fray Marcos de Niza. David J. Weber, ed. Dallas, TX: Southern Methodist University Press.
Hammond, George P., and Agapito Rey, trans.
    1940   Narratives of the Coronado Expedition, 1540–1542. Albuquerque: University of New Mexico Press.
Haury, Emil W.
    1976   The Hohokam, Desert Farmers and Craftsmen. Tucson: University of Arizona Press.
Hedrick, Basil C.
    1978   The Location of Corazones. *In* Across the Chichimec Sea: Papers in Honor of J. Charles Kelley. C. L. Riley and B. C. Hedrick, eds. Pp. 228–232. Carbondale: University of Southern Illinois Press.
Hedrick, Basil C., and Carroll L. Riley
    1974   The Journey of the Vaca Party. University Museum Studies, 2. Carbondale: Southern Illinois University Museum.
    1976   Documents Ancillary to the Vaca Journey. University Museum Studies, 5. Carbondale: Southern Illinois University Museum.
Hodder, Ian
    1986   Reading the Past. Cambridge: Cambridge University Press.
Hudson, Charles
    1976   The Southeastern Indians. Knoxville: University of Tennessee Press.
    1987   An Unknown South: Spanish Explorers and Southeastern Chiefdoms. *In* Visions and Revisions, Ethnohistoric Perspectives on Southern Cultures. George Sabo III and W. M. Schneider, eds. Pp. 6–24. Athens: University of Georgia Press.
Icazbalceta, Joaquín García
    1886   Colección de documentos para la historia de México, Volume 2. Mexico: J. M. Andrade.
    1941   Nueva colección de documentos para la historia de México, Volume 1: Cartas de religiosos de Nueva España. Mexico City: Salvador Chavez Hayhoe.
Jennings, Francis
    1976   The Invasion of America: Indians, Colonialism, and the Cant of Conquest. New York: W. W. Norton.

Jewett, Roberta A.
    1989   Distance, Interaction, and Complexity: The Spatial Organization of Pan-Regional Set-
    tlement Clusters in the American Southwest. *In* The Sociopolitical Structure of Prehistoric
    Southwestern Societies. S. Upham, K. Lightfoot, and R. Jewett, eds. Pp. 363–389. Boulder,
    CO: Westview Press.
Kent, Kate Peck
    1983   Prehistoric Textiles of the Southwest. Albuquerque: University of New Mexico Press.
Kintigh, Keith W.
    1990   Protohistoric Transitions in the Western Pueblo Area. *In* Perspectives on Southwestern
    Prehistory. P. E. Minnis and C. L. Redman, eds. Pp. 258–275. Boulder, CO: Westview Press.
LeBlanc, Steven A.
    1986   Aspects of Southwestern Prehistory: A.D. 900–1400. *In* Ripples in the Chichimec Sea.
    Frances J. Mathien and R. H. McGuire, eds. Pp. 105–135. Carbondale: Southern Illinois Uni-
    versity Press.
Masse, W. Bruce
    1981   A Reappraisal of the Protohistoric Sobaipuri Indians of Southeastern Arizona. *In* The
    Protohistoric Period in the North American Southwest, AD 1450–1700. D. R. Wilcox and W.
    B. Masse, eds. Pp. 28–56. Tempe: Arizona State University Anthropological Research Papers,
    24.
McGregor, John C.
    1965   Southwestern Archaeology. 2nd edition. Urbana: University of Illinois Press.
McGuire, Randall H., and Maria L. Villalpando
    1989   Prehistory and the Making of History in Sonora. *In* Columbian Consequences, Volume
    1: Archaeological and Historical Perspectives on the Spanish Borderlands West. D. H.
    Thomas, ed. Pp. 159–179. Washington, DC: Smithsonian Institution Press.
Mecham, John Lloyd
    1927   Francisco de Ibarra and Nueva Vizcaya. Durham, NC: Duke University Press.
Mignolo, Walter
    1982   Cartas, crónicas y relaciones del descubrimiento y la conquista. *In* Historia de la litera-
    tura Hispanoamericana, Tomo I, Epoca Colonial. L. I. Madrigal, ed. Pp. 57–116. Madrid:
    Ediciones Cátedera.
Milner, George R.
    1980   Epidemic Disease in the Postcontact Southeast: A Reappraisal. Midcontinental Journal
    of Archaeology 5:39–56.
Molloy, Sylvia
    1987   Alteridad y reconocimiento en los naufragios de Alvar Núñez Cabeza de Vaca. Nueva
    Revista de Filologia Hispánica 35(2):425–449.
Nader, Helen
    1990   Liberty in Absolutist Spain, The Hapsburg Sale of Towns, 1516–1700. Baltimore, MD:
    Johns Hopkins University Press.
Nentvig, Juan, S. J.
    1980   Rudo Ensayo (1764). Alberto F. Pradeau and R. R. Rasmussen, trans. Tucson: Univer-
    sity of Arizona Press.
Oblasser, Bonaventure, O. F. M.
    1939   His Own Personal Narrative of Arizona Discovered by Fray Marcos de Niza who in 1539
    First Entered These Parts on his Quest for the Seven Cities of Cibola. Topawa, Arizona.
Och, Joseph
    1965   Missionary in Sonora, the Travel Reports of Joseph Och, S. J., 1755–1767. Theodore E.
    Treutlein, trans. San Francisco: California Historical Society.
O'Gorman, Edmundo, ed.
    1967   *Apologética Historia Sumaria* of Fray Bartolomé de Las Casas. 2 vols. Mexico City: Instituto
    de Investigaciones Historicas, Universidad Nacional Autonoma de Mexico.
Pagden, Anthony
    1982   The Fall of Natural Man. Cambridge: Cambridge University Press.
Pailes, Richard
    1978   The Rio Sonora Culture in Prehistoric Trade Systems. *In* Across the Chichimec Sea: Pa-
    pers in Honor of J. Charles Kelley. C. L. Riley and B. C. Hedrick, eds. Pp. 20–39. Carbondale:
    Southern Illinois University Press.

654 *AMERICAN ANTHROPOLOGIST* [93, 1991

1981   The Upper Rio Sonora Valley in Prehistoric Trade. *In* New Frontiers in the Archaeology and Ethnohistory of the Greater Southwest. C. L. Riley and B. C. Hedrick, eds. Pp. 20–39. Transactions of the Illinois Academy of Sciences 72(4).

Pastor, Beatriz
1983   Duscurso narrativo de la conquista de America. Havana: Casa de las Américas.

Pérez de Ribas, Andrés
1617   Carta del Padre Andrés Pérez de Ribas al Padre Provincial, 13 de Junio 1617. Hubert H. Bancroft Collection, Bancroft Library, University of California, Berkeley.
1638   Temporalidades 2009-1. Memorial al Rey para que no se recenga la limosna de la Misciones y consierva al Senor Palafox en las relaciones a la Compañía, 12 de Septiembre 1638. Archivo Histórico de Hacienda, Mexico City.
1896   Córonica y historia religiosa de la Provincia de la Compañía de Jesús de México (1655). 2 vols. Mexico City: Sagrado Corazon.
1944   Historia de los triunfos de nuestra Santa Fe entre gentes las mas barbaras y fieras del Nueve Orbe (1645). 3 vols. Mexico City: Editorial Layac.

Perrigo, Jynn
1971   Texas and Our Spanish Southwest. Dallas, TX: Banks Upshaw.

Pfefferkorn, Ignaz
1949   Sonora, A Description of the Province. Theodore E. Treutlein, trans. Albuquerque: University of New Mexico Press.

Polzer, Charles W., S. J.
1976   Rules and Precepts of the Jesuit Missions of Northwestern New Spain. Tucson: University of Arizona Press.

Ramenofsky, Ann F.
1987   Vectors of Death: The Archaeology of European Contact. Albuquerque: University of New Mexico Press.

Reff, Daniel T.
1981   The Location of Corazones and Senora: Archaeological Evidence from the Rio Sonora Valley, Mexico. *In* The Protohistoric Period in the North American Southwest, AD 1450–1700. D. R. Wilcox and W. Bruce Masse, eds. Pp. 94–112. Tempe: Arizona State Anthropological Research Papers, 24.
1987a   The Introduction of Smallpox in the Greater Southwest. American Anthropologist 89:704–708.
1987b   Old World Diseases and the Dynamics of Indian and Jesuit Relations in Northwestern New Spain, 1520–1660. *In* Ejidos and Regions of Refuge in Northwestern Mexico. N. R. Crumrine and P. C. Weigand, eds. Pp. 85–95. Anthropological Papers of the University of Arizona, 46. Tucson: University of Arizona Press.
1991   Disease, Depopulation, and Culture Change in Northwestern New Spain, 1518–1764. Salt Lake City: University of Utah Press.

Ricard, Robert
1966   The Spiritual Conquest of Mexico. Lesley B. Simpson, trans. Berkeley: University of California Press.

Riley, Carroll L.
1971   Early Spanish-Indian Communication in the Greater Southwest. New Mexico Historical Review 46(4):285–314.
1976   Sixteenth Century Trade in the Greater Southwest. Carbondale: Southern Illinois University Museum Research Records, 10.
1982   The Frontier People. Center for Archaeological Investigations Occasional Papers, 1. Carbondale: Southern Illinois University.

Santamaria, Francisco J.
1974   Diccionario de Mejicanismos. Mexico City: Editorial Porrua.

Sauer, Carl O.
1932   The Road to Cibola. Ibero-Americana, 1. Berkeley: University of California Press.
1940   The Credibility of the Fray Marcos Account. New Mexico Historical Review 16:233–243.

Sheridan, Thomas E.
1988   Kino's Unforseen Legacy: The Material Consequences of Missionization among the Northern Piman Indians of Arizona and Sonora. *In* The Smoke Signal. Pp. 151–167. Tucson, AZ: Tucson Corral of the Westerners.

Spicer, Edward H.
1962   Cycles of Conquest: The Impact of Spain, Mexico, and the United States on the Indians
        of the Southwest, 1533–1960. Tucson: University of Arizona Press.
1980   The Yaquis: A Cultural History. Tucson: University of Arizona Press.
Sturtevant, William C.
1983   Tribe and State in the Sixteenth and Twentieth Centuries. *In* The Development of Polit-
        ical Organization in Native North America. Elisabeth Tooker, ed. Pp. 3–16. Washington, DC:
        American Ethnological Society.
Thomas, Nicholas
1989   Out of Time. Cambridge: Cambridge University Press.
Udall, Stewart
1987   To the Inland Empire: Coronado and Our Spanish Legacy. Garden City, NY: Double-
        day.
Undreiner, George J.
1947   Fray Marcos de Niza and His Journey to Cibola. Americas 3:415–486.
Upham, Steadman
1982   Polities and Power: An Economic and Political History of the Western Pueblo. New York:
        Academic Press.
Vassberg, David E.
1984   Land and Society in Golden Age Castile. Cambridge: Cambridge University Press.
Wagner, Henry F.
1934   Fr. Marcos de Niza. New Mexico Historical Review 9:184–227.
Weber, David J.
1987   Introduction. *In* The Journey of Fray Marcos de Niza. Cleve Hallenbeck. Pp. vii–1. Dal-
        las, TX: Southern Methodist University Press.
White, Hayden
1978   Tropics of Discourse. Baltimore, MD: Johns Hopkins University Press.
Winship, George P.
1896   The Coronado Expedition. *In* Fourteenth Annual Report, U.S. Bureau of American Eth-
        nology. Pp. 339–613. Washington, DC: Bureau of American Ethnology.
Wood, J. Scott, and Martin E. McAllister
1982   The Salado Tradition: An Alternative View. *In* Cholla Project Archaeology, Volume 1.
        J. J. Reid, ed. Tucson: Arizona State Museum Archaeological Series, No. 161.

7
Silences and Secrets: The Hidden Agenda of Cartography in Early Modern Europe

J.B. Harley

'On a visit to Leningrad some years ago I consulted a map to find out where I was, but I could not make it out. From where I stood, I could see several enormous churches, yet there was no trace of them on my map. When finally an interpreter came to help me, he said: "We don't show churches on our maps." Contradicting him, I pointed to one that was very clearly marked. "That is a museum," he said, "not what we call a 'living church.' It is only 'living churches' we don't show."

It then occurred to me that this was not the first time I had been given a map which failed to show many things I could see right in front of my eyes. All through school and university I had been given maps of life and knowledge on which there was hardly a trace of many of the things that I most cared about and that seemed to me to be of the greatest possible importance to the conduct of my life. I remembered that for many years my perplexity had been complete; and no interpreter had come along to help me. It remained complete until I ceased to suspect the sanity of my perceptions and began, instead, to suspect the soundness of the maps.'

E. F. Schumacher, 'On philosophical maps,' *A guide for the perplexed* (New York, 1977).

Introduction

The present paper picks up a theme explored more fully in the context of the ideological dimensions of cartography.[1] It is concerned with the dialogue that arises from the intentional or unintentional suppression of knowledge in maps. It is based on a theory of cartographic silence. My reading of the map is not a technical one (this already has a voluminous literature) but a political one. The aim in this paper is to probe those silences which arise from deliberate policies of secrecy and censorship and to examine the more indeterminate silences rooted in often hidden procedures or rules. These rules, it can be argued, are a sort of subconscious *mentalité* that mediates the knowledge contained in maps in order to maintain the political *status quo* and the power of the state. Although much of what is said here applies to all periods, including the present,[2] the focus is on early modern Europe. Maps from the sixteenth century onwards offer particularly clear opportunities for the exploration of a new perspective on the changing and reciprocal relationships between the rise of the nation state and the expansion of cartography.[3] The establishment of stability and durability, the primary tasks of each and every nation state,[4] in early modern Europe as at other times, provides the background to this essay. In outlining, first, the theoretical framework, it will be argued that cartography was primarily a form of political discourse[5] concerned with the acquistion and maintenance of power. Examples drawn from the maps themselves will then be used in support of this argument.

Theories about silences in maps

Mapping in the nation-states of early modern Europe offers examples of many types of cartographic silence. As in the history of cartography as a whole it would be possible to construct a broader typology of silences. Silences are contributed by many agents in the map-making process, through the stages of data gathering to those of compilation, editing, drafting, printing, and publication.[6] In assessing silences we must be aware not only of the geographical limits to knowledge but also of the technological constraints to representation, and of the silences in the historical record owing to the destruction of evidence. In the present essay, however, I am not concerned with those silences which arise from geographical ignorance, lack of data, error, the limitations of scale, deliberate design or other aspects of specification and technical limitation.[7] I am dealing here with political silences. An adequate theory concerning the political silences in maps is thus central both to my interpretation of the nature of state cartography and to the ways in which maps were used to maintain and legitimise state power. My theoretical position is derived from two directions. The first concerns a philosophical and, more particularly, a phenomenological, understanding of silences.[8] The second concerns the sociology of power and the idea that knowledge is power.

From the philosophers we learn that silence is a phenomenon 'encountered in every segment of human experience in which utterance takes place.'[9] We learn, too, that utterance is defined as 'any performance employing systematically related signs, sounds, gestures, or marks having recognizable meanings to express thoughts, feelings, states of affairs' and that the 'deployment of any sort of language is counted . . . as an utterance.'[10] This means that although most obvious are the silences which occur in speech and music, they also occur in non-performing arts such as painting and sculpture.[11] In this way, the concept of silences is also applicable to maps. To ignore or downgrade these silences—as both the history of cartography and cartography have done—is to close up an important avenue of historical exploration, one in which maps can be seen to engage both the imagination and the social preconceptions of their readers.[12]

Thus we learn that that which is absent from maps is as much a proper field for enquiry as that which is present. A second insight derived from the philosophical direction is that silences should be regarded as positive statements and not as merely passive gaps in the flow of language. So, allowing for those gaps on the map which make the pattern of lines and points a comprehensible image, we should be prepared to regard silences on maps as something more than the mere absence of something else. I am deliberately insisting on the term 'silences' in the context of maps, rather than the somewhat negative 'blank spaces' of the older literature,[13] for the reason that silence should be seen as an 'active human performance.'[14] Silence can reveal as much as it conceals and from acting as independent and intentional statements, silences on maps may sometimes become the determinate part of the cartographic message. So, just as in verbal communication the silence is more than the mere correlate of what is sounded, in the case of a map the silence is not merely the opposite of what is depicted. The white spaces which abound on the maps of early modern Europe, for example, cannot be explained simply by positing 'fact' against 'no fact'. Silence and utterance are not alternatives but constituent parts of map language, each necessary for the understanding of the other. A cartographic interpretation of silences on a map departs, then, from the premise that silence elucidates and is likely to be as culturally specific as any other aspect of the map's language.[15]

My second insight comes from sociology. This helps us gain an historical understanding of cartographic silence. It involves seeing cartography as a form of knowledge and that knowledge as discourse. In this light, maps are interpreted as socially constructed perspectives on the world, rather than as the 'neutral' or 'value free' representations that, some historians insist, define the rise of state cartography in early modern Europe. This myth of a measurement-based 'objectivity' in maps has yet to be stripped away: the application of the sociological concept of 'power-knowledge' to the history of cartography is another step in that process.[16]

From the sociological literature on the nature of knowledge, I have drawn in this essay on the ideas of Michel Foucault[17] to help interpret the categories of cartographic silence—the intentional and the unintentional—identified below. Two sets of ideas in particular seem of direct relevance: the idea of power-knowledge *(pouvoir savoir)* and the concept of an *episteme*.

1. Foucault constantly stresses the relationship between power and knowledge. For him, this serves to frame the instances of deliberate secrecy and censorship. He writes that:

'We should admit . . . that power produces knowledge (and not simply by encouraging it because it serves power or by applying it because it is useful); that power and knowledge directly imply one another; that there is no power relation without the correlative constitution of a field of knowledge, nor any knowledge that does not presuppose and constitute at the same time power relations.'[18]

While the universality of these assertions may be rejected, it is easier to accept the implication that the map was an instrument of power and that much of the instrumentality of maps in early modern Europe was concerned with power in one form or another. Foucault seems to have accepted the map as a tool of state measurement, enquiry, examination and coercion.[19] In his view, cartographers provide the state with a mass of information which the state, from its strategic position, is able to exploit. Moreover, the state was also frequently able to impose its own rules upon this cartographic knowledge, giving rise to the silences that are induced by those occasions of deliberate secrecy and censorship that recur so often in the history of European state mapping. Elsewhere, Foucault goes on to note that the production of discourse in every society 'is at once controlled, selected, organised and redistributed according to a certain number of procedures.'[20] In the case of cartography, these procedures involved external controls, internal rules, and the regulation of access to knowledge. Thus a state gains power over knowledge.

2. The second set of Foucault's ideas, the *episteme*, helps us interrogate the unintentional silences on maps (the residual 'blank spaces' of the older cartographic literature). As already noted, these silences are 'active performances' in terms of their social and political impact and their effects on consciousness. They are, moreover, a feature of all discourse,[21] part of the cultural codes which underlie all forms of knowledge and which structure 'its language, its perceptual schemata, its exchanges, its techniques, its values, the hierarchy of its practices.'[22] As far as early European maps are concerned, we find that these silences are best understood in terms of 'historical *a priori*' which 'in a given period, delimits . . . the totality of experience of a field of knowledge.'[23] These historical *a priori* form what Foucault once termed an *episteme*:[24] like all other knowledge, cartographic knowledge is similarly delimited, so that while some information is included on the maps, other aspects of life and landscape are excluded according to the *episteme*.

Thus equipped with these philosophical and sociological insights into the meanings communicated by the 'blank spaces' on maps, it seems to me we are in a better position to attempt to unearth the history of those meanings. We may be better equipped, too, to unravel those systems of 'non-formal' knowledge that suffused everyday cartographic practice in early modern Europe, as it does still.

Secrecy and censorship: The intentional silences in maps

By the sixteenth century literary censorship of various kinds was a common aspect of European culture as the emergent nations struggled as much for self-definition as for physical territory.[25] It will be shown here how the production of cartographic knowledge was similarly controlled, selected, organized, and redistributed according to definite procedures. Even in many ancient and traditional societies maps were frequently regarded as privileged knowledge, with access given only to those authorized by the state or its ruler.[26] By the early modern period, cartographic secrecy (maintained by what may be defined as rules of exclusion and prohibition) was clearly widespread and the 'official' cartography of this period furnishes a classic case of 'power-knowledge'.[27] At the very time maps were being transformed by mathematical techniques, they were also being appropriated as an intellectual weapon of the state system. If their study had become, by the end of the sixteenth century, the 'science of princes,' it was because maps were by then recognized as a visual language communicating proprietorial or territorial rights in both practical and symbolic senses.[28] In cartographic terms, however, the exercise of such power could be negative and restrictive. The map image itself was becoming increasingly subject to concealment, censorship, sometimes to abstraction or falsification. It is these deliberate manipulations, willed by individuals, groups, or institutions,[29] that give rise to our category of intentional silences.

Of course, we have to reconcile, map by map, the study of these intended cartographic silences with the complexity of different historical events. The immediate circumstances which led princes, both secular and ecclesiastical, and their advisors, to control cartography by means of censorship and secrecy spanned a wide range of their vital interests. These could be military, commercial, or religious. So, for example, on Jesuit Matteo Ricci's world map published at Peking in 1602, the sacred places of Christianity are suitably annotated while those of Islam appear without comment, the reason for Ricci's silence being that he knew 'the Chinese would be unlikely to be drawn to the religion he was preaching if they knew that deep fissures of belief existed in the Western world from which that religion came.'[30] Reflecting different ways of

59

sharing power within nation states in sixteenth and seventeenth century Europe, the manner in which control over maps and their content was effected also varied. In some states, control centered on the crown and a group of close advisors. In other cases, it was delegated to a bureaucratic institution. In either case, the effects were complex, even paradoxical, while elsewhere policies of secrecy were inconsistently applied. On the maps of sixteenth- and seventeenth-century Europe these aspects of national secrecy are manifested in various ways. Here we shall consider just two ways; first, examples of strategic secrecy; and second, cases of commercial secrecy.

(i) Strategic secrecy
    Some of the most clear-cut cases of an increasing state concern with the control and restriction of map knowledge are associated with military or strategic considerations. In Europe in the sixteenth and seventeenth centuries hardly a year passed without some war being fought. Maps were an object of military intelligence; statesmen and princes collected maps to plan, or, later, to commemorate battles; military textbooks advocated the use of maps. Strategic reasons for keeping map knowledge a secret included the need for confidentiality about the offensive and defensive operations of state armies, the wish to disguise the thrust of external colonization, and the need to stifle opposition within domestic populations when developing administrative and judicial systems as well as the more obvious need to conceal detailed knowledge about fortifications.[31]
    But besides these understandable and practical bases for military secrecy, an increasing number of states adopted a more custodial attitude towards maps of their cities and territories in general independent of such strategic considerations. The Dutch merchant Isaac Massa, for example, who was living in Muscovy in the late-sixteenth century, found it difficult to obtain maps of both Moscow and the Siberian territory only because it would have been a capital offence to supply him with such maps.[32] In the same century, the *Bol'shoy Chertyozh* map (which shows the whole of the Muscovite state) seems to have been drafted in only one copy and to have remained wholly unknown to western European map-makers.[33] Similar policies have been common throughout Europe and can be found, for example, in Prussia in the sixteenth and seventeenth centuries;[34] in late-sixteenth century Italy (map of the Kingdom of Naples);[35] in sixteenth-century Spain (the 'Escorial atlas');[36] in seventeenth-century Switzerland (Hans Conrad Gyger's map of the Canton of Zurich).[37] Herein lies one of the paradoxes of map history. Just as the printing press was facilitating the much wider dissemination of survey data, and just as regional topographical maps were being made for the first time, so, some states and their princes were determinedly keeping their maps secret through prohibiting their publication.
    Why did some states insist upon cartographic secrecy while others allowed the publication of their earliest national surveys? One reason, it may be suggested, is that strong monarchies may have perceived less need for secrecy than did the weak and threatened. Certainly, in strongly-centralised Elizabethan England, surviving documents imply few doubts about the wisdom of publishing Saxton's survey.[38] From the 1570s Saxton's maps were seen by statesmen such as Burghley as an aid to national administration and defence although a few may have taken a different view.[39] Of seventeenth-century France, too, it has been observed how 'maps seem to have functioned in untroubled support of a strongly centralized monarchic regime.'[40] But such an argument fails to explain all. On the contrary, some of these maps became double-edged weapons. Once generally available, they were used to support other sides in political power struggles. In England, for example, Saxton's maps did not (as had been intended) serve solely to strengthen the power of the monarchy. Once published and in circulation, they would surely also have been a contributory factor in the growth of the strong sense of provincial identity and independence which was so successfully articulated against the crown in the Civil War.[41] Likewise, it has been remarked that in the Low Countries the widespread use of maps went hand-in-hand with the nascent bourgeois republicanism of the seventeenth century.[42] With such complex, and sometimes contradictory, aspects in mind we can perhaps begin to glimpse

how, for the cautious monarchy determined to preserve its power, map secrecy came to be regarded as a prudent policy of good government.

(ii) Commercial Secrecy

The rise of map secrecy in early modern Europe was also associated with a second theatre of geographical activity—that of commerce and the rise of monopoly capitalism. In a period when the foundations of the European world economy and its overseas empires were being laid,[43] absolute monarchs were often also 'merchant kings,' pursing economic objectives through the trade monopolies opened up by their navigations.[44] As in the case of the nation state, the essence of empire is control. For such commercial monopolies to survive and for the policies of *mare clausum* to be implemented, there had to be a monopoly of the knowledge which enabled the new lands and the routes to and from them to be mapped. Arguably, the process of monopolization of map knowledge paralleled the secreting and use of craft mysteries in the control of medieval guilds.[45]

The mechanism by which vital cartographic information from nascent overseas empires was censored, regulated and secreted varied considerably. In some countries, it was an *ad hoc* process linked to individual voyages. This seems to have been the case in England where contemporary writers on the navigations were aware of the practice of censorship[46] and knew that new knowledge was controlled in a few powerful hands, those of the sovereign, an inner circle of ministers, or the principal merchants and navigators involved with a venture. For example, the sketch maps and drawings brought back by Drake's voyage round the world (1577–80) became secret documents. Drake had been given express orders that 'none shall make any charts or descriptions of the said voyage,' a prohibition of publication that was to remain in force until 1588. (Fig. 1)[47]

Much more elaborate were the bureaucratic systems set up by the crowns of both Portugal and Spain to regulate the overseas trade and the knowledge on which it depended. Maps quickly became key documents in the launching of the Luso-Hispanic empires. While both the extent to which the Portuguese policy of secrecy actually existed and its effectiveness have been the subject of heated debate,[48] the evidence does suggest the length to which a self-interested and powerful monarchy might go to control and suppress sensitive maps. For instance, the penalty for pilots giving or selling charts to foreigners was to be death.[49] Measures were taken, late in the fifteenth century, by John II of Portugal (1481–1495) to exclude foreigners, especially Genoese and Florentines, from all Portuguese territory, while the Cortes of 1481, in relation to the West African navigation, is said to have

'demanded severe measures for maintaining the secret of the discovered lands. The documents were sequestered; to record new lands on the maps was forbidden; the nautical works became secret books; prohibitory tales were spread; and the navigators forced to keep the oath of silence.[50]

By the beginning of the sixteenth century, Portuguese controls on cartographic knowledge had been further tightened by the establishment of a 'hydrographical repository' within the 'Storehouse of Guinea and the Indies' *(Armazem da Guine e Indias).*[51] This clearly excercised censorship functions. A royal charter of 13 November 1504 prohibited the making of globes and forbade nautical charts to depict the West Africa coast beyond the river Congo. Charts not complying with this provision were required to be taken to an officer of the hydrographical repository to be cleansed of such details. Moreover, such an organization made it possible to insist that nautical charts issued before a voyage were handed back on its completion while the duty of another official was to screen intended recipients lest there might be objections to their handling of charts.[52] Contemporaries alleged the deliberate falsification of charts: it is easy to see how it could have come about in both Portugal and Spain.[53]

The objectives of state control of overseas cartographic knowledge and the regulating mechanisms in Spain were much the same as in Portugal. The Castilian court had set up a special institution in the first decade of the sixteenth century called the *Casa de Contratación* (colonial office in control of shipping, commerce and finance, probably based on the Portuguese model), to oversee exploration and to house, in secrecy, documents of discovery.[54] By

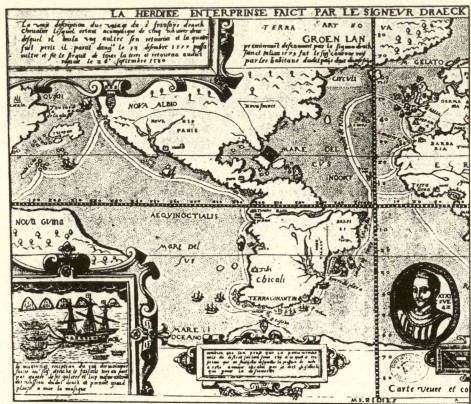

Fig. 1   Part of the world map by Nicola van Sype, showing Drake's circumnavigation and engraved and published at Antwerp, ca. 1583, was probably an unauthorised copy, made from a secret English original and smuggled out of the country. *By courtesy of the British Library (Maps C2.a.7).*

1508 a special geographical and cosmographical department had been created within the *Casa*. It was here that a master world map, the *Padrón Real*, was kept up-to-date by trained chart-makers.[55] The *Casa's* many provisions included the instructions that

> 'Pilots were not to be permitted to make use of any other maps than this, and they were directed, upon finding new islands or lands, new ports or bays, or any other thing—currents or tides, headland or mountains—which might serve the purpose of subsequent identification of localities, to enter the same in the copy of the *Padrón Real* which they carried, reporting all entries made on return, but nothing should be inserted that was not properly attested and sworn to.'[56]

The situation in both Portugal and Spain early in the sixteenth century suggest that the rulers of the nation states of Europe, together with their rising bourgeois merchant classes, were not slow in discovering the value of centralized control in trying to ensure the confidentiality of geographical knowledge about the New World. Rivals of Portugal and Spain copied their navigational institutions. The hydrographic office established at Amsterdam, after the organization of the Dutch merchant companies into the United East India Company in 1602, paralleled the *Casa da Contratación* in a number of ways, including the institutionalization of a secret cartography.[57] Each chartmaker in the Dutch East India Company

> 'was . . . obliged to ensure that the logs from arriving vessels were delivered in good order, and did not fall into the wrong hands. He had to file them in a special room in East India House and had also to keep proper records.

Every six months he had to account for all the improvements he had made in the charts and rutters. The chart-maker was sworn not to disclose any information about his activities to persons not in the employ of the company. He was not allowed to publish, directly or indirectly, any of the company's material without the company's knowledge and comment, and every newly appointed chart-maker had to swear before the mayor of Amsterdam that he would obey these instructions.'[58]

The Dutch East Company had become, in effect, the state's surrogate organ, acting as a ministry with particular responsibility for the eastern colonies. Its map policy was especially cautious when the handing out of charts of newly-explored regions was in question. The practice was to supply pilots with these in manuscript and as required, and to check their return at the end of a voyage. Company officials, such as Plancius and, later, Blaeu, were expected to exercise tight control, even to the point of censoring maps intended for publication. Consequently, maps associated with important voyages, such as those of Tasman to Australia, were effectively being kept secret. (Fig. 2).[59]

Nor were the Dutch monopoly companies alone in adopting such restrictive cartographic practices. In seventeenth-century England, after the Restoration, as trading companies became increasingly monopolistic in structure so they also tended to act as a brake on map publication, if not map-making itself.[60] Once the Hudson's Bay Company (founded in 1670) had acquired its territorial monopoly, its substantial archive—including all the maps—remained all but closed until the late-eighteenth century because of the Company's restrictive policies.[61] These policies meant in practice that the Company 'did not allow details of the geographic pattern of riverways, lakes, and the terrain to become known' for the simple reason that 'such geographic data were considered crucial to the formulation and operation of its trading policies, and thus were commercial secrets.'[62] Particularly interesting is the way the English parliament reacted when faced with these policies. Even when opportunities presented

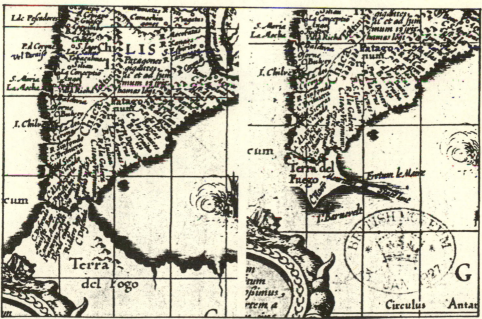

Fig. 2   Tierra del Fuego on two states of Blaeu's *Nova Orbis Terra* (left 1606/1617; right after 1618). Knowledge, available in 1617, on the Straits of Magellan from le Maire's voyage was censored for commercial reasons until after 1618 (see Tony Campbell in reference 59). *By courtesy of the British Library (Maps 920 (262) and Maps 188.j.1(i))*.

themselves to legislate against these practices it was unable to assert itself as the disinterested patron of a 'scientific' knowledge expressed through geographical maps.[63]

Thus the forces impinging upon the cartography of early modern Europe were much more complex than the initially simple notion of power-knowledge allows for. A number of characteristics can be observed. For instance, while it can be claimed that secrecy has been endemic in the history of maps and map-making as well as in the activities of monopoly capitalism, there has been nothing neat or predictable in the timing or the geographical pattern of its imposition. We find that some periods are characterized by 'high security' while in others this has been allowed to slip. When the world limits of the Spanish and Portuguese empires were being demarcated, between about 1515 and 1529, control over secrecy was rigorously enforced but later in the century laxity crept in. (Fig. 3). Another point is the way state policies have been inconsistent. Despite Spain's usual preoccupation with secrecy and control, cartographic caution was thrown to the winds when Charles V of Spain wished to impress foreign crowns with propaganda maps showing the territorial extent of Spanish influence.[64] Nor were the manipulations of one state always meekly accepted by its rivals. These sought to obtain maps as much by espionage,[65] theft and piracy as by direct observation and their own survey. So, Walter Raleigh's collection of New World maps, which had come mainly from Spanish sources, included 'a secret mappe of those partes made in Mexico . . . for the King of Spaine.'[66] Moreover, the strictest policies of cartographic secrecy could be undermined by the ease with which cosmographers and pilots, taking with them their specialist cartographic knowledge, entered the service of rival crowns. There are well-known cases of Portuguese pilots being lured

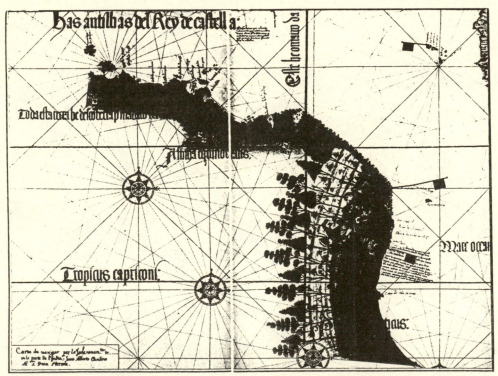

Fig. 3   Brazil on the Cantino Chart, 1502. Anxiety about the Italian spice trade led the Duke of Ferrara to obtain by bribery this map of the 'islands recently discovered in the . . . Indies' from a Portuguese original in Lisbon, from H. Harrisse's facsimile in *Recueil de voyages et de documents pour servir à L'Histoire de la Géographie No 3 Les Corte-Real et leurs voyages au Nouveau-Monde. (Paris 1883). By courtesy of the British Library (Maps 7.e.8).*

into the more lucrative service of Spain, France or England while cartographers such as Cabot, Ribeiro, and Rotz are known to have been the agents by which once confidential maps were given wider currency. Even the *Padrón* of Spanish navigation did not remain secret for ever and its contents were eventually published. Finally, and yet more remarkable, perhaps, were the occasions when ideological conflicts about secrecy emerged in the very institutions set up to enforce it. It has been shown, for example, how there was a protracted debate and even litigation within the *Casa da Contratactión* over the role of patriotism in scientific argument and the role of secrecy in the growth of knowledge.[67] In view of all this, we have to conclude that access to knowledge must be regarded as one of the more complex socio-legal dimensions that structured the development of cartography in early modern Europe.

Epistemological or unintentional silences on maps

A second category of silence on maps is the unintentional silence. This is a silence that does not seem to have been 'explicitly commanded' by the cartographic patrons of early modern Europe yet that was nonetheless instrumental in the diffusion of state power.[68] What commanded the unintentional silence was 'the play of rules which determines within a culture the appearance and disappearance of statements'[69] on maps. So our concern here is with the absence or presence of categories of cartographic detail that cannot be explained by reference to either secrecy or technical factors but by 'historical rules' that are not merely theoretical but observable in forms which varied according to the particular 'social, economic, geographic or linguistic zone' within which a map originated.[70] These 'rules' help to fashion two sets of discourse, the scientific, and the political-social, whose function is to structure the framework within which cartographic knowledge is created.

(i) The scientific discourse in maps

Already in the Renaissance, two 'scientific' characteristics, the 'universal science of measurement and order' and the principle of classification or ordered tabulation,[71] were important underpinnings of map content. From then on, increasingly precise instruments of survey and techniques of mapping contributed to the 'science of measurement' while the way in which cartographic signs were classified and ordered (i.e. set out in tabulated characteristic sheets)[72] points to the adoption of the principle of classification. As scientific progress and increasing technical accuracy marched ahead, few doubts were expressed. State cartography was thus, in the sixteenth century, well on the way to becoming a scientific and technological discourse. Contained within it was the unwritten assumption of an objective world in which the new techniques, being repeatable and transmissible, were always able to be successful in measuring or describing accurately.[73] Today, many historians still accept this model of scientific progress as the standard interpretation of the rise of state cartography.[74] Yet of equal interest are the silences on those allegedly 'objective' products of state mapping. My contention is that while measurement and classification may have fostered objectivity within the terms of reference of the cultural *episteme*, in other respects the maps still remain a subjective perspective on the world of that culture. Standardization, with its Euclidian emphasis on space as uniform and continuous, generates the silences of uniformity. For instance, in many of the topographical atlases of early modern Europe, especially those of the seventeenth century, but even in Mercator's and Saxton's, much of the character and individuality of local places is absent from the map. Behind the facade of a few standard signs on these atlases, the outline of one town looks much the same as that of the next; the villages are more nearly identical and are arranged in a neat taxonomic hierarchy;[75] woodland is aggregated into a few types; even rivers and streams become reduced into a mere token of reality; objects outside the surveyor's classification of 'reality' are excluded. The epistemological force of scientific procedures was, moreover, intensified by their further standardization through map printing—the innovation which saw the start of 'the technologizing of the map'—so that the map images acquire a tidiness and inevitability lacking in the manuscript age.[76] The net result was that the cartographic landscapes of Europe became more generalized, more abstract, and less differentiated in the mode of their respresentation. Their silences are those of the unique.

It is generally accepted that mapping is an activity designed to promote state efficiency and that with good maps the writ of centralized power can be made to run more uniformly over a country as a whole. But we need to ask 'Why was it that it had to be scientific mapping that made this task easier?' If we leave aside all the logistical arguments that have been marshalled in favour of maps—and clearly they persuaded a considerable investment by the rulers of early modern Europe—then there is another side to the explanation: the silences in maps act to legitimize and neutralize arbitrary actions in the consciousness of their originators. In other words, the lack of qualitative differentiation in maps structured by the scientific *episteme* serves to dehumanise the landscape. Such maps convey knowledge where the subject is kept at bay.[77] Space becomes more important than place: if places look alike they can be treated alike. Thus, with the progress of scientific mapping, space became all too easily a socially-empty commodity, a geometrical landscape of cold, non-human facts.

(ii) The political and social discourse in maps

But not all is explained in this way.[78] The paradox is that the socially-empty spaces on the map were not without social consequences. Yet other threads weave through map imagery. In particular, there are those of political consciousness, mediated through patronage,[79] and those of religious values or of social or ethnic attitudes. With the help of these epistemological insights, we can listen to the other silences in our maps.

Political discourse is grounded in an assumption of the legitimacy of an existing political *status quo* and its values. Its utterances through maps as elsewhere, are intended, consciously or unconsciously, to prolong, to preserve and to develop the 'truths' and achievements initiated by the founding fathers of that political system or modified by their successors. However, it can be argued that this cognitive infrastructure itself determines the nature of the technical specification of maps and provides the rules of what is included and excluded on a map. It can also be suggested that political discourse is responsible for differential emphases, through selection and generalisation, which privilege some aspects of 'reality' while others are silenced. Individual cartographers would not have been in the position to control or balance these nuances, even had they been aware of them.

Examples of many different sorts of political and social silences can be found on maps from the early modern period. One category is the toponymic silence. Conquering states impose a silence on minority or subject populations through their manipulation of place-names. Whole strata of ethnic identity are swept from the map in what amount to acts of cultural genocide. While such manipulations are, at one level, the result of deliberate censorship or policies of acculturation,[80] at another—the epistemological—level, they also can be seen as representing the unconscious rejection of these 'other'[81] people by those belonging to the politically more powerful groups.

A similar reading can be made of the silences found in the keys to cartographic signs included on some maps in nearly modern Europe. On Mercator's map of Europe dated 1554, for example, the map-maker chose to identify four ecclesiastical ranks—the Vatican *(Pontifex Romanus)*, the patriarchal sees *(patriarchales)*, the archiepiscopal sees *(archiepiscopales)*, and bishoprics *(episcopales)*—while remaining silent about the four or five ranks of secular status also differentiated and shown on the maps.[82] By implication, the political power acknowledged here is the ecclesiastical one; small settlements (villages) at the bottom of the ecclesiastical hierarchy are of no consequence. Silence thus becomes an 'active performance' giving affirmative support to the political *status quo*.

In yet another group of examples, we can detect how maps were implicated in a discourse of promise—their silences reciprocating eschatological dimensions in the sacred books of particular sects or religions. Thus, in the depiction of the Holy Land inspired by Luther and Calvin, in which a *geographia sacra* was combined with geographical realism (the latter reflecting the scientific discourse in maps), it is events of the Old Testament and the Protestant message of 'Salvation History,' epitomised by the Exodus route, which are emphasized.[83] Left silent are the history and sites of New Testament lore which feature so prominently in the *mappaemundi* of the Catholic Middle Ages.[84]

66

The content and publication of maps may thus be structured by the religious schisms and ideological battles of early modern Europe. The publication of books of town plans of Italy, for example, may have been inhibited in some areas by the aversion of Calvinists to representations of Catholic Rome. Similarly, it may be significant that the ecclesiastic rank of settlements is indicated more frequently on maps of regions south of the Alps (or on the maps of cartographers from countries in which the Roman Catholic Church remained in power, such as Italy, Spain and France) than in the Protestant regions to the north. In contrast, maps containing information about the different sects and adherences of European Christians were more common north of the Alps, where they reflected the religious turmoil of the Reformation, about which maps from the Catholic heartlands of Italy, France and Spain remained silent.[85] Sectarian splits are sometimes discernible in maps whose authors were hotly partisan to one doctrine, for instance through the map's silence about the churches and settlements of the other.[86] (Fig. 4). On yet other maps, including portolan charts, lands which the Ottomans had conquered were shown as if still in Christian hands, while Jerusalem was often depicted as Christian on some of the maps of the Middle Ages long after its fall to Islam.[87]

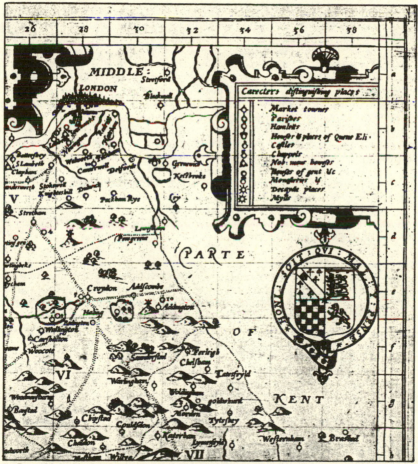

Fig. 4 Part of John Norden's Surrey, 1594. It has been argued that Norden being anti-Catholic, omitted 'Bishop's Sees' from his map. The only one of his maps to show them, Middlesex, 1593, marks by a star rather than a Papists' cross). 'Chappels' (chapels-of-ease) make their appearance, reflecting Norden's attention to ecclesiastical detail. *By courtesy of the British Library (Maps C7c5 (44))*.

The first problem encountered in attempting to integrate the silences in European maps that might have arisen from contemporary perceptions of class or race is the tendency to assume that these perceptions would have been identical amongst all Europeans and throughout the sixteenth or seventeenth century. Even so, it is reasonable to suggest that there was a common conceptual base to European society of the time. For instance, social status and the nature of men's occupation were matters of deep concern both in feudal central Europe and amongst the rising middle ranks or *grande bourgeoisie* of other states which would have influenced map knowledge. Witness the careful ranking of the costumed figures that so often compose the marginal decoration of late-sixteenth and seventeenth century maps such as those of Speed and Blaeu, for instance.[88] While those social distinctions are easily discerned, others may be more subliminal. But the same sort of social taxonomy seems to have underlain the silence in European cartography about the majority social class. For map makers, their patrons, and their readers, the underclass did not exist and had no geography, still less was it composed of individuals. Instead, what we see singled out on these maps are people privileged by the right to wear a crown or a mitre or to bear a coat of arms or a crozier. The peasantry, the landless labourers, or the urban poor had no place in the social hierarchy and, equally, as a carto-graphically disenfranchised group, they had no right to representation on the map. Credentials of social status which gave an individual the right to hold land, also conferred the right to appropriate the most prominent signs in the map-maker's repertoire. The largest (and most eye-catching) pictorial signs on the map turn out to be those associated with feudal, military, legal or ecclesiastical status. A peasant village, lacking strong overlordship or church patronage, recedes into the near-silence of an abstract dot or sign. Moreover, these Europe notions of status were carried into the New World. They are discernible on, in particular, maps of regions where the European culture encountered the Indian culture. They are found, for instance, on maps showing the early English settlement of Virginia. Here the distinction between Indians of the 'better sort' and the common Indian people, frequently made by contemporary writers,[89] is conveyed (as on European maps) by representations of individuals from the privileged upper stratum of Indian society—a Powahatan, Pocahontas or Sus-quehanna chief, for example—while the ordinary men and women are shown massed anony-mously at their feet and, by implication, at their command. Likewise, European hierarchies are found in the settlement signs of maps of the New World. For the two hundred or so Indian settlements that are depicted on John Smith's map of Virginia (1612), a careful distinction is made between 'Kings Houses' (drawn with a visually prominant sign), and 'ordinary Houses' (marked by a relatively insignificant sign), and chief Powhatan's settlement (given the largest sign of all).[90]

Another type of silence found on maps of the New World arises from the tendency to obliterate the uniqueness of the American landscape in favour of a stereotype, a tendency that is more difficult to explain. It could be, of course, simply the result of a lack of information. Faced with empty spaces on the sketches and drafts they were given as models, European engravers would have filled these with the only landscape conventions familiar to them. Alternatively, the stereotype of the American landscape can be seen as a deliberate act of colonial promotion, designed to make the new lands more attractive to settlers or to tempt proprietors and potential investors.[91] But we may also seek explanations of these silences in another direction, at the structural level of Foucault's *epistemes*. Thus, they would be manifesta-tions of yet another way European scientific values were reflected in Renaissance cartography through, especially, measurement and simple landscape classification. So, we could be witness-ing here, once again, the unconscious transposition into American geography of European values and preferences, this time in relation to the landscape. Maps such as those of John Smith ('Lord Baltimore's Map,' 1635) or William Wood ('The South Part of New England,' 1634),[92] seem to show us an already-tamed wilderness, one that has been rendered more acceptable to English eyes. (Fig. 5). There may be a parallel here to the way Theodore de Bry and his assistants transformed John White's paintings of Indians in the Roanoke Colony. We have been told how de Bry 'retained White's meticulous attention to detail in dress, hair style, and body decoration, but changed the faces, postures, and bodies of the Indians in dramatic ways'

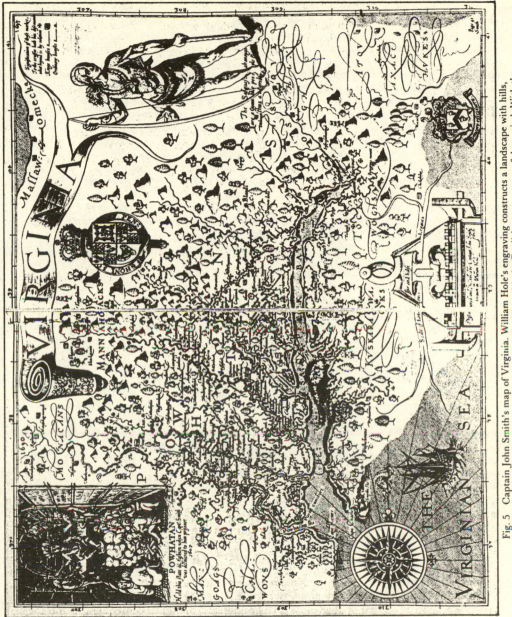

Fig. 5 Captain John Smith's map of Virginia. William Hole's engraving constructs a landscape with hills, rivers, woods and settlements recognisable to eyes familiar with the English county maps of the period. With the royal coat of arms inserted as an emblem of colonial possession beneath the title scroll we see the beginning of a cartographic discourse which ends with maps silent about Indian rights to the territory. The 1625 edition is shown here. *By courtesy of the British Library (Maps 75005(9)).*

and how their 'faces were sweetened, softened, and Europeanized' so that, with their 'new high foreheads, puckered mouths and ringleted hair they resemble the classical figures in the German engraving tradition'.[93] So, too, it seems to have been with the landscape in some of the earliest and most influential printed maps of the regions of North America. In essence, these maps depict a European landscape in European engraving style but far from being actual portraits of America, they really show landscapes whose advent Europe desired and they remain silent about the true America. This sort of cartographic silence becomes an affirmative ideological act. It serves to prepare the way for European settlement. Potential settlers see, on the map, few obstacles that are insurmountable. Least of all does the map reflect the presence of indigenous peoples and their imprint on the land: 'It is as if America were a stage tableau, with the arrival of Europeans as the raising of the curtain and the beginning of action.'[94] In short, such maps are ethnocentric images, and part of the apparatus of cultural colonialism. It is not only that they offer a promise of free and apparently virgin land—an empty space for Europeans to partition and fill—but that the image offered is of a landscape in which the Indian is silent[95] or is relegated, by means of the map's marginal decoration, to the status of a naked cannibal.[96] Through these silences, the map becomes a license for the appropriation of the territory depicted. It is yet another means by which to insist upon the inherent superiority of European technologies and European ways of life.

Conclusions

This essay was designed to illustrate the potential for a history of maps of ideas derived from outside our subject. It has been primarily a theoretical exploration. It should be made clear, however, that neither concepts such as that of power-knowledge nor that of the *episteme* can offer 'provable' generalizations which can be neatly plugged into the 'facts' for this or that map culture. My argument stems from a humanistic standpoint, that it is the role of theory to reveal the complexity of the world rather than to reduce it to the simpler models of the social scientist. Thus, our first conclusion is that, while initially simple and familiar, the notions of power-knowledge and of cartogaphy as a discourse of power with social effects are immensely complex once we start to relate them to specific historical contexts. Faced with a particular map, it is often hard to tell from the historical context whether its silences are the result of deliberate acts of censorship, unintentional epistemological silence, or a mixture of both, or perhaps merely a function of the slowness with which cartographers revised their maps to accord with the realities of the world. The relationships between maps and power, and between maps and other forms of knowledge, were constantly changing. The contribution of cartography in the maintenance of authority throughout the sixteenth and seventeenth centuries was never a constant factor. The complexities were recognized by Helgerson who pointed out that maps could never be ideologically neutral, whatever their use or the consequences of their use and that they could never be 'mere tools' whether of monarchic centralism or any other organization of power. They inevitably entered, he said, 'into systems of relations with other representational practices and, in so doing, altered the meaning and authority of all the others.'[97] It is this constantly shifting terrain between maps and other forms of power-knowledge which still has to be charted within the history of cartography.

A second conclusion is that we are on much surer ground when it comes to the importance of silences. Assuming the world to be a place where human choice is exercised, the absence of something must be seen to be as worthy of historical investigation as is its presence. So it is with cartography. Recently it has been suggested that 'the map that is not made . . . warrants as much attention as the map that is made.'[98] This aphorism can be extended both into the history of map production and into the history of the representational silences in particular maps. We have been able to show, from particular maps, that deliberate acts of censorship and secrecy in the past have indeed resulted in detectable cartographic and historical consequences. But the same is true of the epistemological silences, the 'unthought' elements in discourse.[99] These are also affirmative statements, and they also have ideological consequences for the societies in question. Such silences also help in the reproduction, the reinforcement, and the legitimation of cultural and political values. Finding them expressed geographically on maps points to their universality. There is no such thing as an empty space on a map. Revealed by a careful study of the cartographic unconscious and its social foundations, these hidden agenda have much to offer historians of cartography in coming to an understanding of how maps have been—and still are—a force in society.

The third, and final, conclusion concerns the nature of cartography itself as a form of knowledge. Cartographers may continue to masquerade their products solely in terms of the application of a technical specification—survey instruments, scale, generalization, design, printing, and so forth—but an integral place in the historical interpretation of maps must also be demanded for the cultural choices that were taken for granted in particular societies. Indeed, maps are being read as literary texts[100] rather than as a mechanical replication of technical processes, by an increasing number of scholars. Such an approach has much to commend it, not least as applied to maps of the early modern period.[101] Maps are, in the apt phrase of one cartographer, best viewed as 'a controlled fiction.'[102] This textual viewpoint— reading the map as rhetoric—has important implications for alternative ways in which maps can be used to understand the past. The more we think about the universality of secrecy, of censorship and silence in maps, and the more we continue to reflect upon the epistemological codes of map knowledge, the less convinced we become that map knowledge can be regarded as 'objective' or 'value free.'[103] Maps became part of 'an increasing repertoire of power techniques'[104] and it is a major error to conflate the history of maps with the history of measurement. The essential paradox has been missed. As cartography became more 'objective' through the state's patronage, so it was also imprisoned by a different subjectivity, that inherent in its replication of the state's dominant ideology. The old question of whether particular maps are true or false has not been my concern in this paper. On the contrary, this question has to be downgraded if it is accepted—as I have tried to argue here—that maps are perspectives on the world at the time of their making. My aim in this essay has been to initiate the interrogation of maps as *actions* rather than as impassive descriptions and to persuade historians of cartography to ask the crucial question 'What are the "truth effects"' of the knowledge that is conveyed in maps,[105] both of its more emphatic utterances, and also of its equally emphatic silences?

Acknowledgements

This paper was given in a preliminary form at a seminar in the Department of Geography, York University, Canada in March, 1987; it was subsequently presented at the Twelfth International Conference on the History of Cartography in Paris in September, 1987 and at the 'Geography and the Environment Workshop,' in the University of Chicago, in November 1987; I am grateful for the encouragement and suggestions received on those occasions. I am also indebted to Howard Deller of the American Geographical Society Collection for crucial bibliographical assistance, to Kevin Kaufman for supplying me with references on the early history of cartographic secrecy in Portugal; to David Quinn for a number of other examples of sixteenth and seventeenth century policies of cartographic secrecy; and to Michael Conzen, Catherine Delano Smith, Richard Eversole, Michael Mikos, Denis Wood and David Woodward for commenting on a draft of the essay.

REFERENCES

1. Harley, J. B., *The map as ideology*, forthcoming.
2. An interesting variant of modern censorship is provided by remote sensing from satellites. The resolution of the instruments used for military intelligence is now so extraordinarily fine that satellites for civilian use (LANDSAT I launched in 1972, and LANDSAT V in 1984) have their imagery deliberately degraded; see: Gould, Peter, *The geographer at work* (London, 1985), 162–63, 211–13. For a shift of policy see: Broad, William J., 'U.S. ends curb on photographs from satellites', *The New York Times*, 21 January 1988.
3. For an indication of the importance of this theme see James R. Akerman and David Buisseret, *Monarchs, ministers, and maps: A cartographic exhibit at the Newberry Library* (Chicago: Newberry Library, 1985).
4. Mazzeo, Joseph Anthony, *Renaissance and seventeenth-century studies* (New York, 1964), 148.
5. The word discourse has so many interpretations in linguistic and literary studies that it is necessary to define it here. I take the sense nearest to my own from Hulme, Peter, *Colonial encounters: Europe and the Native Caribbean, 1492–1797* (London, 1986), 2, where he writes of 'colonial discourse, meaning by that term an ensemble of linguistically-based practices unified by their common deployment in the management of colonial relationships.' I am also concerned with how 'linguistically-based practices,' broadly defined as both verbal and non-verbal language and systems of graphic representation including maps, have been used as political instruments. The sense is, therefore, also that of Michel Foucault, *The archaeology of knowledge and the discourse on language*, trans. A. M. Sheridan Smith (New York, 1972), who is concerned with discourse as a social practice with

a set of meanings and effects that can be determined within particular historical societies.

6. Silences can be detected, for example, in most of
the technical stages of map production modelled
by David Woodward: 'The study of the history of
cartography: A suggested framework,' *American
Cartographer,* 1 (1974): 101–15.

7. While he did not specify silences, an excellent
discussion of the difficulty of assigning the
nuances of cartographic representation to particular cultural or technical causes is given by H.
R. Wilkinson: *Maps and politics. A review of the
ethnographic cartography of Macedonia* (Liverpool,
1951), 314–323.

8. I have found Bernard P. Dauenhauer's *Silence: The
phenomenon and its ontological significance* (Bloomington: Indiana University Press, 1980) to be particularly helpful; see also: Max Picard, *The world of
silence,* trans. Stanley Godman (Chicago, 1952). I
owe these references to Dr. Walter Mignolo of the
University of Michigan, Ann Arbor.

9. Dauenhauer, *op. cit.,* 23 (n. 8).

10. *Ibid.,* 4.

11. See Ihde, Don, *Experimental phenomenology* (New
York, 1977) 68, 129.

12. The 'reader-response' to maps in historical contexts has been neglected: for its place in literary
studies see: Iser, Wolfgang, 'The reading process:
A phenomenological approach,' in Tompkins,
Jane, P. (ed.), *Reader-response criticism. From formal-
ism to post-structuralism.* (Baltimore, 1980), 50–51.
The extent to which silences in maps may have
stimulated their readers' participation is worth
pursuing. While early map-makers—unlike Laurence Sterne in *Tristram Shandy* where the reader is
invited to add to the story on a provided blank
page (see: Sterne, Laurence, *The life and opinions of
Tristram Shandy, Gentleman,* ed. James Aiken Work
(New York, 1940), 470—may not have generally
envisaged such participation, it is possible to
investigate its historical effects in the social construction of *terrae incognitae.* I owe the references in
this note to Dr. Richard Eversole.

13. The negative—even derisory—attitude towards
blank spaces on maps was already well established by the eighteenth century most famously in
Jonathan Swift, *On poetry: a rhapsody* (London,
1733), 12 in his well-known lines beginning 'So
geographers in *Afric*-maps . . .' For a modern continuation see Lewis Carroll, 'Bellman's map', *The
hunting of the snark,* quoted by R. A. Skelton in
Looking at an early map (Lawrence, Kansas, 1965),
3.

14. Dauenhauer, *op. cit.,* 4 (n. 8).

15. Recent anthropological research, revealing different cultural and contextual interpretations
given to silence in speech patterns, can serve as a
preliminary warning about the danger of over-
generalizing about the silences in maps. See, for
example, Basso, K. H., '"To give up on words":
silence in Western Apache culture,' in *Language
and social context: Selected readings,* ed. Pier Paolo
Giglioli (London, 1972), 67–86. For a
sociolinguistic example see: Coates, Jennifer,

*Women, men and language: A sociolinguistic account of
sex differences in language* (London, 1986), 33–34. I
owe these references to Dr. Michael Mikos.

16. For an earlier step see; Harley, J. B., 'Maps,
knowledge and power,' in Cosgrove, D. and
Daniels, S. J., (eds.), *The iconography of landscape*
(Cambridge, 1988), 277–312.

17. Among Foucault's commentators and critics I
have found to be particularly helpful for this
paper Merquior, J. G., *Foucault* (Berkeley, California, 1985) and Poster, Mark, *Foucault, Marxism and
history: Mode of production versus mode of information*
(Cambridge, 1984).

18. Foucault, Michel, *Discipline and punish: the birth of
the prison,* trans. Alan Sheridan (New York, 1977),
27.

19. Foucault, Michel, *Power knowledge: Selected interviews and other writings* 1972–1977, ed. Colin Gordon; trans. Colin Gordon, Leo Marshall, John
Mepham, Kate Sopher (New York, 1980), 74–75,
during the interview "Questions on Geography".

20. Foucault, *op. cit.,* 216(n. 5).

21. 'Discourse' here being a word for thought and
knowledge as a social practice: Merquior, *op. cit.,*
18 (n. 17).

22. Foucault, Michel, *The order of things: An archaeology
of the human sciences, trans. Alan Sheridan-Smith* (New
York, 1970), *Preface.*

23. *Ibid.,* xxii, Foucault also argues that the *episteme*
'defines the mode of being of the objects that
appear in that field, provides man's everyday perception with theoretical powers, and defines the
conditions in which he can sustain a discourse
about things that is recognized to be true.'

24. *Ibid.,* xxii.

25. For literary parallels to cartographic censorship,
which help us to view its practice as taken for
granted rather than exceptional in early modern
Europe, see: Patterson, Annabel, *Censorship and
interpretation. The conditions of writing and reading in
early modern England* (Madison, 1984).

26. See, for example, Needham, Joseph, and Ling,
Wang, *Science and civilization in China,* vol. 3, *Mathematics and the sciences of the heavens and the earth*
(Cambridge, 1959), 193; Harley, J. B. and Woodward, David, (eds.), *The history of cartography,* vol.
I, *Cartography in prehistoric, ancient, and medieval
Europe and the Mediterranean* (Chicago, 1987), 254;
and Davenport, William, 'Marshall Islands navigational charts,' *Imago Mundi* 15 (1967), 19–26.

27. In terms of Foucault, *Discipline and Punish,* (23 n),
18, it was also a 'technology of power' closely
enmeshed with the will to dominate in both
domestic and overseas spheres. See also Akerman
and Buisseret, *op. cit., passim* for examples of an
increasing use of maps by the emergent states as
tools of government.

28. Mukerji, Chandra, 'Visual language in science
and the exercise of power: the case of cartography
in early modern Europe,' *Studies in visual communication* 10, n. 3. (1984), 30–45; Sack, Robert David,
Human territoriality: its theory and history (Cambridge, 1986).

29. See: Mann, Michael, *The sources of social power,* vol.

1, *A history of power from the beginning to A.D. 1760* (Cambridge, 1986), 8, where he distinguishes between 'authoritative power,' which 'comprises definite commands and conscious obedience' and 'diffused power' which 'spreads in a more spontaneous, unconscious, decentered way ... not explicitly commanded.' My *intentional* and *unintentional* silences in maps can be allocated to this broad distinction.

30. Spence, Jonathan D., *The memory palace of Matteo Ricci* (London, 1984), 97.

31. For example, in England, the crown had fully grasped the strategic importance of maps by the mid-sixteenth century. In 1551, for example, a chance visit to Portsmouth by a French ambassador en route for Scotland, in the company of an engineer/map-maker, was sufficient to alarm the English authorities into ordering the re-fortification of its castle: *The chronicle and political papers of King Edward VI*, ed. Jordan, W. K., (London, 1966), 97 (26 December 1551). I owe this reference to Peter Barber. In France, the models in the *Musée des Plans-Reliefs*, first constructed after 1668 for Louis XIV, were kept locked away in the Great Gallery of the Louvre and 'few visitors were allowed to see them because examination by a potential enemy could have threatened military security': Rothrock, George A., 'Maps and models in the reign of Louis XIV,' *Proceedings of the annual meeting of the Western Society for French History* 14 (1987), 50; also Konvitz, Josef W., *Cartography in France 1660–1848: Science, engineering, and statecraft* (Chicago, 1987), 93. The same was true of other maps prepared for military purposes. Geoffrey Parker cites the case of the Duke of Alva who had a map of the Franche-Comté made for his pioneer march of 1567 but this was so accurate that he delayed its publication for a decade. See: Parker, Geoffrey, *The army of Flanders and the Spanish Road 1567–1659. The logistics of Spanish victory and defeat in the Low Countries' Wars* (Cambridge, 1972), 83.

32. Keuning, Johannes, 'Isaac Massa, 1586–1643,' *Imago Mundi* 10 (1953), 66–67; Bagrow, Leo, *A history of Russian cartography up to 1800*, ed. Henry W. Castner (Wolfe Island, Ontario, 1975), 51.

33. Bagrow, *op. cit.*, 4–7, (n. 32).

34. Jager, Eckhard, *Prussia-Karten 1542–1810. Geschichte der Kartographischen Darstellung Ostpreussens vom 16. bis zum 19, Jahrhundert. Entstehung der Karten-Kosten-Vertrieb. Bibliographischer Katalog* (Weissenhorn, 1982), 168–71.

35. Valerio, Vladimiro, 'The Neapolitan Saxton and his survey of the Kingdom of Naples,' *The Map Collector* 18 (1982), 14–17. The survey, intended to be produced as an atlas, remained unpublished because it was perceived as a threat to both the interests of Spain and the security of the Kingdom.

36. Akerman and Buisseret, *op. cit.*, 9 (n. 3), although this is debated.

37. Eduard Imhof, *Cartographic relief presentation*, ed. H. J. Steward (Berlin, New York, 1982), 7.

38. Skelton, R. A., *Saxton's survey of England and Wales. With a facsimile of Saxton's wall-map of 1583* (Amsterdam, 1974), 15–18.

39. William Lambarde, the sixteenth-century English historian, for example, had encountered opposition to the publication of a map of beacons in Kent, *See:* William Lambarde, *A perambulation of Kent* (1596), p. 69, where he wrote 'And now, if any man shall thinke that this laying open of the Beacons, is a point not meete to bee made publike: I pray him to give me leave to dissent in that opinion from him. For, as the profit to the Realme and subiect is manifest, in that it speedeth the service, where speed is the most profitable: so there is no secret hereby disclosed, whereof the enimie may take advantage.'

40. Helgerson, R., 'The land speaks: Cartography, chorography, and subversion in Renaissance England,' *Representations* 16 (1986), 51–85.

41. Morgan, Victor, 'Lasting image of the Elizabethan era,' *The Geographical Magazine* 52 (1980), 401–08.

42. Helgerson, *op. cit.*, 81. (n. 40).

43. Wallerstein, Immanuel, *The modern world-system I Capitalist agriculture and the origins of the European world-economy in the sixteenth century* (New York, 1974). *Ibid., The modern world-system II Mercantilism and the consolidation of the European world economy, 1600–1750* (New York, 1980).

44. Cortesão, Jaime, 'The pre-Columbian discovery of America,' *The Geographical Journal* 89 (1937), 29–42.

45. Mukerji, Chandra, *From graven images: Patterns of modern materialism* (New York, 1983), 91.

46. See, for example, Richard Eden's statement in the mid-sixteenth century: 'As touching these trades and voyages, as in manner of all the sciences, there are certain secrets not to be published and made common to all men.' Quoted by E. G. R. Taylor, in 'John Dee and the map of North-East Asia,' *Imago Mundi* 12 (1955), 103: also Best, George, *A true discourse of the late voyage of discoverie, for finding a passage to Cathaya, under M. Frobisher, General* (London, 1578); and Richard Hakluyt who refers to a forthcoming 'very large and most exact terrestriall Globe, collected and reformed according to the newest, secretest, and latest discoueries, both Spanish, Portugall, and English' in *The principal navigations voiages and discoveries of the English nation. A photo-lithographic facsimile with an introduction by David Beers Quinn and Raleigh Ashlin Skelton and with a New Index by Alison Quinn*, imprinted at London, 1589 (Cambridge, 1965), xlviii–xlix.

47. Wallis, Helen, 'The cartography of Drake's voyage,' in Thrower, Norman J. W., (ed.), *Sir Francis Drake and the famous voyage, 1577–1580. Essays commemorating the quadricentennial of Drake's circumnavigation of the Earth* (Berkeley, California, 1984), 121–163.

48. Diffie, Bailey W., 'Foreigners in Portugal and the "Policy of Silence",' *Terrae incongnitae* 1 (1969), 23–34; see also: Cortesão, Armando, *History of Portuguese Cartography*, 2 vols. (Coimbra, 1969–71), II, 76, 116–18.

49. Wallis, Helen (ed.), *The maps and text of the Boke of idography presented by Jean Rotz to Henry VIII now in the British Library* (Oxford, 1981), 40.

50. Cortesão, 'The pre-Columbian discovery of America,' 31 (n. 44); see also, Kimble, George H., 'Portuguese policy and its influence on fifteenth century cartography,' *Geographical Review* 23 (1933), 653–59.

51. Teixeira da Mota, A, 'Some notes on the organization of hydrographical services in Portugal before the beginning of the nineteenth century,' *Imago Mundi* 28 (1976), 51–60.

52. *Ibid.,* 53–54.

53. Stevenson, Edward L., 'The geographical activities of the Casa de la Contratación, *Annals of the Association of American Geographers* 17 (1927), 39–59.

54. Parry, J. H., *The Spanish seaborn empire* (London, 1966), 54–58.

55. Stevenson, *op. cit.,* 41 (n. 53).

56. *Ibid.,* 42.

57. Destombes, Marcel, *Cartes Hollandaises: La cartographie de le compagnie des Indes orientales, 1593–1743* (Saigon, 1941), 5.

58. Schilder, Gunter, 'Organization and evolution of the Dutch East India Company's Hydrographic Office in the seventeenth century,' *Imago Mundi* 28 (1976), 61–78.

59. I owe this point to Professor David B. Quinn: on the so-called 'Secret atlas of the East India Company' see: Wieder, F. C., *Monumenta Cartographica,* V (The Hague, 1933), 145–95. See also Campbell, Tony, 'A descriptive census of Willem Blaeu's sixty-eight centimetre globes,' *Imago Mundi* 28 (1976), 21–50, esp. 27.

60. Crone, G. R. and Skelton, R. A., 'Collections of voyages and travels, 1625–1846,' in Lynam, E. (ed.), *Richard Hakluyt and his successors* (London, Hakluyt Society, 1946), 63–140, esp. 67.

61. Moodie, D. W., 'Science and reality: Arthur Dobbs and the eighteenth-century geography of Rupert's Land,' *Journal of Historical Geography* 2, (1976), 293–309; Williams, Glyndwr, 'The Hudson's Bay Company and its critics in the eighteenth century,' *Transactions of the Royal Historical Society,* 5th Series, 20 (1970), 150–51.

62. Ruggles, R. I., 'Governor Samuel Wegg: intelligent layman of the Royal Society,' *Notes and Records of the Royal Society of London* 32 (1978), 181–99.

63. Williams, *op. cit.,* (n. 61).

64. I owe this point to Professor David B. Quinn.

65. See, for example, Cortesão, Armando, in *Cartografia e Cartógrafos Portugueses dos séculos XV et XVI* (Lisbon: Edição da "Seara Nova, 1935), I: 142–44, describes the acquisition of the Cantino map by the Duke of Ferrara. Alberto Cantino was sent to Lisbon under cover to obtain information on the progress of the Portuguese discoveries. In 1502, a letter from Cantino to the Duke states that he had bribed a Portuguese map-maker, probably one connected to the *Casa da India,* with twelve gold *ducados* to copy a map, probably the official *padrão.* Cantino left Lisbon with the planisphere at the end of October 1502, and through the intermediary of Francesco Cataneo, the duke had the map in his library by December. I owe this reference to Kevin Kaufman.

66. Skelton, R. A., 'Raleigh as a geographer,' *Virginia Magazine of History and Biography* 71 (1963), 131–49.

67. Lamb, Ursula, 'Science by litigation: A cosmographic feud,' *Terrae incognitae* 1 (1969), 40–57.

68. Following the distinction of Mann, Michael, *Sources of social power,* 8 (n. 29).

69. Foucault, Michel, 'Résponse au cercle d'épistémologie,' *Cahiers pour l'analyse* 9 (Summer 1968), quoted by Merquior, *op. cit.,* 81 (n. 17).

70. Foucault, *Archaeology,* 153–4 (n. 5), for a fuller discussion of the concept of the *episteme* as it relates to social constraints on the creation of knowledge.

71. Merquior, *op. cit.,* 46 (n. 17); these two characteristics comprise what Foucault termed the 'classical *episteme.*'

72. The appearance of the characteristic sheet on maps offers a diagnostic criterion for the formalization of this taxonomic tendency: see E. M. J. Campbell, 'The development of the characteristic sheet, 1533–1822,' *Proceedings of the VII General Assembly—XVIIth Congress—of the International Geographical Union* (Washington, 1952), 426–30. For other aspects of the early history of adoption of this device see Catherine Delano Smith, 'Cartographic signs on European maps and their explanation before 1700,' *Imago Mundi* 37 (1985), 9–29.

73. These are, in effect, the assumptions of 'normal science' and they represent an important epistemological thread in the development of cartography.

74. For an earlier statement of this view see Crone, Gerald R., *Maps and their makers: An introduction to the history of cartography,* 1st ed. (London, 1953), xi. Crone writes that 'the history of cartography is largely that of the increase in the accuracy with which ... elements of distance and direction are determined and ... the comprehensiveness of the map content.' That the interpretation persists is demonstrated, for example, by the Foreword by Emmanuel Le Roy Ladurie to Konvitz, *op. cit.,* xi–xiv, where he writes in terms of concepts such as 'enormous progress,' 'Realistic understanding of space,' 'perfection of terrestrial concepts' and concludes that 'The progress of French cartography at the time of the Enlightenment was linked to collaborations between state and science' yet without, in the main, pursuing the ideological implications of the state interest in mapping.

75. See Campbell, E. M. J. Figure 2, (n. 72).

76. For the effects of print culture on social thought with relevance to the argument in this paper see: Ong, Walter J., *Orality and literacy: The technologizing of the word* (London, 1982), esp. 117–23.

77. Foucault sees this as inherent in the process of graphic representation: see Merquior, *op. cit.,* 46–47 (n. 17); Sack, *Human territoriality,* 131, (n. 28) makes the same point in his discussion of

'abstract metrical territorial definition of social relationships', imposed through maps.

78. In relation to the concept of a 'normal science' *episteme* a weakness of Foucault's formulation is that he insists that 'in any given culture and at any given moment, there is always only one *episteme* that defines the conditions of possibility of all knowledge': Foucault, *The order of things*, 168 (n. 22).

79. For an understanding of patronage in the history of cartography in early modern Europe there is much to be derived from Baxendall, Michael, *Painting and experience in fifteenth century Italy: A primer in the social history of pictorial style* (Oxford, 1972). He writes (p. 1): 'A fifteenth-century painting is the deposit of a social relationship. On one side there was a painter who made the picture, or at least supervised its making. On the other side there was somebody else who asked him to make it, provided funds for him to make it and, after he had made it, reckoned on using it in some way or other. Both parties worked within institutions and conventions—commercial, religious, perceptual, in the widest sense social—that were different from ours and influenced the forms of what they together made.'

80. By the nineteenth century the place-names associated with linguistic minorities in many European states were being deliberately suppressed but the origins of such policies as an agent of statecraft still have to be described in the history of cartography: see Ormeling, F. J. *Minority toponyms on maps: The rendering of linguistic minority toponyms on topographic maps of Western Europe* (Utrecht, 1983).

81. Todorov, Tzvetan, *The conquest of America: The question of the other*, trans. Richard Howard (New York, 1984) is a revisionist essay with important ideological pointers to the way we view the silences of the New World cartography of the 'Discoveries' period.

82. Four styles of cross are used to identify ecclesiastical rank. The smallest category of civil settlement is identified by a plain dot while other settlements are shown by pictorial signs. These are not clearly distinguished but range from small to large.

83. For a discussion of the impact of Reformist issues upon the content of maps of the Holy Land, see Delano Smith, Catherine, 'Maps in bibles in the sixteenth century', *The Map Collector* 39 (1987), 2–14: for other examples see Nebenzahl, Kenneth, *Maps of the Holy Land: Images of Terra Sancta through two millenia* (New York, 1986), esp. 70–133.

84. For an analysis of the religious content in *mappaemundi* see Woodward, David, 'Medieval *mappaemundi*,' in Harley, J. B. and Woodward, David (eds.), *The history of cartography*, vol. 1 (Chicago, 1987), 286–370.

85. For example, N. Claudianus' map of Bohemia (1518) may have been prepared for the purpose of showing the distribution and status of Papal and Hussite adherents, since so little topographical information is included; P. de la Beke's map of Flanders (1538), stronghold of Protestanism, concentrates on categories of religious institutions; C.

Radziwiłł's map of Lithuania (1613) for its part distinguishes Orthodox from Roman bishops.

86. Suggestive of such a silence of religous conviction is provided by John Norden, the late-sixteenth and early-seventeenth century English mapmaker. Norden was anti-Catholic and on only one of his county maps, Middlesex (1593), does he show 'bishop's sees' and then with a curious starlike sign rather than a cross (a papal symbol abhorred by some protestants). On the other hand, his unusual inclusion of chapels of ease on most of his other maps can be attributed to his deep interest in ecclesiastical matters. I owe this example to Catherine Delano Smith.

87. Again further contextual research is needed to establish whether we can regard these silences as an action prophesying the ultimate triumph of Christendom or merely a failure to update old images and texts. On the persistence of an old topography of the Holy Land and its meaning see: Katzir, Yael, 'The conquests of Jerusalem, 1099 and 1178: historical memory and religious typology,' in *The meeting of two worlds: cultural exchange between East and West during the period of the Crusades*, ed. Vladimir P. Goss and Christine Verzar Bornstein (Kalamazoo, Michigan, 1986), 103–131; for the continuing consequences of the mental set of the crusaders in Holy Land cartography, see Nebenzahl, *op. cit.*, *passim* (note 83).

88. This may have been an indirect expression of the sumptuary laws which regulated how the members of some European social groups should dress. In the case of England and her colonies it has been suggested that the purpose of these laws was 'that no one would be able to slip over into a status to which he did not belong': *see:* Kupperman, Karen Ordahl, *Settling with the Indians. The meeting of English and Indian cultures in America, 1580–1640* (Totowa, New Jersey, 1980), 3. For a wider discussion of the social significance of dress codes in early modern Europe see Braudel, Fernand, *Civilization and capitalism 15th–18th century*, vol. 1. *The structures of everyday life: The limits of the possible*, trans. Sian Williams (London, 1981), 311–33.

89. Kupperman, *op. cit.*, 2 (n. 88).

90. Key in north-east corner of John Smith's 'Virginia,' 1612. For a detailed description of this influential map and its various printed states see Verner, Coolie, 'The first maps of Virginia, 1590–1673,' *The Virginia Magazine of History and Biography* 58 (1950), 3–15.

91. For a somewhat later example of the deliberate use of maps in this way see De Vorsey, Louis Jr., 'Maps in colonial promotion: James Edward Oglethorpe's use of maps in "selling" the Georgia Scheme,' *Imago Mundi* 38 (1986), 35–45.

92. For reproductions see Schwartz, Seymour I., and Ehrenberg, Ralph E., *The mapping of America* (New York, 1980), Chapter 4, 'Permanent colonization reflected on maps: 1600–1650,' 84–109.

93. Kupperman, *op. cit.*, 33 (n. 88).

94. *Ibid.*, 1.

95. This silence, like others, cannot be regarded as an historical constant. By the nineteenth century it

has been pointed out that even popular maps were showing the location of Indian tribes in the American West and Southwest. This 'probably confirmed in the reader's mind an image of the . . . [region] as a place heavily peopled by hostile Indians': *The mapping of the American Southwest*, ed. Reinhartz, Dennis, and Colley, Charles C., (College Station, Texas, 1987), 67.

96. For a discussion relevant to the depictions of scenes of cannibalism on early manuscript and printed maps of the New World see Kolata, Gina, 'Are the horrors of cannibalism fact—or fiction,' *Smithsonian* 17, no. 12 (1978): 150–170; for wider implications see also Arens, William, *The man-eating myth* (New York, 1979).

97. Helgerson, *op. cit.*, 81 (note 40).

98. Monmonier, M. S., 'Cartography, geographic information, and public policy,' *Journal of Geography in Higher Education* 6, no. 2 (1982), 99–107.

99. The notion of the 'unthought' *(impensé)* is that of Foucault.

100. In the cartographic literature see, notably, the two recent essays by Wood, *see:* Wood, Denis, and Fels, John, 'Designs on signs: Myth and meaning in maps,' *Cartographica* 23, no. 3 (1986): 54–103; and Wood, Denis, 'Pleasure in the idea: The atlas as narrative form,' in *Atlases for schools: Design principles and curriculum perspectives*, ed. Carswell, R. J. B., de Leeuw A. J. A., and Waters, N. M. *Cartographica* 24, no. 1 (1987, Monograph 36), 24–45.

101. Helgerson, *op. cit.* n. 40, is an example of how 'The new historicism' in literary studies has brought

maps within its purview as an aspect of represen-tation; it is taken for granted that the map would be read as any other text: I owe this point to Dr. Richard Eversole of the University of Kansas at Lawrence.

102. Muehrcke, Phillip C., *Map use. Reading, analysis, and interpretation* (Madison, 1978); 103. Foucault, *Archaeology*, Chapter 6, 'Science and Knowledge,' 178–195 (note 5), refuses to make a distinction between 'science' and 'ideology.' This places him apart from traditional marxism in which 'science' and 'ideology' have always been regarded as sep-arate categories of knowledge. It is this latter position, derived from positivist science, which has established itself within cartography (and the history of cartography), and is reflected, for example, in the assumed major cleavage between 'propaganda maps' and 'truth maps.' For similar conclusions about the artificiality of this divide, taking examples from present-day maps, see Axelsen, Bjørn, and Jones, Michael, 'Are all maps mental maps?' *GeoJournal* 14, no. 4 (1987): 447–64, and (much earlier) Wood, Denis, *I don't want to, but I will. The genesis of geographic knowledge: A real-time developmental study of adolescent images of novel environments* (Worcester, Mass., 1973), *passim*.

104. Mann, Michael, *op. cit.*, 524–25 (n. 29). While he does not mention cartography specifically it is clearly part of 'the infrastructure available to power holders' and is among 'the social inven-tions that have crucially increased power capacities.'

105. The notion of 'truth effects' is that of Foucault.

8

English Charting of the River Amazon
c. 1595–c. 1630

Sarah Tyacke

In the late sixteenth century the northern part of South America, called Guiana by contemporaries and stretching from the river Orinoco to the Amazon river, became the focal point of North European attempts at trade and settlement in South America.[2] The valuable, if illicit, tobacco trade with the Spaniards on the Orinoco and elsewhere, the hope of another American empire of gold and silver, and the strategic prospect of an overland river route to the Pacific Ocean all attracted the enterprising French, Dutch, English and Irish to the shores of this territory. Slightly later the more mundane but profitable planting of tobacco and sugar appealed to those intent on settlement along the Guianan rivers. For the most part this area had remained unoccupied by the Spaniards whose own earlier coastal explorations had ceased;[3] neither did the Portuguese, settled to the south in Brazil, see any reason to extend their actual control as far north as the Amazon basin.

Some of the earliest adventures and settlers to Guiana were the English whose original surveys of this little known coast and hinterland survive from the 1590s onwards. In all, six[4] English manuscript charts survive from the period c. 1595-1630 which cover Guiana or its parts. These, the earliest and most detailed charts of Guiana and of the Amazon river in particular, were surveyed by the ships' masters in command of vessels sent out by, amongst others, the English courtiers Sir Walter Ralegh and Sir Thomas Roe. Derived as they apparently were from original surveys these charts provide primary information about the extent of exploration and settlement. (Fig. 1) Much of this information cannot be gathered from later charting by the Portuguese, or the Dutch, nor can it be found in the written accounts of the area's history. Later historians of the Amazon have referred to this lack of coherent written sources and discussion of these early charts of the Amazon may help to elucidate what J. A. Williamson once called, 'some obscure enterprises in the period 1611-20'.[5] The charts themselves also reveal the Thameside chartmakers' abilities to draft charts where no foreign prototypes existed.

In 1619 Captain Matthew Morton 'an expert sea-man in the discoverie of this famous River [Amazon]'[6] wrote to his kinsman William Moreton of Moreton in Cheshire telling him that 'wee goe to make a plantatio[n] in the river of Amazones. Wee leave there 100 men this yeare and wee meane to plant sugar canes and to ereckt ingenies [engines?] for makinge suger.' Morton was to 'stay in a pinnes for discovringe the river and the cost.'[7] The project underway was that promoted by Captain Roger North which did not materialize, in the face of the Spanish ambassador's hostility, until 1620. Morton could not afford to await the fleet's departure and so he sailed for the East Indies as commander of the *Verity* instead.[8] His part in North's plans however reveals his use as an explorer, and presumably as a surveyor, of the river which he had already visited. At Sir Thomas Roe's charge, Morton had sailed up the Canal do Norte or northern channel of the river Amazon and had settled groups of colonists along its banks in 1611 and probably on at least one other subsequent occasion. As a result of this he had commissioned a chart of his explorations from the chartmaker Gabriel Tatton[9] (d. 1621). (Fig. 2) A second chart also survives copied from a survey which seems to have been based on the discoveries made in the Amazon by Morton's contemporary Captain Thomas King.[10] (Fig. 3) Both King's and Morton's expeditions were financed by Sir Thomas Roe and his associates.

Roe himself had set sail for the Amazon in 1610 with two ships and provisions for two pinnaces. The only account of his voyage is that printed by Edmund Howes in his continuation of John Stow's *Annales or Chronicle of England* (1615) where Howes writes 'in the end of April Roe fell in with the river he first discovered and entred his shippe two hundred miles,

Key

1. A chart of northern South America showing the coastline from the mouth of the Amazon river to Puerto Bello probably drawn by Sir Walter Ralegh c. 1596.
British Library, Additional MS. 17940 A.

2. A chart of northern South America showing the coastline from Cayenne ('river of Chilliana') to Puerto Bello probably drawn c. 1596.
In the collection of the Duke of Northumberland.

3. A chart of 'Guiana' showing the coastline from the river Amazon to the island of Margarita drawn by Gabriel Tatton c. 1613.
British Library, Additional MS 34240.

4. A chart of 'Guiana' showing the coastline from the river Amazon to the island of Margarita. A revised version of chart (3) apparently drawn about 1616 during Sir Walter Ralegh's preparations for his last voyage to Guiana in 1617.
In the Archivo General de Simancas *M.P.y.D. IV-56.*

5. A chart of the rivers Amazon and Xingu drawn by Gabriel Tatton in 1615.
In the collection of the Duke of Northumberland.

6. A chart of the river Amazon up to the junction of the Tapajos river, drawn c. 1618-24, showing the explorations of Thomas King.
Bibliothèque National D. 2654.

The above list includes only those charts which cover Guiana or its parts; more general charts of the Atlantic, West Indies, or South America, which include the coastline of Guiana, are not listed here.

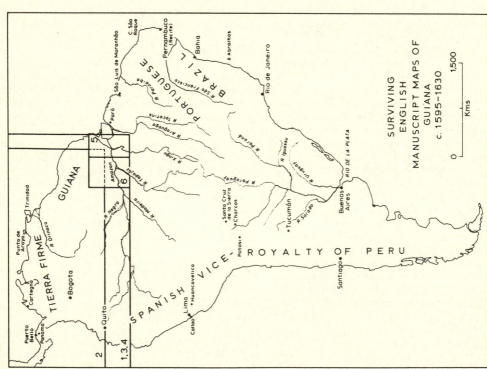

Fig. 1. Modern map showing English chart coverage of Guiana.

and then with boates one hundred more, and made divers Journeyes into the Mayne among Indians . . .' After further explorations in Guiana itself, Roe returned to England in 1611 and sent two more expeditions to the Amazon 'to make further discoveries, and maintained 20 men in River of Amazones who', as Howes relates, 'are yet [in 1614] remaining there and supplied'. Although Howes does not give the names of the ships' masters responsible for these two ventures an historical note, written at the time of Captain Roger North's proposals for a settlement about 1618, supplies an identification: 'Matthew Morton planted people in June an. 11. [anno 1611] on the river of Amazons at S^r. Roe's charge about 6 yeares since. Tho. King was then there . . . also under the charge of Roe'.[13] Morton may also have gone to the river again in 1614 on board the *Lions Clawe* of London.[14] The Spaniards had got wind of this activity and referred in a document dated 24 May 1615 to one 'Thomas Rey' who had established a notable fort at the mouth of the river of Amazons, 'where he makes great and profitable returns.'[15] In 1616 the Portuguese, making an attempt to counter these settlements, also reported that the natives had told them that about '120 leagues up river from our fort [presumably Belem] there was a colony of Englishmen, with wives and children'.[16] The report also mentioned that on the north bank was 'a strong point and village peopled by the Dutch who had already built sugar mills.' This activity caused grave concern to the Spaniards who appreciated the strategic consequences of this invasion, for 'with time and opportunity to navigate up river they [the interlopers] could cause great trouble to neighbouring provinces; for this river and its branches cross the whole mainland including Peru reaching almost to the Southern Sea.'[17]

The results of the surveys undertaken by Matthew Morton and Thomas King are preserved in two charts of the river Amazon, showing the lower reaches of the river. These would surely have confirmed the Spaniards' worst fears. The earlier chart in terms of survey information, was drawn for Matthew Morton by the Thameside chartmaker Gabriel Tatton, in 1615. This chart shows the course of the Canal do Norte from Cabo do Norte up the river Xingu to a stated 2°50'S, a distance of some 270 statute miles. The other shows the results of Thomas King's explorations, presumably in the period 1611 to 1618, as far south as the river Tapajos in 3°S, a distance of some 350 statute miles.

Earlier English charts of Guiana notably that drawn by Sir Walter Ralegh in about 1595[18] and the 'Indyan carde' thought to have been drawn for William Downe the master of the *Discoverer* on Lawrence Keymis's voyage of 1596,[19] do not provide any survey information about the mouth of the Amazon. The map, at least drawn in part by Ralegh, gives, as one would expect, only a generalised view of the Amazon river showing the northern channel to the Rio Negro and beyond to Peru. The second chart, which is in the style of a professional chartmaker, ends abruptly at 'the river of Chilliana' presumably the river on which the present town of Cayenne stands, west of Cabo Orange—named *Cape Cecil* by Keymis. Downe is in fact recorded by Keymis as, having 'fel with this land [Guiana] somewhat to the southward of Cape Cecyll', as indeed had Keymis, so that the unfinished coastline on the chart remains a mystery.[20] In any case it would seem that the English had not reached the mouth of the Amazon in 1596. The earliest definite notice of the English trading on the Amazon seems to be from the year 1599.[21] Presumably at some point after Keymis's expedition, the English extended their activities southwards. The first Dutch expedition is recorded as reaching *Cape North* (Cabo do Norte) and the mouth of the Amazon in 1598. The Dutch expedition, which was recorded in a journal written by A. Cabeliau, reached the Amazon and traded with the natives in 1598. The earliest Dutch charts of the Guianan coastline seems to come from this voyage, one of which bears the inscription 'Pieter Cornelisz van Petten, 1598',[22] but these two charts do not extend southwards to the Amazon river. Similarly although the English chronicler Samuel Purchas records the voyages, amongst others, of John Leggatt in 1606, and of Robert Thornton in the *Santa Lucia* to the Amazon in 1607-08, no charts have apparently survived from that period. In the case of Thornton's expedition it was claimed that the ship had spent ten weeks in the river[23] and a later chart, evidently based on his discoveries, was included in the sequence of manuscript maps of Guiana compiled about 1636 for Robert Dudley's *Arcano del Mare*.[24] (Fig. 4) Thornton's voyage was undertaken, with the assistance of Dudley, at the charge of the Grand Duke of Tuscany who was Dudley's patron during his exile

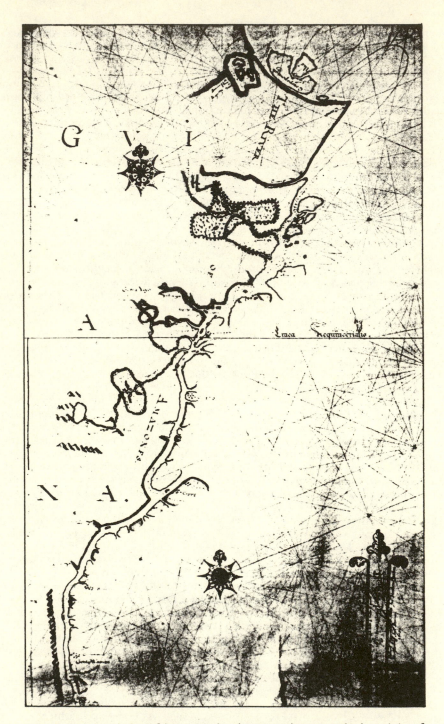

Fig. 2. Gabriel Tatton's chart of the Amazon, based on Morton's survey. By kind permission of the Duke of Northumberland.

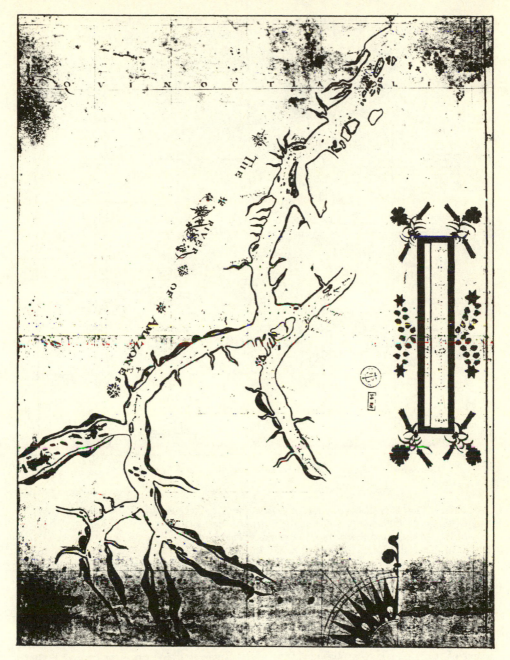

Fig. 3. The 'Thomas King' chart. By kind permission of Biblothèque Nationale, Paris.

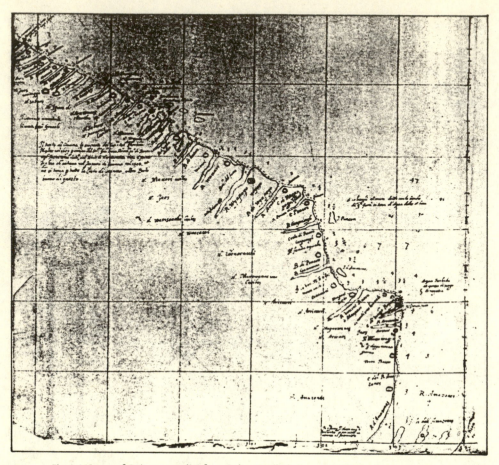

Fig. 4. MS map of Guianan coastline from Robert Dudley's *Arcano c.* 1636: detail. (North to top).

in Florence. The chart shows the port of *Chiana,* the river Araguari (*Arrowari*) south of Cabo do Norte (named *C. di Vincent Pinčon*), and the northern channel of the river Amazon.

As might be expected there are no Portuguese charts of the Amazon from this early period. Not until the establishment of the fort at São Luis de Maranhão in 1615, and the fort of Belem on the right bank of the Para in 1616, did the Portuguese apparently consider mapping the estuary in response to the interloping activities of the foreigners. Even then the earliest chart to survive, which was based in part on Portuguese sources, was apparently copied and revised in about 1620 by a Dutch cartographer.[25] The information given on this unfinished chart shows a generalized river mouth and the northern channel unnamed. The Portuguese fort of Belem on the Para and the Dutch ones of Materu and Nassau on the right bank of the river Xingu are shown. The situation depicted on the chart reflects the period from before the Portuguese attack of 1623 on these two substantial Dutch forts. There seem to be no other pre-1620 charts of the Amazon to survive in Dutch or Portuguese archives.

The earliest general chart to include the Amazon in other than a conventional way, was Gabriel Tatton's chart of the whole of Guiana,[26] which seems to have been drawn to record English exploration there, possibly in connection with Robert Harcourt's claim of 1613. The chart includes the mouth of the Amazon from Cabo do Norte or *Point Perilous*[27], so named by

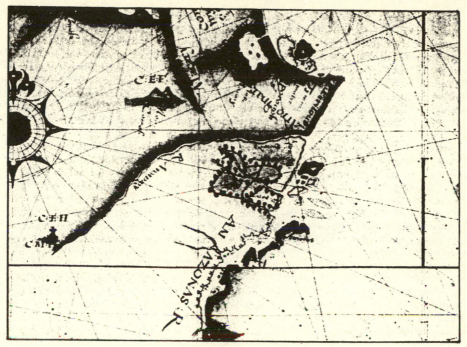

Fig. 5. Tatton chart of 1613: detail (North to top.)

Robert Harcourt's brother who was left to explore the region between 1609 and 1612, to a cross in 0°40′S up the northern channel. (Fig. 5) The symbol is used elsewhere on the chart to indicate the extent of exploration and in this case is named as the place *Manheno*. Neither Robert Harcourt nor his brother seem to have ventured up the north channel of the Amazon this far. Robert Harcourt actually states, that having anchored to the north of Cape North, he did 'forbeare to make particular discovery of this coast intending (if God spare me) to make a perfect discovery of the river Amazones'.[28] They knew, presumably from conversations with the Indian chief Leonard Ragapo, that the rivers *Arapoco* (Anauerapuca) and *Arrawary* (Araguari) flowed into the northern channel of the Amazon but no more. The name *Manheno* does not occur on the Tatton and 'King' charts of the river nor does it occur in any written sources. The only time it re-appears is on a close copy of this chart drawn in pen and ink for Sir Walter Ralegh's last voyage to Guiana in 1617.[29] In so far as it is possible to determine where *Manheno* was it would seem to be up river from the village of *Matianos* which was shown on the Ilha do Para. It was probably somewhere on the Ilha Grande do Gurupá. The source for this part of Tatton's chart remains unclear, although it could be conjectured that it came from Roe's own voyage of 1610.

A curious feature of these charts and of that drawn by Tatton for Matthew Morton in 1615 is the prominence of detail in the hinterland behind the village of *Sapanow*, which seems to have been near the mouth of the Canal do Gurijuba. An intricate system of rivers bordered by swamp and trees is shown. It was evidently important enough for inclusion on a chart otherwise bereft of detail inland. The presence of this feature on both charts suggests a common source to which Tatton had access, for it is evident from the difference in delineation of the coastline higher up river and in the placenames, that the Tatton chart of 1615 could not have served as the exact model for the general undated chart—presumably that common source was an earlier survey drawn either at the time of Roe's expedition or possibly by Morton himself on his subsequent voyages.

The chart drawn by Gabriel Tatton for Matthew Morton in 1615 was presumably copied from Morton's own surveys of the northern channel of the Amazon recording the navigable channels up the Canal do Norte and along the tributary, the river Xingu (Fig. 2). As such it is a record chart evidently made for presentation. It is in the Duke of Northumberland's collection at Alnwick Castle and may have come into the family's possession through the association of Henry, Earl of Northumberland (1564-1632), with the Amazon ventures. The Earl's brother Captain George Percy (1580-1632) intended going to the Amazon with one Captain Bud in 1615, and wrote to his brother asking for financial support.[30] Whether the chart was intended for Morton's own use or for one of his backers, presumably Roe, is not however clear.

The chart records the extent of Morton's exploration from Cabo do Norte in 1°15'N to a native village called *Ama* at 2°50'S up the Xingu river, which is unnamed.[31] It is drawn on a stated scale of 20 English leagues to a degree and is approximately on a scale of 1:700,000 but this is variable. Native villages, and some topographical features are shown but, as one would expect from a pilotage chart, the main information shown is hydrographical: that is soundings, shoals or sandbanks, anchorages and the direction of the river with occasional prominent landmarks, such as the hills on the left bank of the Xingu, presumably the Sierra do Tapará. Unlike today, the approach to the river was evidently made by raising Cabo do Norte, and then hugging the west bank of the mouth of the Amazon, by sailing along a shallow channel of some three to seven fathoms in depth between the mainland and the islands of Bailique, Jabarú and Curuá. The first anchorage was off the island of Curuá opposite the village of Sapanow. This channel is now described, cautiously, in the *Admiralty Pilot* as, 'partly blocked by shoals' but 'it is much frequented by coasting vessels, and it is reported that it can be used by vessels of deep draught'.[32] In the case of the *Lions Clawe* which was a mere 74 tons there was evidently little problem.[33]

The chart then shows the Canal do Norte up to its junction with the Xingu river and the Canal do Gurupá, neither of which are named. Evidently much of the delineation of the river bank is generalized; numerous river mouths are omitted presumably because they were not important to Morton. At the conjunction of the Xingu and Canal do Gurupá however there is a curious omission, the main channel of the river Amazon. This may reflect the mistake, that some explorers seem to have made, in thinking that the Xingu was the main channel, or merely that Morton had succeeded in missing it.[34] As the chart was drawn for Morton himself it presumably reflects accurately what he saw and thought was important, and therefore the probability is that the mistake occurred at the survey level rather than at the chart-making stage.

In terms of planimetric accuracy[35] the problems of assessment are obvious. Few of the natural features and place-names can be identified with any great certainty and certainly not with any measurable precision. It is a hazardous process therefore to attempt to compare Tatton's cartography with that of, say, the modern Brazilian charts or maps of the river[36] (Fig. 6). Even so some obvious distortions present themselves. A peculiarity seems to be the coastal trend from Cabo do Norte to the river Araguari; it trends south-south-west instead of bulging eastwards and then running almost due south. To judge from the soundings on the chart, the ship passed some thirty to forty miles from the coast. Although Cabo do Norte is marked as a cape on both the modern map and Tatton's chart, it is evident from the *Admiralty Pilot* that it is in fact scarcely higher than the surrounding low-lying, wooded banks. Indeed it is not at all clear whether the present position of Cabo do Norte can even be identified with Morton's *Cape Curço*. Furthermore the constant flooding of the river bank has meant the continual shifting of shoals. As it would appear that the coastline may well have altered since 1615, it is impossible to say whether the coastline was accurately charted or not. The Xingu river, however, shows a distortion of direction which cannot be explained by later changes. It trends north-south instead of north north-west-south-south-east but again why this should be so is not clear. It seems to be too great a distortion to be merely the result of charting on the basis of an uncorrected compass.[37] As soundings are shown up the Xingu, Morton presumably surveyed the river himself rather than relying on verbal reports, so that we might expect the chart to accurately reflect his survey—the more so as it was actually drawn for him. On the other hand a discrepancy of a compass point or two may not have concerned a ship's master who had a river bank to guide him.[38]

The chart is drawn on the plane projection and shows latitudes; in so far as any natural features can be identified they seem to be in their true latitudes to within 10 minutes up to *Sapanow*. By Point Macapá and thereafter the latitudes are 25 minutes out.[39] The discrepancy seems to arise between *Sapanow* and Point Macapá where the coastline has been compressed on the Tatton chart, making the Equator cross the middle of the island of Para, instead of passing through Macapá a misplacement of nearly half a degree to the south. Thereafter the distances seem to be roughly accurate although the latitudes retain the discrepancy. Without some written evidence it seems impossible to determine whether the compression of the coastline is the surveyor's or the chartmaker's mistake. Presumably the survey was done with a common English sailing compass, log and line, and possibly some latitude observations. Whether the chartmaker worked from a rough survey given him by Morton or from sketches and a collection of bearings and distances run cannot be ascertained.

The most prominent land feature, as on the earlier Tatton chart (fig. 5), is the swamp area behind the village of *Sapanow*. Although shown in more detail, the precise implications are still not clear. Beyond this swampy area is shown a 'Steel Mine'. The term 'Steel Mine' probably indicates a mine where high-grade ore for smelting steel could be found. Well into the seventeenth century such mines were called 'Steel Mines'.[40] This chart contains the only reference to the presence of such a mine on the Amazon and may indicate one of the activities of the settlers Morton left in 1611. Tatton's chart marks thirty-seven village and river names[41] only some of which re-occur on later maps or in later written descriptions. Morton's naming of the villages is the earliest known, and his survey evidently found its way into the most comprehensive, printed description of the Amazon published ten years later in 1625 by the Flemish historian Jan de Laet. In his *Nieuwe Wereldt* De Laet describes the course of the Amazon in detail and cites Robert Harcourt as his source for the description up to the rivers Anauerapucu and Araguari. He then goes on to give information from what he calls 'the most relevant chart or description of this river which we have yet seen'.[42] This seems to be Tatton's chart or one very much like it. De Laet seems to have read off the names of the villages and their corresponding latitudes from the chart. For example, writing of the east side of the river Xingu he says that 'in the height of one degree and 50 minutes is *Huaman* a settlement of the Indians; and in the height of two degrees and 20 minutes to the south of the Line a town of the Indians of the Womian nation.' At 1°50'S along the east bank of the Xingu, Tatton marks the village of *Huaman* and at 2°20'S the *Genta Womian*. This correlation may be further demonstrated by De Laet's use of the Morton place names *Aropoya*, *Corpoppy*, and *Capitan* near the present day town of Gurupá.

How did De Laet come into possession of this information? It is possible that an account or indeed a similar chart to that made by Tatton had found its way into the archives of the Dutch West India Company and that De Laet had access to it.[43] De Laet's *Nieuwe Wereldt* was of course written as a guide for the Dutch West India Company, of which De Laet was a director. He was also a friend of Sir Thomas Roe. Roe returned to England in 1611 and was next recorded in December 1613 at Flushing, then an English cautionary town. His purpose there was noted as 'going for Captane Flood's Companye, who died lately in Frislande . . .'[44] Presumably he was anxious to get in contact with Captain Flood's ship's company for one of his ventures, possibly for the Amazon, which the date might suggest.[45] Whether he knew De Laet then is not known but he certainly came to know him personally, as is revealed many years later by a letter from him to De Laet on 12 February, 1640/1.[46] In it he promised to help De Laet's son Samuel, obtain naturalization in England. The means of obtaining the information may have been much simpler of course: in a period of co-operation between the Dutch and the English on the Amazon, charts may have been passed from Morton to his Dutch contemporaries out there.

Tatton also marks a number of villages and river names along the west bank of the Canal do Norte which do not appear elsewhere. They were presumably discovered by Morton or he had received verbal reports of them from the coastal Indians. Along what Tatton calls the river *Woakathy*, which seems to be in the region of the river Mazagdo, he marks a native village called *Comoo*. This may be the area in which Captain Roger Fry later established a fort in 1631 which was called *Cumau* and which was described as being near *Mocopo*, presumably Macapá.[47] He also shows further up the river beyond a marshy area the village of *Parraroia*. On the *Wocapoco*, which may be identified as the river Prêto or possibly the Pedreiro, he marks the villages of *Oparoka, Parao, Corawica, Paropa* and *Maranowite*. These names are not recorded elsewhere. No indication is given of any European settlement up these rivers although Morton's settlers are known to have grown tobacco and presumably built, what later Portuguese accounts and maps called, fortified buildings or 'casas fortes' in this region south of the river Anauerapucu.[48]

Tatton's chart also shows the positions of various Indian villages, along the Canal do Norte itself, in which fortified trading posts were later built by the English, Dutch and Irish. The first was *Sapanow* which seems to have been on a little island possibly near the mouth of the Canal do Gurijuba and is described, by a later prospective colonist Jesse de Forrest in 1623, as a village of three long houses built on stilts by the river.[49] It was the first port of call having, as Tatton's chart records, a good anchorage of some seven fathoms. The second large settlement was at *Sapanapooke* on the Ilha do Para opposite the river Anauerapucu. The third settlement Tatton records was at the village of *Coropokery* which he shows as a peninsula (possibly this was an island as shown on the 'king' chart) on the Ilha Grande de Gurupá. The absence of forts of any kind especially in the region of the Xingu river where the Dutch built the two forts of Materu and Nassau may suggest that Morton's survey of *c*. 1614 was made before they were built, and, indeed, before the fort of 'Thomas Rey' was constructed. The chart does however show the placename *Comaranowa* in 2°30′ south up the Xingu, which may be identifiable as the village called *Komerou* by the Dutch where they built their fort of Nassau.

The second chart of the Amazon based on Thomas King's survey is now in the Bibliothèque Nationale (Fig. 3). The chart is evidently a copy of another and was again apparently drawn by a professional chartmaker, possibly John Daniel (fl. 1612-42) or his apprentice Nicholas Comberford (fl. 1626-1670). The approximate scale is 1:1¼ mill and is variable. The geographical extent shown is from the river Araguari in the north to the confluence of the Amazon and the river Tapajos. Whenever the chart was actually copied, it records Thomas King's survey which probably took place before 1618.[50] Little if anything is known about King. He may be identifiable as the shipowner and sailor of Uphill Somerset, who died in 1628 and who was described in his will as 'a man imployed often in travaile at sea and to have born many dangers . . .'.[51] Unfortunately no evidence seems to survive to connect this King with the Amazon captain. As he went to the Amazon at Roe's charge between 1611 and 1618, his mission was presumably like Morton's—that is to settle colonists and to explore the river. The extent of exploration shown is considerably more than that on the Tatton chart and the place-names shown are different. The difficulties of interpretation however are similar and, indeed, made worse by the evident gross distortion of the river Amazon in the region of what may be Monte Alegré and beyond. In contrast to the Tatton chart, this one is evidently a copy of another, and it exhibits some rather peculiar characteristics which probably derive from the copyist as distinct from the surveyor. For example the uncoloured quadrant compass rose has evidently been put on by mistake. If it had been finished the logic of the drawing would mean that the North point would have been pointing either East or South. The finished coloured rose shows its North point correctly. The latitudes given are also erroneous to such a degree that they cannot be attributed to observational error. The Equator is misplaced by a degree to the North while the apparent locality of the Tapajos river is placed in 6°30′S instead of about 3°S.[52] Although it is difficult to determine, it seems that the latitude scale was placed on the chart independently of the geographical content. The square grid used for copying does not coincide with the lines of the degree divisions on the latitude scale. This would normally be the case if the scale of the geographical area shown was actually based on the latitude scale. The piece of vellum would be divided into however many degrees of latitude were to be shown and then the geographical area plotted on that basis. The source or reason for these erroneous latitudes is unknown.

The major geographical distortion is however near the river Tapajos. From the vicinity of Monte Alegré the river is shown trending due south straight into the Tapajos river which is shown bearing a south-south-east direction instead of a south-south-west direction. What may be identifiable as the river Arapiuns and the two main channels of the Amazon are also swung round to the west approximately 45°. It seems difficult to imagine that this was owing to compass error of any sort and so it is tempting to think that, perhaps, the copyist was so anxious to include all the survey on his one piece of vellum that he deliberately altered the rivers' directions[53] (See Fig. 6).

The place names recorded on the chart are in some cases English, perhaps implying a longer familiarity with the Canal do Norte than is reflected on the Tatton chart.[54] What may be the island of Bailique is called, descriptively enought, *Lung Island;* Point Macapá is called *Red cliff* (the Dutch named it *Roode hoeck*) again presumably describing the ridge of rocks on which present day Macapá stands. The other English place-names are more difficult to identify although they certainly indicate particular areas of English interest, and possibly the location of plantations. *Porsalls Creek* on the left bank of the Channel is shown as being opposite what may be the southern end of the Ilha do Para. This would indicate that it was meant to represent a river, possibly the Prêto or the Pedreiro as Tatton's river *Wocapoco* may do also. 'Porsalls creek' was presumably named after one of the Purcell brothers whose part in the settlement of the Amazon has been described by Dr. Joyce Lorimer.[55] Philip and James Purcell were Irish traders based at Dartmouth. James Purcell was one of sixteen to twenty men carried out by Matthew Morton in late 1611 or 1612 and he and his brother are subsequently recorded on the river. It was presumably on 'Porsalls Creek' that Purcell and Roe's other settlers first established their plantations and built what became known as the 'Taurege' fort. Philip Purcell is again recorded on the Amazon with another Irish adventurer Bernard O'Brien in about 1624.[56] He built the fort of *Mandiutuba* on the right bank of Canal do Gurupá which is shown on the chart presumably as *Manatobe* and, when this fort was attacked and destroyed in April 1625 by the Portuguese, Purcell retreated to a river called by the Portuguese the 'rio de Felippe', which was described as being another branch of the Amazon. The most likely place for Purcell's retreat was to the Canal do Norte and the forts and fortified dwellings on the west bank, which had been established between 1610 and 1624 by himself, Captain Roger North and others. A number of these settlements seem to have been destroyed by the Portuguese including the Irish fort on the *Taurege* in 1625. During this engagement James Purcell was captured and taken to Belem but was eventually transported back to Europe in 1626. In 1628 he returned to the Amazon and rebuilt the Taurege fort only to be captured once again in its defence in 1629. The first 'Taurege' or 'Torrego' fort was presumably built by 1623 when Jesse de Forrest recorded the Irish plantation on what he called the Taurege creek. A chart of the Amazon, drawn much later for the atlas of Johannes Vingboons about 1665 but apparently showing the situation on the river about 1628 shows the 'fort op de Torego' which could well be on the same river as the 'King' chart's *Porsalls Creek* and Morton's *Wocapco*, both of which are shown opposite the Ilha do Para.[57]

The chart also shows the position of *Materu,* now presumably Pôrto de Moz, on the right bank of the river Xingu where the Dutch built their fort, which was destroyed in 1623 by the Portuguese. The only actual depiction of a fort, however, is that placed up the main channel of the Amazon river on the north bank beyond the confluence of the Xingu and Canal do Norte. It is merely called 'the fort' and was presumably built on Roe's instructions by the colonists taken out by King. Its location cannot be determined with precision. It is shown on the river bank between two rivers apparently some 15 leagues apart with mountains rising behind it. The problem of identification is made worse by the gross distortion of the river and its tributaries at this point. The course of the Amazon has been drawn trending due south into what seems to be the river Tapajos instead of due south, east and then north. Up the river Tapajos, which may be identified by the apparently large Indian settlement on its banks which is called *Tapio,* is marked an anchorage and the name, 'Thomas King'. The other channels shown are presumably the various meanderings of the Amazon at the junction of the Tapajos and the main river. That being so, the fort seems to be in the vicinity of Monte Alegré with the Sierra Jabocal rising behind it. There is no other evidence for an English fort in this area. The Dutch under Pieter Adriansz had established a fort upstream from the Paru in 1616 probably on the site of what was later called *Destierro* now near modern Almeirim. This fort was presumably the one reported by the Portuguese in 1616. From the position shown on King's survey the fort does not seem to be Adriansz's as it is too far up river.[58] Portuguese sources however record only the Hollanders or the Flemmings in this area. On a map drawn about 1623 they recorded that the Flemmings went to the river *Gurupatuba,* possibly the Maicuru, to trade with the Tapajos Indians,[59] and a later map of 1630 shows a fort apparently at the mouth of the Maicuru, (*Corpotibes*) which was said to be Dutch, and which the Portuguese had destroyed, presumably in 1623.[60] On the other hand 'Thomas Rey', presumably Roe, was reported in 1615 as having built a fort at the mouth of the Amazon and, a year later, the Portuguese were aware of an English colony 120 leagues up river from Belem. This fort is presumably one of the settlements placed on the Amazon by Roe in the period 1610 to 1618.

The chart also shows Thomas King's explorations of the various branches of the Amazon river and of the Tapajos river which he does not name. The settlement of *Tapio* may be in the region of present day Santarem. Written evidence of Dutch or English explorations and settlements in this area is scanty. In 1616 Pieter Adriansz was recorded by Colonel Scott's

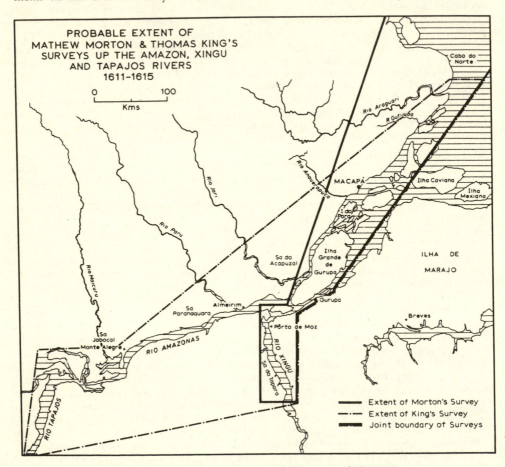

Fig. 6. Modern map showing the extent of the Morton and King surveys.

manuscript 'History of the Amazon' written about 1660,[61] as 'having been as high as the entrance of the strait, they feared they might be in a wrong Channel, returned back again, and between the River *Coropatube* (Maicuru?), and the river *Ginipape* (Paru) on a peninsula by a little river on one side, and an Arme of the Amazones on the other side they built a fort'. The 'strait' was presumably the mouth of the Tapajos which is about 10 miles wide. In the 1620s the English are recorded as attempting a settlement on the banks of the Tapajos, which the Portuguese chronicler Christoval de Acuña seems to be describing in 1639, in the following manner: 'that in times past an English ship of great burden ascended it [the Tapajos], those people intending to make settlement in this province and to prepare harvests of tobacco.'[62] The Indians apparently drove them out. This chart seems to suggest that the area had been explored by the English at some point before 1618. King's furthest point of exploration up what may be the one of the main channels of the Amazon is a river mouth labelled *Pennepaneura*. This place or tribal name has yet to be identified but was presumably somewhere in the region between Tapajos and Obidos.

The interest of both these charts lies in their contribution to a period of obscure and confused history on the Amazon river: an important period however when the English, Irish and Dutch first explored and settled the river. (Fig. 6) Although the settlements lasted a mere twenty years, the enterprises involved hundreds of settlers on plantations scattered along 300 miles of the river. The Portuguese took over ten years to conquer the region from 1620 to 1633. Their own charting, which seems to have been begun by Antônio Vicente Cochado, the Pilot-Major on the first exploratory advance up the river in 1616, records the sites of the various forts they found and destroyed. The charts date from about 1620 onwards but are drawn in so generalized a way that identification of places is very difficult. By comparison these two earlier English charts, as records of hydrographical survey, provide a relatively clear picture of the Canal do Norte and the main river, although again much of their apparent information about settlements is difficult to interpret and must remain elusive. At least it is clear from the charts that the river Tapajos was reached and the main channels of the Amazon explored in the region near Monte Alegré by the English in the second decade of the seventeenth century.

Table 1.

The River Amazones. Gabriell Tatton made this Platt for Mathewe Morton in Ratcliff Ann° Domini 1615. A scale of 20 Inglish Leagues, every League into 3 miles or parts [=160mm] 850× 500mm. *In the collection of the Duke of Northumberland.*

Modern Area	Toponomy
	Place and Tribal names
Coast of Guiana—	
south to Cabo Norte	Maiacary
	The Lake of Maiacary
	Coropoporough Iles
	C. Curco
River Amazon—	
Canal do Norte—west bank	R. Arrowary
	R. Marmhion
	The Steel mine
	Sapanow
	Arracores
Area of the	
River Anauerapucu and	Matarem
southwards	Roakery
	Anarapook
	R. Woakathy
	Comoo
	Parraroia
	Genta Yayo
	[R.] Wocapoco
	Oparoka
	Parao
	Corawica

	Paropa
	Maranowite
River Xingu—west bank	R. Toquia
	R. Apahow
River Amazon—	
Canal do Norte—east bank	Arracores
	Arrowas
	Sapanapooke
	Matiana
	Coropokery
River Xingu—east bank	Capitan
	Corpappy
	Arropoya
	Matorion
	Huaman
	Comaranowa
	Ama
	Genta Womian

Table 2.
The River of Amazones. A scale of Fiftie English Leagues 50[= 187 mm] 670 x 530 mm.
Bibliothèque Nationale, Paris pf. 166. Div. I.p. 4

Modern Area	Place Names
River Amazon	
Canal do Norte—west bank	Arowary [river]
	Lung Island
	Saparno
	Red Cliff
	Hog Island
	Porsalls Creeke
	Caripacara [island]
	Not Creeke
River Amazon main branch	The fort
	Pennepaneura
River Amazon—east bank	Tapio
	[Anchorage of] Thomas King
Canal do Norte—east bank	The River Para
at junction with the Amazon river	Corapopi
opposite Ilha Grande de Gurupá	Manatobe
	Arapore
River Xingu—east bank	The R of quyamenna
	Matarro
	Chingu

References

1. A version of a paper presented at the VIIIth International Conference on the history of cartography, Berlin 1979. The author would like to thank Professor D. B. Quinn, Max Guedes, Joyce Lorimer, Gunther Schilder, Marcel Destombes and Tony Campbell for their generous advice.
2. Joyce Lorimer has described the history of English trade and settlements in Guiana in her unpublished thesis 'English trade and exploration in Trinidad and Guiana' (Liverpool 1973) which has provided much of the historical background for this discussion. Hereinafter referred to as J. Lorimer (1973).
3. The earliest Spanish chart of the coastline seems to date from the 1560s. A reproduction is to be found in Koeman, C. (ed.) *The History of the cartography of Suriname 1500-1971.* (Amsterdam, 1973) fig. 2.
4. See fig. 1. and accompanying key. I am indebted to Mr. C. Cromarty who drew fig. 1. and 6. A chart of the river Orinoco dated 1629 drawn by a Dutch mapmaker, but which includes a scale of English leagues and may therefore be based on an English survey, survives in the Rijksarchief (the Hague) at Leupe 653- 'Caerte van de River van Orinoque gelyck de selve is sareckende vant begins el tot St Thomas de la guane toe Ano 1629'.
5. J. A. Williamson: *English colonies in Guiana and on the Amazon 1604-1668* (Oxford, 1923) p. 60.
6. Morton was described as such by John Smith in *The true travels, adventures and observations of Captaine John Smith.* (London, 1630) p. 49.
7. Letter to William Moreton Esq. of Moreton, Cheshire from Matthew Morton dated London, 5 May 1619. British Library, Additional MS 33935 f. 27.
8. Letter to William Moreton, 19 November 1619 from Mathew Morton. British Library Additional MS 33935 f. 32.
9. See fig. 2. Compare with fig. 6. Fig. 2. By kind permission of Duke of Northumberland.
10. See fig. 3. Compare with fig. 6. Fig. 3. By kind permission of Bibliothèque Nationale, Paris.
11. Edmund Howes (ed.) *The Annales, or Generall Chronicle of England, begun first by maister John Stow* . . . (1615). p. 946.
13. British Library, Lansdowne MS 160 f. 109 dated 15 March 1618. Cited as a reference in J. Lorimer (1973).

14. Public Record Office E. 190/820/1 entry in the Port Books for 27.6.1614. Seems to refer to the *Lions Clawe* of London, to Matthew Morton and to [*?*] Knighte. As the entry is very faded the transcription may be incorrect. Cited as a reference in J. Lorimer (1973).

15. Transcripts of manuscript documents in the Archivo General de Indias, Seville, held in the British Library Department of Manuscripts Additional MS 36320. f. 186. 'Thomas Rey' may mean Thomas King whose name in Spanish would indeed be 'Rey' or it may, as usually stated, refer to Roe himself.

16. Printed in Studart, Guilherme, barão de: *Documentos para a historia do Brasil especialmente a do Ceará, 1608-1625.* Quarto volume (Fortaleza-Ceará, 1921). pp. 8-10. 'No. 232 4 de Septembro de 1616—Carta Regia sobre a expedicao de Francisco Caldeira—Codice da Bibliotheca de Eduardo Prado'. I am indebted to my colleague Harold Whitehead for his translation of this and the following quotation.

17. *Documentos para a historia da conquista e colonisacão da costa de leste-oeste do Brasil.* (Rio de Janeiro, 1905). pp. 207-209. 'Carta del L. do D. Francisco de Texada y Mendoza sobre la poblacion del Rio Marañon . . . y de lo que contiene un Memorial del Padre Xptoval de Acuña sobre el descubrimiento del Rio de las Amazonas . . . 14 Feb. 1617.

18. British Library Additional MS. 17940 A. Comparison with the maps in Walter Ralegh's commonplace book of about 1616 (British Library Additional MS. 57555) seems to corroborate that the place-names of the map of Guiana are in his hand. In 1596 Thomas Hariot, writing to Cecil, refers to Ralegh having taken his principal chart of Guiana to Cadiz leaving him to draft a chart from Ralegh's notes and writings. Some pencilled additions showing the west coast of northern South America are not in Ralegh's hand. (See fig. 1. No. 1.).

19. This chart is now in the Duke of Northumberland's collection. It was formerly in the possession of Boies Penrose and is reproduced in B. Penrose *Travel and discovery in the Renaissance 1420-1620* (Cambridge, Massachusetts, 1952) Opp. p. 108. R. A. Skelton thought it was the work of Thomas Hood but this attribution seems doubtful. Its association with Downe rests on the report of 31 July 1596 that Sir George Trenchard and Sir Ralph Horsey, assistants to the Lord Lieutenant of Dorset, took possession of the 'plott or discovery of the Indies voyage . . . being in the custody of one Samuel Mace and William Downe'. The items 'an Indyan carde [chart of the West Indies?], with two others not perfected' were sent to Robert Cecil. They are not present in the collection at Hatfield House. (See fig. 1. No. 2).

20. Lawrence Keymis: *A relation of the second voyage to Guiana.* (London, 1596.) p. 25. Downe told Keymis that he had sailed up the *Wiapoco* (Oyapock), which does not appear on the map. Keymis himself relates (p. 2.) that he first anchored in the mouth of the *Arrowarie* (Araguari), which is also not shown. Apart from the absence of information to the south of the 'river of Chilliana', the chartmaker has placed the Equator passing through the mouth of the river Orinoco—an error not made on earlier or contemporary English charts.

21. Letter to Juan de Harra in Lisbon from Alvaro Mendez de Castro dated 16 January 1599 reporting the presence of the English on the Amazon. British Library Additional MS 36317 f. 237.

22. These charts are reproduced in Venezuela—British Guiana Boundary Arbitration: *The case of the United States of Venezuela . . .* vol. 4. Appendix, atlas. (Baltimore, 1898) pl. 57 and 58.

23. William Davies: *A True relation of the travailles and most miserable captivity . . .* (London, 1614) Sig. D. 3.

24. Fig. 4. One of a series of manuscript charts showing the Guianan coastline and mouth of the Amazon. This one includes a MS note indicating that it was drawn after the voyage of Robert Thornton to Guiana. Robert Dudley, self-styled Duke of Northumberland, supplied Thornton with charts for the voyage and evidently received information on Thornton's return. The MS atlas is in the Bayerische Staatsbibliothek, Munich, Icon. 139 f. 52b.[v] The MS note (not printed in the published *Arcano* of 1648) is as follows: 'Il porto di Chiana fu scoperto dal Cap[ne]: Rob[to]: Thertono Inglese nel 1609 . . . Instructioni dato dal Duca di Northumbria . . . il primo Inglese ch'entrava nel Imperio di Guiana nel 1594 . . .'. The area showing the mouth of the Amazon was revised on a later chart 'La Carta megliore p il Rio de las Amazones come fu scoperto et posseduto gia d'Olandese' (f. 58[r].) This was based on Hessel Gerritsz' map in De Laet's *Nieuwe Wereldt* (1625).

25. Reproduced in A. Cortesão *Portugalia Monumenta Cartographica.* vol. 5. (Lisbõa, 1960.) pl. 601A.

26. British Library Additional MS 34240N. fig. 5 shows detail of Amazon river.

27. So named on Tatton's chart.

28. Harcourt anchored at $2\frac{1}{2}$°N 'by certaine islands called Carripapoory' which were probably the Ilha de Maracá. In *A relation of a voyage to Guiana* by Robert Harcourt 1613. Edited by C. A. Harris. Hakluyt Society, Series II, no. LX. (London, 1927.) p. 70.

29. See fig. I. no. 4.

30. Percy Papers X (1611-1617), f. 220. The letter is quoted in full in J. Shirley: 'George Percy at Jamestown 1607-12,' in *Virginia Historical Magazine,* July 1949 p. 242.

31. See fig. 6 for the probable extent of the Morton and King Surveys.

32. *South America Pilot Pt. I.* 9th edition. (London, 1945) p. 75.

33. The burthen is given in the entry in the Port Book 27.6.1614, Public Record Office E.190/820/1.

34. Some idea of the problems of navigating in the river may be gained from the *South America Pilot* (London, 1864) p. 281, where it is remarked that 'the uniform aspect of the banks of the Amazons, the resemblance between all the islands . . . and the almost entire absence of objects of recognition, renders it impossible to give fixed direction for navigating this river. It will, therefore, be necessary to employ a pilot . . . to prevent mistaking one channel for another.' De Laet (1625) p. 463 indicates that the river shown on Morton's survey south of Gurupá is not the main channel.

35. The methods used to assess planimetric accuracy and their inherent problems have been widely discussed

recently. See for example J. H. Andrews 'Motive and method in historical cartometry' (paper presented to the History of Cartography Conference, Greenwich 1975). Subsequent experimental work has been done by J. C. Stone and A. M. D. Gemmel: see 'An Experiment in the comparative analysis of distortion on historical maps' in *Cartographic Journal* (June 1977) pp. 7-11; and by Joan Murphy in 'Measures of map accuracy assessment and some early Ulster maps' in *Irish Geography* (1978) vol. 11. pp. 88-101. See also W. Ravenhill's various historical studies, notably his use of vector analysis in 'The Accuracy of early maps? Towards a computer-aided method' *Cartographic Journal* (June 1974) pp. 48-52. Owing to the absence of sufficient data on these two charts quantitative analysis of them is not possible.

36. Tatton's chart (and the 'King' chart) was compared with Mapo do Brasil politico 1:2,500,000. Rio de Janeiro, 1958. 4 sh. Compare figs 2, 3 and 6.

37. Ralegh recorded that the variation at 7°N off the coast of Brazil in 1595 was 7° easterly. See Robert H. Schomburgk (ed.). Walter Ralegh *The Discovery of the large, rich, and beautiful Empire of Guiana*, Hakluyt Society Series I, vol. 3. (London, 1848) p. 196 and note. For the year 1600 Dr. van Bemmelen constructed an 'Isogonen—Karte' for the world which was included in *Observations made at the Royal Magnetical and Meteorological Observatory at Batavia*. vol. XXI. 1898, (Batavia, 1899). He concluded, on the basis of his compilation of references to magnetic variation in journals of the period, that the variation in the region of the mouth of the Amazon was about 7°E. The compass used however may have been partially corrected for the London variation of 11.1/4° easterly. It was common, as William Borough records in 1585, to offset the compass wires half a point to the East. See his edition of *A Discourse of the variation of the compass or magneticall needle* (London, 1585.) Sig. G. Such a chart would obviously exhibit only a slight discrepancy in comparison with a chart drawn on the basis of true North, if the variation in the particular region concerned was about 7° East.

38. The distortion may of course be the result of the chartmaker's mis-interpretation of whatever sources he had at his disposal.

39. A Table of latitudes of points which seem to be identifiable, compared with modern values.

Place	Morton-Tatton Chart	Brazil 1:2,500,000
Ilha Maraca (*Iles Coropoporough*)	2°	2°
Cabo do Norte (*Cape Curco?*)	1°50'N	1°40'N
Mouth of river Araguari (*Arrowary*)	1°15'N	1°15'N
I. Baillique? (southern end?)	1°N	0°55'N
Mouth of Gurijuba (*Sapanow?*)	0°50'N	0°50'N
Point Macapá	0°20'N	0°5'S
Ilha do Para (southern end)	0°5'S	0°30'S
Ilha Grande de Gurupa (southern end)	1°5'S	1°30'S

There are no possible points of identification in the Xingu river.
The 'King' chart seems to exhibit the same compression of distance between *Saparno* and Point Macapá. Its latitudes are of course quite erroneous.

40. Schubert, H. R. *History of the British Iron and Steel Industry*. (London, 1957.) p. 318. The author notes the use of 'mines of steel' for a mine producing good quality ore in 1631.

41. See the list of place names transcribed from the chart in Table I.

42. J. De Laet *Nieuwe Wereldt* (1625) p. 462. He refers to 'De pertinentste Kaerte ofte ontwerpinghe van dese rieviere die wy als noch hebben konnen sien . . .' He also refers to another chart which seems to be Hessel Gerritsz's chart of the Amazon river which De Laet included in the 1625 edition of his *Nieuwe Wereldt* (1625). It named, according to De Laet, the places *Wayecorpap*, *Mannetibi*, and *Corpappi* amongst others, which are shown on Gerritsz's map. Tatton's exhibits a different set of names which are also included in De Laet's description as follows:

Morton-Tatton, 1615	De Laet, 1625	Morton-Tatton, 1615	De Laet, 1625
R. Arrowary	River Arraway	Matiana	Matiana
Sapanow	Sapeno or Sapenou	Coropokery	Corropokery or Corpecari
Arracores	River Arrowas	Matorion	Matorion
	Paricores	Aropoya	Aropoya
Arrowas	Arrowen	Corpappy	Corpoppy
Matarem	Matarem [village]	Capitan	Capitan
Roakery	Roakery	Huaman	Huaman
Anarapook	Anarcaprock	Genta Womian	Womian
Sapanapooke	Sapanapoock		

43. If this was the case, the chart is not recorded in the Dutch West India Company Collection at the Rijksarchief (the Hague) by F. C. Wieder. In discussing the Johannes Vingboon's chart of the Amazon (dated after 1660) he identified a possible source for the Boca del Para section of the chart (Leupe 684) but remarked that another, unidentifiable, source had been used for the Canal do Norte. F. C. Wieder *Monumenta Cartographica* (The Hague, 1925-33). p. 111. Recent investigations (in 1977) at the Rijksarchief have not brought such a chart to light, although a later one showing the lower Amazon *c.* 1675 (Leupe 2153) indicates that it was copied from an earlier original not now known. A note to the place-names reads: 'N.B. ox desij sijn niet in de orgeneele'.

44. *Dictionary of National Biography* (London 1909) entry for Roe.
45. At least some of the Amazon ventures were apparently set in train at Flushing. In a report dated 31 Jan. 1638 by a Dutch adventurer to the Amazon Jacob Van Reese the north channel of the Amazon is described thus: 'Concerning this land, where the Irish and the English had their plantations, enough is known already in Flushing, where most of their expeditions were financed and fitted out'. Rijksarchief (the Hague) in the collection of Wassenaer van Rosande. I am indebted to Christopher Hibber for this translation and to my colleagues in the Map Room of the Rijksarchief for their help and advice during my visit.
46. J. A. F. Bekkers: *Correspondence of John Morris with Johannes de Laet 1634-49*. [Assen:] 1970. Item 25A. Manuscript is at Utrecht University MS 986 f. 411.
47. J. A. Williamson: *English colonies in Guiana and on the Amazon 1604-68*. (Oxford, 1923.) p. 137. An identification of European forts in the Amazon region must be tentative. It is possible that with the aid of these, and other charts, excavations may provide more solid evidence of where the forts were.
48. See Max Justo Guedes: *Brasil-Costa Norte. Cartografia portuguêsa vetustíssima* (Rio de Janeiro, 1968). pl. 19 and p. 66. Captain Guedes has made a thorough study of the chartmaking of the Portuguese of the Amazon in the period 1616-1633. See also his 'Ações navais contra os estrangeiros na Amazônia 1616-1633' in *História naval Brasileira*. vol. 1. pt. 11 (Rio de Janeiro, 1975) pp. 589–616.
49. E. J. De Forest: *A Walloon Family in America . . . together with a voyage to Guiana being the Journal of Jesse de Forest and his colonists 1623-1625*. (Boston, 1914.) p. 223. The manuscript journal which includes a map of the northern channel of the Amazon is in the collection of the British Library, Sloane MS179B.
50. Thomas King may have gone to the Amazon after 1618. The situation shown on the map indicates however a date before 1623 when the Portuguese destroyed the forts in the Xingu and Amazon.
51 Public Record Office PROB 11/154/95. Signed 11 Feb. 1622/3.
52. It is assumed that the branch of the river which bears the village name *Tapio* may be identifiable as the Tapajos.
53. It is interesting to note the presence of swimming women in one of the river's branches—presumably the legendary Amazons.
54. See table 2 for toponomy.
55. J. Lorimer (1973). Chapter VII.
56. J. A. Williamson (1923). p. 105, and T. G. Matthews 'Memorial autobiografico de Bernardo O'Brien' in *Caribbean Studies* (1970) X. i. pp. 89-106. Bernard O'Brien's tale (Seville, A.G.I. est. 147. caj. 5. leg. 21) has been translated into English by John Hemming who kindly gave me a copy. O'Brien records that in 1624 a Dutch ship came to the Amazon and he left Philip 'Porzel' in charge of the fort he had built, while he took tobacco and cotton back to Europe. On O'Brien's return in 1629 he claimed to have rebuilt the fort on land called *Toherego*, *i.e.* the Taurege.
57. Johannes Vingboon's atlas in the Vatican Library, vol. II. sh. 3. Reproduced in F. C. Wieder *Monumenta Cartographica* vol. IV. (The Hague, 1932) p. 83.
58. In view of the evident distortion however it may still be meant to indicate Adriansz's fort.
59. Max Guedes: *Brasil-Costa Norte* (1968) pl. 13 and p. 56.
60. A. Cortesão: *Portugalia monumenta cartographica*, vol. 4. pl. 471. A reproduction of chart 24 in Joao Teixera I's atlas, 1630. Library of Congress, Washington, Case 9, D. 6., Deck 1.
61. John Scott 'History and Description of the river Amazones'. Bodleian Library, Rawlinson MS A. 175 ff.355. Quoted in J. A. Williamson (1923) p. 68.
62. C. R. Markham (ed.) *Acuña's New Discovery of the Amazons*, 1639. Hakluyt Society, Series I (London, 1859) p. 127. De Laet also refers cryptically to an Englishman exploring the main river of the Amazon in the 1630 French edition of *Nieuwe Wereldt* p. 571.

9
The Influence of Father Ricci
on Far Eastern Cartography

Helen Wallis *

The cartography of the European Renaissance reveals the stages by which men learnt over a short period of years to assimilate a new world of ideas. There followed a second, more dramatic, confrontation of old and new when European missionaries carried to the Far East the scientific learning of their age. Preeminent among these missionaries was Father Matteo Ricci, called by the Chinese 'Hsi-ju', the Wise Man from the West, or Western Scholar. "In Ricci the civilization of the Far West was for the first time meeting that of the Far East", Father Pasquale d'Elia, S.J., wrote in his last article on Ricci, published two years before his death; he describes the encounter as a "happy meeting of minds".[1]

The purpose of this paper is to illustrate Ricci's influence on Far Eastern cartography through a study of two recent acquisitions of the British Museum. In 1961 the late Sir Percival David, Bart., and Lady David presented the Museum with the munificent gift of a terrestrial globe made in China in A.D. 1623 by the Jesuit Fathers Manuel Dias the younger and Nicolo Longobardi. As the earliest known Chinese terrestrial globe, this work ranks with Father Ricci's world map as one of the two most important examples of early European cartography in China. While it is clearly derived in many features from Ricci's map, the globe incorporates later geographical knowledge, thus forming a sequel and complement to Ricci's work. The influence of the globe, which is in manuscript, was limited. That Longobardi and Dias had made a globe was not known until about 1938, when the son of a Parisian antique dealer discovered this one in Peking. Sir Percival David, on being shown its photograph while on a visit to Paris, immediately ordered the globe, and it reached his home at Henley just after the outbreak of the Second World War. The second acquisition is an example of the Shōhō world map, 1645, which the Museum purchased from Japan in 1963. This map, the earliest world map published in Japan, traces its descent from one of Ricci's world maps, and for many years it was the prototype of most Japanese world maps, other than those expressing the Buddhist idea of the world. Through the medium of the Shōhō map Ricci's influence in Japan reached over many generations.

Ricci entered China at Macao as a Jesuit missionary in 1582. Some time before the end of 1584 he made his first map of the world, a Chinese version of the European world map hanging on the wall of the mission room. No example of this map, which Father d'Elia calls the "first edition"[2], is known to survive, although some idea of what it was like may perhaps be gained from the copy made by Ricci's friend Chang Tou-chin in 1623.[3] Nor are any examples known of Ricci's second world map, which was made at Nanking in 1600 at the request of an important mandarin, and was twice the size of the first. Ricci's third world map, made to fit a folding screen twelve feet by six feet comprising six panels, and published at Peking in 1602, is preserved in the Vatican Library. It was reproduced by Father D'Elia in a magnificent facsimile edition in 1938.[4] Two other examples are in Japan, and a fourth is in the possession of Mr. Philip Robinson in

* For help with the study of the Chinese globe I wish to express my thanks to my colleague Mr. E. D. Grinstead of the British Museum, to Mr. H. D. Talbot of the University of Hong Kong, and to Mr. J. V. Mills, with whom I began my earliest work on the globe. The study of the Shōhō map owes much to Mr. K. B. Gardner, Keeper of Oriental Printed Books and Manuscripts in the British Museum, to Professor Nobuo Muroga of Kyoto and Professor Hiroshi Nakamura of Tokyo, who have made this a collaborative work, uniting East and West.

[1] Pasquale M. d'Elia, *Recent discoveries and new studies (1938-1960) on the world map in Chinese of Father Matteo Ricci SJ*, Monumenta Serica, vol. XX (1961), p. 161.
[2] More properly, the first version, since Ricci's later maps were engraved on wood, not copper, unlike the first, and each was from a different wood block.
[3] D'Elia (ed.), *Fonti Ricciane*, II (1949), tav. VIII.
[4] D'Elia, *Il Mappamundo cinese del P. Matteo Ricci S.I.* (1938).

London.[5] A later reprint, completed after 1644, hangs on the wall in the Royal Geographical Society, London.[6] (Fig. 1). In 1603 Ricci made a fourth and still larger version of his map, printed on eight panels, instead of six, an example of which survived in Korea before the Second World War.[7]

Ricci made this series of world maps to show the Chinese what the world was really like and to disabuse them of the traditional belief still held by many Chinese that the world was a square plain mainly comprised of Chinese territories. In a marginal note on his map of 1602, he wrote: "I should have made a globe, but because it was an inconvenient form for a map I was obliged to convert the sphere into two dimensions and turn circles into lines".[8] Before 1585 Ricci had made for a scholarly friend, Wang P'an, prefect of Chao-ch'ing, and two other Chinese, three terrestrial globes, "entirely in their language and script", claiming that these and the astronomical instruments which he had also made were absolutely new in China.

This claim was unjustified. In 1267 the Persian astronomer and geographer Jamal-ud-Din had presented Kublai Khan with a terrestrial globe and six other astronomical instruments. We learn from an accompanying description that the globe was a round ball made of wood, seven parts of which were coloured green and represented water, and three parts of which were coloured white and represented land.[9] It is improbable that Ricci had heard about this globe. He may never have realized that his terrestrial globe was not the first in China. He did discover later that the Chinese had knowledge of astronomical instruments. At Nanking in 1600 he was shown at the College of Chinese Mathematicians various instruments, including a celestial globe dating from the Yuan dynasty in the thirteenth century;[10] but, as Dr. Needham points out, Ricci, like others after him, underestimated Chinese scientific knowledge. Ricci was not aware that early in the fifteenth century the Chinese were producing world maps which surpassed those of western Europe, the most remarkable being the Korean world map of 1402 by Chüan Chin, based on the map of Li Tse-min, c. A.D. 1330.

Ricci's maps transformed the Chinese picture of the world. They illustrated the division of the earth into its five "celestial features", the Equatorial zone, the two Tropical and the two Polar zones. They displayed its terrestrial features as five continents, Europe, Africa, North and South America, Asia and Magellanica (the southern continent). By means of lines of latitude and longitude the position of each place could be exactly calculated, whereas the Chinese checker-board divisions represented distances. Ricci's sources were the first and later editions (published from 1570) of Abraham Ortelius's *Theatrum Orbis Terrarum*, the maps of Gerard Mercator and, for the third version of the world map, the large world map by Peter Plancius, 1592. The projection follows that of Ortelius's "Typus Orbis Terrarum", published in the *Theatrum* (1570), but Ricci centres his map on the meridian of 170° E, which passes east of New Guinea. By placing China and its surrounding territories towards the centre of the map, he made a reasonable concession to his Chinese readers. This arrangement sets America on the eastern borders of the map, a fact which was later to confuse the Japanese, who saw America as one of the "western countries".[11] Such a difficulty does not arise when the continents are displayed on a globe. To convey the idea of the sphericity of the earth on a flat map, Ricci included insets of the polar regions and diagrams of the armillary sphere, the

---

[5] See D'Elia (1961), p. 108-9.
[6] J. F. Baddeley, *Father Matteo Ricci's Chinese world-maps, 1584-1608*, Geographical Journal, vol. L (1917), p. 254-70; E. Heawood, *The relationship of the Ricci maps*, ibid., p. 271-6.
[7] This map was examined in 1936 by Professor Ayusawa Shintarō. His latest article on it, including a reproduction, appears in *Chirigakushi Kenkyū* (1957).
[8] D'Elia (1938), tav. IV.
[9] Walter Fuchs, *The Mongol Atlas of China by Chu Ssu-pen and the Kuang-yü-t'u* (1946), p. 4-5. In the discussion which followed this paper M. Marcel Destombes pointed out that the records of native Chinese globes show that they comprised only the top half of the earth, and that, curiously enough, in the work of the Persian astronomer Al-Bīrūnī in the eleventh century there is a reference to the fact that he had constructed a globe which comprised only one hemisphere.
[10] Joseph Needham, *Science and Civilization in China*, III (1959), pp. 367-9, 456.
[11] A statement in the Zōho Kai Tsūsho Kō reads: 'America lies east of Japan on a map, but geographically it is one of the Western countries, Japan being the country situated in the farthest east'. See Nobuo Muroga and Kazutaka Unno, *The Buddhist world map in Japan and its contact with European maps*, Imago Mundi, XVI (1962), p. 60.

FIG. 1. RICCI'S WORLD MAP OF 1602, REPRINTED AFTER 1644 (CENTRAL PORTION ONLY). *Courtesy of the Royal Geographical Society.*

FIG. 2. MANUSCRIPT TERRESTRIAL GLOBE BY LONGOBARDI AND DIAS, 1623. *Courtesy of the British Museum.*

celestial spheres and the seasons. The globe which was made in 1623 by Nicolo Longobardi, Ricci's successor as Superior General of the China Mission, in collaboration with Manuel Dias, can thus be regarded as the completion of Ricci's work.[12]

Like Ricci, Longobardi and Dias were dedicated to the propagation of Christianity. Expelled from China in the persecution of 1616, the Fathers returned in 1621 eager to continue their work.[13] "We try various ways to return to our former freedom", Dias wrote. "The second is through mathematics, for which we now have sufficient books and instruments. We are undertaking [the reform of] the Calendar and similar projects which up to now have been impossible".[14] Through the exposition of western science the Fathers hoped to win acceptance for western religion.

23 inches (59 cm.) in diameter, the globe is made on a scale of 1 : 21 million, which is large enough to convey a picture of the world in some detail. Like the globe of Jamal-ud-Din, it also is a round ball of wood. The geographical features are painted in lacquer on the wooden surface. The sea is green; the continents are distinguished by different colours. Asia, it may be significant, is in yellow (imperial yellow?) edged with red. Land and sea are not represented in their true proportions, for the southern regions contain the continent of Magellanica. The large title cartouche, which obliterates the continent in the eastern hemisphere, lies south of China, thus giving that country pride of place (Fig. 2).

In certain major and minor features the globe diverges from Ricci's map. Some of these differences appear in areas in whose delineation Ricci was evidently following Plancius. This may suggest that Longobardi and Dias were using one of the earlier versions of Ricci's map. A narrow strait, like Mercator's Strait of Anian, divides northern Asia from North America, whereas Ricci on his later maps depicts a wide expanse of ocean, as on Ortelius's map of the Pacific, 1589, and as on Plancius's world map, 1592.[15] Similarly the Arctic coast of North America resembles that on Ortelius's world map of 1570. Ricci shows two gulfs, following Ortelius's map of America, 1587, appearing in the edition of the *Theatrum* published in 1592, and Plancius's world map, 1592. In areas of which Longobardi and Dias had personal knowledge or for which they had access to new sources, notably eastern Asia and the Pacific, the globe incorporates many improvements. The outline of China is more accurate than on Ricci's map, although there is less detail in inland geography. Japan, Korea, and the islands of the East Indies are better delineated. The most remarkable of the improvements lies in the shape of New Guinea. Ricci names it New Guinea and draws it as a peninsula connected by a neck of land to the southern continent. Longobardi and Dias show it as an island named Little Java. Its remarkably accurate outline reveals knowledge of the discovery of Torres Strait by Torres in 1606. We know that Father Giulio Aleni, an associate of Longobardi and Dias, had information about this discovery. He drew New Guinea in a similar shape on his manuscript world map of 1623,[16] and on the maps of the Far East and Pacific in his world geography *Chih-fang wai-chi*, 1623 (see Fig. 3), and he wrote that about ten years before 1623 a ship had discovered that New Guinea was not joined to Magellanica, as was first thought, but was an island lying from 1 °S to 12 °S, 165°-190° E in longitude.[17] As Longobardi, Dias and Aleni had been working together in 1612, they could have learnt of the discovery from the same source, or one from another. Probably in 1623 the three Fathers consulted each other and used the same authorities. They were associating with the same group of Chinese scholar converts, including the three most eminent, known as the "Three Pillars of the Christian Religion in China". Of these, both Li Chih-tsao (Leo) and Hsü Kuang-ch'i (Doctor Paul) had been intimate friends of Ricci, helping him with the publication of his world maps, and after Ricci's death in 1610 they had continued their scientific work

[12] For a fuller study of the globe, see Helen Wallis and E. D. Grinstead, *A Chinese terrestrial globe A.D. 1623*, British Museum Quarterly, vol. XXV (1962), p. 83-91.

[13] Details of the lives and works of the two Fathers are given in Louis Pfister, *Notices biographiques et bibliographiques sur les Jésuites de l'ancienne mission de Chine, 1552-1773*, I (1932), p. 58-66, 106-11.

[14] Manuel Dias, *Relatione delle cose piu notabili scritti negli anni 1619, 1620, 1621 dalla Cina* (1624), p. 16.

[15] Ricci's first map of 1584, as reproduced in 1623, shows a narrow strait.

[16] Aleni's manuscript world map is preserved in the Ambrosiana Library, Milan, and was formerly called the Ambrosiana map.

[17] *T'ien-hsüeh ch'u-han* (Christian works, first series), Peking, 1630, vol. XIV, ch. 4, f. 16b, quoted by d'Elia (1938), p. 225.

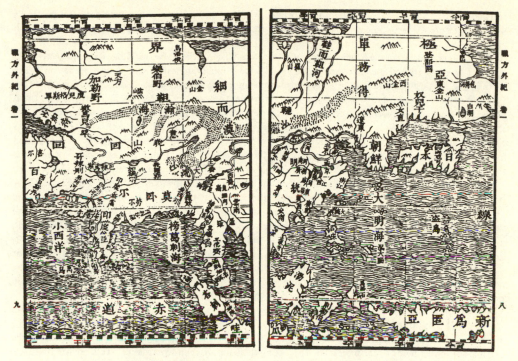

FIG. 3. MAP OF ASIA AND THE WESTERN PACIFIC IN ALENI'S WORLD GEOGRAPHY, 1623. A REPRINT.

with Longobardi, Dias and Aleni as Ricci's successors. The third, Yang T'ing-yün, Grand Mandarin of Hangchow, a late convert and godson of Li Chih-tsao, was in 1623 helping Aleni with his World Geography, as Li Chih-tsao records in his preface to the work. Any or all of these Chinese scholars could have sponsored the construction of the globe, or advised in the actual making of it.[18] It may even have been intended as a present for the Emperor or was perhaps commissioned by him, as Sir Percival David believed; for the Emperor T'ien-ch'i was himself a great carpenter and lacquerer, and the globe is said to have come from the Imperial Palace at Peking.

From the globe the Chinese must have gained a truer idea of distances and of relationships between places and regions than from any of the earlier maps or globes made in China. The explanatory legend shows the Fathers' concern to convey the facts of world geography to the Chinese and to correct the idea that the earth was flat. Little knowing that Chinese astronomers were writing of the sphericity of the earth in the 2nd century B.C., and that they must have known of it as early as the 4th century B.C., the Fathers write: "Chinese scholars, seeing only a flat surface, said that the earth was flat. Westerners, using the principle of the parallels, travelled far and wide over the oceans. Some went from west to east without interruption until they finally returned to their starting-point." Ships in full sail served to remind the Chinese how the Fathers themselves had come to China. The Fathers explain how eclipses reveal differences in time and, therefore, in longitude, and how this proves that the earth is spherical; and, accordingly, "We have made a model in the shape of a spherical ball." They set out the theory of the five zones of latitude, and describe the five continents in terms similar to Ricci's. In discussing the relativity of compass directions, of north and south, they labour their points as if expecting to encounter resistance. The traditional Chinese concepts of Yin and Yang made the force of opposites an overwhelming feature in daily life and every ritual ob-

---

[18] See Wallis and Grinstead (1962), p. 84-5.

servance. In the Chinese mind Yang was associated with hot and south and Yin with cold and north. It would, therefore, be very difficult for the Chinese to accept the fact stated on the globe, that "the south can also be cold".

The Fathers also expounded their theory of the earth's place in the universe. Like Ricci, they wrote in terms of an earth-centred universe, and made use of a traditional Chinese idea in their explanation: "The earth is like the heavy turbid yolk of an egg concentrating in one place". Ricci had used the analogy of the yolk in an egg on his map of 1602. As Needham has shown, the analogy of the yolk in a hen's egg and that of the spherical cross-bow bullet were the two oldest expressions in Chinese cosmological thought for the shape of the earth floating in the midst of the vast heavens. We find it in the *Commentary on the Armillary Sphere* by the great 1st century astronomer Chang Heng.[19] This metaphor of the egg had also appeared in the cosmological ideas of the Orphic philosophers of ancient Greece, and in earlier Greek writings near the end of the fifth century B.C.[20] It is clear from the description of the original mounting of the globe, which is given in the title legend, that it was set on a vertical axis, as in the Ptolemaic system.[21] The Fathers have been criticised for withholding from the Chinese the new helio-centred astronomy of Copernicus and Galileo, but, as D'Elia has pointed out,[22] this criticism does not take into account their difficulties in coming to terms with the full implications of the Copernican revolution, nor their great interest in Galileo's work, even after the Injunction of 1616 against Galileo. The last page of Dias's treatise on the sphere *T'ien-wen lüeh* (1615) gives the first references in Chinese to Galileo's discoveries, and Dias concludes with the hope that one of Galileo's telescopes would soon arrive in China.[23] The Fathers, notably Schreck, had been appealing to Galileo to send to China the results of his discoveries, which were necessary for their work in reforming the Chinese calendar.

It is of special interest that in one scientific theory the authors of the globe were ahead of scientists in Europe, and that this they owed to the Chinese. They refer in the title legend to the parallel between the attraction of the lodestone for particles of iron and the effect of gravitational force: "The centre of the earth is the lowest point. All objects having mass by their nature tend towards it." This remarkably early conception of terrestrial magnetism was entirely derived from Chinese work on the magnet.

The authors end the title legend with a religious reference to the Creator or King of Creation: "So we can deduce the origin [of heaven and earth] in the King of Creation." To this they add the date (1623) and their names in Chinese. If the King of Creation represents God in a Christian sense, it would suggest that the globe was made at the request of one of the Christian scholar converts; but to the Chinese the term would mean something quite different from a personal Creator. As Needham points out, the expression used, *tsao hua chê* (Author of Change), or *tsao wu chê* (Author of Things), is a very old one in Chinese thought, going back to the 4th century B.C.[24]

The globe reveals the achievements and limitations of Jesuit Renaissance science. It gave the Chinese a true picture of the world as it was then known. Yet the Fathers themselves accepted only part of the new learning, not understanding the Copernican theory sufficiently to present it to the Chinese in place of the earth-centred cosmology traditional both in Europe and China. They failed also to appreciate the antiquity and the achievements of Chinese science. They claimed western scientific discoveries as the natural outcome of Christian thought and civilisation. The Chinese disputed this claim. To them the western knowledge was 'new' knowledge, and they objected to the term 'western' being applied to it, reserving this term for the Christian religion.

---

[19]   Needham, III (1959), p. 217-8.
[20]   G. S. Kirk and J. E. Raven, *The Pre-Socratic Philosophers* (1957), p. 45-8; W. K. C. Guthrie, *Orpheus and Greek Religion* (1952), p. 93-5.
[21]   A new stand made for the globe when it reached Europe set it on an axis of $22\frac{1}{2}°$, in the Copernican system, as appears in the photograph (Fig. 2.)
[22]   D'Elia, *Galileo in China* (1960), p. 51-6.
[23]   D'Elia, *Galileo* (1960), p. 18-19.
[24]   Needham, II (1956), p. 564, 581. Needham (II, 581) shows that the highest spiritual being ever known or worshipped in China had not been a Creator in the Hebrew sense.

The assimilation of the 'new' knowledge demanded some intellectual flexibility, and also a motive for accepting the new ideas. The Chinese gained no practical advantage from Ricci's geographical teachings, which became increasingly misunderstood and distorted. How little was the influence which his maps exerted on Chinese cartography can be seen from a map of the 'Chinese dominions' or 'universe', published in 1818. It shows the Indian Ocean as the Little West Sea in the extreme south-west corner, and the Atlantic Ocean, including the island of America, as the Great West Sea in the extreme north-west corner (Fig. 4). With its distortions it conveys a true psychological picture of the world as it impinged on the Chinese, a self-sufficient people living in isolation. That it is difficult to tell whether Chinese maps were intended to be maps of China, maps of the Chinese empire, or maps of the world, is significant. Ricci's report of the five continents was described by official Chinese historians of the 17th and 18th centuries as 'vague and fictitious',[25] and a 'wild fabulous story'.[26] The Rites controversy, which led to the missionaries' loss of imperial favours, had contributed to the declining interest in western science. The Friars who formed the rival sect of missionaries contested the Jesuits' sympathetic approach to Chinese culture, and to their use of science for the propagation of Christianity. "I, for my part, would prefer to see our Friars in China with Crosses around their Necks, rather than with Maps and Clocks in their Hands", Friar Navarrete declared before the Royal Judge in Manila, 1656-57.[27] It is fortunate that, despite this Chinese revulsion from western science, persons in high places should have considered the globe made by Ricci's successors to be worthy of preservation.

Ricci's map exerted a greater influence on Japanese cartography than on Chinese because, being exempted from the prohibitions directed against works of Christian propaganda, it was available to be copied, and so came to be transmitted in a simplified form through the publication of the Shōhō map of 1645 and that map's many derivatives. Various European maps and atlases were introduced into Japan in the late 16th and early 17th centuries, among them Ricci's map. According to Baddeley, examples of the map of 1600 were sent to Japan by the Jesuit Fathers in China;[28] and it is probable that one was in use at the Academy of Mathematicians founded in the Church at Kyoto in 1605 by Father Carlo Spinola, S.J.[29] Ricci's map achieved the widest circulation because its place-names and legends were written in Chinese characters, which could be read by the educated Japanese. After the prohibition of Christianity and the exclusion of all foreigners except Dutch and Chinese by the Shogunate Government in 1638, works such as Aleni's *Chih-fang wai-chi* of 1623 and Ricci's religious writings were on the list of prohibited books, but no restriction was placed on world maps because of their usefulness. This included Ricci's map, which was considered to have no direct connection with Christianity. When, for example, a restrictive order on imports was issued at Nagasaki in 1668, world maps could still be imported because they were "convenient and useful".[30] In later years Ricci was often mistakenly regarded as an Asian, but this misconception had its origin in *Sairan Igen*, a book on world geography written in 1713 by the celebrated scholar and high Shogunate Government official Arai Hakuseki.[31] It is perhaps significant that the Jesuit sign IHS on Ricci's map at Kyoto University has been rubbed off.

[25] *Ming Shih* (1740), 326/7b-9b, quoted by Kenneth Ch'en in *Matteo Ricci's contribution to, and influence on, geographical knowledge in China*, Journal of the American Oriental Society, LIX (1939), p. 355.

[26] *Huang Ch'ao Wên Hsien T'ung Kao*, 289/14ab, quoted in Ch'en, p. 356.

[27] Navarrete's *Controversias*, quoted in J. S. Cummins, ed. *The Travels of Friar Domingo Navarrete 1618-1686* (Hakluyt Society, 1962), I, 150n.

[28] Baddeley, *Geographical Journal*, vol. L (1917), p. 263.

[29] The statement that the map was in use at the Academy of *Princes* at Kyoto appears to have arisen from a confusion between the Academy of Princes and the Academy of Mathematicians. See Arimichi Ebizawa, *Nanban Gakutō no Kenkyū (Studies of the Catholic School of Science in Japan)* (Tokyo, 1958), p. 51. For this reference and much other information I am indebted to Professor Nobuo Muroga, who points out that there is no clear evidence in the Japanese records to show when Ricci's map was first introduced into Japan.

[30] "Nagasaki Oboegaki", quoted by Yasuhiko Komiya in his *Nikka Bunka Kōryūshi* (History of Cultural Intercourse between Japan and China), Tokyo, 1955. (A reference kindly supplied by Professor Nobuo Muroga).

[31] I am indebted to Professor Nobuo Muroga for this information about the Shogunate Government's policy on the circulation of world maps.

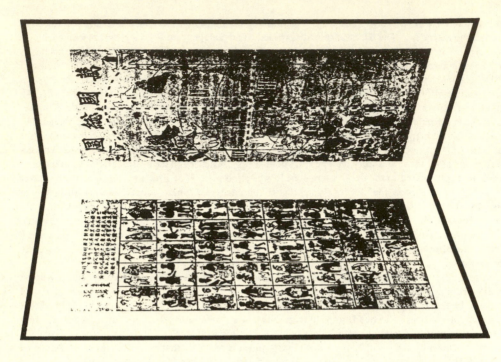

FIG. 6. THE SHŌHŌ WORLD MAP AND ACCOMPANYING SHEET
BEARING THE PICTURES OF FOREIGNERS, 1645. *Courtesy of the British Museum.*

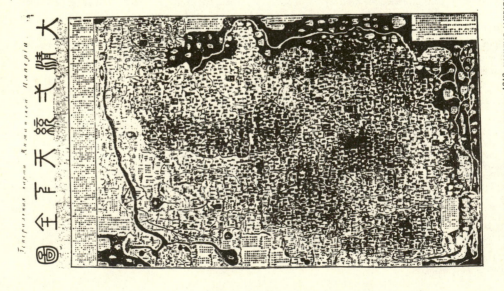

FIG. 4. A UNIVERSAL MAP OF THE CHINESE EMPIRE, 1818, SHOWING AMERICA
AS AN ISLAND IN THE NORTH-WEST CORNER. *Courtesy of the British Museum.*

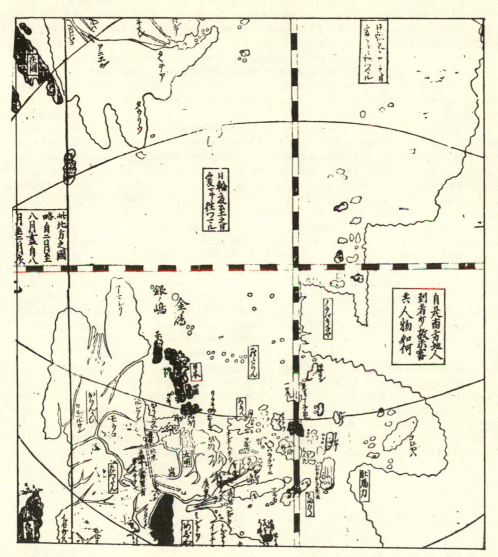

FIG. 5. THE SHŌHŌ WORLD MAP, 1645. *Courtesy of the British Museum.*

This free circulation explains why the unknown author of the Shōhō map had an example of Ricci's maps (or a derived version) available to copy when, in 1645, seven years after the period of Japan's self-imposed isolation had begun, he set about making a map depicting western knowledge of the world entitled *Bankoku Sōzu*, Map of the World.[32] This, the first true map of the world printed in Japan, was very different from the ancient Buddhist map of India, purporting to be a map of the world, which first appeared in the printed edition of an old Japanese encyclopaedia, the *Shūkaishō*, in 1642.[33] Following the outlines of Ricci's map, the author of the Shōhō map depicted the five continents of the world. The southern continent with the projecting peninsula of New Guinea is identical in form with Ricci's (see Fig. 5). The same oval projection is used, with the central meridian sited east of New Guinea. The graduations of latitude and longitude in black and white represent five-degree intervals, but the author evidently did not understand the geographical principles behind this decorative device, as he has not drawn the meridian lines at regular intervals, and he marks 170 degrees to the west of the prime meridian and 160 degrees to the east.

Although Ricci's map was its main source, the Shōhō map appears very different in purpose and conception from the remarkable scientific exposition of world geography which Ricci's map exemplifies. Ricci's map and the globe of 1623 pay special attention to the continents and their relationships, and to the place of the earth in the universe. The Shōhō map is popular rather than educational, decorative rather than scientific. It is accompanied by a sheet displaying forty pictures of the peoples of the world (see Fig. 6). Printed from sets of wood-blocks (five in number for the map, each about eleven inches wide), the two sheets form a two-fold screen, a simplified and popular version of the gorgeous six-fold and eight-fold Nanban screens much used by the nobility in the preceding years. The colour has been added by hand, and the map may be an example of "Nagasaki-e" (Nagasaki Pictures), the colour-prints from wood-blocks which were sold to travellers as products of Nagasaki art. The sheet of pictures bears the imprint: "Published at Nagasaki Harbour in the *hinoto tori* (cock) year of the Shōhō era". The cyclical date 丁 酉 *(hinoto tori)* is wrong, as the Shōhō era had no 丁 *(hinoto)* year, although the 酉 *(tori)* element in the date corresponds to 1645. This mistake in the date has led scholars to doubt both date and place of publication. It has been suggested by Sadakichi Misumi,[34] followed by H. Ikenaga,[35] that the map was published at Kyoto between 1651 and 1669, for these scholars then knew of no map published at Nagasaki before 1764. They conjectured that the author of the Shōhō map gave a false date and place of publication in order to avoid being suspected of being a Christian by the anti-Christian government of the time. A Shōhō type map formerly preserved at the Saidaiji Temple, Nara, bears the imprint: "Shimo Honnōji-mae [Kyoto], Eya Shōbei" (Shōbei, seller of pictures in front of Honnoji temple), and this also seemed evidence in favour of Kyoto as the place of publication of the map of 1645; but the fact that the map by Shōbei, unlike that of 1645, displays the Tropics of Cancer and Capricorn, and that it has additional place-names, shows that it is a revised edition.[36] The motive attributed to the author's deception in giving a false imprint seems doubtful, as there was no prohibition on the publication of world maps throughout the Edo period. Unless decisive evidence in favour of its publication at Kyoto comes to light, the Shōhō world map may yet win acceptance as the earliest Japanese printed map of the world drawn by a painter of Nagasaki and published at Nagasaki in 1645.

---

[32] George H. Beans, *A List of Japanese Maps of the Tokugawa Era* (Jenkintown, 1951), p. 11-12.

[33] See Muroga and Unno (1962), p. 51-2 and fig. 2.

[34] Sadakichi Misumi, "Bankoku Sōzu ni tsuite" (On the General Map of all the Countries of the World), *Bungei shunjū*, July, 1933.

[35] H. Ikenaga, *Collection Ikenaga* (1933), notes to pl. 133.

[36] I am indebted to Professor Nobuo Muroga for this information. Professor Hiroshi Nakamura, who supports the theory that the map of 1645 was published at Kyōtō, gives details of the Saidaiji world map in *Nanban Byōbu Sekaizu no Kenkyū* (A Study of World Maps on Nanban Folding Screens), *Kirishitan Kenkyū*, vol. IX, 1964. The map, unfortunately, is now missing from the Saidaiji Temple, Nara, and is believed to have been lost in the period of post-war confusion, Professor Muroga reports. He has very kindly sent me a copy of a photograph taken twenty or thirty years ago.

The correspondence between the names of peoples on the accompanying sheet and the place-names on the map suggests that the two sheets were made by the same artist as companion works. The corners of the map are also decorated, carrying drawings of four ships, Chinese and Japanese at the top (from left to right), Dutch and *Nanban* (Spanish and Portuguese) at the bottom (although, curiously, these European ships are also Japanese in style[37]). Probably the idea of illustrating the map with pairs of foreigners was inspired by the decoration of Dutch maps with vignettes in the margins depicting foreign couples, as well as views of cities.

The same interest in the peoples and countries of the world is shown on the map. Countries are distinguished by different colours, as on the maps of Blaeu, and their names are given usually in *hiragana*, not in *katakana*, and are enclosed in boxes. The fact that the names are in *kana* (Japanese syllabic letters) suggests that the map and picture were published for popular use and were intended to enlighten the general public. Only educated people could read Chinese characters. Foreign names were usually written in *kana* because it was much easier to express them phonetically, but it is significant that the names for the islands round Japan are also in *kana*. Place-names in China are written in Chinese characters. Another name in Chinese characters is Maletur, a name attached to the projection of the southern continent opposite Java. The characters are given as on Ricci's map, although in the wrong order, showing that the author was copying directly from Ricci. In certain other features the author's divergencies from Ricci clearly are intentional, and point to the use of another source, European in language and origin. The Great Wall of China is marked and carries the legend "There is a stone wall here extending for 1300 *li*". The Chinese called it "the 10,000 *li* wall", but European maps such as that published in Ortelius's *Theatrum Orbis Terrarum*, 1592, give the length as 400 leagues. The author of the Shōhō map, using a European source, seems to have translated miles directly into *li*. The Islands of Gold and Silver, which had appeared in the seas east of Japan on Portuguese maps of the 1580s and later Dutch maps, are marked on the Shōhō map, although they are not on Ricci. The Cape of Good Hope is named "Kapo chi boha esupeunshiya" (the second "u" being presumably a copying error for "ra"). This is the Portuguese form, whereas Ricci called it "Big Wave Mountain", which scholars have interpreted as a representation of the older Portuguese name "Cape of Storms". Other names seem to be Portuguese in form, such as Ingeresu for England.[38]

Five editions of the Shōhō map and picture were published, the latest dated 1652, as Professor Hiroshi Nakamura has shown.[39] This example of the edition of 1645 is the only one in Europe. The map had great influence, and derived versions went on being published until as late as 1708. An example of these is the world map entitled "Bankoku Sōzu" of smaller size published at Nagasaki in 1671, with the pictures of foreigners displayed on the same sheet (Fig. 7). The map is circular, and not drawn on a true projection, and the "graduations" are purely decorative. Such maps were intended for the illustration of popular handbooks. Other maps derived from the Shōhō map but modified in terms of traditional Buddhist cosmography were even more bizarre, as appears from the "Bankoku Zu", a map of all countries. c. 1744[40].

The many world maps published in Japan in the hundred years after 1645 testify to the great interest of the newly awakened middle classes in the new knowledge of the world, and to their curiosity about foreign countries, despite the Government's policy of seclusion. Through this chink in the closed door the Japanese peered at the outside world, while the Chinese were still looking inward, absorbed in the problems of their own great empire. Thus Ricci's geographical teachings brought western knowledge to Japan more effectively than to China, because they reached more receptive minds, in a wider group of the community. Divorced from their Christian context, they were assimilated into a native Japanese form of cartography, although much simplified in the process.

---

[37] Professor Nobuo Muroga points out that this is one factor arguing against the author being one of the painters of Nagasaki, as he would have been familiar with European ships, whereas the painters of Kyoto would not.
[38] The author is making a fuller study of this map and its sources in collaboration with Mr. K. B. Gardner.
[39] Professor Nakamura has kindly provided this and much other information by letter, and the results of his researches are now published in *Nanban Byōbu no Kenkyū* (1964).
[40] Muroga and Unno (1962), fig. 12.

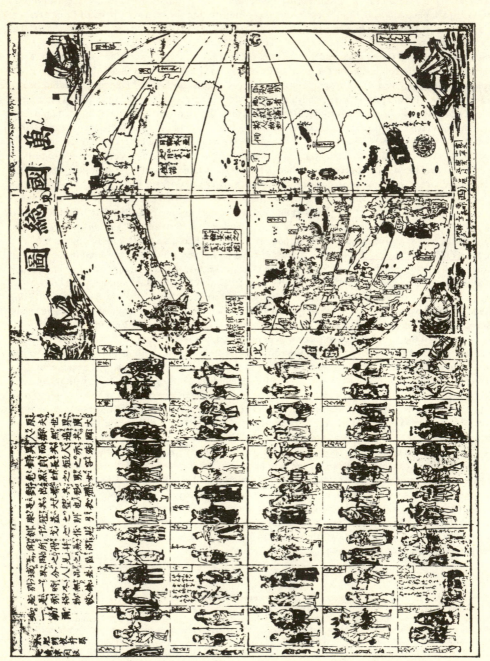

FIG. 7. BANKOKU SÕZU. MAP OF THE WORLD, 1671. *Courtesy of the British Museum.*

10

Amerindian Contributions to the Mapping of North America: A Preliminary View

Louis De Vorsey

This annexed Mappe, . . . will present to the eie, the way of the mountaines and current of the rivers, with their severall turnings, bays, shoules, isles, inlets, and creekes, the breadth of the waters, the distances of places and such like. In which Mappe observe this, that as far as you see the little Crosses on rivers, mountaines, or other places, have beene discovered; the rest was had by information of the *Savages,* and are set downe according to their instructions.

Captaine John Smith, 1612

The manifold contributions of Amerindians to the exploration and mapping of North America have been largely ignored in the literature of the history of cartography. Two notable exceptions to this generalization are the Eskimo and Aztec traditions, which have attracted the attention of a number of able cartographic scholars.[1] This essay will not attempt to include these rich traditions but rather will take a preliminary view of the contributions and maps of the native peoples who inhabited the continent between Mexico and the arctic slope homelands of the Eskimo.

It is clear from the narratives and journals of scores of explorers, from Columbus onward, that Amerindian cartographers and guides in every region of the continent contributed significantly to the outlining and filling of the North American map. Columbus, for example, relied on Indian geographic information from the outset of his landings in the New World and, when available, Indian drawn maps as well. Justin Winsor called attention to an incident in which Columbus took an elderly Indian onboard his ship 'since the savage could draw a sort of chart of the coast.'[2] A century later while coasting off the shores of New England, Captain Bartholomew Gosnold gained important perspectives from a chalk drawing of the coast which local Indians prepared for him.[3] Later Samuel de Champlain frequently had Indians sketch rivers and areas for him during his explorations.[4] In his account of his explorations of the St. Lawrence Valley and adjacent country during 1611, Champlain included the following remarks which provide an excellent insight into the nature of the Amerindian assistance he was receiving:

I had much conversation with them regarding the source of the great river [St. Lawrence] and regarding their [Huron] country, about which they told me many things, both of the rivers, falls, lakes, and lands, and of the tribes living there, and whatever is found in those parts. Four of them assured me that they had seen a sea, far from their country, but that the way to it was difficult, both on account of enemies, and of the wild stretches to be crossed in order to reach it. They told me also that during the preceding winter some Indians had come from the direction of Florida, beyond the country of the Iroquois, who were familiar with our ocean, and friendly with these latter Indians. In short they spoke to me of these things in great detail, showing me by drawings all the places they had visited, taking pleasure in telling me about them. And as for myself, I was not weary of listening to them, because some things were cleared up about which I had been in doubt until they enlightened me about them.[5]

Explorers of the continent's interior such as La Salle also benefited from Indian cartographic ability. Henri Joutel told of how La Salle's party, 'were informed by one of the Indians that we were not far from a great River, which he described with a Stick on the Sand and shew'd it had two branches, at the same time pronouncing the word Cappa, which as I have said is a nation near the Mississippi.'[6] Herman Friis has reported 'at least thirty direct references to Indian-made maps and some ninety-one descriptive statements of a geographical nature by Indians' in the published journals of the famous Lewis and Clark expedition.[7] Friis further noted that these intrepid western explorers had 'faithfully copied most of the maps the Indians traced out for them on a swept-sand surface, on a smooth bark and on a leathern chart.' Similar instances can be recounted for almost every region of the continent from the West Indies in the fifteenth century to the Pacific coastlands in the nineteenth.

Rather than inventory additional similar instances and examples of Amerindian geographic and cartographic expertise at this point it would be valuable to examine a single exploratory adventure in some detail. The original British exploration of the Chesapeake Bay region in eastern Virginia and resulting first published map of the area will be shown to form something of a model through which the complex process of Amerindian contribution to the mapping of North America may be better understood and appreciated.

It will be recalled that Raleigh's sixteenth century attempts to plant colonies on North America's mainland had failed and it was not until 1607 that a viable Virginia colony took first root on the James River estuary. In large measure the original thinking regarding the Virginia colony appears to have been predicated on the strongly held belief that North America was, in these latitudes, an isthmus with the Pacific Ocean in easy reach of the Atlantic. As a result, the Colony's Charter included rights of expansion 'into the land throughout from sea to sea west and north-west.' The colonists were instructed to lose no time in seeking some river or pathway by which 'you shall soonest find the other sea.'

Captain John Smith, Virginia's governor in 1608–9, was to become known as the colony's first historian and author of the first detailed printed map to show the area with any degree of accuracy in 1612. Cartographic scholars have been unstinting in their praise of this map and it is universally acclaimed as one of the most influential pieces of cartography in the history of the United States.[8] Coolie Verner notes that Smith prepared his map as a response to the London Council's 1606 instructions which directed:

> You must observe, if you can, whether the river on which you plant doth spring out of mountains or out of lakes. If it be out of any lake, the passage to the other sea will be more easy, and it is like enough, that out of the same lake you shall find some spring which runs the contrary way towards the East Indian Sea.[9]

An examination of Smith's map reveals that it incorporates and acknowledges the significant input of Amerindians who guided, instructed, and informed him and his associates as they painstakingly explored the wilderness during the first months and years of Virginia's founding. In the map's legend Smith included a small black maltese cross symbol which is explained by a caption which states, 'Signification of these marks, to the crosses hath been discovered—what beyond is by relation.' Figure 1 is a version of the Smith map to which I have added shading to the areas upstream of these crosses on the map. This shaded area is further explained by Smith in his published 'Description of Virginia,' which the map was intended to accompany. In this elaboration Smith wrote that the shaded area was mapped 'by information of the Savages and . . . set downe according to their instructions.'[10] Thus, it can be seen that a large portion of this important map is the direct product of Amerindian contributions to the exploration and mapping of Virginia.

The manner and circumstances in which these contributions were made are worthy of examination in that they combine to form, along with Smith's map, what can be termed a model of the processes through which Amerindians contributed so significantly to the history of North American mapping. With such a model in mind topics worthy of further study in that history may be suggested and occasional gaps in the available records of particular exploratory efforts may be more intelligently filled. Ultimately a fuller appreciation of the active role played by Amerindians in the mapping of North America should take form to fill the void now present in the literature of the history of exploration and cartography.

Captain Gabriel Archer, one of the first party to explore Virginia under the explicit instructions of the Virginia Company, wrote an account of an expedition up the James River.[11] When they were about 34 miles upstream from the site of Jamestown, Archer's party encountered eight Indians in a dugout or 'canoa'. After making friendly contact and communicating the exploring party's intent through sign and gesture, Archer reported that one of the indians evidenced an understanding. In Archer's words the Indian 'offered with his foote to Describe the river to us: So I gave him a pen and paper (shewing first ye use) and he layd out the whole River from Cheseian [Chesapeake] bay to the end of it so farr as passadge was for boats.'[12] Archer took this Indian cartographer in company as he proceeded up the

Fig. 1 Captain John Smith's Map of Virginia with area derived from Amerindian sources shaded.

James into the interior. Further upstream he had an opportunity to test the Indian's cartographic image as he describes in the following passage:

> I caused now our kynde consort that described the River to us to draw it againe before kyng Arahatec, who in everything consented to his draught, and it agreed with his first relation. This we found a faythfull fellow, he was one that was appointed guyed for us.[15]

When Archer and his party reached the falls of the James, at the site of Richmond, the same cartographically gifted Indian was described as follows:

> Now setting upon the banck by the overfall beholding the same, he began to tell us of the tedyous travell we should have if wee proceeded any further, that it was a Daye and a half journey to Monanacah and if we went Quiranck, we should get no vittailes and be tyred, and sought by all means to Disswade our Captayne from going any further: Also he told us that the Monanacah was his Enmye and that he came downe at the fall of the leafe and invaded his countrye.[14]

In apparent respect of this persuasive intelligence the exploring party chose to terminate their survey and return to their settlement on the James estuary.

This was not, however, to terminate the flow of geographic intelligence from Archer's cartographically gifted guide. Archer went on to note:

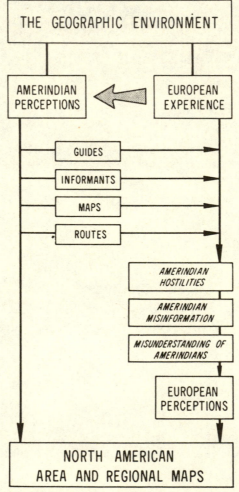

Fig. 2   Diagram summarizing Amerindian contributions to the Mapping of North America.

So farr as we could discerne the River above the overfall, it was full of huge Rocks: About a myle off it makes a pretty bigg island; It runnes up between highe Hilles which increase in height one above another so farr as we sawe. Now our kynde Consort's relatyon sayth (which I dare well beleeve, in that I found not any one report false of the River so farr as we tryed or that he tolde us untruth in any thing ells whatsoever) that after a Day's journey or more, this River Devydes it selfe into two branches which both came from the mountaynes Quirank. Here, he whispered with [to] me that theer Caquassan [copper?] was gott in the bites of Rocks and between Cliffes in certayne vaynes.[15]

It seems safe to conclude that this whispered intelligence concerning the mineral wealth of the interior was to stimulate the zeal of those who followed Archer into Virginia's interior.

Through Archer's engaging account we have an episode which forms an important segment of a verbal model of the manner in which countless American Indians contributed in substantial degree to the mapping of North America. Archer's 'Kynde Consort' exhibits an outstanding talent for geographic observation and cartographic depiction. The latter talent executed with foot or pen, a versatility shared by few if any modern cartographers! While it can't be said with absolute certainty that the actual 'manuscript' produced by this particular Indian found its way into the published Smith map, it is clear that Indian observations, images, and even manuscripts did influence its final form and content.

Several significant processes of information flow took place between the Indians and Virginians during the explorations which contributed to Smith's map. One of these processes involved the information flow from European to Indian which went on simultaneously with the flow from Indian to European. Captain John Smith was taken captive by Indians during the summer of 1607. One aspect of that captivity, the heroism of Pocahontas is well known in literature and fable. Another aspect is less colourful but more germane to what can be termed the information flow from European to Indian. In writing of his captors presenting him to their chief, Smith told how he:

. . . presented him with a compass diall, describing by my best meanes the use thereof: whereat he so amazedly admired, . . . he suffered me to proceed in a discourse of the roundness of the earth, the course of the sunne, moone, starres and plannets.

At another point in his confinement Smith described how another Indian chief:

took great delight in understanding the manner of our ships, and sayling the seas, the earth and skies, and of our God: What he knew of the dominions he spared not to acquaint me with, as of certaine men cloathed at a place called Ocanohonan, cloathed like me: the course of our river, and within 4 or 5 daies journey of the falles, was a great turning of salt water.[17]

Clearly there were two-way flows of geographical information going on in these Indian—European exchanges. It is obvious that the Indians as well as the Europeans were benefitting from these exchanges in many ways and particularly in terms of their cartographic skills. It further seems reasonable to hypothesize, that as our data base of Indian maps is increased through the much needed cartobibliographic project recently begun by G. Malcolm Lewis, regional and temporal differences which can be attributed to the adoption of European cartographic convention and geographic knowledge by the Indians will be discovered.[18] It is certainly a point to be kept in mind as research into this branch of the cartographic tree proceeds.

This is not to imply, of course, that these information flows were universal or not without impediment. As with any cross-cultural exchange, geographic and cartographic communication between Indians and Europeans depended on many things. Important among these was trust and confidence as stressed in the following extract from John Lawson's 1709 'Account of the Indians of North Carolina':

They will draw Maps very exactly of all the Rivers, Towns, Mountains and Roads, or what you shall enquire of them, which you may draw by their directions, and come to a small matter of latitude, reckoning by their day's journeys. These Maps they will draw in the Ashes of the Fire, and sometimes upon a Mat or Piece of Bark. I have put a Pen and Ink into a savage's Hand, and as he has drawn me the Rivers, Bays, and other Parts of a Country, afterwards I have found to agree with a great deal of Nicety: But you must be very much in their Favour, otherwise they will never make these Discoveries to you; especially if it be in their own Quarters.[19]

and European groups involved. While on this point it is tempting to speculate that the competition and tension which marked European imperial relationships, one with another in

Lawson's caveat suggests another hypothesis which awaits the necessary cartobibliographical data to allow its testing. This is, that frequency and relative accuracy of Indian derived geographic information and maps will reflect the state of affairs existing between the Indian North America, may also have had a role in the nature and production of Indian maps.

At least two Indian drawn maps in the Library of Congress Geography and Map Division's Faden Collection are clearly the product of Anglo-French rivalry and warfare in the Ohio Valley during the mid-eighteenth-century. The first of these is titled 'Copy of A Sketch of the Monongahela, With the Field of Battle, Done by an Indian' and the other is 'Map of the Country About the Mississippi Drawn by Chegeree (the Indian) Who Says He has Travelled Through the Country.'

George Washington saw extensive service in this region before and during the French and Indian War (as the conflict was known to the colonists). His account of his expedition to the French fort at Le Boeuf in 1753–4 provides a vivid glimpse of the important military intelligence which Indians provided for their allies in both verbal and cartographic form. Washington wrote of a conference he held with the Indian leader known as Half King in the following:

> He informed me that they [the French] had built two Forts, one on Lake Erie, and another on French-Creek near a small Lake about 15 Miles asunder and a large Waggon Road between; they are both built after the same Model, but different in Size; that on the Lake the largest. He gave me a Plan of them, of this own drawing.[20]

In the post-war period, when western land acquisition became one of Washington's major preoccupations, he again benefitted from Indian cartographic skill. While examining land along the lower reaches of the Kanawha River, in what is today West Virginia, on November 16, 1770, Washington made the following entry in his diary:

> Here it was for the 2nd time the old Indian with me spoke of a fine piece of Land and beautiful place for a house, and in order to give me a more lively idea of it, chalked out the situation upon his Deer skin.[21]

In this case Amerindian cartography was contributing to the choice of settlement sites in the frontier zone on the eve of its occupation by whites. An analysis of such events would be valuable in badly needed studies aimed at an understanding of Amerindian environmental and landscape perception.

Other Indian-drawn maps arose from and reflected Indian versus Indian tensions. A well known example of such a map accompanies the 'Account of Lamhatty' in the collection of the Virginia Historical Society in Richmond. Lamhatty appears to have been a Creek Indian living along the Alabama River when he was captured by a marauding band of Tuscaroras from distant North Carolina. As a captive he was treated as a slave and eventually sold to Shawnees living even further afield. During a hunting expedition in the valleys of the Blue Ridge, Lamhatty escaped and made his way down the Mattapony River to the white settlements below the Fall Zone, arriving during the Christmas season of 1707. The naked and wretched Lamhatty was befriended and nursed back to health. During his stay in the settlements he was interviewed by Robert Beverly. On the reverse side of the manuscript 'Account', which Beverly wrote summarizing Lamhatty's narration, is a map which appears to have been drawn by the Indian with the names of rivers, villages, and other features added by Beverly. A facsimile of this novel example of Amerindian cartography was prepared and published in 1908.[22]

The colourful and often controversial Baron De Lahontan made much use of Amerindian cartography in his extensive travels through North America's heartland during the late seventeenth-century. In a published essay on the Indians he provides an indication of how important maps were to the Indians themselves as follows:

> They are as ignorant of Geography as of other Sciences, and yet they draw the most exact Maps imaginable of the Countries they're acquainted with, for there's nothing wanting in them but the Longitude and Latitude of Places: They set down the True North according to the Pole Star; The Ports, Harbours, Rivers, Creeks and Coasts of the Lakes; the Roads, Mountains, Wood, Marshes, Meadows, etc. counting the distances by Journeys and Half-Journeys of the Warriors and allowing to every Journey Five Leagues. These chorographical Maps are drawn upon the Rind of your Birch Tree; and when the Old Men hold a Council about War or Hunting, they're always sure to consult them.[23]

Indian versus Indian tension could also impede or block the production of maps entirely as William Gerard De Brahm, Britain's Surveyor General of America's southern colonies, discovered during his explorations of East Florida. On his large scale map titled 'East Florida

East of the 82nd degree of Longitude from the Meridian of London . . .' he included the following as a caption placed near the West bank of the Indian River inland from Cape Canaveral:

> Surveyor Gen: Camp March 7, 1765—Thus far the Surveyor General carried on his Survey by land from St. Augustine guided by Sahaykee a Creek Indian, who meeting some Hunting Indians made difficulties and out of fear to disobaye the Nation refused to continue as far as the Haven of Spirito Santo which stop'd the Surveyor-General who must have fallen in with many Hunting Ganges of Semiolokee [Seminoles] of which that of the Indian Headman called Cowkeeper was only within one [day's] journey to the Southward of him.[24]

De Brahm also wrote of what he termed the Creek Indian's 'natural knowledge in Geometry.'

Even during periods of peace and amity not all Indian to white geographic and cartographic communication was clear and unimpeded. Simple misunderstanding of message due to linguistic limitations doubtless clouded the exchange on frequent occasions. This seems particularly to have been the case when the Europeans were operating under strongly held preconceptions regarding New World geography. John Lederer, the first European to record observations of Virginia's upper Piedmont and Blue Ridge, is probably typical of many early explorers in this regard. Lederer, in common with many of his age, was convinced, as Smith had been earlier, that the Pacific was within easy reach of the Atlantic in the latitude of Virginia. During his second expedition in 1670 Lederer met four 'stranger-Indians' whom he felt came from California. In discussing this hypothesis he wrote:

> . . . from whence we may imagine some great arm of the Indian Ocean or Bay stretches into the Continent towards the Apalataean Mountains into the nature of a mid-land Sea . . . To confirm my opinion in this point, I have heard several Indians testifie, that the Nation of Rickohockans, who dwell not far to the Westward of the Apalataean Mountains, are seated upon a land, as they term it, of great Waves; by which I suppose they mean the Sea-shore.[25]

Cumming and Rights are probably correct in suggesting that Lederer's eagerness to find confirmation for his geographic theory caused him to misinterpret the Indian sign language meaning mountain ridges.[26]

It could easily be that Captain John Smith was prey to similar misunderstanding when he wrote of 'a great turning of salt water' in the quotation mentioned above. As more thorough analyses of early maps based on Indian supplied data are forthcoming additional similar misunderstandings will doubtless come to light. Certainly the problems and difficulties inherent in even the simplest Indian-White verbal and graphic information exchange should be kept in mind by anyone attempting to delve into the topic of Amerindian contributions to the mapping of North America.

In concluding this preliminary view of Amerindian contributions to the mapping of North America the accompanying diagram should prove helpful. The large block labled 'The Geographic Environment' represents New World areas being actively explored by Europeans. During the exploratory process both 'Amerindian Perceptions' and 'European Experience' serve as information bases from which eventual maps could flow. As shown in the diagram and discussed in the essay above, 'Amerindian Perceptions' were being altered through contacts with the Europeans and their culture. Amerindian perceptions, however, were of fundamental importance in the exploratory process which contributed to the 'North American Area and Regional Maps which are of main concern here. As the diagram shows Indians served as guides and informants and drew maps of *areas* being explored and mapped by the Europeans. 'Routes' is included in the diagram but not discussed explicitly in the essay. Had space been available it would have been possible to show how the pre-existing Amerindian trail networks influenced European perception and appraisal of territory and its eventual mapping.

Just as the Amerindians contributed positively to the mapping of the continent so too did they impede the process at times. Such impediments are suggested by the italic-lettered blocks captioned 'Amerindian Hostilities,' 'Amerindian Misinformation,' and 'Misunderstanding of Amerindians.' All of these elements then, some negative and some positive, can be seen to outline in diagrammatic form the way in which countless Amerindians contributed to the mapping of North America.

(This paper was read at the *VIIth International Conference on the History of Cartography*, Washington D.C., U.S.A., August 1977.)

NOTES

1. For the Aztec see, Eulalia Guzman, 'The Art of Map-making Among the Ancient Mexican,' *Imago Mundi*, 3 (1939), 166; and Howard F. Cline, 'The Ozoticpac Lands Map of Texcoco 1540,' *The Quarterly Journal of the Library of Congress* XXIII (1966) 77–115. For the Eskimo, John Spink and D. W. Moodie, *Eskimo Maps of the Canadian Arctic*, Cartographica Monograph 5 (1972).
2. Justin Winsor, *Christopher Columbus* (Cambridge, 1892), 442.
3. Gabriel Archer, 'The Relation of Captaine Gosnols Voyage to the North Part of Virginia . . . 1602,' in Samuel Purchas, *Hakluytus Posthumus or Purchas His Pilgrimes* XVIII, [Reprinted by AMS Press, Inc., (New York, 1965)] 304.
4. Samuel de Champlain, *The Works of Samuel de Champlain*, ed. H. P. Biggar, I, (Toronto, 1922–26) 153, 159, 335.
5. *Ibid.* II, p. 191.
6. Henri Joutel, *A Journal of La Salle's Last Voyage* (New York, 1962), 142.
7. Herman Friis, 'Geographical and Cartographical Contributions of the American Indian to Exploration of the United States Prior to 1860,' (Unpublished Paper), 6–7. For examples, see volume VIII of the *Original Journals of the Lewis and Clark Expedition* (New York, 1904).
8. Coolie Verner, 'The First Maps of Virginia, 1590–1673,' *The Virginia Magazine of History and Biography* 58 (1950), 6–12; E. M. Sanchez-Saavedra, *A Description of the Country, Virginia's Cartographers and Their Maps 1607–1881* (Richmond, 1975), 13.
9. Verner, *op. cit.* 6.
10. Captain John Smith, 'The Description of Virginia,' *Travels and Works of Captain John Smith*, I, ed. Edward Arber (Edinburgh, 1910), 55.
11. A Gentleman of the Colony [Captain Gabriel Archer?], 'A relaytion of the Discovery, etc. 21 May-22 June 1607,' *Travels and Works of Captain John Smith*, I, ed. Edward Arber (Edinburgh, 1910), xl-lv.
12. *Ibid.*, xli.
13. *Ibid.*, xliii.
14. *Ibid.*, xlvi.
15. *Ibid.*, xlvii.
16. Captain John Smith, 'A True Relation of Such Occurrences and Accidents of Noate . . .,' *Travels and Works of Captain John Smith*, I, ed. Edward Arber (Edinburgh, 1910), 15.
17. *Ibid.* 16.
18. J. Malcolm Lewis, 'Toward a cartobibliography of North American Indian maps and mapping,' Personal Correspondence, September, 1976.
19. John Lawson, *A New Voyage to Carolina*, ed. Hugh Talmadge Lefler (Chapel Hill, 1967), 214. (Underlining added for emphasis).
20. John C. Fitzpatrick (ed.), *The Diaries of George Washington 1748–1799* I (Boston and New York, 1925), 49.
21. *Ibid.*, 439.
22. David I. Bushnell, Jr., 'The Account of Lamhatty,' *American Anthropologist* new series X (1908), 568–74.
23. Baron De Lahontan, *New Voyages to North America* II [Reprint of 1703 English edition] ed. by Reuben Gold Thwartes (New York, 1900), 427.
24. British Public Record Office, London, C.O. 700 Maps—Florida 3. For a discussion of De Brahm's activities see Louis De Vorsey, Jr. (ed.), *De Brahm's Report of the General Survey In the Southern District of North America* (Columbia, 1971).
25. William P. Cumming (ed.) *The Discoveries of John Lederer* (Charlottesville, 1958), 25–6 & 120. (I am indebted to Professor Cumming for suggesting this incident and reference).
26. *Ibid.* p. 120. Captain Thomas Yong, an early British explorer of Delaware Bay and River wrote of how he had mistakenly assumed an Indian sign language message to mean ten days when in reality the Indians had intended to convey ten weeks. See 'Relation of Captain Thomas Yong, 1634,' Albert Cook Myers (ed.) *Narratives of Early Pennsylvania, West Jersey, And Delaware, 1630–1707* (New York, 1940) 40. Temporal as well as geographic relationships were subject to misunderstandings.

11

Indicators of Unacknowledged Assimilations from Amerindian Maps on Euro-American Maps of North America:
Some General Priciples Arising from the Study of La Verendrye's Composite Map, 1728–29

G. Malcolm Lewis

From the earliest contacts, Amerindians have transmitted to Euro-Americans spatially-arranged information about the lands, coasts, waters, places, routes and resources of North America.[1] The information was usually solicited from them by aliens engaged in exploration and discovery and, in most cases, it would appear to have been given in good faith. It was transmitted by speech, sign and gesture, pictographs, models and, most commonly, by a combination of two or more of these. Speech usually involved one or more translations and neither the vocabularies nor syntaxes were well suited to communicating spatially structured information. Though widely used and effective indigenously, sign and gesture were evanescent and, from a Euro-American perspective, their meaning was often obscure. Pictographs and, to a lesser extent, models were more permanent, easily copied and potentially well suited to communicating spatially structured information. Indeed, some pictographs were map like and *maps* were used by Indians throughout the continent in transmitting spatially-structured information to Euro-Americans.[2] In 1540, for example, Hernando Alarcón (b. *c.* 1500) persuaded an Indian to 'set me downe in a charte as much as he knew concerning' the Colorado River.[3] In the following year Indians represented the course of part of the St. Lawrence River for Jacques Cartier (1491–1557) 'with certaine little stickes which they layde upon the ground in a certaine distance, and afterwards layde other small branches between both representing the Saults'.[4]

In using *maps* to communicate with Euro-Americans, Indians were employing or adapting an indigenous technique. Though difficult either to prove or refute, some prehistoric North American rock art is considered by some to incorporate terrestrial *maps* and the evidence for celestial *maps* is much stronger.[5] Indians not only made *maps* they sometimes valued them sufficiently to store them. Early in the eighteenth century Joseph Lafitau (1681–1746), a Jesuit missionary, reported that the Iroquois made 'exact maps' and kept them 'in their public treasury to consult them at need'.[6] In the nineteenth century, Indians are known to have made and used *maps* indigenously in, among other activities, planning raids, religious practices and communicating with each other on journeys and in the course of hunting expeditions.[7] Some Indians still preserve *maps* as part of their cultural tradition and they are sometimes interred with the dead.[8] Indeed *maps* and *mapping* are so much parts of some Indians' ways of structuring their worlds that they actually dream *maps*.[9]

Most of the extant and reported examples of Indian *maps* were made in the course of communicating with explorers. Regrettably, a high proportion of the extant ones are transcripts, made to preserve what appeared at the time to be information content but with little concern for whatever appeared to be either merely style or irrelevant. In early post-contact times a *map* was often the most appropriate mode of communication but, increasingly through time, information was also solicited by Euro-Americans in that mode. Although many were requested merely to establish the best route for the next stage of a journey into a *terra incognita* and others were collected for their ethnographic value as artefacts, the information content of many *maps* was considered to be sufficiently important for it to be assimilated onto the maps of Euro-American explorers, early Euro-American mapmakers and, since the mid eighteenth century, American, Hudson's Bay Company and Canadian surveyors. Assimilation often resulted in representations as *terrae cognitae* of what, on the basis of Euro-American experience alone, were *terrae incognitae*. In a few cases assimilation was acknowledged as, for example, on John Smith's *Virginia* (1612), where Maltese crosses on each of the main rivers mark the points beyond which the content 'is by relation', and, more specifically, in the previous year, on the 'Velasco' map (Frontispiece, upper) of the northeast seaboard, where 'all the blue [of the interior] is done by the relations of the Indians'.[10] In many cases, one suspects that assimilation occurred without acknowledgement but establishing this in the absence of appropriate ancillary evidence is difficult.

Given that assimilation certainly did occur, that it was probably widespread and that, before the late eighteenth century at least, it was usually unacknowledged, three questions arise:

By what processes did information from Indian *maps* become assimilated onto Euro-American maps?

What were the consequences of assimilation for content, shape and reliability?

Are there any general diagnostic characteristics on the bases of which unacknowledged assimilations might be suspected, as a preliminary to testing by means of content analyses conducted in wider contexts?

The processes of assimilation were almost always unrecorded and can only occasionally be inferred. Hence, the consequences of assimilation can rarely be demonstrated conclusively. Among the exceptions are the extant letters, maps and derivative maps stemming from the attempts made in 1728 and 1729 by the French Canadian Pierre Gaultier de Varennes et de la Vérendrye (1685–1749) to solicit information from Indians about the waterways and features in the Euro-American *terra incognita* to the west and northwest of Lake Superior. In the first part of this paper these are examined for what they reveal about the processes and consequences of assimilation. This leads to the formulation of a set of non toponymic diagnostic characteristics. Each of these is used to isolate one or more possible cases of assimilated content on late sixteenth- or early seventeenth-century Euro-American maps.

The Case Study

1. Sequence of assimilation

By the end of the first quarter of the eighteenth century, the upper Great Lakes' region was at the western edge of the Euro-American *terra cognita*. Neither the French, nor the employees of the Hudson's Bay Company to the north, had any reliable information about the geography and ethnography of the area between the head of Lake Superior and the Pacific coastline but hopes of finding a practical route across the *terra incognita* were about to stimulate westward exploration undertaken in conjunction with fur-trading activities. In 1728, after only one year's experience in the area, Pierre Gaultier de Varennes et de la Vérendrye (sometimes called Boumois) (1685–1749) assumed from his brother, Jacques-René Gaultier de Varennes (1677–1757), command of the 'poste du Nord', military posts on the north shore of Lake Superior, and of the fur-trading activities in their hinterlands.[11] Almost immediately, he began to solicit from Indians information about the geography of the area to the west of Lake Superior.

In 1728 and 1729, at posts at the mouths of the Nipigon and Kaministiquia Rivers, La Vérendrye received information in *map* form, supplemented by gestures and narratives received in the course of interrogations, from three different Cree Indian sources; Tachigis, Auchagah (also spelled Ochagach, Ochakah and Ochagac) and a group of three chiefs which included La Marteblanche. This was supplemented by information, not in *map* form, received from another group of Crees (Pako *et al.*), a Monsoni, a slave Indian (perhaps of Mandan origin) and one other unspecified Indian. The information was summarized in a report written during the winter of 1729–30, which La Vérendrye presented to Charles, Marquis de Beauharnois de la Boische (1671–1749), governor general of New France, when he visited Quebec in 1730.[12] It was supposedly accompanied by the *map* 'traced for me by Auchagah' but an extant map, which appears to be in La Vérendrye's own hand, contains no reference to the Indian and seems to represent features in areas beyond those included in Auchagah's *map* as described in

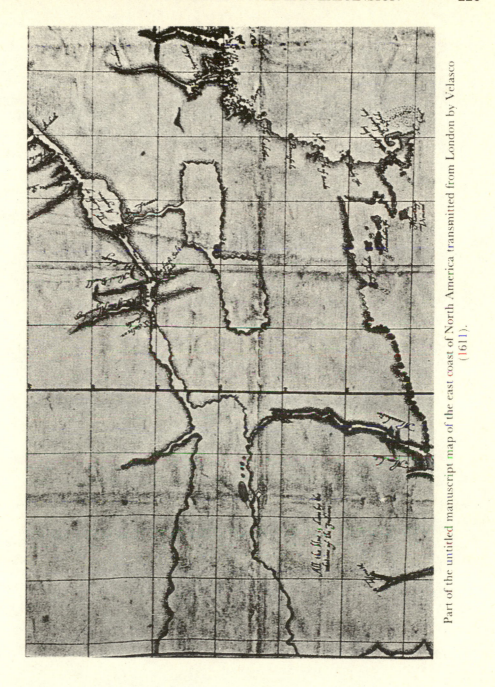

Part of the untitled manuscript map of the east coast of North America transmitted from London by Velasco (1611).

Part of Block's untitled manuscript map of the east coast of North America (1614).

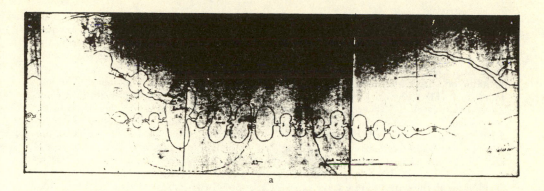

a

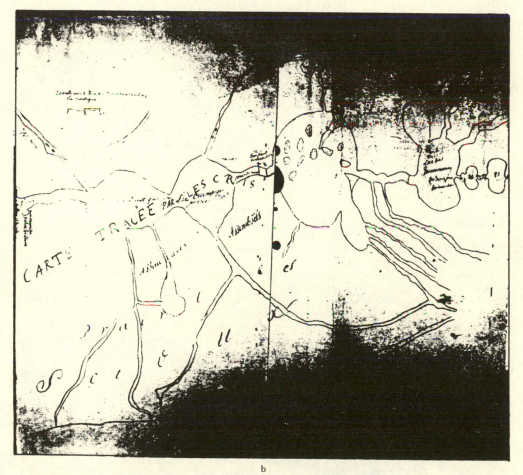

b

Fig. 1   La Vérendrye's composite map (1728–29)—apparently in his own hand: (a) right side; (b) left side.
N.B. b. is reproduced 40 per cent larger in linear dimensions than a.

the report.[13] Collation of the extant map with the several Indian *maps* as described in the report suggests that it was a composite. Interestingly, it is on two sheets of paper of unequal dimensions which have been stitched together. The right-hand sheet (Fig. 1a), covering the area between the northwest shore of 'Lac Superieur'[14] almost as far as 'Lac de Tecacamiouen' (= Rainy Lake), agrees very closely with Auchagah's *map* as described in the report and contains one bar scale: 'Echelle pour les lac [Superieur] jusqua Tacacamiouen'.[15] The left-hand sheet (Fig. 1b), which is stylistically somewhat different, albeit transcribed in the same hand (i.e. apparently La Vérendrye's), is only partly integrated with the content of the right-hand sheet, has two different bar scales and contains a bold legend: CARTE TRAC'EE PAR LES CRIS. It is a reasonable inference that most of this part of the map was derived from the *map* made by La Marteblanche *et al.*, i.e. 'Les Cris' of the legend.[16] For the area beyond Lake of the Woods (unnamed) La Vérendrye notes that their map agreed 'with the one made by Auchagah' but it was evidently preferred by him, doubtless because La Marteblanche *et al.* lived 'towards the outlet of' that Lake and were presumably better informed about those parts. The lower part of the left-hand sheet was almost certainly derived from a third source. The description in La Vérendrye's report of the drainage network as represented on the *map* drawn by Tachigis 'with a piece of charcoal' agrees in every detail with that on the composite map in the area covered by the legend 'Prairies Scioux'.[17]

Further evidence that La Vérendrye's composite map was that referred to in his report as having been 'traced' by him for Auchagah is to be found in a letter dated 15 October 1730 from Beauharnois to Jean Frédéric Phelypeaux, Comte de Maurepas (1701–1781), minister of marine in Paris. It accompanied 'a copy of a map . . . made by the savage Auchagah' but refers to it as 'the savages' [n.b. plural] map, on which there are three scales'.[18] This was clearly the composite map, though it may have been a second state, redrawn by Gaspard Chaussegros de Léry (1682–1756), a military engineer with the Department of Marine in New France. De Léry is referred to twice by Beauharnois in the letter and a version of the composite map has survived which appears to be in his hand.[19] The letter also refers to two derivate maps drawn by De Léry: a reduction of 'the savages' map, on which there are three scales? '. . . [showing] the whole course of the river [of the West] from the height of land beyond Lake Superior to above California'; and a tracing 'from the Sieur de l'Isle's map on a loose sheet [of] the course of that river reduced according to the map'.[20] It is not clear whether these were transmitted with Beauharnois' letter but versions of both, apparently in De Lery's hand, have survived. The first is a transformation of the composite map in which the left-to-right scale has been standardized but the top-to-bottom scale remains essentially the same[21] (Fig. 2). The second is a manuscript copy of the North American part of Guillaume De l'Isle's *Carte d'Amerique* (1722) on which is pasted a simplified but otherwise unchanged version of the transformed map[22] (Fig. 3). On this the pasted-on part is not given a scale but the map has a graticule and the scaling is clearly according to the scale as indicated on the transformed map: '50 Lieues de 20 au degre'.

Recapitulating, none of the three *maps* drawn by Indians for La Vérendrye has survived.

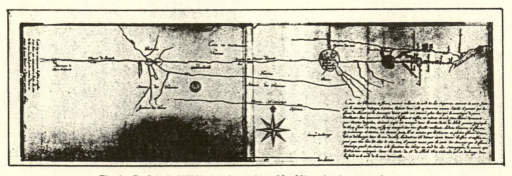

Fig. 2   De Léry's (1730) transformation of La Vérendrye's composite map.

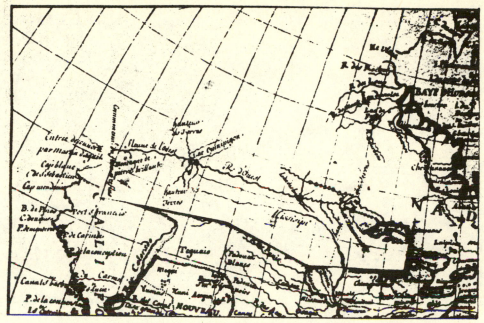

Fig. 3 The part of De Léry's copy (1730) of Delisle's *Carte d'Amerique* ... (1722) containing the pasted-on transformation.

Indeed, there is no reason to suspect that they were ever forwarded from the poste du Nord at or near which they were made. Three, apparently contemporary, derivatives have, however, survived:

i. a composite map, probably in La Vérendrye's own hand;

ii. a transformed map, clearly derived from the composite map by a process involving an attempt at scale standardization along the left-to-right axis and almost certainly in de Léry's hand;

iii. an amended map, also apparently in de Léry's hand, consisting of a somewhat simplified version of the transformed map pasted onto a transcript of an earlier map of North America.

In the context of this paper, the significance of these derivatives is that the amended map became incorporated and ultimately accommodated on Euro-American maps, on which it should, therefore, be possible to establish those stylistic elements which were Indian in origin.

Philippe Buache (1700–1773), who, as a former employee of the Depôt des cartes et plans de la Marine and the Premiere Géographe du Roi, had access to the composite, transformed and amended maps, included the composite map as an inset on his *Carte Physique des Terreins les plus éléves de la Partie Occidentale du Canada* (1754), acknowledging that it was 'tracee par le Sauvage Ochagach et autres'.[23] This, however, was not an incorporation, let alone an accommodation, in that it was neither a part of or relatable to the main map. Genuine, but only indirectly acknowledged incorporation had, however, occurred on Jacques Nicolas Bellin the elder's (1703–1772) *Carte De L'Amerique Septentrionale* ... (1743)[24] (Fig. 4). This contained the legend 'Ici suivant le report des Sauvages Comence le Flux et reflux' and it presented for the first time on a printed map the three most distinctive elements of the composite map, which were to recur, with modifications, on maps of western North America almost until the end of the eighteenth century. These were:

13

Fig. 4   Part of Bellin's *Carte de L'Amerique Septentrionale* (1743).

'Riviere' . . . [and] 'Fleuve de l'Ouest';
'Montagne de Pierres Brillantes';
'Comence du flux et reflux'.

The recurrence of the three elements, often as bold items, in relatively empty areas on maps of the western part of the continent implied that for half a century they were perceived by map makers to be important, yet their pattern and location changed considerably through time and they each eventually disappeared. Scholars have never reached a consensus concerning their geographical referents. They have failed to do so because they have not recognized that the original information was derived from Indians via a complex sequence of assimilation by persons who had little understanding of Indians as informants, of Indians' spatial concepts or the properties of their *maps* and whose judgement was influenced by hopes of finding a relatively short and easy route westward to the Pacific across the Euro-Americans' *terra incognita*.

2. Processes of assimilation

Although the precise details must remain conjectural, an appreciation of the several processes which in sequence brought about assimilation is necessary in order to assess the influence of the Indian inputs on the printed maps of a decade or more later. The sequence of processes was as follows:
 i. interpreting information received from Indians: by La Vérendrye, in the course of interrogating a number of different Indians over a period of not more than three years;
 ii. mosaicing information received from several sources: apparently entirely by La Vérendrye;
 iii. transforming the mosaic according to some concept of scale: by De Léry, perhaps with instructions from or in consultation with Beauharnois, who had met and presumably interrogated La Vérendrye;

14

iv. incorporating the transformation into an existing map of a wider area derived from a different source: by De Léry, using De l'Isle's (1722) map as a base and perhaps with instructions from or in consultation with Beauharnois;

v. accommodating the original incorporation on other maps: by Bellin, who almost certainly had access to the original incorporation and perhaps to the transformed and composite maps, and by later map makers, who almost certainly did not.

i. *Interpreting.* In interpreting information received from the Indians, La Vérendrye and De Léry, like many Euro-Americans both before and after them, seem to have assumed that essentially straight lines on their *maps* represented linear features on the ground which either maintain a constant direction or, over longer distances, approximated to parts of great circles. This, however, was not so. Straight lines—and, indeed, smooth curves—usually symbolized linkages between points and did not represent course—or route—details. In this respect, Indian *maps* had much more in common with modern public-transport-users' guides than with topographic maps.

La Vérendrye also assumed that Indian *maps* were drawn approximately to constant linear scale and that they could, therefore be given bar scales. Furthermore, De Léry accepted La Vérendrye's bar scales as the bases for transformation and incorporation. Indians, however, had no absolute metric for distance. They usually expressed it in terms of intervals of time—numbers of days, camps, pauses, smokes etc.—but there is no evidence that they scaled their *maps* even according to these relative metrics. Certainly Indians never placed bar scales on their *maps* and the three on the composite map were almost certainly introduced by La Vérendrye on the basis of travel times as given to him in days for journeys between stated points. Although his report to Beauharnois of 1729/30 gave eight such distances in leagues (together with five in days and two in fractions of other distances), he was almost certainly converting according to the conversion factors then generally employed by Canadians: 7.5 leagues for one day's travel upstream and 15 leagues for one day's downstream.[25] These, however, were only crude approximations, failing to take into account variables such as mode and season of travel, unsuspected hazards and anticipated obstacles confronted *en route,* purpose of journey, volume and weight of baggage or the age, sex, physique and morale of those travelling.[26] Furthermore, they were approximations based on the experience of Canadians. Indians, with their greater familiarity with terrain and their environmentally better-adjusted lifestyle could, when necessary, travel faster and, usually wishing to please, they probably gave their fastest travel times in communicating distances to Euro-Americans.

Association features as represented on Indian *maps* with known or supposed features on the ground was difficult. Very typically, Indians caricatured the shapes of features which were culturally or locally important, symbolized others and omitted the remainder. Those omitted were culturally or strategically less significant but could be just as large or even larger than some of those included. On La Vérendrye's composite map, for example, most of the lakes are represented as oval or bean-shaped, the largest representation being approximately ten times larger in linear dimensions that the smallest. In reality most of the lakes thus represented are neither oval nor even 'chunky' in plan but sinuous and branching, with highly irregular coastlines. Furthermore, the range in size among those represented is far greater than a ratio of one to ten might be interpreted to imply. On the map these lakes were merely symbolized, perhaps with the symbol varying in size according to some measure of relative importance other than size. Lake of the Woods (unnamed) and 'Lac Tecacamioueg' (= Rainy Lake) are partial exceptions in that they are represented as basically oval but with distinctive ornamentations: a lobe to the upper left on 'Lac Tecacamioueg' to represent the bay heading in what is now named Manitou Sound; and a lobe to the lower right on Lake of the Woods, representing what is now Big Traverse Bay (Fig. 5). Lake of the Woods is also ornamented with a long point, caricaturing the Aulneau Peninsula, and by ten islands in the upper half, signifying (but not caricaturing) the hundreds of islands which occur in the northern and eastern parts of the Lake.

In retrospect at least, features which were caricatured can be idfentified with a reasonable certainty. Conversely, features which were symbolized are difficult to identify. Occasionally, symbols may be wrongly interpreted as caricatures and vice versa. The hour-glass shape to the

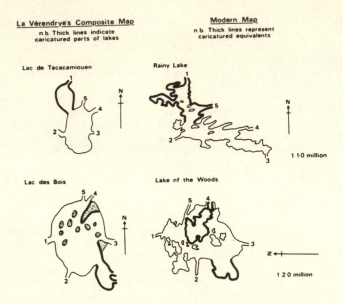

Fig. 5   Caricaturizations of Lac de Tecacamiouen and Lac des Bois on the composite map.

left of the unnamed Lake of the Woods on the composite map has usually been interpreted to be a caricature of Lake Winnipeg, with the constriction supposedly caricaturing the one-mile-wide Narrows which connect the Lake's southern and northern basins. Yet in size the two ovals are each very little larger than several of the symbols representing much smaller lakes between Lake Superior and Lake of the Woods. Interpreted as two symbols, rather than one caricature, the two shapes could well have been intended to represent Sand and Tutu Lakes: two relatively small lakes on the Winnipeg River, a short distance downstream from Lake of the Woods and well above the discharge into the southern end of Lake Winnipeg. The legend 'Riviere d'Ouest qui se Lac Ouinipigon passen trois jours de marche', which appears within and occupies virtually the whole of these two symbols tends to confirm this interpretation. The travel time of three days between Lake of the Woods and Lake Winnipeg is of a similar order to that of six days to cross Lake of the Woods and descend the Winnipeg River to Lake Winnipeg as reported by Auchagah and to the distance of 100 leagues from the outflow of Lake of the Woods down the Winnipeg River to Lake Winnipeg as given by La Marteblanche and his two fellow chiefs.

Indians usually supplemented solicited maps orally and gesturally with names and descriptions of specific features and conditions and many of these were added to the maps by interrogators or incorporated in the course of transcription. If the names and descriptions had been both unique and stable over long periods of time this would have facilitated the attribution of representations to referents. Different groups of Indians, however, used different names and descriptions for the same feature. Conversely, but equally confusingly, different features were often named or described by different Indians in identical or similar ways. For example, taken out of its spatial context, the 'Riviere au Vermillon' of the composite map could have been any one of several rivers, some of which still retain names derived from the redness of their beds, their water or the much valued sources of ochre to which they led. Therefore, unless the spatial context is already fairly clear, the name may not serve to establish the referent.

Because of cultural and linguistic differences, Indians and Euro-Americans often appeared to describe in the same way features which were essentially different and located far from each other. To La Vérendrye and the French in the second quarter of the eighteenth century, for example, Indian reports of the 'Commencement du flux et du reflux' were usually assumed to

16

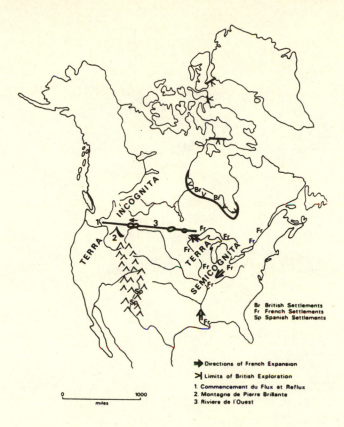

Fig. 6   Strategic significance of the three-element image *circa* 1730.

refer to a tidal point on the Pacific coast (Fig. 6). In retrospect, however, the referent seems much more likely to have been one of several hydrological phenomena in the Lake Winnipeg region, where the behaviour of surface water was unusual as perceived by Cree Indians from around Lake of the Woods (Fig. 7). Similarly, the Montagne de pierre brillants, which was reported by the Indians to shine day and night, suggested to the French and later Euro-Americans a spectacular and majestic snow-capped mountain peak located far to the west of Lake Winnipeg, perhaps somewhere on the continent's primary watershed. In retrospect, it seems much more likely that the Indians were referring to one of several locally exceptional landscape features, geological outcrops or other topographic phenomena located within the Lake Winnipeg region: almost certainly one with mythical associations, because La Vérendrye reported that it was 'the Dwelling of the Spirit' which 'no one ventures to go near . . .' (Fig. 8).

ii. *Mosaicing*. Mosaicing two or more Indian maps was very difficult. The absence on them of equivalents of graticules, grids or neat lines, their failure to conserve distance, or direction, or shape and the absence—or, at best, paucity—of unambiguous toponymic and environmental content together made mosaicing at best an exercise in guesswork and at worst an indulgence in wishful thinking.

In mosaicing three maps, La Vérendrye certainly made one and probably two serious mistakes. The part of the composite map derived from Auchagah undoubtedly represents what in reality is the essentially straight route between Lake Superior and Lake of the Woods. Likewise, the part from Lake of the Woods down the 'Riviere' and 'Fleuve de l'Ouest' as

17

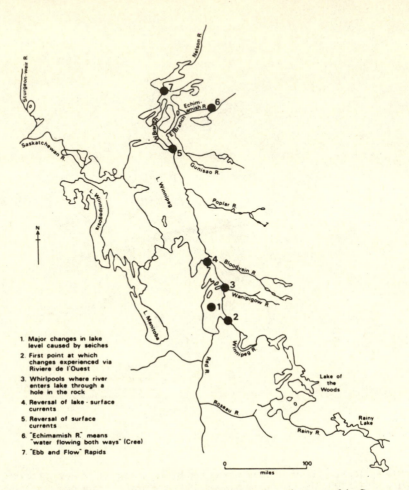

1. Major changes in lake level caused by seiches
2. First point at which changes experienced via Rivière de l'Ouest
3. Whirlpools where river enters lake through a hole in the rock
4. Reversal of lake - surface currents
5. Reversal of surface currents
6. "Echimamish R." means "water flowing both ways" (Cree)
7. "Ebb and Flow" Rapids

Fig. 7   Seven hydrological features, of which any one could have given rise to the report of the Commencement du Flux et du Reflux.

'Trac'ee Par Les Cris (= La Marteblanche *et al.*) represents an essentially straight route, whether one interprets it in the traditional manner as leading to the north end of Lake Winnipeg or, more restrictively, as terminating at the discharge of the Winnipeg River into the southern end of that Lake. The actual route from Lake Superior to Lake Winnipeg, however, involves an approximately 55° change in direction at the southern end of Lake of the Woods. In mosaicing Auchagah's and La Marteblanche *et al*'s representations of the two parts of the route La Vérendrye presented the latter's as a straight-line extension of the former's. A far better representation can be achieved by introducing a 55° rotation at the critical point (Fig. 9).

La Vérendrye also joined to the part derived from La Marteblanche *et al.* Tracchigis' representation of the rivers further west. The latter probably represented all the rivers draining the Prairie-Plains from the lower Saskatchewan River south to the upper James River. If the map made by La Marteblanche *et al.* is interpreted not as in Figure 9 but restrictively, then La Vérendrye appears to have mistakenly linked representations of the Saskatchewan, Dauphin and Red River drainage systems to Tetu and Sand Lakes; the two small lakes on the Winnipeg River which are more than 50 miles to the southeast of Lake Winnipeg (Fig. 10).

18

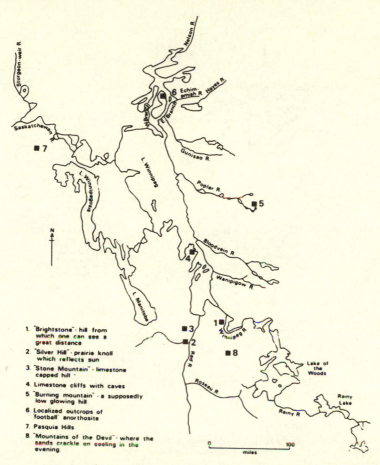

1. "Brightstone" - hill from which one can see a great distance
2. "Silver Hill" - prairie knoll which reflects sun
3. "Stone Mountain" - limestone capped hill
4. Limestone cliffs with caves
5. "Burning mountain" - a supposedly low glowing hill
6. Localized outcrops of 'football' anorthosite
7. Pasquia Hills
8. "Mountains of the Devil" - where the sands crackle on cooling in the evening

Fig. 8   Eight topographical and geological features, of which any one could have given rise to the report of the Montagne de Pierre Brilliante.

iii. *Transforming*. We do not know how De Léry transformed the composite map. Inspection indicates that he somehow derived and added a fourth bar scale and that he rescaled the map along the long axis only. Even in that direction, however, rescaling was along the rivers only, the shapes and relative sizes of the lakes remaining essentially the same on the transformed as on the composite map. De Léry almost certainly had access to La Vérendrye's report to Beauharnois of 1729/30 which contained Indians' estimates of distances: five in day's travel; eight in leagues; and two as fractions of other distances.[27] It is also possible that De Léry had seen La Vérendrye's report of the previous year. The limits of the route intervals for which these times, distances and proportions were reported were, however, often imprecise and sometimes unusable for the purpose of reasonably precise transformation. All were apparently the estimates for actual and complex routes via rivers and lakes. Yet the composite map represented these as essentially straight lines. Furthermore, stated intervals often terminated not at points but within large areas. 'Lac Tecacamioueg' (= Rainy Lake), for example, which has a long axis of more than 60 miles, was used as a terminal 'point'. Likewise, although the composite map marked 'Prairies' and 'Islets de bois', it did not indicate where the forests ended

19

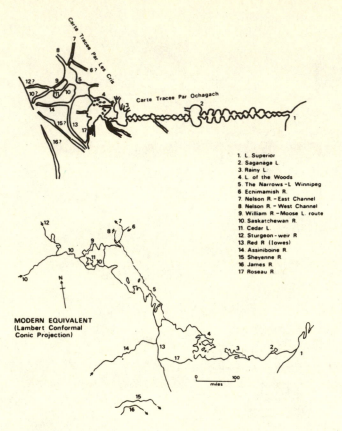

1. L. Superior
2. Saganaga L.
3. Rainy L.
4. L. of the Woods
5. The Narrows -L. Winnipeg
6. Echimamish R.
7. Nelson R. - East Channel
8. Nelson R. - West Channel
9. William R - Moose L. route
10. Saskatchewan R.
11. Cedar L.
12. Sturgeon - weir R.
13. Red R (Iowes)
14. Assiniboine R.
15. Sheyenne R.
16. James R.
17. Roseau R.

MODERN EQUIVALENT
(Lambert Conformal
Conic Projection)

Fig. 9 The composite map modified by a 55° clockwise rotation of all the content to the left of Lake of the
Woods interpreted fairly conventionally.

and the prairies began. Hence, Pako's reported statement that wood was to be found for 'about two hundred leagues' along the Fleuve de l'Ouest was of little value in rescaling.[28] Hydrological and topographical features mentioned in the report were not necessarily related correctly to representations on the composite map. For example, three of the stated intervals terminated at the inflow of the 'Fleuve de l'Ouest' into 'Lac Ouinipigon' but, as indicated already, the hour-glass-shaped representation on the map may have been intended not as a caricature of Lake Winnipeg but as symbolizations of Sand and Tetu Lakes. For these and similar reasons De Léry's transformation along the long axis could not have been based on a rigorous application of the principles of proportion. Deliberately, or as a consequence of false interpretations, it resulted in the features most distant from Lake Superior being represented as much further away than they really are.

　　iv. *Incorporating.* Incorporating a transformed map onto an existing Euro-American map of a wider area almost inevitably introduced new errors as well as perpetuating those which had already been introduced in the interpreting, mosaicing and transforming processes.

　　De Léry's incorporation was defective in several respects; most notably in the east-west orientation of 'Riviere . . .' and 'Fleuve de l'Ouest' in its course beyond Lake of the Woods. This made manifest an error which was implicit on the transformed map: the representation of a great river which flowed west towards the Pacific Ocean. Although the representation stopped short of showing it as actually flowing into the Ocean and omitted the westward-pointing flow

20

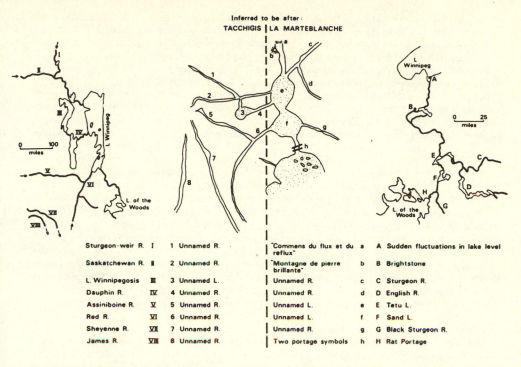

Sturgeon-weir R.	I	1	Unnamed R.	"Commens du flux et du reflux"	a	A Sudden fluctuations in lake level
Saskatchewan R.	II	2	Unnamed R.	"Montagne de pierre brillante"	b	B Brightstone
L. Winnipegosis	III	3	Unnamed L.	Unnamed R.	c	C Sturgeon R.
Dauphin R.	IV	4	Unnamed R.	Unnamed R.	d	D English R.
Assiniboine R.	V	5	Unnamed R.	Unnamed L.	e	E Tetu L.
Red R.	VI	6	Unnamed R.	Unnamed L.	f	F Sand L.
Sheyenne R.	VII	7	Unnamed R.	Unnamed R.	g	G Black Sturgeon R.
James R.	VIII	8	Unnamed R.	Two portage symbols	h	H Rat Portage

Fig. 10   A possible false mosaicing of the La Marteblanche and Tacchigis components of the composite map.

(?) arrows of the transformed map, the placing of 'hauteur des Terres', to the north, east and south precluded any other interpretation. The serious scaling errors on the transformed map were further distorted in the process of incorporation. The stated scale of '500 Lieues de 20 au degre' on the transformed map clearly indicated that the type of league used was the lieue commune (= the pre-1635 lieue marine) of 25 to one degree of latitude (and of longitude at the equator). If oriented east-west at the equator the approximately 800 lieues between the mouth of the 'Riviere Nantohouaganne' (= Pigeon River) on 'Lac Superieur' and the 'Commencem.' du flux et reflux' would have occupied 32° of longitude. But at 47°30' N (the latitude of the River's mouth—not actually represented—on De l'Isle's *Carte d'Amerique* ... (1722) such a linear distance would have occupied 47° of longitude. This would have placed the 'commencem.' ...' approximately 12° west of the Pacific coastline of what is now the state of Washington. In representing it one or two degrees east of the coast and onlyt 34° west of the mouth of the Riviere Nantohouaganne', De Léry was either deliberately distorting the geometry or ignoring the scale as indicated on the transformed map. In doing so he avoided what would have been a nonsensical representation and came slightly closer to the truth but achieved a set of spatial relationships which was still a gross distortion of reality as we now know it.

The incorporation involved only three linkages with elements on De l'Isle's *Carte d'Amerique* ... (1722): the 'Riviere Nantohouaganne', and the unnamed but indisputable 'Riviere Kamanestiquouia' with 'Lac Superieur', which were essentially correct, and the 'Fleuve Missisipi' with the middle Mississippi somewhere near the site of what is now Dubuque, Iowa. The latter resulted in a representation which involved the upper Mississippi crossing a clearly marked 'hauter des Terres' and rising approximately 20° to the west of its actual source. In retrospect, the representation of the upper Mississippi can be seen as far less satisfactory than that on the transcript of the *Carte d'Amerique* ... (1722) over which it was pasted.

On the whole, the errors arising in the process of incorporation were probably less serious than those which had already been introduced in the course of transformation.

v. *Accommodating*. Accommodating the incorporation on printed maps which were compiled from a mix of sources occurred in two stages: initial; and subsequent.

Bellin's initial accommodation of 1743 (Fig. 4) although almost certainly derived from De Léry's incorporation, differed from it in several respects. Among these the following are noteworthy. Arrows on the 'Riviere ...' and 'Fleuve de l'Ouest' now clearly indicated that it supposedly flowed west. Its linearity and east-west orientation were retained but the axis was moved northward from approximately 47°30′ to 50°00′ north. 'Lac des Bois' and 'Lac Tecacamiouen' (the latter unnamed) were enlarged in relation to almost all the other features derived from the incorporation. The source of the Mississippi was moved approximately 20° to the east into the longitude of 'Lac des Bois'. 'Lac Ouinipigon' was still both small and located far to the west. Most interestingly, the river draining north from 'Lac des Bois', which flowed to the edges of both the composite and transformed maps and terminated abruptly on De Léry's paste-on incorporation, was connected northwards to a large 'Lac des Assiniboels'. A lake by that name to the northwest of Lake Superior had been represented on maps since at least 1678 and Lake Winnipeg is most likely to have been the original referent for this. If so, Bellin was unknowingly representing Lake Winnipeg twice on the same map. Both representations were derived from information supplied by Indians but at different times, by different groups and via different sequences of assimilation. Ironically, the older of the two representations was somewhat nearer to reality in terms of position, relative size and, to a lesser extent, linkages.

3. Some consequences of assimilation

The case study reveals that much of the spatially-arranged information which had been honestly transmitted by the Amerindians and which at the time of transmission was true according to their concepts and cultural conventions, was filtered out, falsified or remained ambiguous in the course of assimilation (Fig. 11). Yet what survived was of particular interest to the aliens in that it related to a *terra incognita* which, like most *terrae incognitae*, was perceived to be of potential strategic significance. Information about it was, therefore, much valued. Ironically, the less that was known, the more it was valued and the higher the proportion that was Indian in origin (Fig. 12). In retrospect, that information when assimilated onto Euro-American maps can be seen as weakly integrated, of low reliability, difficult to verify and slow to be revised.

Some of the characteristics of the original information did, however, survive assimilation and these provide the diagnostic characteristics upon which to detect possible Amerindian information on printed maps which lack acknowledgements of sources and for which supporting contemporary documentation has not been found.

Some Diagnostic Characteristics of Information Transmitted by Amerindians in Map *Form*

Arising from the case study six non-toponymic diagnostic characteristics emerge.

1. Irregular linear features.

Because they were cognized and represented topologically, rivers, coastlines, routes and, though less frequently represented, boundaries, almost all of which are now known to be irregular, usually appeared on Indian *maps* as essentially straight or gently curved lines. Thus, in representing as straight the then most frequently used canoe route between Lake Superior and Lake of the Woods. Auchagah was not reflecting ignorance of hydrological detail but adopting the normal mode for structuring information about linear features. In 1602 Miguel, a southern Plains or west Gulf Coast Indian, drew for Spaniards what is now probably the oldest extant *map* to have been made by an Indian for Europeans.[29] It represents an area that includes San Gabriel, New Mexico, either the middle Arkansas valley or the Texas coastal plain, and probably parts of Mexico. The trails (caminos) are represented without exception as regular and straight and the rivers (rios), though symbolically sinuous are, likewise, straight overall.

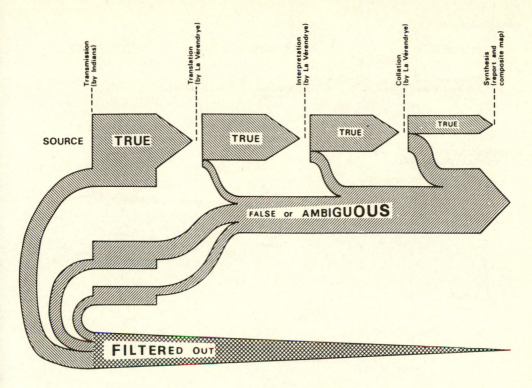

Fig. 11   The changing balance between true and false or ambiguous information in the course of assimilation.

Changes in line direction on the map occur only at nodes. Similarly, in or around 1767 two Chipewyan Indians represented as essentially straight almost 4000 miles of coastline between Fort Churchill, on the southwest coast of Hudson Bay, and the mouth of the Coppermine river, at the head of what is now Coronation Gulf: a coastline which is characterized by several major peninsulas, has much irregular detail and involves an approximately 100° change in direction at the Boothia Peninsula (Fig. 13).[30] Hence, occurrences on Euro-American maps of essentially straight representations of geometrically complex linear features within contemporary *terrae semicognitae* may be considered as possible indicators of Amerindian assimilations.

The representation as an essentially straight line on Vincenzo Maria Coronelli's *Partie Occidentale du Canada ou de la Nouvelle France ...* (*c.* 1685) of the approximately 700 mile-long stretch of the Mississippi River between just above the 'Saut de St. Ant. de Padoue' (= present-day Minneapolis) and the confluence of the 'Riv. des Ilinois, ou Seignelay' (= Illinois River) should be examined as a possible Amerindian assimilation, even though Louis Jolliet and Jacques Marquette had explored part of it in 1672 and Jean-Louis Hennepin the whole of it in 1679[31] (Fig. 14).

2. Networks

Networks which in reality are asymmetrical in pattern were frequently represented by Indians as approximately symmetrical. This characteristic probably reflected the tendency of the human mind to impose a simpler order on reality than actually exists, thereby focussing on essentials and increasing memorability. The tendency is manifest in a mid nineteenth century Iowa Indian's representation of the drainage networks in the upper Mississippi and lower Missouri catchments[32] (Fig. 15) and, likewise, in a Blackfoot Indian's representation of the upper Missouri and its tributaries earlier in the century.[33] Both represented an axial element as

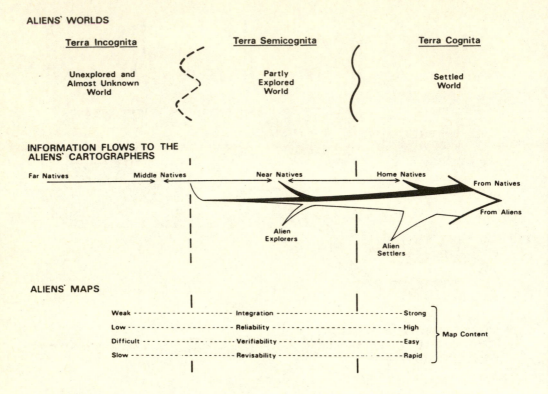

Fig. 12   Information flows to the aliens' map makers.

essentially straight (the Mississippi-Wisconsin Rivers in the Iowa's case, with what is now considered to be the upper Mississippi represented as a tributary of the main axis) and essentially straight tributaries which join the main axis at approximately equal angles.

Symmetry is often to be found on early printed maps as, for example, on Nicolas Sanson d'Abbeville's *Le Nouveau Mexique, et La Floride* . . . (1656)[34] (Fig. 16), where the whole of south-central North America is shown as being drained by a series of rivers which converge on a 'Bahia del Spirito Santo' without any suggestion of the Mississippi River. Sanson's map reveals another characteristic of networks as represented by Indians. Because rivers were the natural routeways through much of the continent and native boats (mainly but not exclusively canoes) were both light and portable, boats were frequently carried across watersheds at portages which had been chosen because they were short, easy and would reduce journey times on regular routes. Because Indian *maps* often failed to distinguish between the riverine and portage elements of route networks (or because Euro-Americans failed to recognize such distinctions when they were made) drainage networks as derived from their *maps* frequently appear unnatural. Rivers appear to anastomose, even at the macro scale, whereas in nature this is rare, even at the micro scale. This is a characteristic of La Vérendrye's composite map, on which rivers appear to cross each other and to bifurcate downstream. There are good examples of downstream bifurcation on Cornelius Wytfliet's *Florida et Apalche* (1597)[35] (Fig. 17) and of both downstream bifurcation and river-course crossings on Sanson's *Le Nouveau Mexique, et la Floride* . . . and in both cases the occurrences are within Euro-American *terrae semicognitae*.

24

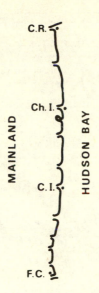

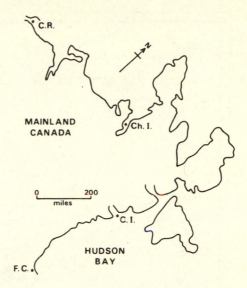

According to Meatonabee and Idotly - azee
(ca. 1767) - two Chipewyans

According to a Modern
Composite Projection

C. I. Chesterfield Inlet   Ch. I. Chantry Inlet
C. R. Mouth of Coppermine River   F. C. Fort Churchill

Fig. 13   The west coast of Hudson Bay and the north coast of mainland Canada according to an eighteenth-century map by two Chipewyan Indians and a modern map.

3. Discrete enclosed spaces.

Indian topological representations of relatively small, clearly bounded spaces often paid no regard to boundary details but employed the simplest of enclosing shapes: the circle. It was sometimes used to symbolize settlements, where the use of the proportional-size principle to denote relative population or relative importance can often be inferred but is difficult to prove. An Iroquois representation of their villages (castles) towards the end of the seventeenth century certainly suggests this principle.[36] Likewise, the map painted on deer skin by an Indian cacique around 1720, a copy of which was dedicated to the Prince of Wales (later George II), which showed native tribal areas inland from South Carolina as circles.[37] Circles, or other simple enclosed shapes, were most commonly used to represent lakes and this tradition continues to be used widely among Canadian Indians in making *maps* with which to register their trapping rights.[38] Such representations are known from the earliest post-contact times, as in Auchagah's depiction of most of the lakes on his part of La Vérendrye's composite map, where long, sinuous, bifurcating and in general irregularly-shaped lakes are represented as bean shaped and where difference in size may have been intended to represent differences according to some order of importance.

Complex, small- to medum-sized lakes occur along the rivers throughout the shield lands to the north of the Great Lakes. Samuel Champlain's representation of these as tadpole-like in shape on *Carte de la Nouvelle France* . . . (1632) suggests that he was using information received from Indians[39] (Fig. 18). Indeed, as Europeans had not even begun to explore the area at that date it is difficult to imagine otherwise.

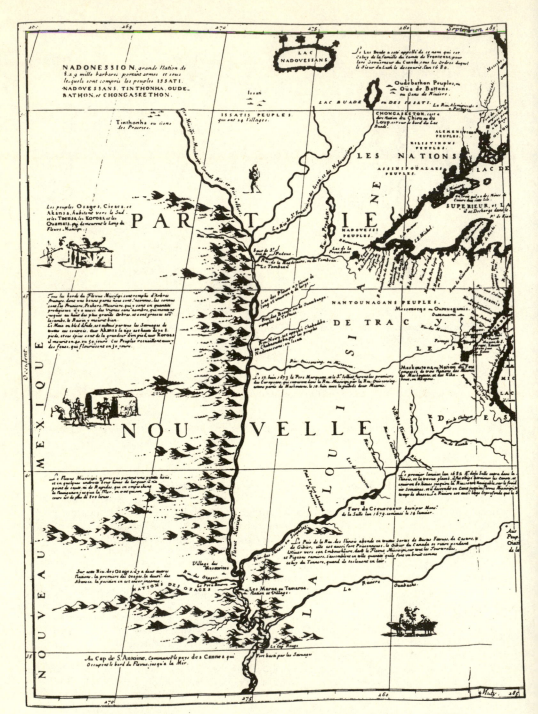

Fig. 14   Part of Coronelli's *Partie Occidentale du Canada ou de la Nouvelle France . . .* (c. 1685).

26

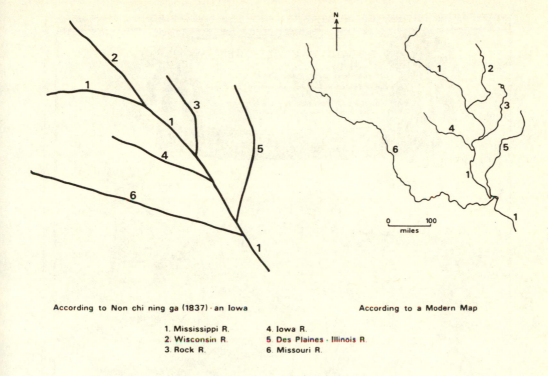

According to Non chi ning ga (1837) · an Iowa   According to a Modern Map

1. Mississippi R.	4. Iowa R.
2. Wisconsin R.	5. Des Plaines · Illinois R.
3. Rock R.	6. Missouri R.

Fig. 15   Hydrography of the upper Mississippi and lower Missouri catchments according to a mid nineteenth-century map by an Iowa Indian and a modern map.

4. Caricaturization and exaggeration.

Indians often emphasized regionally unusual or locally important features on their *maps* by means of caricaturization and/or exaggeration. As already reasoned, La Marteblanche and his two fellow Cree chiefs almost certainly caricatured 'Lac de Tecacamioueg' (= Rainy Lake) and Lake of the Woods (unnamed) as they appear on La Vérendrye's composite map: two lakes which were culturally important and well known to the three chiefs as being close to their villages (Fig. 1b). Whether or not they were responsible for exaggerating their extents in relation to the features further east is less clear because of the uncertainty concerning what precisely was derived from Auchagah and what from La Marteblanche *et al.* They achieved the caricatures by modifying the essentially bean-like symbol for lakes to show selected bays, peninsulas and islands. The Southern Ojibway of the area around Leech Lake, Minnesota, possess migration charts made on birch bark which represent the route via which they believe they received their religion. These, likewise, combine caricaturization and exaggeration. Typically, a few small lakes are represented by circular symbols, whereas culturally-important Leech Lake is caricatured, departing from being circular by the addition of three major peninsulas[40] (Fig. 19). Lake Superior, which is represented as bullet shaped also contains a caricature: a long and large intrusion at its left-hand end, which is obviously intended to represent the locally important, landscape-wise exceptional but regionally insignificant bay bar at Fond du Lac.

There would appear to be an example of this kind of caricaturization combined with exaggeration on John Foster's *A Map of New England* (1677)[41] (Fig. 20). Winnipesaukee Lake (unnamed), at that date beyond the limit of English settlement, is represented as far too large in

27

Fig. 16 Part of Sanson's *Le Nouveau Mexique et La Florida . . .* (1656)

relation to everything else on the map. Furthermore, the representation caricatures a long narrow peninsula (= Moultonboro Neck), some of the many islands, the two small lakes (= Winnisquam and Silver) below the outflow of the main lake via the Winnipesaukee River, and the sharp change in direction of that River near what was to become Northfield. Nothing else on the map equals the boldness of these representations. As with 'Lac des Tecacamioueg' and the unnamed Lake of the Woods on La Vérendrye's composite map the exaggerated size

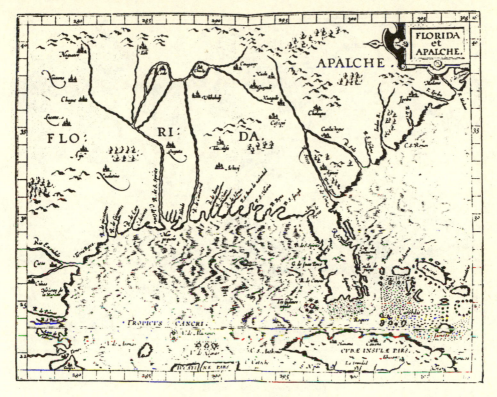

Fig. 17   Wytfliet's *Florida et Apalche* (1597).

could either have been Indian in origin or a consequence of mosaicing: in this case, presumably of an Indian *map* to a primarily Euro-American map.

5. Duplication.

Exaggeration of size could be either an intrinsic characteristic of Amerindian *maps* or a consequence of mosaicing, whereas duplication resulted from mosaicing, incorporating or accommodating. The accommodation of De Léry's transformation of La Vérendrye's composite map in Bellin's *Carte de l'Amerique Septentrionale* . . . (1743) (Fig. 4) either contained or unknowingly implied a duplication. According to most retrospective reinterpretations, Lake Winnipeg was the most likely referent, for 'Lac des Assiniboils'.[42] Bellin's 'Lac Ouinipigon' was represented as being far to the southwest of his 'Lac des Assiniboils' yet, according to whether one accepts the traditional interpretation or the one proposed earlier in this paper, the referents were either Lake Winnipeg or Tetu and Sand Lakes. Quite clearly, the traditional interpretation indicates a duplication. Equally, however, the new interpretation implies one because, if it had been represented, the true Lake Winnipeg would have been to the left of 'Lac Oouinipigon', i.e. even further away from 'Lac des Assiniboils'.

The untitled manuscript map of the east coast of North America and the St. Lawrence valley which Don Alonso de Velasco sent from London to King Philip II of Spain in 1611 may contain a major duplication[43] (Frontispiece Upper). It is unusual for that period in distinguishing in colour between content derived from different sources. Although 'All the blue is done by the relations of the Indians' there is no indication of how many native sources were used. There are three non contiguous sets of features represented in blue, two of which could well have resulted from

29

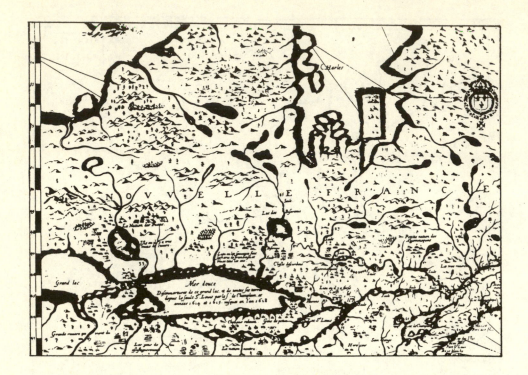

Fig. 18   Part of Champlain's *Carte de nouvelle france* . . . (1632).

representations of the same referent as derived from two different Indian sources. The St. Lawrence River, knowledge of which had been obtained from European sources, is represented as flowing from the northeastern corner of a large lake. The lake, which is represented in blue (i.e. on the basis of information derived from Indians), is quite clearly the eastern part of Lake Ontario. Likewise, what are clearly representations of Lac St. Pierre and the lower Richelieu River are based on European sources but the latter is shown as rising in the lower of two linked lakes both of which are outlined in blue. They are arranged en echelon and oriented approximately east-west. The representation of the two lakes is distinctive but in orientation and form it is quite unlike the long, narrow, meridionally-oriented Lake Champlain in which the Richelieu actually rises. Rather, the shape and relations of the representation suggests a small-scale, correctly oriented caricature of Lakes Erie and Ontario which, however, has been falsely linked to the St. Lawrence River, is out of place and far too small in relation to virtually every other recognizable representation on the map. If so, then the eastern edge of Lake Ontario is represented twice.

6. Discontinuities of style.

Incorporation and accommodation of Indian *maps* almost inevitably gave rise to juxtapositions of contrasting styles, though some map makers managed to minimize this. For example, whilst the incorporation by De Léry of La Vérendrye's composite map contrasts stylistically with that of his transcription of De l'Isle's map (1722) which he used as a base (Fig. 3), the contrast is less obvious on Bellin's accommodation of 1743 (Fig. 4). Though the networks on the latter remain virtually unchanged, the bead-like chains of small lakes have disappeared and, though still unrealistically long and remaining essentially straight, the 'Riviere' and 'Fleuve de l'Ouest' have visual weights and detailed styles similar to those of the other major

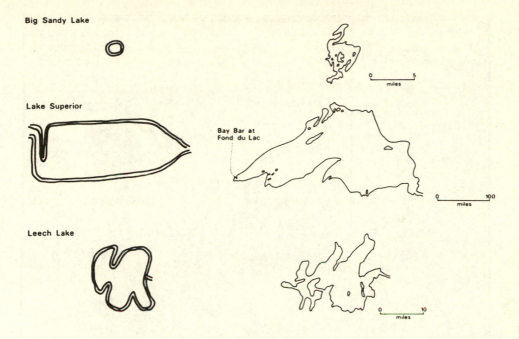

Fig. 19 A lake symbol and caricatures of two specific lakes on a Southern Ojibway midé migration chart.

rivers. Only the unexplained but apparently conflicting arrows and the frequent stream anastomoses continue to give grounds for suspicion.

Discontinuities of style are often quite blatant. For example, the Dutch 'Figurative Map' (c. 1614) of Northeastern North America, which has usually been ascribed to Adriaen Block, shows the coastline and lower parts of the main rivers in fair detail[44] (Frontispiece, Lower). Along and adjacent to these linear elements, features and settlements are named and it is fairly easy to establish most of the referents. To the north, however, the representation of the drainage system upstream from 'De schants Quebec' is gross in style, contains two anastomoses and does not link with what appears to be the eastern end of Lake Ontario, i.e. the lake which is in part represented on the extreme left centre of the map to the immediate upper left of the 'Nie' in 'Nie Vneder Landt'. Furthermore, what in terms of shape, orientation, linkage and name ('Het Meer Vand Irocoisen' = Lake of the Iroquois) could reasonably be interpreted as a representation of Lake Champlain, is represented as being far too the east—rather than somewhat to the north—of the Hudson River. The suspicion of a different origin for this content is reinforced by the conspicuous chain of hill symbols which almost surround the 'Meer'. There are no such symbols elsewhere on the map yet, from the perspective of the Hudson valley, of which the Dutch had some experience, the area is not particularly hilly. Conversely from the perspective of the middle St. Lawrence valley it is spectacularly so. It would appear, therefore, that a different origin for the representation of features on the upper part of the map is virtually certain and that an Indian source or sources would seem to be highly likely.

Forward

The ideas developed in this paper should be seen as a first step in what could become an exciting sector of research in the history of cartography. They must first be tested and modified in the course of further case studies conducted in a North American context. At this stage the objectives should be to recognize further characteristics and to establish the cultural and

31

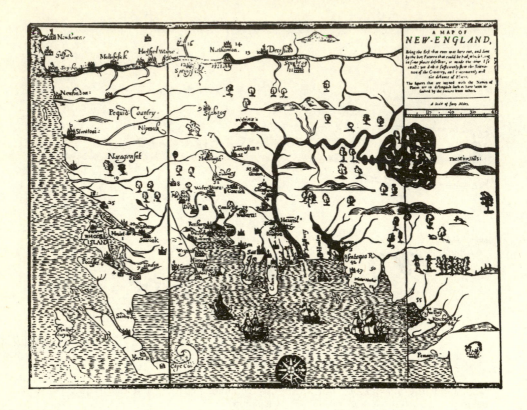

Fig. 20   Foster's *A Map of New England . . .* (1677).

temporal ranges of each. Second, the diagnostic power of the characteristics needs to be tested with reference to Euro-American maps for which contemporary documentation concerning content and compilation is extant. If this step proves positive the third must be to assess the extent to which the characteristics of Amerindian *maps* are valid for the *maps* of other preliterate peoples, both historic and prehistoric. Finally, and most significantly, if the third step proves positive, and it is possible to recognize a set of characteristics which is universally syndromic of the *maps* of pre-literate peoples, it should be possible to begin developing a cognitive history of cartography, perhaps within the framework of Piagetian genetic epistemology. The recognition of this possibility is not new[45] but the suggested way forward is.

ACKNOWLEDGEMENT

*This paper stems from research on the *maps* and *mapping* activities of North American Indians and Inuits from prehistoric times to the present. A version was read at the Eleventh International Conference on the History of Cartography, Ottawa, Canada, 1985. Funding from the Newberry Library, Chicago, the History of Cartography program, Madison, the Canadian High Commission, London, the Social Science Research Council (now the Economic and Social Science Research Council) and the Research Fund of the University of Sheffield is gratefully acknowledged.

REFERENCES

1. This paper is only concerned with the influence of Amerindian *maps*. Inuits also made *maps*, information from which was sometimes incorporated on Euro-American maps of the Canadian Arctic and Alaska: see Spink, John and Moodie, D. Wayne, 'Eskimo maps from the Canadian Eastern Arctic', *Cartographica Monograph*, 5 (1972), 1–98.

2. Because they differ in several important respects from post-Renaissance European and Euro-American maps, the map-like pictographs of Amerindians and transcripts thereof are referred to in this paper as *maps*.

3. Alarcón, Hernando, The relation of the navigation and discovery . . ., in Hakluyt, Richard (1600), *The third and last volume of the voyages, navigations . . .* (London: George Bishop, Ralfe Newberie and Robert Barker, 1600), 438.

4. Cartier, Jacques, The third voyage of discovery . . ., in Hakluyt (1600), 235.

5. Wellmann, Klaus F, *A survey of North American Indian rock art* (Graz, Austria: Ackademische Druck und Verlagastalt, 1979); the Index contains entries under each of the following: map as rock art design; game trails; ground plan of house or lodge; and astronomical motifs. Aveni, Anthony F. (ed.), *Archaeoastronomy in Pre-Columbian America* (Austin and London: University of Texas Press, 1975); see especially Mayer, Dorothy, Star-patterns in Great Basin petroglyphs, 107–130.

6. Lafitau, Joseph F., edited and translated by Fenton, William N. and Moore, Elizabeth M., *Customs of the American Indians . . .* (Toronto: the Champlain Society) 2 (1977), 130.

7. Military examples are described among the Comanche by Dodge, Richard I., *The hunting grounds of the great west* (London: Chatto and Windus, 1877), 414 and among coastal Indians of British Columbia by Sproat, Gilbert M., *Scenes and studies of savage life* (London: Smith, Elder and Co., 1868), 191–192. An example used by a Delaware preacher is described in Heckewelder, John, An account of the history, manners and customs of the Indian natives . . ., *Transactions of the Historical and Literary Committee of the American Philosophical Society* 1 (Philadelphia, 1819), 288–290 and reconstructed in Lewis, G. Malcolm, 'The indigenous maps and mapping of North American Indians, *The Map Collector* 9 (1979), 26. Examples of maps on birchbark used by Passamaquoddy Indians on hunting expeditions are reproduced in Mallery, Garrick, Picture-writing of the American Indians, *Tenth Annual Report of the Bureau of Ethnology for 1888–9* (Washington, D.C.: Smithsonian Institution, 1893), Figs. 457 and 458.

8. Some of the birchbark pictographs in Southern Ojibway medicine bundles have recently been shown to incorporate *maps* of the St. Lawrence and Great Lakes drainage system, via which the Indians believed they received the Midé religion; Dewdney, Selwyn, *The sacred scrolls of the Southern Ojibway* (Toronto: University of Toronto Press for the Glenbow-Alberta Institute, 1975), 57–80. In 1947, a large book containing drawings, including *maps*, made after 1891 by her brother, the Oglala Sioux, Amos Bad Heart Bull, was buried with Mrs. Pretty Cloud; Blish, Helen H., *A pictographic history of the Oglala Sioux* (Lincoln: University of Nebraska Press, 1967), Preface. In 1979, the missing corner of a Beaver Indian skin *map* was said to have been cut off and buried with the body of someone 'who would not easily find his way to heaven . . .'; Brody, Hugh, *Maps and dreams* (London: Norman and Hobhouse, 1982), 267.

9. As recently as 1979 Beaver Indians produced a 'magnificent dream map' on hide at a public hearing organized by the Northern Pipeline Agency. Preserved in bundles, such maps are only opened 'for very special occasions'; Brody, *op. cit.*, 266–267.

10. Smith, John. *Virginia: discovered and discribed by Captayn John Smith 1606, graven by William Hole* (London, 1612). De Velasco, Don Alonso (1611). Untitled map of the east coast of North America, MS, Estado. Leg. 2588, fo. 22, Archivo General de Simancas, Simancas, Spain.

11. *Dictionary of Canadian Biography*, 3 (University of Toronto Press: Toronto, Buffalo and London, 1974), 245–254.

12. *Pierre Gaultier de Varennes et de la Vérendrye, Joint à lettre de M. de Beauharnois du 10 octobre 1730. Suite du memoire du Sieur de la Vérenderei touchant la découverte de la Mer de l'Ouest*. Original with English translation reproduced in Burpee, Lawrence J., 'Journals and letters of Pierre Gaultier de Varennes de la Vérendrye and his sons', *The Publications of the Champlain Society*, no. 16 (Toronto: Ballantyne Press, 1927), 43–66. Burpee would appear to have used either transcripts in the Public Archives of Canada included in Correspondence Generals, vol. 16, 'Posts in the western country, 1679–1759' or Margry, Pierre (ed) *Decouvertes et etablissements des francais dans l'ouest et dans le sud de l'Amerique Septentrionale* (Paris: Maissonneuve, 1879–88), 6 vols. According to Zoltvany, Yves F. in *Dictionary of Canadian Biography*, 3 (1974), 253, 'Correspondence, memoirs, maps and the journals kept by La Vérendrye are found in A[rchives] N[ationales] Col.[onies], B; C¹¹ᴬ; C¹¹ᴱ; E; F³; [and] Section Outre-Mer, Dépôt des fortifications des colonies. Important items will also be found in Archives du ministère des Affaires etrangères (Paris), Mem[oires] de doc[uments], Amerique, 8; B[ibliothèque] N[ationale], NAF 9286 (Margry)'.

13. Manuscript map without title but often referred to by a legend on the left hand part: *Carte Tracée Par Les Cris*. Photographic Print, Public Archives of Canada, National Map Collection H2/902:[1728–29].

14. Legends and topographic and tribal names which appear in quotation marks are rendered according to their form on the appropriate map.

15. Burpee, *op. cit.*, 52–55.

16. *Ibid.*, 55–60.

17. *Ibid.*, 48–49.

18. *Ibid.*, 64.

19. [Probably De Lery, Chaussegros in 1730], *Carte copiee, sur celle tracée par le sauvage Ochagach et autres*, Archives Nationales, Colonies E, Carton 263—Dossier La Veranderie no. 18.

20. Burpee, *op. cit.*, 64.

21. [Probably De Léry, Chaussegros in 1730], *Cours des Rivieres et fleuve, courant a Louest du nord du Lac Superieur . . .*, Depôt des Cartes et Plans de la Marine, Service Hydrographique, Bibliothèque 4044B, no. 84.

22. [Probably De Léry, Chaussegros in 1730], Untitled manuscript map in which a version of the transformation of La Vérendrye's composite map is pasted on a manuscript base map of North America derived from Guillaume De l'Isle (1722), *Carte d'Amerique . . .* (Paris), Bibliothèque Nationale, Department des Estampes Series Vd, vol. 22.

23. Buache, Philippe, 'Réduction de la carte tracée par le sauvage Ochagach et autres, . . .', insert on *Carte physique des terreins les plus élevés de la partie occidentale du Canada* (Paris, 1754).

24. Bellin, Jacques Nicolas, *Carte de l'Amerique Septentrionale pour servir à l'histoire de la Nouvelle France* (Paris, 1743).

25. Karpinski, Louis C. (1926–27), Photographic reproduction of 'Tire de la Relation de la N.^{lle} france en 1657 et 1658', Scrapbook 3, Newberry Library, Chicago.

26. In the Rocky Mountains, for example, the ratio of fast to slow travel times could be as much as 4:1. 'They measure distances by a day's journey. When an Indian travels alone, his day's journey will be about 50 or 60 English miles, but only 15 or 20 when he moves with the camp'; De Smet, Pierre J., *Letters and sketches with a narrative of a year's residence among the Indian tribes of the Rocky Mountains* (Philadelphia: M. Fithian, 1843).

27. Burpee, *op. cit.*, 44–58.

28. *Ibid.*, 45.

29. Untitled contemporary transcript (31×43 cm) in the Archivo General de Indias, Seville, Spain. Reproduced in Lewis, G. Malcolm, 'Indian maps: their place in the history of Plains cartography', *Great Plains Quarterly* 4 (Lincoln, Nebraska, 1984), 101.

30. Meatonabee and Idotly-Azee (Chipewyans *c.* 1767), 'A draught brought by two Northern Indian leaders call^d Meantonabee & Idotyazee, of ye country to ye northward of Churchill river', MS, 150×72 cm., G.2/27, Hudson's Bay Company Archives, Winnipeg.

31. Coronelli, Vincenzo Maria, *Partie occidentale du Canada ou de la Nouvelle France . . .* (Paris, 168 [sic]).

32. Non-Chi-Ning-Ga (Iowa Indian, 1837). Untitled map of tribal migrations in the upper Mississippi and Missouri drainage basins, MS, 104×69 cm, RG 75, map 821, tube 520, Cartographic Branch, National Archives, Washington, D.C. Reproduced in Lewis, *op. cit.*, 94.

33. Ac Ko Mok Ki (Blackfoot Indian, 1801), Untitled map of the upper Missouri River and its tributaries, contemporary MS transcription by Peter Fidler, 37×48 cm, E.3/2, fos. 106d–107, Hudson's Bay Company Archives, Winnipeg. Reproduced and interpreted in Moodie, D. W. and Kaye, Barry, The Ac Ko Mok Ki map, *The Beaver* 307:4 (Winnipeg, 1977), 5–15.

34. Sanson, Nicolas, *Le Nouveau Mexique, et la Floride: . . .* (Paris, 1656).

35. Wytfliet, Corneille, *Florida et Apalche* (Louvain, 1597).

36. Ackentijaekon *et al.* (two Cayuga and one Susquehannock Indian, 1683). Untitled map of the Susquehanna and Hudson-Mohawk Rivers, contemporary MS transcription by Robert Livingston, endorsed 'This draugt is taken from 3 Indians . . . 7th of September 1683', Livingston Indian Records, Franklin D. Roosevelt Library, Hyde Park, New York.

37. Indian Cacique (*c.* 1720). This map describing the scituation of the several nations of the Indians to the N.W. of South Carolina was coppyed from a Draught drawn & painted on a deer skin by an Indian cacique and presented to Francis Nicholson Esqr, Governor of South Carolina . . ., MS, 83×115 cm; Sloane 4723, Department of Manuscripts, British Museum, London.

38. Several modern examples are reproduced in Pentland, David H., *Cree maps from Moose Factory* (Regina: published by the author, 1978).

39. Champlain, Samuel, *Carte de la Nouvelle France, augmente depuis la derniers, servant a la navigation faicte en son vray meridien . . .* (Paris, 1632).

40. Figure 19 is derived from the transcript of Red Sky's migration chart as reproduced in Dewdney (1975), fig. 47.

41. Foster, John, *A map of New England . . .* (Boston, 1677).

42. A lake, associated with which is the name Assiniboels, occurs on Jolliet, Louis, *Nouvelle decouverte des plusieurs nations dans la Nouvelle France*, MS (1673–74), John Carter Brown Library, Providence, Rhode Island. According to Ruggles this was 'the first definite occurrence of the Lake of the Assiniboels upon the map of Canada, which through an involved metamorphosis evolved into the Manitoba Lakes', i.e. Lakes Winnipeg, Winnipegosis and Manitoba, see Ruggles, Richard I. and Warkentin, John, *Historical Atlas of Manitoba . . .* (Winnipeg: The Historical and Scientific Society of Manitoba, 1970), 36.

43. De Velasco, *op. cit.* (1611).

44. Block, Adriaen (*c.* 1614), Untitled map of northeast North America, MS, Algemeen Rijkarchief, The Hague, The Netherlands.

45. Earlier statements of the idea are to be found in Pentland, David H., 'Cartographic concepts of the Northern Algonquians, *Canadian Cartographer* 12 (1975), 149–160 and Wood, Denis, 'Now and then: comparisons of ordinary Americans', *Prologue: The Journal of the National Archives* 9 (Washington, D.C., 1977), 151–161.

12

Ayurvedic Medicine in Goa According to the European Sources in the Sixteenth and Seventeenth Centuries

John M. de Figueiredo

The purpose of this paper is to review a cross-cultural exchange of medical knowledge between India and Portugal which took place in the Portuguese territory of Goa in the sixteenth and seventeenth centuries. This exchange of knowledge represents the beginning of the professionalization of medicine in Goa and was a forerunner of the development of tropical medicine as a science in the Baconian sense (i.e., derived from experimentation rather than solely from empirical observation). This review will draw attention to a number of new European sources for the study of *Ayurveda* (medicine). Given the scarcity of Indian sources, these European sources help to extend our understanding of that cross-cultural exchange.

The origin of *Ayurveda* (medicine) was attributed by the ancient Hindus to Brahma, the source of truth and knowledge. *Ayurveda* was a chapter in the *Atharva-Veda* in which medicine had a magic character. The various illnesses were thought to be caused by devils and cured by magic formulae and procedures. Most probably the content of the medical courses taught in the Indian schools was obtained from the classic textbooks (*samhitas*) of Charaka, Suśruta and Vagbhāta.[1] However, the study of medicine was not restricted to schools alone. Medicine was regarded as a craft or skill transmitted from one generation of medical practitioners (*vaidyas*) to another as part of the family heritage. Thus, the *vaidya* would learn his trade at home, from his father, and, upon the latter's death, he would receive his "book of secrets" or collection of prescriptions, together with empirical knowledge acquired while collaborating in the practice of the elder's profession.

Before the conquest of Goa by the Portuguese in 1510, Goa had been

---

[1] Kaviraj Kunja Lal Bhishagratna, trans. and ed., *An English Translation of the Suśruta Samhita*, 3 vols. (Varanasi: Chowkhamba Sanskrit Series Office, 1963); Kaviraj Avinash Chandra Kaviratna, trans. and publ., *English Translation of Charaka Samhita*, 4 vols. (Calcutta: 200 Cornwallis Street, 1890–1925); Claus Vogel, ed., *Vagbhāta's Astanghrdaya Samhita* (Wiesbaden: F. Steiner, 1965).

ruled by several Hindu dynasties, including the Kadambas (eleventh to thirteenth centuries) and the emperors of Vijayanagara (fourteenth to fifteenth centuries). Surviving records of the practice of *Ayurveda* in Goa under these various ruling families are fragmentary. Those available suggest that many centuries before the arrival of the Portuguese in India, medicine was taught in Goa in institutions of higher learning called *agraharas* and in settlements of Brahmans called *brahmapuris*. The *agraharas* and the *brahmapuris* were centers for advanced study and teaching of all branches of knowledge, including medicine; they were communities of learned Brahmans whose scholarship attracted students from distant places and different religions.[2] For example, an inscription of 1099 states that while the Kadamba King Guhalladēva III reigned in Goa, the village of Priol (in Ponda, Goa) was honored by the presence of two Brahmans, Agemaryo and his son Nag Devaryo, who taught and practiced medicine there; and for this reason, the village acquired a certain fame.[3] Another inscription during the reign of Guhalla-dēva commemorates the establishment of a *brahmapuri* of twelve families of Brahmans, devoted to learning, in the neighborhood of Gopakapattana (Goa Velha in Tissuari, Goa) near the temple of Sarasvati.[4] The same record refers to an officer named Kelina who received the approval of Guhalla-dēva III to establish charitable institutions at the city of Gopaka (Goa Velha).[5] Queen Kamala-dēvi, the wife of the Kadamba King Permadi or Śivachitta (1147/48–1178), promoted the advancement of learning in the Kadamba kingdom of Goa by establishing a number of *agraharas*.[6] According to an old Goan tradition, Madhava Mantri, who held the post of Governor of Goa under the Emperor of Vijayanagara from 1379–80 until some time between 1387 and 1390, established an *agrahara* in Manchalapur, formed by the villages of Goali (Goalim) and Mauli (Moula) in Tissuari, Goa, and a *brahmapuri* in Velha Goa at the site of the Church of Trindade.[7]

The settlement of Arabs in Goa had started as early as the eighth century A.D. Over the centuries the Muslims gained political power and their influence culminated in 1489 with the annexation of Goa into the sultanate of Bijapur. From this sultanate, Goa was seized by the Portuguese in 1510. By the time of the annexation, Arabic medicine had evolved into an organized

[2] George M. Moraes, *The Kadamba Kula: A History of Ancient and Medieval Karnataka* (Bombay: B. X. Furtado & Sons, 1931), pp. 287–300.

[3] Santana inscription of Tribhuvanamalla (Guhalla-dēva III) (1099 A.D.). The original Sanskrit text of this inscription has perished. A Portuguese translation is in the Goa Historical Archives, Panjim, Goa, Monções do Reino, n. 97, p. 561. This translation was published by P. Pissurlencar, "Inscrições pré-portuguesas de Goa (Breves notas)," *O Oriente Português*, 1938, *22:* 400–403.

[4] Inscription of Tribhuvanamalla (Guhalla-dēva III) (1107 A.D.). Published by G. H. Khare, "Kadamba Tribhuvanamalla Kalina yeka tamrapatta," *Bharata Itihasa Samsodhaka Mandala Quarterly, 31* (4): 45. See also P. B. Desai, "Copper-plate grant of Kadamba Tribhuvanamalla, Saka 1028," *Epigraphia Indica*, 1953, *30:* 71–76.

[5] Khare, "Kadamba Tribhuvanamalla."

[6] J. F. Fleet, "Inscriptions relating to the Kadamba Kings of Goa," *J. Bombay Branch Roy. Asiatic Soc., 9:* 224, 295.

[7] Arquivo Nacional da Torre do Tombo, Lisbon, Portugal, Corpo Cronológico, Part III, Packet 11, n. 107.

body of knowledge, largely based on the writings of Avicenna and Averroes. It was the Arabs who "established the first apothecary shops, founded the earliest school of pharmacy and produced the first pharmacopoeia."[8] Like the records of *Ayurveda,* surviving records of the practice of Arabic medicine in Goa are fragmentary. It is known, however, that by the eleventh century A.D. there were charitable institutions in Goa, such as the mosque founded by Sadano, the Arab prime minister of the Kadamba King Jayakēśi I (1050–80), which dispensed medical attention and care for the poor, the infirm and the pilgrims.[9]

Hindu and Arab records of medical practice were largely lost during the Christianization of Goa in the sixteenth and seventeenth centuries and with one exception, the existing Indian sources are conspicuously silent on the exchange of medical knowledge between India and Portugal.[10] The single exception is the work, *Bhāva Prakāśa,* written in the sixteenth century, whose author, Bhāva Miśra, blames the Portuguese for the introduction of syphilis into India, and calls it *firangi roga,* the "European illness."[11] Since contemporary Indian sources are few, Portuguese and other European sources fill an important gap by documenting not only the prestige and sophistication of Ayurvedic physicians and their healing methods but also the ambivalence of the Portuguese rulers toward these native healers.

It is well known that European medicine was introduced in India by the Portuguese. The old city of Goa (Velha Goa) was one of the major centers of teaching and practice of European medicine in India during the sixteenth and seventeenth centuries.[12] Indian physicians, however, both Hindu and Muslim, continued to play an important role in the practice of medicine in Goa even after its conquest by the Portuguese in 1510. Soon after the conquest and for a considerable period of time thereafter, due to the scarcity of Portuguese physicians, the Portuguese noblemen and missionaries needing medical attention turned to the *vaidyas* (Hindu Ayurvedic physicians), usually Goans, speaking the native Goan language, Konkani, and to the *hakims* (Muslim physicians). In fact, the Goan *vaidyas* were preferred to the few European practitioners because of the *vaidyas'* more accurate knowledge of the treatment of tropical diseases. The Portuguese called these Hindu

[8] Philip K. Hitti, *The Arabs* (Chicago: Gateway, 1956), p. 141.

[9] Goa charter of Jayakēśi I (1053 A.D.). The original Sanskrit text of this charter was published by Pissurlencar, "Inscrições pré-portuguesas," pp. 387–91. A Portuguese translation is in the Goa Historical Archives, Panjim, Goa, Monções do Reino, n. 93, p. 1396. This translation was published by Filipe Neri Xavier, *Descripção do Coqueiro, Arequeira e Moedas da Goa* (Goa, 1870), pp. 61–65; and in the *Gabinete Litterario das Fontainhas,* 1: 16. See also Moraes, *Kadamba Kula,* pp. 394–400; M. G. Dikshit, "Panjim plates of Jayakēśi I," *Indica,* The Indian Historical Research Institute Silver Jubilee Commemoration Volume (Bombay, 1953), pp. 89–94.

[10] Joaquim Heliodoro da Cunha Rivara, *Ensaio Histórico da Língua Concani* (Nova Goa: Imprensa Nacional, 1858).

[11] Bhāva Miśra, *Bhāvaprakaśani Ghantuh,* ed. Brahma Śankara Miśra (Banaras: Jayakrishna Das Haridas Gupta, 1949), pp. 34–35.

[12] Alberto Carlos Germano da Silva Correia, *História do Ensino Médico na India Portuguesa* (Nova Goa: Imprensa Nacional, 1917).

physicians *panditos,* a word derived from the Sanskrit *pandit,* which means "scholar"; by derivation, Indian medicine (*Ayurveda*) was designated as *ciência de pandito,* the science of *panditos.*[13]

The contact between the two cultures resulted in some interchange between the two groups' physicians. For example, an epidemic said to be of cholera morbus took place in the city of Goa in 1543. It was so devastating that Governor Martim Afonso de Sousa convened a meeting of all physicians (both Indian and Portuguese) and ordered that an autopsy of one of the victims be performed. Gaspar Correia reports that, during this epidemic, the Goan *panditos* saved many patients by giving them native drugs and medicine.[14] In the famous Colégio de São Paulo, the Jesuit college in Goa and the first Catholic university in the East, an Indian physician, a Brahman, was treating patients in 1548.[15] Another *pandito* was the family physician to the Governor of Goa, António Moniz Barreto, in 1574.[16] Also it is recorded that in 1564, Goan Hindus, apparently attracted by Catholicism, or disillusioned by their own doctors, brought their sick children to the Colégio de São Paulo; Father Francisco de Sousa notes that these Hindus would promise St. Paul to devote their children to Christ if he would give them life and health.[17] According to Jan Huyghen van Linschoten, a Dutch voyager who lived in Goa from 1583–1588, the *panditos* were the physicians of the Portuguese Viceroy, the Archbishop, and of numerous members of the Portuguese aristocracy and clergy in Goa, who patronized them more frequently than they did their fellow Portuguese physicians.[18]

The fame of Goan *panditos* attracted the attention of Filippo Sassetti, an Italian traveler who lived in Goa from 1583–1588. In 1586, Sassetti wrote to Francesco I, the Grand Duke of Tuscany:

> At the end of last summer, I succeeded in collecting some seeds to send to Your Highness, but I might as well have done nothing at all, because the plants together with the medicine came to me more quickly than the seeds, which one can only hope to see bear fruit; however, such as they may be, I have protected them this spring from the corruption that the excessive humidity, with the great heat of this land, causes in all things. I have found here among these Gentiles [Hindus] other Hippocrates, Galens and Dioscorides who discuss this faculty with much thoroughness ["*gentilezza*"]; and concerning that doctor, Niganto,

---

[13] Sebastião Rodolfo Dalgado, "Pandito," in *Glossário Luso-Asiático* (Coimbra, Portugal: Imprensa da Universidade, 1919–1921), pp. 155–57.

[14] Gaspar Corrêa, *Lendas da Índia,* ed. Rodrigo José de Lima Felner, 4 vols. (Lisbon: Typ. da Academia real das sciencias, 1858–1866), 4: 288.

[15] Josef Wicki, ed., *Documenta Indica,* 15 vols. (Rome: Tipografia Pius X, 1948), 1: 254.

[16] Goa Historical Archives, Panjim, Goa, Livro do Pai dos Christãos p. 83; Joaquim Heliodoro da Cunha Rivara, ed., *Archivo Portuguez Oriental* (Nova Goa: Imprensa Nacional, 1857–76), Fascículo V, Parte II, n. 773, p. 899; António de Silva Rego, *Documentação para a História das Missões do Padroado Português no Oriente, India,* 12 vols. (Lisbon: Agencia Geral do Vltramar, 1958), 12: 273.

[17] Francisco de Sousa, *Oriente Conquistado a Jesus Christo pelos Padres da Companhia de Jesus da Província de Goa* (Lisbon: Oficina de V. Da Costa Deslandes, 1710), 2: 2.

[18] Arthur Coke Burnell and P. A. Tiele, eds., *The Voyage of John Huyghen Van Linschoten to the East Indies,* 2 vols. (London: Hakluyt Society, 1885), 1: 230.

who writes on this matter of simples as they require, I have translated from that Gentile [Hindu] physician's work that he writes about most of the things I send to Your Highness, and with this will be whatever else I have been able to discover about their quality and virtue. I do not doubt that if someone who had a good knowledge of the matter of simples, with good principles of philosophy and medicine, came here, he would greatly advance medicine. And an artist who knew well how to draw and paint plants might offer much delight with their representation; because the great degree of originality in this area is unimaginable . . .[19]

In this passage, Sassetti takes the title of the work he translated, *Nighantu,* to be the name of the author. While the translation itself has perished, the description given in the letter clearly shows that *Nighantu* was a dictionary of Ayurvedic terms, a compendium on medicinal plants and their therapeutic effects. His interest in Hindu medicine led Sassetti to study Sanskrit and to translate this work into Italian. It is obvious that such handbooks were commonly used in Goa in the sixteenth century by the Goan "Hippocrates, Galens and Dioscorides" (i.e., medical practitioners).

Sassetti's hope that "someone with a good knowledge of the matter of simples, with good principles of philosophy and medicine" would come to India had already been fulfilled in 1534, when the famous Portuguese physician Garcia d'Orta arrived in Goa and started his investigations of Indian medicine. Orta was physician to several successive viceroys and governors at Goa, where he conducted a lucrative practice until his death in 1568. By cooperating with Hindu and Muslim physicians, he collected from them a wealth of information on Indian drugs and healing methods. He tested these drugs and methods on his own patients and reported his findings in the classic *Colóquios dos simples e drogas he cousas medicinais da India,* published at Goa in 1563.[20]

Garcia d'Orta was relatively impartial in his description of Ayurvedic medicine. He wrote that the Indian physicians of his time "cure the dysentery well, can tell whether there is fever or not from the pulse, and whether it is weak or strong, and what is the humor that offends, whether it is blood or heat or phlegm, or melancholy; and they give a good remedy for obstruction."[21] He praised his Goan colleagues for the high degree of their scholarship and effectiveness, and called them "excellent scholars" and "great physicians, both Arabs and Gentiles [i.e., Hindus]."[22] He was also ready to

[19] Filippo Sassetti, *Lettere* (Milan: 1874), p. 342, dated 23 January 1586. The passage from Sassetti's letter was kindly translated by Mr. Lawrence Venuti, Department of English and Comparative Literature, Columbia University. See also Angelo Gubernatis, *Storia dei Viaggiatori Italiani nelle Indie Orientali* (Leghorn, 1875); Angelo Gubernatis, *Matériaux pour servir à l'histoire des études orientales en Italie* (Paris, 1876), p. 313.

[20] Garcia d'Orta, *Colóquios dos Simples e Drogas da Índia,* 2 vols. (Goa, 1563; Lisbon; Imprensa Nacional, 1895). See also Conde de Ficalho, *Garcia da Orta e o seu Tempo* (Lisbon, 1886); Silva Carvalho, *Garcia d'Orta* (Coimbra, Portugal; Imprensa da Universidade, 1934); Charles R. Boxer, *Two Pioneers of Tropical Medicine: Garcia d'Orta and Nicholas Monardes* (London: Hispanic and Luso-Brazilian Councils, 1963).

[21] D'Orta, *Colóquios dos Simples e Drogas da Índia,* 1: 151–52; 2: 137.

[22] *Ibid.,* 1: 151–52;.2: 136.

hand over his patients to his Indian colleagues when he was unable to cure the ailment: "When we find that our patients do not appreciate our gentle medicines, we deliver them over to Malabars [i.e., Indians] to be given their stronger medicines."[23] When asked if he had learned anything from them, he replied: "Yes, many things, but first I try the medicines of my doctors, and when I find them useless, I take them to the Brahmans of this land."[24] Unlike Sassetti, he was unaware of the written sources of Ayurvedic medicine (e.g., the writings of Charaka, Suśruta, and Vagbhāta) and as a result, he commented that Ayurvedic physicians never bled, could not interpret the color and the flow of urine, knew nothing of anatomy, and, in general, cured strictly "according to experience and custom."[25] Nevertheless, his admiration for Indian medicine led him to introduce into the *Colóquios* an Ayurvedic physician who came to his house to treat his servants: Orta has him describe the use of the Indian plant Triputa ("Turbid") to reduce inflammation.[26]

Not all of the Portuguese-trained physicians were as thorough and unbiased as Garcia d'Orta was, and some of them denounced the *panditos* as being merely the Asian counterparts of the Portuguese faith healers, or *curandeiros*. In 1618 the municipal council at Goa promulgated a decree that "no person of any religion, category, or nationality can exercise the medical or the surgical profession without passing a qualifying examination given by the *Físico-Mór* (chief physician) or the *Cirurgião-Mór* (chief surgeon), and they will be obliged to take out the certificate of examination, so that those found practicing without this certificate will be fined twenty *pardaos*."[27] The municipal council also decided that the number of Hindu physicians thus licensed to practice should be limited to thirty, and that the certificate of proficiency which they received from the chief physician or the chief surgeon would have to be endorsed by the *Câmara* (municipal council) as well, so as to ensure that the number of thirty should never be exceeded. A number of these *cartas de examinção*, dated 1613–1622, have already been published.[28] The areas of medicine covered and the types of examination are unknown. However, as Charles R. Boxer has noted, these certificates gave the holders unrestricted license to practice medicine in any part of the Portuguese empire, which seems to imply that European medicine rather than Ayurvedic was meant.[29] Obviously these restrictions placed on the practice of medicine by Hindu physicians were motivated by political considerations.

[23] *Ibid.*, 2: 15.
[24] *Ibid.*, 2: 139.
[25] *Ibid.*, 2: 137.
[26] *Ibid.*, 2: 332.
[27] "Postura dos Fizicos, Cirurgiões, Sangradores, e Boticários," dated Goa, 3 November 1618, in Viriato A. C. R. de Albuquerque, *O Senado de Goa, Memória Histórico-Arqueológica* (Nova Goa, 1909), pp. 423–25.
[28] John M. P. de Figueiredo, "The practice of Indian medicine in Goa during the Portuguese rule, 1519–1699," *Luso-Brazilian Review*, June 1967, *4*: 51–60.
[29] Charles R. Boxer, "Some remarks on the social and professional status of physicians and surgeons in the Iberian World, sixteenth-eighteenth centuries," *Revista de História* (São Paulo, Brazil), 1974, *100*: 197–215. Cf. p. 207.

Ayurvedic Medicine in Goa   231

In spite of these barriers, the practice of Ayurvedic medicine continued to flourish in Goa during the seventeenth century. We find the following reference to Hindu medicine in the book *Breve Relação das Escrituras dos Gentios da India Oriental,* found in the Jesuit archives in Goa and thought to have been written sometime in the seventeenth or eighteenth century:

> All the opinions of Pithagoras, and of other men who flourished among these Gentiles are treated in it [i.e., the book *Vaidakastra* or *Doctrine of Medicine*], and they teach them in school, from which many graduate, and they come to the lands of the Portuguese, and they are examined by the *Físico-Mór,* a man from Europe, whom I often heard stating that the said Brahmans called *Panditas* cure better than the European physicians who practice in India. I knew a friar of St. Augustine, of the Portuguese nation, who taught medicine in Portugal, and lectured on it for sixteen years, who after coming to India treated some Portuguese patients, all of whom passed away; seeing this happening, the said priest called the *Panditas* and asked them how they went about curing their patients; they replied that the properties and the composition of the drugs were well taught in the books; however, this was not sufficient to heal the patient unless his complexion, and the ruling humor, and the connection with the local climate were first known, and that they ordered their remedies according to these principles. Knowing they were giving him a good reason, the Priest took some information from them in order to succeed in curing, and according to this and his science he later made wonderful cures.[30]

In 1602, Father Sebastião Gonçalves, a Jesuit missionary, noted that the Goan *panditos* studied medicine in the *agraharas:* "They [Goan Hindus] also study medicine in their universities; they call their doctors *panditos,* and India is well provided with them. They cure with simple remedies, quite unlike our [i.e., European] physicians."[31] Johann Albrecht von Mandelslo lived in Goa in 1639 and refers to the Goan *panditos* as follows: "There are among them [Goan Hindus] some very able physicians, who are so highly respected at Goa, that they are permitted to have their umbrellas carried with them, which is a privilege allowed only persons of quality: nay the Portuguese, even the Viceroy himself and the Archbishop, make use of them, rather than of those of their own Nation. They never eat but with those of their own sect, though they were ready to starve."[32] In 1620 the patients of the Convent of Madre de Deus in Goa were treated by a *pandito* named Rama Boto.[33] In 1628, the Portuguese soldiers wanting to take sick leave from the Army presented letters written by the *panditos,* a situation which created some

---

[30] *Breve relação das escrituras dos gentios da India Oriental e dos seus costumes,* in Collecção de Notícias para a História e Geografia das Nações Ultramarinas, que vivem nos domínios portuguezes, ou lhe são vizinhas: publicação pela Academia Real das Sciencias (Lisbon: Typ. da Academia, 1812), pp. 52–53.

[31] Sebastião Gonçalves, *Primeira parte da História dos Religiosos da Companhia de Jesus,* ed. Josef Wicki, 3 vols. (Coimbra, Portugal: Atlantida, 1962), 3: 66–67.

[32] *The Voyages and Travels of J. Albert de Mandelslo in to the East Indies,* trans. John Davies, 3 vols. (London: J. Starkey and T. Basset, 1669), 2: 85.

[33] Goa Historical Archives, Panjim, Goa, Cartas Patentes e Alvarás, n. 7, p. 178v.

concern to the officials of the Army.[34] The prestige of these "Panditos, who understand the pulse well and are quite skilled in herbs" ("*Panditos, q'entendem bem do pulso, e são bons herbolarios*"), as Father Fernão de Queyroz refers to them,[35] seems to have reached a peak in 1644, when the Portuguese Viceroy of Goa, the Count of Aveiras, informed the King of Portugal that in the absence of Portuguese physicians, the important position of *Físico-Mór* (chief physician) in Goa was being exercised by a Goan.[36]

Hindu healing methods were so popular in Goa that, according to Jean Baptiste Tavernier, Portuguese physicians learned therapeutic procedures from Ayurvedic medicine and commonly used them in 1666 in Goan hospitals.[37] A *pandito* was called to cure the French physician Gabriel Dellon in 1674–75 when he failed in his suicide attempt while he was in prison by order of the Goan Inquisition.[38] Giovanni Francesco Gemelli Careri, an Italian physician and traveler, noted in his *Giro del mondo* that in 1695 the doctors from Portugal used to study the treatment of "cholera" and other tropical diseases with the *panditos* because European methods of diagnosis and treatment were unsuitable for this purpose:

> A man in India must be very regular in eating, or he will fall into some incurable distemper; or at least such as must be cured after the country fashion with fire; experience having shown that European medicines are of no use there... For this reason the physicians that go out of Portugal into those parts, must at first keep company with the Indian surgeons to be fit to practice; otherwise if they go about to cure those distempers, so far different from ours after the European manner, they might kill more than they might cure.[39]

It would appear that every attempt was made by the Portuguese physicians to learn the therapeutic "secrets" of their Hindu colleagues, as the following incident, witnessed by Niccolo Manucci in 1683 and described in his *Storia do Mogor*, illustrates: "There was a Hindu practitioner who knew a perfect cure for scrofula. The chief physician wanted to learn his secret, and sent the poor fellow to prison. He was informed that he would not recover his liberty until he had taught his secret to the physician. The timid Hindu resolved to die in prison rather than to divulge his secret."[40]

---

[34] Joaquim Heliodoro da Cunha Rivara, *Archivo Portuguez Oriental*, p. 1242.

[35] Fernão de Queyroz, *Conquista Temporal, e Espiritual de Ceylão*, ed. P. E. Pieris (Colombo, Ceylon: H. C. Cottle, Government Printer, 1916), p. 85; *The Temporal and Spiritual Conquest of Ceylon*, trans. Father S. G. Perera, 3 vols. (Colombo, Ceylon: A. C. Richards, 1930), 1: 110.

[36] Arquivo Histórico Ultramarino, Lisbon, Portugal, Caixa 17, Papeis avulsos relativos a India. The word "negro" in this letter refers, in all probability, to a native of Goa.

[37] Jean Baptiste Tavernier, *Travels in India*, trans. orig. French ed. 1676 by V. Ball, 2 vols. (London: Macmillan, 1889), 1: 198–99.

[38] Gabriel Dellon, *Relation de l'Inquisition de Goa* (Paris: Daniel Horthemels, 1699), p. 126. The first edition of this book was published in Leyden in 1687.

[39] *Giro del mondo del dottor D. Gio. Francesco Gemelli Careri* (Venice: P. G. Malachin, a spese de G. Maffei, 1719); *A Voyage Round the World by Dr. John Francis Gemelli Careri*, trans. from Italian (London: Churchill, 1732), part III, book I, chapter I, p. 188. See also, Surendra Nath Sen, *Indian Travels of Thevenot and Careri* (New Delhi: National Archives of India, 1949), pp. 161–62.

[40] Niccolo Manucci, *Storia do Mogor or Mogul India, 1653–1708*, trans. with intro. and notes by William Irvine, 4 vols. (London: J. Murray, 1907–08), 3: 136.

Their conversion to Catholicism in the seventeenth century precluded the Hindu physicians from practicing *Ayurveda*, seen as a religious belief. This barrier, compounded by the exodus of Goan Hindus to neighboring lands in order to escape from discrimination and conversion, eventually led to the downfall of *Ayurveda*. Unlike other Hindus, some *panditos* continued to practice their religion and their profession and remained influential in Goan society at least until the end of the century. This can be inferred from the complaints of the Portuguese people settled in Goa that the scarcity of Portuguese physicians forced them to use Indian physicians instead. In 1687 Christóvão de Sousa Coutinho wrote that "in Goa *panditos* and surgeons are not missing."[41] In 1688 the Portuguese Governor of India, Dom Rodrigo da Costa, wrote to Dom Pedro II, King of Portugal, requesting physicians because their lack led the residents of Goa to resort to "Gentile physicians called *Panditos* and some native surgeons who cured only with their little experience."[42] Dom Rodrigo da Costa died in 1691 "because there was no physician in Goa who could cure him."[43] Again in 1691, the residents of Goa submitted to Dom Pedro II a petition for physicians and surgeons because the death of the physician Simão de Azevedo and of the chief surgeon Francisco Antunes led them to resort to "Gentiles with some experience called *panditos* who cure in medicine."[44]

Other *panditos* emigrated from Goa to neighboring lands, such as Kerala, where they could safely pursue their trade. The language spoken by these emigrants and their descendants was Konkani, the language of Goa. This is seen in a testimonial written in Konkani, and signed by three Brahman doctors—Ranga Bhātta, Vinayaka Pandita, and Apu Bhātta—on 20 April 1675. These *panditos*, like other Konkani-speaking emigrants settled in Kerala, detested the Portuguese and were happy to see them attacked by the Dutch.[45]

Among the Dutch who distinguished themselves in the assaults on Portuguese Malabar was Henricus Van Rheede Van Draakenstein, Lord of Mijdrecht, and owner of a castle at Draakenstein near Utrecht. In 1669 Van Draakenstein was appointed Governor of Malabar, a post he accepted in 1671.[46]

Van Rheede wrote a monumental work on Indian botany, the *Hortus Indicus Malabaricus*, published in Amsterdam from 1678 to 1703 in twelve volumes. To produce this work, he had Indian doctors draw up lists of plants. He then employed people to collect specimens with their leaves and fruits, and assigned three painters to make accurate drawings of the samples. After

[41] Joaquim Heliodoro da Cunha Rivara, *O Chronista de Tissuary* (Nova Goa, 1866), 8: 204. Dated 8 December 1687.

[42] Goa Historical Archives, Panjim, Goa, Monções do Reino, n. 53, p. 326. Dated 31 October 1688.

[43] University of Coimbra Library, Coimbra, Portugal, Papéis vários, Códice 584, pp. 173–74.

[44] Goa Historical Archives, Panjim, Goa, Monções do Reino, n. 55B, p. 366. Dated 23 January 1691.

[45] Joaquim Heliodoro da Cunha Rivara, trans., and A. de Magalhães Basto, ed., *Viagem de Francisco Pyrard de Laval*, 2 vols. (Oporto: Livraria Civilização, 1944), 2: 33.

[46] "Van Draakenstein," *Biographie Universelle* (Paris: L. G. Michaud, 1824), 3: 456–61; P. J. Veth, "Hendrik Adriaan van Rheede tot Draakenstein," *Koloniaal Instituut te Amsterdam, Gids*, 1887, 3: 423–75, 4: 113–61.

this, the three Konkani-speaking doctors mentioned above personally supervised the completion of the manuscript for two years. In addition, they wrote out a testimonial in Konkani for Van Rheede giving their approval of the work and a verification of its authenticity which the latter reproduced in his book along with a Latin and Portuguese translation (see Appendix). In his association with the Konkani-speaking *panditos*, Van Rheede was impressed by their texts on medicine and botany in which the names of the specimens were followed by extensive and accurate descriptions of the morphology, properties, and therapeutic indication of each.[47]

As stated earlier, Ayurvedic medicine was seen by the Portuguese as a quasi-religious entity derived from Hinduism. Portuguese intolerance against religions other than Christianity attained its peak in the seventeenth century but gradually declined in the eighteenth and nineteenth centuries. This allowed many Ayurvedic physicians to return to Goa and safely continue their trade. Ayurvedic medicine survived in Goa partly as an added skill of Hindu physicians trained in Western medicine, partly as a trade of Hindu families devoted to faith healing, and partly as a "secret" kept as a privilege by both Hindus and Christians and transmitted verbally from one generation to the next.

APPENDIX

Testimonial of Three Hindu Physicians on Van Rheede's *Hortus Indicus Malabaricus* (20 April 1675)

Konkani Text:

Svasti śri Śalivahana śaka 1597 rakśasa Samvatśara chaitra bahulla 10. Kochi rajpattanim baisike Ramgabhātta tatha Vinayaka Pandita Apubhātta tega vaidya tanim Kochicha Cumdora Andorika Phanddre (Henricus Van Rheede) Teacha niropana hea Malabara deśantu aśile okshadhamatra vruksa, vali, zhaddakhandda ollaktelea manusyanka musaro devunu te te ganvantu pet Ttavuna, tim tim vokhadam annavuna tea tea zharhachem phala, phula, pana, bija, samasta tea tea rutukallavari sampaduna tim tim chitarilim. Tea uparanta amim amagelea vaidya granthacha Nighantta pramannim team team okshadhache gunna va anubhavana zo zo gunna amakam kallelo to va team okhadanchim nanvam palleunu aji doni varksam sakalli sanje amim lagi ravunu ho livru sambadana dila. Tem lattika ashi mhannushaka nazo ashi mhannu amim amanchi nisanni karnu dili. Tem satya mhannu manuchem zaido mhannu Nagara barpana hem baravunu dilam. Śri. Rangabhātta. Vinayaka Pandita. Apubhātta.

Translation:

Hail! The Śalivahan year 1597, Rakśasa Samvatśara, Chaitra Bahula 10. In the royal city of Cochin, by the orders of Henricus Van Rheede, Commander of Cochin, the

[47] M. J. Sinks, *Indisch Natuuronderzoek*, Kolonial Institut te Amsterdam, Mededeeling, n. 6, Afdeeling Handesmuseum, n. 2 (Amsterdam, 1915), pp. 14–24.

Ayurvedic Medicine in Goa   235

three doctors Ranga Bhātta, Vinayaka Pandita, and Apu Bhātta gave information on the medicinal trees, creepers, and plants of this Malabar country to men who could spot them, and sent the men to the right places and the proper medicines fetched, as well as got the specific flowers, leaves, and seeds collected and drawn at the right season. After this, for two years, we stayed near morning and evening and had this book completed, with information concerning the virtues of the several medicines, according to our doctors book, the *Nighantu,* or their qualities as known to us by experience, also examining the medicines' names. That this may not be said to be false, we gave our signature to it. We have also written this out in Nagari letters that it may be taken as true. Prosperity! Ranga Bhātta. Vinayaka Pandita. Apu Bhātta.

13

The Pre-History of Modern Science in Japan: The Importation of Western Science During the Tokugawa Period

Yabuuti Kiyosi

Introduction

THE manner in which Japan embarked on rapid development after the Meiji Restoration and followed swiftly in the steps of Europe and America was indeed sufficient to astonish the world. Under the Meiji government, with its slogan of "Civilization and Enlightenment", policies were adopted which took the West as their models, not only in political organization but in every branch of study, and all of them produced notable results. Again, the results produced by the uniting of the energies of the Japanese people for the purposes of "enriching the state and strengthening its armed forces" brought victory to Japan in the Sino-Japanese and Russo-Japanese wars, and scarcely forty years after the Restoration Japan had succeeded in advancing to the position of one of the most powerful states in the world. Many reasons, of course, may be put forward in explanation of this miracle. Among them, one of the most important was the fact that Japan rapidly adopted the science and technology of the West, digested them thoroughly, and employed them in the development of the state. It was in the middle of the 16th century that Japan first made contact with European civilization, but throughout the three centuries of the rule of the Tokugawa Shogunate a strict policy of national seclusion was enforced, and only a modicum of knowledge of European science was transmitted to Japan through the only trading-port, Nagasaki. There was thus a great difference, both in quality and quantity, in the importation and assimilation of western science before and after the Meiji Restoration. However, the reasons for Japan's success in rapidly assimilating western science after the Restoration can be traced far back into the Tokugawa period. In this short essay I propose to give an account of how western science was imported during the Tokugawa period, and to analyse its influence and significance in relation to Japan's success in modernization after the Restoration [1].

1. *On the Foundations of Chinese Civilization...*

The first intercourse with Europeans in the mid-16th century took place with the Portuguese and the Spaniards. These Europeans were called *Nambanjin* (Southern Barbarians) by the Japanese, and from them they gained a fragmentary knowledge of western science, particularly of astronomy and medicine [2]. Later, the Dutch took part in trading with Japan, but as a result of the policy for the suppression of Christianity the *Nambanjin* were forbidden to visit Japan, and with the strict enforcement of the policy of seclusion by the Tokugawa Shogunate in 1639 Nagasaki became the only trading-port, and the Dutch were the only Europeans who were allowed to enter it. Only a small number of Dutchmen were allowed to spend periods of residence on the small island of Dejima in Nagasaki, and to engage in a limited trade. The Dutch were called *Kômô-jin,* or "red-haired people", and the western civilization which they brought with them was also called *Kômô.* The Japanese were deeply interested in those aspects of western civilization which were of practical utility, that is, in the natural sciences, and the humanities remained almost unstudied throughout the three centuries of the Tokugawa regime. During the early years of the enforcement of the policy of seclusion the importation of western science took place through Nagasaki, and the principal agents of its introduction were the official interpreters (Tsûshi) who lived in Nagasaki and were in direct contact with the Dutch. It was almost impossible for non-authorized persons to study the Dutch language, and these interpreters were the sole expositors of western science. They had little understanding of western science, but some of them were able to acquire the respect of the world with the help of western medicine [3]. Edo, the centre of political power,

---

[1] The author has published an article entitled "Edo Jidai ni okeru Seiyô Kagaku no Yunyû" (The Importation of Western Science during the Tokugawa Period), *Kagakushi Kenkyû*, No. 43, pp. 1-4, 1957. The present essay is an expanded version of this article, incorporating the results of later study. On the subject of the concrete content of science and technology, chiefly in the Tokugawa period, the reader is referred to the volumes of the *Meiji-zen Nihon Kagakushi* (History of Japanese Science before the Meiji Restoration) published since the war by the Nihon Gakushi-in. Volumes have already been published dealing with the history of mathematics, the history of astronomy, the history of medicine, and many branches of technology. The publication of this series is still in progress.

[2] EBIZAWA YÛDÔ, *Namban Gakutô no Kenkyû* (A study of the *Namban* School of Japanese Sciences), 1958.

[3] For example, such figures as Yoshio Kôgyû, the propagator of the Yoshio school of surgery, and Narabayashi Chinzan of the Narabayashi school. On the importation of western medicine, chiefly through Nagasaki, see KOGA JÛJIRÔ, *Seiyô Ijutsu Denraishi* (A History of the Transmission of Western Medicine to Japan), 1942.

was situated at a great distance from Nagasaki, and at first it was in an unfavourable position in the matter of assimilating western science. The state of communications at this period made the journey to Nagasaki far from easy, and only a little knowledge was to be acquired from the visits of the Dutch who came to pay their respects to the Shogun once in every two years on the average [4]. These visiting Dutchmen comprised the head of the Dutch factory, doctors, and others, and they were obliged to answer all kind of questions by the Japanese in their eagerness to acquire knowledge. The doctors, in particular, being, as it were, in the position of representatives of European natural science, were questioned not only about medicine but about all the other branches of natural science. These questions, of course, were put to the Dutchmen through the interpreters (Tsûshi) who accompanied them. This state of affairs continued until the latter half of the 18th century, and for a long time the knowledge of Dutch among the residents of Edo, and, of course, their knowledge of western science, was much inferior to that of the Nagasaki interpreters. However, in the course of time, a slowly accumulated understanding of western civilization produced an increased interest in western civilization among many people. In particular, after positive studies of western science were given encouragement by the Shogun Yoshimune about the year 1720, favourable conditions were brought about for a more radical absorption of western science among the scholars of Edo. The translation of the *Kaitai Shinsho* [5] at Edo by a body of scholars centered on Maeno Ryôtaku and Sugita Gempaku was a concrete result of these more favourable conditions. Aoki Kon'yô was the first to learn Dutch in Edo, but his studies did not go beyond the collection of a few hundred Dutch words. His pupil Maeno Ryôtaku went to study at Nagasaki, where he deepened his knowledge of the Dutch language, and Sugita Gempaku's translation of the western work on anatomy was in large measure dependent on Maeno Ryôtaku's knowledge of Dutch. In his later years Sugita Gempaku wrote his famous *Rangaku Koto-hajime* [6] in which he described the introduction of western science to Edo and its later development. *Rangaku*, or "Dutch learning", the subject of this

---

[4] The Dutch visited Edo in this manner 116 times in the 218 years between 1633 and 1850. In 1790 the times appointed for these visits were changed, and thereafter one visit was made every five years. ITAZAWA TAKEO, *Nichi-ran Bunka Kôshô-shi no Kenkyû* (Studies in the History of Cultural Intercourse between Japan and Holland), 1959, pp. 80-128.

[5] The *Kaitai Shinsho* was a work on anatomy based on a Dutch translation of a work written in German by J.A. Kulmus. The translation was begun in 1771 and was published in 1774.

[6] OGATA TOMIO has written a detailed commentary on the *Rangaku Koto-hajime*. See the edition of the *Rangaku Koto-hajime* published in the Iwanami Bunko series. For an English translation of the *Rangaku Koto-hajime*, see E. MA, "The Impact of Western Medicine on Japan, Memoirs of a Pioneer, Sugita Gempaku, 1733-1817", in *Archives internationales d'histoire des sciences*, XIV, pp. 65-84, 253-273 (1961).

work, meant the study of western learning through the medium of imported books written in the Dutch language, and since, as we have already noted, Holland represented the West in Japan at this period, Dutch learning was regarded as identical with the learning of the West. Sugita Gempaku wished to deliver western learning, hitherto monopolized by the interpreters, into the hands of the scholars so that they might undertake more profund researches, and the word *Rangaku* was first used by Sugita Gempaku and his coadjutors with this purpose clearly in mind. The *Kaitai Shinsho* was published by this group of scholars in 1774, and represents a turning-point in the importation of western science during the Tokugawa period. After this date Dutch learning advanced rapidly.

The core of learning in Japan before the rise of Dutch learning was, of course, the learning of the Chinese. Generally speaking, Chinese learning was more concerned with man and human society than with the realm of Nature. This tradition of Chinese learning was represented by the name "Confucianism", and its ideals were those of "cultivating one's person and regulating one's house". Under the Sung dynasty the doctrines of Confucianism were provided with new philosophical foundations by Chu Hsi, and these Neo-Confucian doctrines, adopted as the state orthodoxy by the Tokugawa Shogunate, became guiding principles in the maintenance of the Tokugawa regime. Under the influence of internal political unity and economic prosperity the Shogunate's encouragement of the learning of the Neo-Confucian school brought about a rapid advance in studies of the learning of the Chinese, and this tendency first manifested itself during the Genroku period (1688-1703). At the same time, the influence of Chinese learning was confined to the humanities, but also affected the spheres of science and technology employed for practical purposes [7]. About this time Miyazaki Yasusada was active in the sphere of agricultural science, Kaibara Ekken and Inô Jakusui in the study of material medica, Shibukawa Harumi in the study of astronomy, Seki Takakazu in the study of mathematics, and Nagoya Gen'i and Gotô Konzan in the study of medicine. These scholars took the Chinese literature of science and technology as their point of departure, and made original contributions to its development. Again, in China new studies of the Confucian tradition were made by a number of scholars after the time of Chu Hsi, and the influence of these new schools of Confucianism extended to Japan. The Neo-Confucianism of Chu Hsi

[7] For a detailed account of the increased interest in applied science and technology in the middle Tokugawa period, see SUGIMOTO ISAO, *Kinsei Jitsugaku-shi Kenkyû* (Studies in the History of Realist Learning in the Tokugawa Period). 'Realism' (*jitsugaku*) was originally imported into Japan along with the philosophy of Chu Hsi, and the word was at first used only in the philosophical sense, but it later came to have the meaning of the morality used in maintaining society, and gradually came to be used of applied science and technology.

was the chief instrument of ideological control in the latter years of the Tokugawa Shogunate, but the Confucianism of Wang Yang-ming, a Chinese Confucian of the Ming dynasty, was perhaps more popular among scholars who were not employed by the Shogunate. Again, the *Kogaku,* or Ancient Learning, school of Confucianism arose in Japan, a parallel development to the appearance in China of the text-criticism school of the Ch'ing dynasty which opposed itself to the philosophical Confucianism of the Sung and Ming dynasties and returned to the tradition of the Han dynasty in making critical studies of the texts of the Confucian classics. As famous representatives of the Ancient Learning school of Confucianism, we may name Itô Jinsai (1627-1705), a private scholar resident in Kyôto, and Ogyû Sorai (1666-1728), a native of Edo. The members of the Ancient Learning school of Confucianism differed to some degree in their view of the world from the Confucians of the Sung and Ming dynasties. In contrast to the Neo-Confucians, who sought to explain the natural world and human society by means of the same principles, the members of the Ancient Learning school treated these two spheres separately, and provided an intellectual background favourable to empirical studies of Nature [8]. Such physicians as Nagoya Gen'i and Gotô Konzan adopted the same ideological position as the Ancient Learning school of Confucianism, rejecting metaphysical theory and advocating empiricism in medicine, and, like the Ancient Learning school, they advocated the study of the ancient texts, considering the study of the *Shang Han Lun,* an ancient medical work written under the Han dynasty, to be of the first importance [9]. Hereupon arose the new *Kohô-ha,* or Ancient Prescription school of medicine, a name employed in contradistinction to the existing tradition of medicine, styled the *Gosei-ha* or Latter Day school, which was based on the infinitely elaborate medical theory of the Chinese. This Ancient Prescription school flourished chiefly in Kyôto, the city which produced Itô Jinsai, but the influence of Ogyû Sorai was the source of an important stimulating effect on Sugita Gempaku's Dutch studies [10]. At this point we may give an account in concrete terms of some of the ways in which Chinese science exercised an influence in certain branches of science in Japan.

After the closure of the country by the Tokugawa Shogunate, the only foreigners who entered the port of Nagasaki were the Dutch and

---

[8] MARUYAMA MASAO has established this point by his studies of the Confucianism of Itô Jinsai and Ogyû Sorai in the first chapter of his *Nihon Seiji Shisô-shi Kenkyû* (Studies in the History of Political Thought in Japan), 1952.

[9] FUJIKAWA YÛ, *Nihon Igakushi* (History of Japanese Medicine), p. 29 and p. 342, 1941.

[10] SATÔ SHÔSUKE, *Yôgaku-shi Kenkyû Josetsu* (An Introduction to the Study of the History of Western Learning), 1964, pp. 43-70. The stimulus from the Confucianism of Ogyû Sorai which affected Sugita Gempaku came from Ogyû Sorai's writings on military science.

the Chinese. The Chinese, in particular, were allowed considerable freedom in visiting the port, and Chinese books were continually being imported along with other goods in the China trade. These included. besides technical and scientific works belonging to the Chinese tradition, Chinese translations of western scientific works and studies of them by Chinese scholars. In regard to the latter, it needs hardly be said that the importation of any books which mentioned Christianity, and in particular any which were inscribed with the name of the Jesuit missionary Matteo Ricci (Chinese name Li Ma-tou), was strictly forbidden. Other books, however, could be imported at will, and Chinese publications had an immediate effect on Japan, not only in the field of studies of the Chinese classics, but also in the newer departments of scholarship. In mathematics [11], the *Suan Fa T'ung Tsung*, a Chinese work on mathematics written under the Ming dynasty, was imported into Japan at the beginning of the Tokugawa period, and on the basis of it Yoshida Mitsuyoshi published his *Jingôki* in 1627. This became one of the "best sellers" of the time, and made a great contribution to the raising of the level of mathematical knowledge among the Japanese. In the Genroku period appeared Seki Takakazu, the greatest of the Japanese mathematicians, who took the Chinese *T'ien yüan shu* (a species of algebra) as his starting-point and produced studies of mathematics which were of outstanding quality. He is known as the Japanese Newton [12], and he succeeded in producing the formula for infinite expansion which is now arrived at by means of the infinitesimal calculus, and established the very original form of mathematics which was known to later ages as *Wasan*. In the field of astronomy, Shibukawa Harumi [13] produced a new astronomical table, and in 1684 a new calendar was brought into use with the support of the authority of the Shogunate. Up to that time the *Semmyô-reki* or *Hsüan Ming Li* (a Chinese calendar devised under the T'ang dynasty) had been in use in Japan for 800 years since the age of the rule of the Imperial court, and because of the decline of the court and continuous civil war it had been retained in use although errors had been discovered in it. Shibukawa Harumi took the *Shou Shih Li*, a calendar of the Yüan dynasty, as his starting-point, and, after making a few corrections in it, produced the calendar known as the *Jôkyô-reki*. At that time the Ch'ing dynasty in China had adopted an astronomical table based on western astronomy, but knowledge of this kind was not fully

---

[11] On the subject of the history of mathematics, in addition to the series of publications by the Nihon Gakushi-in issued in recent years, there is ENDÔ TOSHISADA, *Nihon Sûgakushi* (A History of Japanese Mathematics), Revised and Enlarged Edition, 1960.

[12] D. E. SMITH, *History of Mathematics*, 1925, 2nd volume, p. 701. For the life of Seki Takakazu there is HIRAYAMA AKIRA, *Seki Takakazu*, 1959.

[13] NISHIUCHI TADASHI, *Shibukawa Harumi no Kenkyû* (A Study of Shibukawa Harumi), 1940.

known when Shibukawa Harumi carried out his revision of the calendar. Shibukawa Harumi left many works, and his *Nihon Chôreki*, a study of the chronology in Japanese history, is worthy of notice as a clear manifestation of national consciousness among the Japanese. He believed that a specifically Japanese calendar existed in Japan before the importation of the Chinese calendar, and reconstructed the chronology of Japanese antiquity from the *Nihon Shoki*. Contentions such as these, which sought to establish the independent character of Japanese culture, were incorporated in the rise of systematic Shintoism in the Tokugawa period, and as the age proceeded they became the means of producing a powerful national consciousness. Not only was Shibukawa Harumi an eminent astronomer, but he was at the same time a pupil of Yamazaki Ansai, the founder of the Suika sect of Shintô. When the calendar was to be changed in the Jôkyô period (1684-1687) it had been proposed that the *Ta T'ung Li* of the Ming dynasty should be adopted, and the putting into use of Shibukawa Harumi's *Jôkyô-reki* is worthy of note as a reflection of nationalism in the sphere of science. It is needless to say that the development of nationalism among the Japanese during the Tokugawa period greatly facilitated the uniting of the energies of the Japanese people around the Emperor after the Meiji Restoration.

In the field of medicine, the new developments constituted by the Ancient Prescription school took place as described above. This Ancient Prescription school devoted all its attention to therapeutic practice in accordance with simple theory, and an especially notable scholar of this school was Yamawaki Tôyô of Kyôto (1705-1762). He learned medicine from Gotô Konzan, and in 1754 witnessed the dissection of the body of an executed criminal, publishing his work on the anatomy of the human body, entitled *Zôshi*, five years later on the basis of his experience. This was fifteen years before the commencement of Sugita Gempaku's translation of a western work on anatomy under the title of *Kaitai Shinsho*, and is a most noteworthy event in the history of Japanese medicine. The medicine of China (as well as that of Japan, which was a continuation of it) was principally concerned with therapeutics, and it neglected anatomy, the proper basis of medicine. Yamawaki Tôyô was in the tradition of the Ancient Prescription school, a school which revered empiricism, but he noticed that the Chinese anatomical drawings were extremely crude, and that they differed from reality. Further, he himself possessed Dutch books on anatomy, and he felt that he would like to witness an actual dissection of the human body. It happened that he had the opportunity of seeing the dissection of the body of an executed criminal, but the dissection was performed by the member of the outcaste class who discharged the office of executioner, and consequently Yamawaki Tôyô was unable to make a thorough examination of the interior of the human body with his own hands. Consequently, the *Zôshi* contained a number of errors, but it constituted an advance in Japanese medicine in that it dared to criticize the traditional medicine of China.

In the Genroku period notable advances were made in the study of all branches of Chinese learning in Japan, but at the same time Japanese scholars began to be critical of Chinese learning. As time went on it became known that there was a form of learning other than Chinese learning, particularly in the field of science, namely the western learning known through Holland, and later still it became known that the learning of the west was superior to that of the Chinese. Yoshimune, the eighth Shogun of the house of Tokugawa, gave encouragement to productive industry in an attempt to restore the finances of the Shogunate, and he took steps to promote studies which would be of practical utility. With the aim in mind of making an accurate calendar in order to bring prosperity to agriculture, the centre of the national economy, he gave encouragement to the studies of astronomy which were necessary for this undertaking. Nakane Genkei, who made use of this opportunity, proposed that the prohibition of the importation of certain books should be relaxed in order to provide an environment in which such studies could be carried on, and this proposal was adopted by Yoshimune. The prohibition of the importation of books was applied to Christian works and Chinese works treating of Christianity or inscribed with the name of Matteo Ricci, and because of this prohibition there were some who thought it prudent to refrain from reading works on western science written in classical Chinese. With the exception of the interpreters of Nagasaki the scholars of this period had practically no knowledge of Dutch, and Nakane Genkei performed his task by reading the works of Mei Wên-ting, a subject of the Ch'ing dynasty who had studied western astronomy, and he presented copies of these works to the Shogunate after adding annotations showing how the classical Chinese text should be construed in Japanese. However, Yoshimune realized the necessity of reading Dutch books for the purposes of practical studies, and he ordered a number of scholars to apply themselves to the study of Dutch. Aoki Kon'yô, whom we mentioned above, was one of these scholars. These developments paved the way for the translation of the *Kaitai Shinsho* and the rise of Dutch studies. On the subject of the reasons for the sudden development of Dutch studies before the translation of the *Kaitai Shinsho*, Sugita Gempaku said in his *Rangaku Koto-hajime* : "I think it probable that since Chinese studies are written in highly ornamental style they made only slow progress, while Dutch studies were lucid and made rapid progress because they were written in real and plain language. Or, the rapid progress in Dutch studies might have been due to the Chinese studies which had developed our minds before-hand." [14] Sugita Gempaku gives two

---

[14] The quotation is from the translation by E. MA, *op. cit.*, p. 264.

reasons—the fact that the Dutch books described reality in plain language which made understanding easy, and the fact that the academic level of the Japanese scholars who were in contact with Dutch learning had been raised by their studies of Chinese learning. When a civilization is to be accepted into a country, the assimilation of that civilization will not be accomplished smoothly unless the ground is prepared to rival the civilization already accepted in that country. The seed will not grow if the soil is untilled. Only after the traditional science of China had been fully digested and even been the object of criticism was it possible for Dutch learning to put down its roots. However, under the conditions of national seclusion enforced by the Tokugawa Shogunate the development of Dutch studies was by no means smooth, nor did it attain to any great heights. Its progress was extremely slow, and we shall now trace its course in the period following the publication of the *Kaitai Shinsho*.

2. *Dutch Learning after the* Kaitai Shinsho

After the translation of the *Kaitai Shinsho*, Ôtsuki Gentaku, a pupil of Sugita Gempaku, wrote a treatise on the Dutch language in 1781 which was published under the title of *Rangaku Kaitei*, and in this way the generality of scholars were provided for the first time with a textbook for learning the Dutch language. After learning a number of Dutch words in Edo, Ôtsuki Gentaku spent some time at Nagasaki, where he studied under Shitsuki Tadao, the author of the first grammar of Dutch written in Japanese and the most accomplished scholar among the Dutch interpreters. After the publication of the *Rangaku Kaitei* it became possible to study Dutch outside Nagasaki, but the linguistic abilities of the Nagasaki interpreters who were in contact with the Dutch retained their value throughout the Tokugawa period. Yoshio Kôgyû was one of the Nagasaki interpreters who assisted in the translation of the *Kaitai Shinsho*, and the first edition of that work included a preface written by him. Later, another interpreter, Baba Teiyû, made translations of Dutch documents, principally dealing with astronomy, under the direction of Takahashi Kageyasu, an official in charge of astronomy in the Shogun's administration. Again, the Dutch had a factory at Nagasaki in which Dutch physicians were resident, and Japanese students were going to Nagasaki to learn medicine and the Dutch language right up to the end of the Tokugawa period. Among these Dutch physicians there were scientists of the first rank such as von Siebold [15] who contributed

---

[15] For a detailed life of Siebold, see KURE SHÛZÔ, *Shiiboruto Sensei, sono Shôgai oyobi Gyôseki* (Dr. Siebold, His Life and Work), 1926.

to the raising of the level of scientific knowledge in Japan. Von Siebold was originally a German, but he had been sent out as a physician in the service of the Dutch East India Company for the special purpose of studying natural history in the Orient. He was resident at Nagasaki for six years from 1823, and in addition to training a large number of first-class students, he published a great volume of work on the flora and fauna of Japan after his return to Germany. Let us now give a simple account of studies of western science in a number of scientific fields in the period after the publication of the *Kaitai Shinsho*.

First, in the field of mathematics, very little influence was exercised by the West. The appearance of the great mathematician Seki Takakazu had established the *Wasan* school of mathematics in Japan, and the *Wasan* tradition was transmitted by specially designated "masters" in a manner similar to the traditions of the tea ceremony and flower-arrange-ment [16]. Seki Takakazu, as the founder of the school, became the first master of his tradition of learning, and a successor chosen from among his pupils succeeded to his knowledge of all the secrets of *Wasan* ma-thematics, thus becoming the second master in the tradition. In this way Seki Takakazu's tradition of mathematical knowledge was transmitted from generation to generation down to the end of the Tokugawa period. Mathematics became analogous to one of the polite arts. Old forms of notation were employed, and the objects of study remained almost un-changed. If we suppose that science is brought into being in response to the demands of society, we have some grounds for asserting that the society of the Tokugawa period had practically no need of the higher mathematics of the West.

The conditions for the development of astronomy were comparatively favourable. In the political thought of China, and in that of Japan which was a continuation of it, importance was attached to the making of an accurate calendar and the prediction of astronomical phenomena such as the eclipses of the sun and the moon. However, in such astronomical work as the prediction of eclipses, the correctness or otherwise of the calculations made could be confirmed by observation. Consequently, the supreme order given by the Tokugawa Shogunate to its officers in charge of astronomical matters was that, in the event of their predictions being proved inaccurate, they should prepare a new astronomical table and revise the existing calendar. These officers were continually worrying over changes in the calendar. In 1774 and 1792 the Nagasaki interpreter Motoki Ryôei translated Dutch books containing the heliocentric theory of Copernicus, but the professional astronomers in the service of the

---

[16] A detailed account of the croft-guild character of the *Wasan* tradition of mathe-matics is given in OGURA KINNOSUKE, *Nihon no Sûgaku* (Japanese Mathematics) in the Iwanami Shinsho series.

Shogunate had practically no interest in such theoretical questions. Again, between the years 1798 and 1802 Motoki's pupil, Shitsuki Tadao, produced a translated work in three books entitled *Rekishô Shinsho* in which he introduced Newton's theory of gravitation, but this work, too, failed to attract the attention of the Shogunate's astronomers. Like all officials in feudal society these astronomers were holders of hereditary offices, and not only were there mediocre personalities among their successors, but they were so content in their secure hereditary tenure that they showed practically no interest in the development of western astronomy, except insofar as it related directly to the calendar. The men who introduced the heliocentric theory to the world at large were scholars of the town such as Shiba Kôkan and Yamagata Bantô. Shiba Kôkan [17] received instruction from Ôtsuki Gentaku, although he acquired only a very slight knowledge of Dutch, and he heard of the heliocentric theory from Motoki Ryôei during a visit to Nagasaki. He was a very fine painter, and painted in oils in the western manner. He was also the first Japanese to make copper engravings, a technique which he learned from a Dutch book. Yamagata Bantô [18] was a personality who exhibited considerable financial acumen as a merchant of Ôsaka, and besides acquiring the traditional learning of the Confucians he read such books as the *Rekishô Shinsho* and also bought Dutch books and Dutch furniture. By the beginning of the 19th century, when these two scholars were active, a knowledge of western science had been widely diffused among the generality of the educated classes and the rich merchants. The merchants, who were chiefly concentrated in Ôsaka, saved the Shogunate and the feudal lords from financial crises with the aid of their ample economic resources, but, unlike the citizens of the cities of Renaissance Italy, they did not, in the end, attain the stature of political power-holders. Merchants who offended against the Shogunate's policies were at once sentenced as criminals and expropriated of their wealth, and, in some instances, were even put to death. No matter how enlightened an ideology they may have possessed, their ideology was subject to limitations in the nature of their situation, and they were never anything other than dependents of the feudal order.

However, since the time of the Shogun Yoshimune plans had been made for the compilation of a calendar by means of the methods of western astronomy, but it was during the Kansei period (1789-1800)

---

[17] The representative works of Shiba Kôkan are given in NAKAI SÔTARÔ, *Shiba Kôkan*, 1942. On the subject of his life and thought there is an article by KURODA GENJI, "Shiba Kôkan no Shizen Kagaku-teki Gyôseki ni tsuite" (On Shiba Kokan's Work in the Natural Sciences), in *Bijutsushi Kenkyû*, No. 6, 1952.

[18] There is a detailed biography by KAMEDA JIRÔ, *Yamagata Bantô*, 1943, but for a study which accords high value to his "realism", see MATSUURA OSAO, *Kinsei Nihon ni okeru Jitsugaku Shisô no Kenkyû* (A Study of Japanese Realist Thought in the Tokugawa Period), 1963.

that the plan was realized in a revision of the calendar. Among the pupils of Asada Gôryû, a private scholar of astronomy who lived in Ôsaka, there were two named Takahashi Yoshitoki and Hazama Shigetomi [19], and they were the principal persons involved in this revision of the calendar. Hazama Shigetomi, being a merchant of Ôsaka, had his services commissioned by the Shogunate, while Takahashi Yoshitoki was appointed to the office of astronomer in the service of the Shogunate. Neither of them could read Dutch, and they sought guidance in the *Li Hsiang K'ao Ch'eng*, a Chinese compilation based on western astronomy. Nevertheless, they obtained telescopes and other observational instruments from the Dutch, and adopted western methods of astronomical observation. At this time Iwabashi Zembei was well-known in Ôsaka as a maker of telescopes, and the making of scientific instruments in Japan had advanced to some degree. In his later years Takahashi Yoshitoki learned Dutch, and made an abstract of a Dutch translation of a treatise on astronomy by the French astronomer, Lalande. Again, Hazama Shigetomi gave assistance to the poor artisan Hashimoto Sôkichi, sending him to Edo to study, and causing him to learn Dutch. With the passage of time Hashimoto Sôkichi became the leading spirit in Dutch studies in the Kyôto-Ôsaka area. Inô Tadataka [20], the first scientific cartographer of Japan, was, in form at least, a pupil of Takahashi Kageyasu (son of Yoshitoki), an astronomer in the service of the Shogunate, but his studies were also much influenced by Takahashi Yoshitoki and Hazama Shigetomi. He went round the whole of Japan making his cartographical surveys, employing such western scientific instruments as the quadrant, the transit and the telescope.

Takahashi Kageyasu was not only an accomplished scholar, but also an able administrator. He was not satisfied with the mere discharge of his duties as an official astronomer, but undertook the direction of the work of Inô Tadataka, and in 1807 he set up a geographic bureau in the office of the official astronomers of the Shogunate and presided over the making of a map of the world. He also obtained permission to set up a bureau for the translation of Dutch books in the office of the official astronomers of the Shogunate, and he collected about him such students of Dutch as Baba Teiyû. It was he who took up the idea of translating into Japanese a Dutch version of the Encyclopedia written by the Frenchman Chomel, a work which he believed would be beneficial to Japanese industry. However, his ambition was cut short, for he was implicated in the famous Siebold incident, and died in prison in 1815. The Siebold incident is the name given to the discovery of maps of Japan

---

[19] WATANABE TOSHIO, *Hazama Shigetomi to sono Ikka* (Hazama Shigetomi and his Family), 1943, contains references to Asada Gôryû and Takahashi Yoshitoki.

[20] ÔTANI RYÔKICHI, *Inô Tadataka*, 1917. This work contains fairly detailed references to Takahashi Yoshitoki and Takahashi Kageyasu.

and other articles whose export was forbidden among the goods which Siebold was to take with him on leaving Japan, as a result of which Siebold and his pupils were subjected to investigation by the officers of the Shogunate, and Takahashi Kageyasu and Habu Genseki, who had given Siebold the forbidden articles, were arrested and died in prison. The effect of this incident was to put a stop to the spread of interest in the West in Japanese society. By this time, however, it was impossible to shake the conviction of the superiority of western science. Previous to this, in 1811, a Russian warship had visited the island of Hokkaidô and in 1822 an American vessel had entered the port of Uraga, near Edo. These incidents indicated that the Shogunate's policy of national seclusion was approaching a crisis. The Shogunate and the feudal lords devoted all their attention to the superior science and technology of the West, and in particular to the question of coastal defence with the help of western military technology. After the Siebold incident, the arrest in 1839 of a number of students of the Dutch language, which is known as the *Bansha no Goku* incident, represents a turning-point in the assimilation of western learning in Japan. The bureau for the translation of Dutch books, which had been established under the office of the official astronomers of the Shogunate (an office considered to be of great importance in traditional Chinese political theory) was removed from the control of the official astronomers in 1856 and established as an independent office with the new title of "Office for the Inspection of Foreign Books". The new office carried on its translation work over an even wider field than before. However, before this, in 1842, Shibukawa Kagesuke, a son of Takahashi Yoshitoki, who had succeeded to the headship of the house of Shibukawa and who was one of the official astronomers, carried out the final revision of the calendar under the Tokugawa Shogunate with the assistance of another official astronomer, Yamaji Kaikô. This calendar was worked out from an astronomical table based on Lalande's work on astronomy.

Let us next consider the field of medicine. During the Tokugawa period no licence was needed for the practice of medicine in Japan. For the intelligentsia, who could read with ease medical works written in classical Chinese, the practice of medicine was always at hand as a means of making a livelihood. What is more, men who had only the slightest knowledge of European medicine or pharmacy could make a living as doctors of the *Namban* or *Kômô* schools of medicine. Whereas the Chinese tradition of medicine was chiefly concerned with internal medicine, European medicine was first adopted for its surgical methods of treatment. European surgical appliances were used, and hemostasis practised. It need hardly be said that with the translation of the *Kaitai Shinsho* the assimilation of western medicine entered a new age. Western medicine, which had hitherto been known only in a fragmentary fashion, was learned in an increasingly coherent form as translations of Dutch medical works became available. In 1793, Ôtsuki Gentaku, the leading figure among the students of the Dutch language in Edo, translated a work by L. Heister which he published under the title of *Yôi Shinsho,* and by means of this translation a knowledge of western surgery was introduced into Japan for the first time. Again, in 1793 Uragawa Genzui, a pupil of Katsuragawa Hoshû, one of the collaborators in the translation of the *Kaitai Shinsho,* introduced western internal medicine by the publication of a work entitled *Seisetsu Naika Sen'yô.* This was a translation of a book by J. de Gorter. Similar translations of other works dealing with the various branches of medicine were published one after another [21]. However, the learning of medicine could not be dependent on books alone, and it was necessary to receive direct instruction from specialists. Von Siebold, whom we have mentioned above, performed great services in this regard. With the permission of the Shogunate he established a hospital at Nagasaki, and at the same time he gave instruction in medicine and natural history to students who had come to Nagasaki to pursue their studies. There were many fine scholars among his pupils, including some who wrote scientific papers in Dutch. One of them, Takano Chôei [22], translated a book on physiology, the first to be published in Japan. Later he was involved in the *Bansha no Goku* incident and fled from place to place pursued by the agents of the Shogunate, and finally, finding himself unable to escape from them, he committed suicide. While he was in hiding he translated a western work on military science, but under the conditions of crisis which prevailed in Japan in the second half of the 19th century it was impossible for scholars to devote themselves to the study of this subject alone. However, another of the pupils of Siebold, Itô Gemboku, established an educational institution in Edo, styled the Shôsendô, where he spent his whole life training the Dutch scholars of the last years of the Tokugawa period. About the same time Tsuboi Shindô, who had learned western medicine in Edo, became a famous figure as a scholar and teacher. One of his pupils, Ogata Kôan [23], built a school in Ôsaka named the Tekijuku and trained many students. Ogata Kôan was a famous physician, but besides the pupils who came to the Tekijuku to study western medicine there were many who gathered there with the intention of learning Dutch and gaining an understanding of western civilization in its wider aspects. Fukuzawa Yukichi, the great popular educator of the early Meiji period

[21] This work was followed by the *Ganka Shinsho* (1815) and *Baisô Shinsho* (1819) translated by Sugita Rikkei, and the *Karin Sankasho* (1823) translated by Aoji Rinsô. They treated the subjects of ophtalmology, syphilis and obstetrics respectively.

[22] TAKANO KÔUN, *Takano Chôei Den* (Biography of Takano Chôei), 1943.

[23] OGATA TOMIO, *Ogata Kôan Den* (Biography of Ogata Kôan), 1942.

who founded Keiô Gijuku University, was one of the pupils of the Tekijuku.

Let us add some remarks on translated books dealing with the various branches of science, omitting western military science, the study of which flourished in the last years of the Tokugawa Shogunate. The *Rigaku Teiyô*, produced in 1852 by Hirose Genkyô, a student of Dutch medicine, was a translation of a work by N. Isfording on physics, originally written as an introduction to the subject for the use of students of medicine [24]. This work deserves attention since it shows that the Japanese had attained a clear consciousness of the fact that western science was of a systematic character, built upon deep foundations, and that even in the case of such a subject as medicine, preparatory knowledge of various other subjects, such as physics, was necessary. Previous to this, in 1825, *Kikai Kanran*, physical learning in the broad sense, was written by Aoji Rinsô and later enlarged in 1851 by his pupil Kawamoto Kômin. In the field of chemistry, Udagawa Yôan wrote the *Seimi Kaisô*, the pioneer work in this branch of chemistry, in 1837. In 1833 he wrote the *Shokugaku Keigen*. In this work he broke free from the Chinese tradition of studies of materia medica, and showed forth a new way in the study of botany.

In this way progress was made in introducing and in studying western science, but, as we have noted above, the Siebold incident and the *Bansha no Goku* incident which followed it were the occasion of great changes in studies of Dutch learning. These changes are perhaps most clearly indicated by changes in the social classes from which the students of Dutch learning were drawn. The class origins of the students who received instruction from Siebold when he was in Japan between 1823 and 1829 were as follows.

Physicians	Members of the Military Class	Others	Unknown	Total
43	1	2	6	52

Practically all his students were physicians [25]. Among the 406 students who attended the Shôsendô founded in Edo in 1840 by Itô Gemboku, however, there were as many as 179 who were members of the military

---

[24] Since western learning was in general of a theoretical character, learning of this kind was designated by the word *kyûri*, a term employed by the Neo-Confucians. At the end of the Tokugawa period physical science in the western tradition was called *kyûrigaku*. YAJIMA SUKETOSHI, "Hompô ni okeru Shoki no Butsurigaku-teki Kenkyû" (Early Studies in Physical Science in Japan), in *Kagakushi Kenkyû*, No. 2, pp. 33-78, 1942 ; and YAJIMA SUKETOSHI, "Hompô ni okeru Kyûrigaku no Seiritsu" (The Rise of *Kyûrigaku* in Japan), in *Kagakushi Kenkyû*, No. 7, pp. 62-97, 1943 and No. 8, pp. 40-67, 1944.

[25] From data in KURE SHÛZÔ, *op. cit.*

class [26]. Many of them were members of the military class who had been sent to Edo from the domains of feudal lords in distant parts of the country. A similar state of affairs prevailed in Ogata Kôan's Tekijuku in Ôsaka. Although both Itô Gemboku and Ogata Kôan were physicians the instruction given in the schools which they established was centered on instruction in the Dutch language. Nagayo Sensai, who spent six years at the Tekijuku, studied under Pompe van Meerdervoort, and played an important part in the administration of medicine in the early Meiji period, speaks of the Tekijuku in his *Shôkô Shishi* in the following terms : "Although the Tekijuku was originally a school of physicians, in fact it was a place for the study of the reading of Dutch books. The students were not all physicians, but included students of military science, students of gunnery, students of materia medica and students of chemistry, for in these days all who aspired to Dutch learning entered the Tekijuku in order to prepare themselves." Fukuzawa Yukichi, whom we have mentioned above, was a member of the military class who belonged to the Nakatsu fief, and although he studied at the Tekijuku he learned nothing at all about medicine.

The aspiration to study Dutch learning on the part of many members of the military class in the last years of the Tokugawa Shogunate was a most natural development, since the military class had long performed ruling-class functions in the administration of the Shogunate at Edo and they were the class which felt most keenly the need to acquire western learning, as a means of saving the situation in that time of national crisis. The fact also provides a key to the understanding of the reasons for the implementation of a strenuous policy for importing western learning after the Meiji Restoration. One of the reasons for the fact that the Meiji Restoration is not to be described as a "revolution", although it caused a great change in Japan, is the fact that no radical change was made in the ruling class as a result of the Restoration. After the Restoration the Shogun and the feudal lords were deprived of their political power, but in their place the military class, including many members of the lower ranks of the military class, took an active role as the backbone of the administrative apparatus of the Meiji government. These members of the military class had had personal experience of the superiority of western science and technology in the times of crisis in the last years of the Tokugawa regime. If we ignore this fact we shall be unable to explain the smooth development of western science and technology in Japan after the Meiji Restoration.

[26] HARA HEIZÔ, "Rangaku Hattatsushi Josetsu" (An Introduction to the History of the Development of Dutch Learning), in *Rekishi Kyôiku*, Vol. 11, No. 3.

3. *Western Learning under the Shogunate and the Feudal Lords*

After 1840 a marked change took place in studies of western learning. The visits of Russian and American vessels shook the foundations of the power of the Tokugawa Shogunate, hitherto supported by the policy of national seclusion. The news that the mighty Ch'ing dynasty in China had been defeated by a small force of the British Navy in the Opium War filled the Shogunate and the feudal lords with fear of the West. As well as ordering the feudal lords to take the most stringent measures for coastal defence, the Shogunate also appointed certain of its retainers to study western methods of gunnery. It was on the instructions of the Shogunate that in 1850 the Commissioner at Shimoda, Egawa Tarô-zaemon, built a reverberatory furnace at Nirayama in the province of Izu with the help of which cannon were cast. Gun emplacements were built at a number of places in the vicinity of Edo. But a more important incident took place in 1853, when Perry entered the port of Uraga, in command of an American naval force. In contrast to previous visits by foreign vessels, Perry arrived in Japan determined to cause the Japanese to open the country and to use force if it should be required. When Perry re-visited Japan in the following year, the Shogunate was no longer able to resist his demands, and a Treaty of Friendship was signed between Japan and the United States of America. Once a treaty had been signed with one country, it was impossible to refuse similar requests for treaties on the part of other nations, and accordingly Japan entered into diplomatic relations with Russia, Britain, Holland and others, and a number of ports were declared open to trade. In this way the Shogunate's policy of national seclusion was completely overthrown. Among the members of the military class in the service of the feudal lords, however, there was an increasing number who steadfastly maintained that the barbarians should be expelled from Japan, and who opposed themselves to the Shogunate in the name of the Imperial house. Ironically enough, however, the traditional arms in use in Japan were quite unequal to the purpose of expelling the barbarians, and this policy could not be put into effect except with the help of studies of western military science and by means of artillery and other western fire-arms. Studies of western learning centered on military technology were pressed forward, and in addition to books written in Dutch, books in English, French and German came to be read, while the word *yôgaku* (western learning) took the place of *Rangaku* (Dutch learning) as the term used to denote the learning of the west.

Studies of western learning, conducted under the Shogunate, began with the bureau for the translation of Dutch books in the office of the astronomers of the Shogunate. The translation of Chomel's Encyclopedia which had been originally planned by this bureau was held up by the death in prison of Takahashi Kageyasu, but was completed in 1845. It was published with the title of *Kôsei Shimpen* [27]. In addition to this work a number of other works were produced by the bureau, such as the *Yôchishi* of Aoji Rinsô and the *Kaijô Hôjutsu Zensho* translated by Sugita Rikkei and Sugita Seikei. After the conclusion of the Treaty of Friendship between Japan and America, intercourse with foreigners became more frequent, and it was planned to establish an institution for the study of western learning in which retainers of the Shogunate who had acquired knowledge of language would be trained, and in which studies of western learning would be carried on, chiefly in the field of military technology. In 1854, however, the bureau for the translation of Dutch books in the office of the astronomers of the Shogunate was established as a separate institution, with the title of Office for the Inspection of Foreign Books. The aims of this institution were to translate foreign books dealing with gunnery, the building of gun emplacements, fortifications, the building and navigation of vessels of war, navigation and surveying, naval and military training, mechanics, geography and natural productions, and the condition of foreign countries, while at the same time instruction was to be given in foreign languages. Astronomical works of no immediate importance were regarded as being of a secondary nature. The title of the Office was changed in 1862 and again in the following year, and it extended its instruction on western learning to an even wider field. In the first years of the Meiji period this institution was absorbed into the newly established Tokyo Imperial University, and several of its instructors played leading roles in the cultural activities of the Meiji period.

While the Office for the Inspection of Foreign Books and its successors were concerned with the study of western learning through the medium of linguistic studies and books, the medical training given at naval establishments at Nagasaki with the assistance of the Dutch produced a greater effect from the point of view of practical utility [28]. Stimulated by the arrival of Perry, the Shogunate applied to the Dutch for the purchase of a steam-ship, as a result of which they were presented with a steam vessel by the Dutch in 1855, and practical training in navigation commenced with the assistance of Dutch naval personnel. The Shogunate sent 37 of its retainers to Nagasaki as students, headed by Katsu Rintarô, who later represented the Shogunate on the occasion of the surrender of Edo castle, and with the addition of members of the

---

[27] In ITAZAWA TAKEO, *Nichi-ran Bunka Kôshô-shi no Kenkyû* (Studies in the History of Intercourse between Japan and Holland), pp. 264-297, there is printed a piece entitled *Kôsei Shimpen Yakujutsu-kô* (An Inquiry into the Translation of the *Kôsei Shimpen*). Sixty-eight fascicules of the original translation have been preserved.
[28] For an outline of these, see NUMATA JIRÔ, *Yôgaku Denrai no Rekishi* (The History of the Transmission of Western Learning), 1960, pp. 168-172.

military class sent from the fiefs of the feudal lords the total number
of students reached 129. The course of instruction lasted four years,
and was fairly successful in terms of results. When a Japanese mission
was sent to the United States by the Shogunate in 1860 to ratify the
Treaty of Friendship, the party of representatives sailed in a vessel
of the American navy, but the American vessel was preceded by the
Kanrin Maru, navigated under the command of Katsu Rintarô. The
Kanrin Maru was a newly-built Dutch ship which had arrived at Nagasaki in 1857, and which had been purchased by the Shogunate.

Alongside the activities of the naval training establishments at
Nagasaki, Pompe van Meerdervoort, who arrived in Japan in 1857
along with service personnel sent from Holland, stayed for five years
in Nagasaki before returning home in 1862 and made a lasting contribution to medical education in Japan. It was he who first established the
modern medicine of the West in a systematic manner, and he taught the
theory and practice of medicine in a most clear and systematic fashion,
from the basic sciences of physics and chemistry to basic medicine and
clinical medicine. In his school were trained the representative figures
in the medicine of the early Meiji period, men such as Matsumoto Ryôjun, Ishiguro Chûtoku and Hashimoto Kôjô, the founders of military
medicine in the early Meiji period, Shiba Ryôkai, a scholar in the tradition of Tokyo Imperial University, Satô Shôchû, the founder of Jun-
tendô Hospital, and Nagayo Sensai, the first head of the Public Health
Bureau under the Meiji government. It is said that when Pompe van
Meerdervoort first came into contact with these students, he found that
these chosen members of the Japanese aristocracy of talent were almost
totally devoid of knowledge and had failed to acquire the most elementary concepts from their reading of the Dutch medical literature [29]. It
need hardly be said that it was only with the aid of Pompe van Meerdervoort's erudition and exertions that the splendid results of this school
of medicine were obtained. However, when we view the state of the
naval training establishments at this time and the work of Pompe van
Meerdervoort in medical education, we are left with the impression that
by this time western science and technology were no longer considered
miraculous. It was, of course, impossible to build up in Japan the modern
science established by Galileo and Newton. However, it is a much easier
undertaking to imitate something which has been completed and to
follow in the footsteps of the advanced countries of the West than to
create the whole from the beginning. The rapid development which took
place in Japan after the Meiji Restoration was carried out under the easy
conditions of Japan's role as an imitator. However, it was necessary for

---

[29] In ITAZAWA TAKEO, op. cit., p. 54, extracts are given from writings produced
by Pompe van Meerdervoort himself.

the state to implement forceful policies in order to bring about a positive assimilation of science and technology. It may be legitimate for us to take the view that the military class, who had given Japan three hundred years of almost complete peace and unity during the Tokugawa period, used their excellent political abilities in building anew the prosperity of the Meiji period.

The policies pursued by the Shogunate after the opening of the ports were linked by their results with the policies of the Meiji government. While western science and technology were being assimilated at home in a most positive manner, students were being sent abroad to study, even during the period of the Shogunate. The dispatch of the Kanrin Maru enabled many of the military class to see the actual situation of America. In 1862 the Shogunate sent a mission to Europe for the first time. Fukuzawa Yukichi, who was a member of both these missions, published his *Seiyô Jijô* (The Situation of the West) on his return to Japan. At the end of 1862 the first students sent abroad were dispatched by the Shogunate to Holland aboard a Dutch merchant ship. This first group of students were sent to learn navigation and gunnery, but one of them was Nishi Amane, the man who first used the word *tetsugaku* (philosophy) in Japan, and he studied law in Holland. Several more groups of students were sent abroad before the fall of the Shogunate. A similar state of affairs prevailed in the domains of the feudal lords. For example, a party of students including Itô Hirobumi and Inoue Kaoru went to study in England in 1866 without the permission of the Shogunate. They came from the Môri fief, a feudal domain which was strongly opposed to the Shogunate. Itô and Inoue later became politicians who bore the chief burdens of responsibility in the Meiji government. Itô Hirobumi was several times Prime Minister, and drafted the Meiji Constitution. Outstanding figures were also sent to England from the Satsuma fief. These two fiefs were supporters of the policy of expelling the barbarians, and they attacked a British warship, but in return were fiercely attacked by the British warship. However, England's skilled diplomatists looked beyond the impending fall of the Shogunate and they gave assistance to the Satsuma and Nagato fiefs. In the event, the Meiji government was dominated by members of the military class from the Satsuma and Nagato fiefs and we may take the view that the amicable relations between England and Japan which characterized the Meiji period were brought into being during the last years of the Tokugawa Shogunate.

Let us now give a simple account of studies of western learning carried on in the domains of the feudal lords [30]. In the Nagato fief the granting of official recognition to studies of Dutch medicine in 1839

[30] See NUMATA JIRÔ, *op. cit.*, pp. 173-189.

marks the beginning of the adoption of Dutch learning. However, because of the necessity of improving coastal defence which had resulted from Perry's visit, new teaching facilities were established in 1855 with the aid of which western military science was studied in addition to western medicine, and in 1857 an enlargement of the *Meirinkan*, the chief educational institution in the fief, caused studies of western military science to flourish even more. The studies of western learning carried on in the domains of Nagato's partner, Satsuma, were of an even more practical nature. In the Satsuma fief the building of sailing ships of the western type had been carried on for some time, the first ship being completed in 1854. Satsuma also planned to build a steam-ship, although the attempt was not successful, and between 1860 and 1867 the fief purchased no less than 17 foreign vessels. Some of these vessels were used as warships, and the remainder employed mainly in carrying on trade with other fiefs. In 1852 work was started on the construction of a reverberatory furnace. In due course this was used in casting cannon, and orders for these cannon were received from other fiefs. While devoting efforts to improvements in military technology, the rulers of the Satsuma fief did not neglect to make use of western learning in causing industry to flourish in the territory over which they had control. In the institution called the *Shûseikan*, set on foot in 1857, not only were cannon cast, but glass and electrical machines were also manufactured, and it is said that the workers who were employed there numbered more than 1,200. The making of cut glass, for which Satsuma is still famous, began at this period. The place in the island of Kyûshû which came second to Satsuma in studies of western learning was the Nabeshima fief in the Saga area. About 1834 the rulers of the Nabeshima fief had sent some of their retainers to Nagasaki to learn gunnery from the famous gunner Takashima Shûhan, and since that time studies of military technology flourished in that fief. Among the fiefs of the feudal lords the Nabeshima fief sent the greatest number of students to the naval training establishments at Nagasaki, the total number amounting to no less than 48, and it is also said that the level attained by these students was of the highest. The fief went on to build a reverberatory furnace, and embarked on the casting of cannon. It need hardly be said that it was also very positive in the assimilation of western medicine. The Echizen fief and the Matsushiro fief may also be mentioned as notable for their studies of western learning. In the case of the Matsushiro fief, the lord of the fief was appointed to the supreme council of the Shogunate in 1841, and with his experience of the burden of responsibility for coastal defence he devoted great efforts to the sphere of military technology. We may think it natural that Sakuma Shôzan, the great student of western learning in the last years of the Tokugawa regime, should have come from this fief. His main efforts were directed to the development of new industries with the help of Chomel's Encyclopedia. He was the possessor of a very enlightened ideology, but in 1864 he was assassinated at the hands of the party favouring the expulsion of the barbarians.

4. *Conclusion*

As we have said above, the importation of western learning during the Tokugawa period was made possible only by the prior assimilation of Chinese science. In general the learning of China provided the guiding principles for the maintenance of the feudal order, and it penetrated deeply into the minds of the intellectual class, drawn chiefly from among the military class (the ruling class throughout the Tokugawa period) and the merchants. Classical Chinese performed a function similar to that of Latin in mediaeval Europe, and it was common for scholarly works to be written in this medium. This applied also to the translations made of western scientific books written in Dutch. The rise of the so-called "nationalist scholarship" of Kamo no Mabuchi, Motoori Norinaga, and their successors did something to direct the attention of the Japanese to the anomalous character of this situation, and their studies of Japan's national literature combined with the religious traditions of Shintô to have a powerful effect on the development of Japanese nationalism. However, these nationalist scholars attempted to destroy the tradition of reverence for China, but in regard to the learning of the west the attitude which they displayed was, if anything, a liberal one.

A new age in the development of studies of western learning in the Tokugawa period was ushered in by the translation of the *Kaitai Shinsho*. The year 1840 marks another great turning-point, and after this time the stage is set for the Meiji Restoration. We can discern a change in the class origins of students of western learning in the periods marked by these two turning-points. In the words of Fukuzawa Yukichi, "The studies of Dutch learning carried on in the eighty or ninety years from the Hôreki and Meiwa periods (i.e., since 1751) were carried on by physicians, but the studies of Dutch learning carried on since the Kôka and Kaei periods (i.e., since 1844) have been carried on by members of the military class." Thus the military class, who were the ruling class in the Tokugawa period and who brought about the Meiji Restoration and held the real power as members of the Meiji government, also played the leading role in the assimilation of western learning. This may provide us with a key to the explanation of the success of the Meiji government's policy for rapid Europeanization.

There is, however, some dispute as to whether studies of western learning in the Tokugawa period tended to push the feudal order towards its destruction or not. While such writers as Itô Tasaburô and

Numata Jirô [31] emphasize the contributions which western learning made to the strengthening of the Tokugawa feudal regime, others, such as Takahashi Shin'ichi [32] and Tôyama Shigeki [33], point out that students of western learning possessed the functions of critics and conquerors of feudalism, although they admit that they were brought into a condition of dependence on the feudal order. That is to say, the latter writers are of the opinion that western learning was anti-feudal or critical of feudalism. Further, scholars of this school of thought have maintained that this anti-feudal character of western learning was broken and suppressed by two incidents—the Siebold incident and the *Bansha no Goku* incident—and that thereafter Japan went down the steep slope which led to the absolutism of the Meiji government. Criticizing these two views, Satô Shôsuke [34] has produced a refutation of the theory of Numata Jirô in the following terms. Whereas Numata Jirô considers western learning to have been "the system of western European natural science grafted on to the Confucian view of natural science [35]", Satô Shôsuke takes up the thought of Ogyû Sorai and of Sugita Gempaku, who was influenced by Ogyû Sorai, and points out that the beginnings of modern technical and scientific thought, differing from the Confucian view of natural science, are to be discerned therein. Again, in opposition to Numata Jirô, who holds that the rulers of the Tokugawa Shogunate took up western learning in order to preserve feudalism, Satô Shôsuke maintains that the encouragement of western learning was carried out against the background of an acknowledgement of the superiority of western learning which extended throughout the whole of Japanese society, and that it is wrong to attach exclusive importance to the encouragement of western learning by the ruling class.

On the other hand, Takahashi Shin'ichi, whose views differ from those of Numata Jirô, holds that the group of students of western learning who gathered around Watanabe Kazan in the Tempô period (1830-1845) constituted the first free academic body in Japan, and maintains that the modern national consciousness brought into being through this body, as well as the beginnings of scientific thought which developed from the basis of this national consciousness, was pitilessly destroyed in

---

[31] NUMATA JIRÔ has written *Bakamatsu Yôgakushi* (A History of Western Learning in the Last Years of the Tokugawa Shogunate), 2nd ed., 1942, and *Yôgaku Denrai no Rekishi* (The History of the Transmission of Western Learning), 1960.

[32] TAKAHASHI SHIN'ICHI, *Yôgakuron* (On Western Learning), 1939.

[33] See the section entitled *Sonnô Jôi Shisô to Nashionarizumu* (The Ideology of the Movement for Revering the Emperor and Expelling the Barbarians and its Relation to Japanese Nationalism) in TÔYAMA SHIGEKI, *Sonjô Shisô to Zettaishugi* (The Ideology of the Movement for Revering the Emperor and Expelling the Barbarians and its Relation to Absolutism), 1948.

[34] SATÔ SHÔSUKE, *op. cit.*

[35] NUMATA JIRÔ, *Bakumatsu Yôgakushi* (A History of Western Learning in the Last Years of the Tokugawa Shogunate), p. 27, 1952.

the period following the *Bansha no Goku* incident, and that western learning was then directed into channels in which it would serve as technology and knowledge to be used in a revisionist reorganization of feudalism into absolutism. Again, Tôyama Shigeki holds that although the students of western learning were the only potential source of a modern national consciousness in the late Tokugawa period, they were subjected to unfeeling suppression at the hands of feudal authority after the *Bansha no Goku* incident, and that after that time the anti-feudal view of the world which characterized western learning was emasculated and students of western learning were obliged to be content to occupy the position of lackeys serving the maintenance of the feudal order with studies of a technological character in the fields of armaments production and the development of industry. As opposed to the views of these two scholars, Satô Shôsuke has carried out a detailed examination of the *Bansha no Goku* incident, which he conceives to have consisted in a struggle between the conservative and progressive elements in the bureaucracy of the Shogunate, and has maintained that the policies advocated by Watanabe Kazan and his associates were actually put into effect as the policies of the Shogunate. He is thus totally opposed to the view espoused by Takahashi and Toyama—that the spirit of western learning was broken and suppressed.

The history which the present writer has traced in the preceding pages inclines him to agree with the opinion of Satô. While we agree that reactionary policies were forcefully carried out by the Shogunate, as in the case of the *Bansha no Goku* incident, enlightened policies such as the setting up of naval training establishments at Nagasaki and the dispatch of students overseas were adopted by the Shogunate. Further, the effecting of these policies was greatly stimulated by the opening of Japan which resulted from Perry's visit. The policy of national seclusion which had been the support of the feudal order headed by the Tokugawa Shogunate had disintegrated altogether, and the times were moving swiftly in the direction of the Meiji Restoration. It need hardly be said that the setting up of naval training establishments and the dispatch of students overseas were carried out with the idea that they would serve to maintain the feudal order headed by the Shogunate in its time of crisis. However, there is no doubt that among the progressive bureaucrats of the Shogunate there were some who had gained the impression that the maintenance of the Shogunate had now been rendered impossible by the collapse of the policy of national seclusion. Had it not been so, it would scarcely have been possible for such events as the surrender of Edo castle and the restoration of political authority to the Imperial house to have occurred in conditions which were more or less those of peace.

It need not be said that the acceptance of a foreign civilization requires that the civilization of the receiving country should have attained some degree of advance. In this matter Japan had Chinese science as a basis for the assimilation of western learning during the Tokugawa period. However, if an even more foreign civilization is to be assimilated, this civilization will scarcely take root unless its assimilation is pushed forward under considerable pressure. The western learning assimilated during the Tokugawa period under the political conditions of national seclusion was extremely poor in content, in spite of the extraordinary efforts made by the Japanese. This fact is made known to us in a most striking way by the words of Pompe van Meerdervoort which we have quoted above. However, a change came about in this situation in the last years of the Shogunate, when the country was opened and the learning of the west freely admitted. For the Japanese it was by no means difficult to accept western science and technology and to follow in the footsteps of the advanced nations. The heart of the matter was the question of the leaders needed to push forward the policy for an intensive assimilation of the new science and technology. As we have already noted several times, the military class of the late Tokugawa period, who were acquainted with the superiority of western science and technology, remained in their ruling-class position after the Meiji Restoration, and were thus able to carry out their plans for "Civilization and Enlightenment" and for "Enriching the State and Strengthening its Armed Forces". Although feudalism disappeared as a result of the Meiji Restoration, may we not be permitted to say that the political order in which the Shogun was regarded as absolute had merely been replaced by the deification of the Emperor? May we not be permitted to say that the new rulers of Japan succeeded in driving the energies of the nation in the direction of Europeanization by methods which scarcely differed at all from those of the feudal period?

14

Chinese Astronomy and the Jesuit Mission:
An Encounter of Cultures

Joseph Needham

IN the history of intercourse between civilizations there seems no parallel to the arrival in China in the 17th century of a group of Europeans so inspired by religious fervour as were the Jesuits, and at the same time so expert in most of those sciences which had developed with the Renaissance and the rise of capitalism. The year 1600 is a turning-point, for after that time there ceases to be any essential distinction between world science and specifically Chinese science. But the part which the Jesuits played in Chinese astronomy had many links with the Asian astronomy of past centuries, and has much to teach us about the mutual impact of Chinese and Western thought.

The coming of the Jesuits was by no means (as it has often been made to appear) an unmixed blessing for Chinese science. Let us make a provisional balance-sheet of the merits and demerits of their contribution, before illustrating some of its items from contemporary documents. In the first place, the European methods for the prediction of eclipses were greatly superior to the traditional empirical Chinese methods. This was first demonstrated for the solar eclipse of 15 December 1610, when Sabbathin de Ursis was acting as the principal Jesuit astronomer after the death of Matteo Ricci.[1] Secondly, the Jesuits brought a clear exposition of the geometrical analysis of planetary motions, and of course the Euclidean geometry necessary for applying it. This had many other uses, as (thirdly) in gnomonics and the stereographic projections of the astrolabe, and in surveying. A fourth contribution was the doctrine of the spherical earth and its division into spaces separated by meridians and parallels. Fifthly, the new 16th-century algebra of the time of Vieta was made available to the Chinese, with many new computing methods, and ultimately mechanical devices such as the slide-rule. Sixthly, by no means the least valuable transmission was the most up-to-date European technique of instrument-making, graduating of scales, micrometer screws, and the like. The spread of the telescope was the climax of this.

(1) CHINA AND THE DISSOLUTION OF THE CRYSTALLINE SPHERES

On the other hand, the world-picture which the Jesuits brought was that of the closed Ptolemaic-Aristotelian geocentric universe of solid concentric crystalline spheres.[2] Hence they opposed the indigenous Hsüan Yeh doctrine of the floating of the heavenly

---

[1] Comedy sometimes attended Jesuit predictions. In 1636 they stated that Jupiter would pass between two stars in Cancer and then begin a phase of retrogradation. Some of the Chinese officials thought this presaged a calamity by fire so they falsified the observations, but the explosion of a large powdermill near Peking confirmed strikingly the exactness of the Jesuits.

[2] See especially Aristotle, *De Caelo*, Bk. 2. There is a charming story of one of the friends of the Jesuits, Chhü Thai-Su, accepting a prism of rock-crystal and decorating its case with an inscription to the effect that this was a piece of the very material of which the sky is composed.

bodies in infinite space, and the irony was that they did so just at a time when the best minds in Europe were breaking away from the closed Aristotelian system. Hence also (second) they obstructed the spread of the Copernican heliocentric doctrine in China, for after all they could not but be sensitive to the condemnation of Galileo by the Church. It followed, thirdly, that they substituted an erroneous theory of the precession of the equinoxes for the cautious Chinese refusal to form any theory at all about it. Fourthly, they completely failed to appreciate the equatorial and polar character of traditional Chinese astronomy, and therefore, confusing the *hsiu* divisions with the zodiac, equalized the duodenary equatorial divisions when there was no need to do so. Fifthly, in spite of the advance to equatorial co-ordinates which was just being made by Tycho Brahe, the Jesuits imposed the less satisfactory Greek ecliptic co-ordinates upon Chinese astronomy, which had always been primarily equatorial, and actually constructed in Peking an ecliptic armillary sphere.

A fascinating glimpse of this paradoxical situation is seen in letters which Ricci wrote on 28th October and 4th November 1595, enumerating the 'absurdities', as he called them, of the Chinese. They say, he wrote, that

(1) The earth is flat and square, and that the sky is a round canopy; they did not succeed in conceiving the possibility of the antipodes.

(2) There is only one sky (and not ten skies). It is empty (and not solid). The stars move in the void (instead of being attached to the firmament).

(3) As they do not know what the air is, where we say that there is air (between the spheres) they affirm that there is a void.

(4) By adding metal and wood, and omitting air, they count five elements (instead of four)—metal, wood, fire, water and earth. Still worse, they make out that these elements are engendered the one by the other; and it may be imagined with how little foundation they teach it, but as it is a doctrine handed down from their ancient sages, no one dares to attack it. [3]

(5) For eclipses of the sun, they give a very good reason, namely that the moon, when it is near the sun, diminishes its light. [4]

(6) During the night, the sun hides under a mountain which is situated near the earth. [5]

[3] The arguments in favour of the Aristotelian elements were not a whit better. Trigault, however, related with pride the triumph of the Four elements over the Five in the lectures and pamphlets of the Jesuits. Yet this was almost contemporary with the epoch-making work of Jean Rey and John Mayow in Europe, and within half a century the whole edifice of element-theory was finally exploded by Robert Boyle.
[4] Ironical. It will be remembered that this is the ancient Yin-Yang influence theory which one or other of Ricci's interlocutors must have fished out of the *Lun Hêng*.
[5] A relic of the legendary cosmology which Ricci must have obtained from some uneducated acquaintance rather than from anyone skilled in astronomy.

Here we see the elements of superiority in European science at the turn of the 16th and 17th centuries imposing a fundamentally wrong world-picture, that of the solid spheres, on the fundamentally right one which had come down from the Hsüan Yeh school, of stars floating in infinite empty space. [6]

The point is worth looking at a little more closely. Five years after these words had been written by Ricci in his letter home, William Gilbert was saying in his *De Magnete:*

Who has ever made out that the stars which we call fixed are in one and the same sphere, or has established by reasoning that there are any real, and, as it were, adamantine spheres? No one has ever proved this, nor is there a doubt but that just as the planets are at unequal distances from the earth, so are these vast and multitudinous lights separated from the Earth by varying and very remote altitudes—they are not set in any sphaerick frame or firmament. The intervals of some are from their unfathomable distance matter of opinion rather than of verification; others less than they are yet very remote, and at varying distances, either in that most subtile quintessence, the thinnest aether, or in the void . . . It is evident then that all the heavenly bodies set as if in destined places are there formed into spheres, that they tend to their own centres, and that round them there is a confluence of all their parts. And if they have motion, that motion will rather be that of each round its own centre, as that of the Earth is, or a forward movement of the centre in an orbit, as that of the Moon is . . . But there can be no movement of infinity and of an infinite body, and therefore no diurnal revolution of that vastest Primum Mobile.

Twenty years earlier, Giordano Bruno, in his *De Infinito Universo,* had been pointing the same moral, in his usual more violent way:

The difficulty proceedeth from a false method and a wrong hypothesis—namely of the weight and immovability of the Earth, and the position of the Primum Mobile, with the other seven, eight, nine, or more, spheres, on which stars are implanted, impressed, plastered, nailed, knotted, glued, sculptured or painted —and that these stars do not reside in the same space as our own star, named by us Earth.

Thus was the ' false method ' and ' wrong hypothesis ' in cosmology introduced to China. But did any stimulus come back in exchange?

[6] It is unfortunate that Cronin, in a widely-read and moving book published in 1955, still seeks to perpetuate the Jesuit legend of the backwardness of Chinese cosmology and astronomy.

Most of the scholastics, following Aristotle, had held that a plurality of worlds was an impossibility. But in the 17th century the doctrine rapidly gained ground, and it was accompanied by a great proliferation of ' scientific ' romances of interplanetary travel. Among the literary works in which these themes were set forth there are certain coincidences which hint that the scepticism of the Chinese as to the solid spheres had not been without influence. Thus, for example, Francis Godwin, in *The Man in the Moone; or, A Discourse of a Voyage Thither, by Domingo Gonsales, the Speedy Messenger* (1638), one of the earliest scientific romances, makes his narrator fly to the moon in a machine propelled by wild geese. From there the earth looks like any other planet, and after some time the narrator, ' free of that tyrannous lodestone, the Earth ', and acquiring another sort of lodestone, as antidote to the earth's attraction,[7] floats down safely, arriving precisely in China, where he meets both mandarins and missionaries. Both the Chinese and the lunar people speak a tonal language. In less romantic form, the same idea was urged by John Wilkins, in his *Discovery of a World in the Moon, tending to prove that 'tis probable that there may be another habitable World in that Planet* (also 1638), and Christian Huygens (1698). But the Chinese theme occurs again in the amusing political satire of Daniel Defoe, *The Consolidator; or Memoirs of Sundry Transactions from the World in the Moon* (1705), who mentions both Godwin and Wilkins. So far as China is concerned the satire is double-edged, for while many exaggerated stories are told of Chinese inventions and discoveries,[8] the Chinese devotion to natural law and good custom is used to contrast the political absolutism of European governments.[9] The Consolidator, or 'Apezolanthukanistes', is a real anticipation of the aeroplane; it has wings and carries enough fuel to last out the voyage to the moon. The ambivalent attitude of European to Chinese science is well seen, for while Defoe speaks of the ' gross and absurd ignorance of the Chinese of the motions of the heavenly bodies ', the interplanetary aeroplane could only be supposed to have been made and used by people well versed in astronomy and mechanics. Yet a third recurrence of the Chinese theme is found in Miles Wilson's *History of Israel Jobson, the Wandering Jew*, who visited all the planets and allegedly wrote the account of his travels in Chinese

---

[7] It will be recalled that just such a device was imagined by H. G. Wells in his *First Men in the Moon.*

[8] Printing and gunpowder are of course referred to, and the construction of very large ships, but there is also mention of storm and tide prediction, and imaginary inventions such as typewriters and dictaphones are described.

[9] The Chinese polity is said to be based on the belief that ' Natural Right is superior to Temporal Power ', an heretical doctrine for the West, ' long since exploded by our learned doctors, who have proved that kings and emperors came down from heaven with crowns on their heads, and that all their subjects were born with saddles on their backs.'

(1757). Indeed, it is hardly possible to take up any seventeenth-century book dealing with the idea that there are other peopled solar systems besides our own, without finding some reference to China. For example, in the *Entretiens sur la Pluralité des Mondes* written by B. de Fontenelle in 1686, the subject is discussed in the guise of evening conversations with a great lady at a country house. After many passing mentions of China, the narrator says:

Je viens de vous dire, répondis-je, toutes les nouvelles que je sçay du Ciel, & je ne croy pas qu'il y en ait de plus fraîches. Je suis bien fâché qu'elles ne soient pas aussi surprenantes et aussi merveill-euses que quelques Observations que je lisois l'autre jour dans un Abrégé des Annales de la Chine, écrit en Latin, & imprimé depuis peu. On y voit des milles Étoiles à la fois qui tombent du Ciel dans la Mer avec un grand fracas, ou qui se dissolvent, et s'en vont en pluye, & cela n'a pas esté veu pour une fois à la Chine. J'ay trouvé cette Observation en deux temps assez éloignez, sans compter une Étoile qui s'en va crever vers l'Orient, comme une fusée, toujours avec grand bruit. Il est fâcheux que ces spectacles-là soient reservez pour la Chine, & que ces Pays-cy n'en ayent jamais eu leur part. Il n'y a pas longtems que tous nos Philosophes se croyoient fondez en expérience pour soutenir que les Cieux et tous les corps Celestes estoient incorruptibles & incapables de change-ment, & pendant ce temps-là d'autres hommes à l'autre bout de la Terre voyoient des Étoiles se dissoudre par milliers; cela est assez différent.

Mais, dit-elle (Mme la Marquise), n'ay-je pas toûjours oüy dire que les Chinois estoient de si grands Astronomes?

Il est vrai, repris-je, mais les Chinois y ont gagné à estre separez de nous par un long espace de Terre, comme les Grecs et les Romains à en estre separez par une longue suite de siècles; tout éloigne-ment est en droit de nous imposer . . .

So here again, with bantering tone, a European expositor of post-Renaissance cosmology, while gently making fun of the Chinese reputation for wisdom in such matters, hints that indeed they had long known of the birth and death of stars (novae, meteors, etc.) which European tradition had made immutable; and of the almost infinite distance and diversity of those lights which European tradi-tion had supposed truly fixed to a revolving crystal sphere. In a word, specific investigations might be worth making to ascertain whether the complete disbelief of the Chinese in the solid celestial spheres of the Ptolemaic-Aristotelian world-picture, which became evident to the Jesuits as soon as they began to discuss cosmology in China, was not one of the elements which combined in breaking

5

up medieval views in Europe, and contributed to the birth of modern astronomy. For such a suggestion there is contemporary evidence in the words of Christopher Scheiner, seeking about 1625 to show that the realm of the stars had a fluid nature.

The peoples of China (he said) have never taught in any of their innumerable and flourishing academies that the heavens are solid; or so we may conclude from their printed books, dating from all times during the past two millennia. Hence one can see the theory of a liquid heavens is really very ancient, and could be easily demonstrated; moreover one must not despise the fact that it seems to have been given as a natural enlightenment to all peoples. The Chinese are so attached to it that they consider the contrary opinion (a multiplicity of solid celestial spheres) perfectly absurd, as those inform us who have returned from among them.

And we may take as another example the words of Nieuwhoff (1665) who found the idea of a plurality of worlds very Chinese. [10]
In any case, the height of irony is reached when we find Wells Williams, in 1848, reproaching late Chhing popular writers for their belief in solid celestial spheres, under the impression that this was a primitive Chinese doctrine still persisting.

(2) THE IMPERFECT TRANSMISSION

The sincere (and well-justified) admiration of Ricci himself for the instruments of Kuo Shou-Ching is known to us. But such was the decadence of the late Ming period, and so convinced were the Europeans of their scientific superiority, that the accounts of Chinese astronomy which got through to 17th-century Europe were mainly unfavourable. One or two relevant passages are worth looking at. Thus Trigault wrote:

They have some Knowledge also of Astrologie and the Mathematikes: In Arithmetike and Geometry antiently more excellent, but in learning and teaching confused. They reckon four hundred Starres more than our Astrologers have mentioned, numbring certaine smaller which do not always appeare. Of the heavenly Appearances they have no rules: they are much busied about foretelling Eclipses, and the courses of Planets, but therein very erroneous; and all their Skill of Starres is in a manner that which we call Judiciall

---

[10] Nieuwhoff had accompanied the Dutch ambassadors to Peking in 1656. In the second part of the book which he wrote about this embassy and about China he said: ' Et les opinions qu'ont quelques-uns (des Chinois) dans la physique, conformes à celles de Democrite et de Pythagore touchant la pluralité des Mondes, monstrent assés combien ceux de cette Nation se plaisent a l'étude des choses naturelles '.

Astrology, imagining these things below to depend on the Starres. Somewhat they have received of the Westerne Saracens, but they confirme nothing by Demonstration, only have left to them Tables, by which they reckon the Eclipses and Motions.

The first of this Royal Family (the Ming) forbad any to learne this Judiciall Astrology but those which by Hereditary right are thereto designed, to prevent Innovations. But he which now reigneth mayntayneth divers Mathematicians, both Eunuches within the Palace and Magistrates without, of which there are in Pequin two Tribunals, one of Chinois, which follow their owne Authors, another of Saracens which reforme the same by their rules, and by conference together. Both have in a small Hill a Plaine for contemplation where are the huge Mathematicall Instruments of Brasse before mentioned: One of the Colledge nightly watcheth thereon as is before observed. That of Nanquin exceeds this of Pequin, as being then the Seat Royall. When the Pequin astrologers foretell Eclipses, the Magistrates and Idoll Ministers are commanded to assemble in their Officiary Habits to helpe the labouring Planets, which they think they do with beating brazen Bels, and often kneelings, all the time that they thinke the Eclipse lasteth, lest they should then be devoured (as I have heard) by I know not what Serpent.

Another passage, from Lecomte, is of much interest as giving an eye-witness account of that nightly observation which had been going on for perhaps three millennia.

They still continue their Observations. Five Mathematicians spend every Night on the Tower in watching what passes over head; one is gazing towards the Zenith, another to the East, a third to the West, the fourth turns his eyes Southwards, and a fifth Northwards, that nothing of what happens in the four Corners of the World may scape their diligent Observation. They take notice of the Winds, the Rain, the Air, of unusual Phenomena's, such as are Eclipses, the Conjunction or Opposition of Planets, Fires, Meteors, and all that may be useful. This they keep a strict Accompt of, which they bring in every Morning to the Surveyor of the Mathematicks, to be registered in his Office. If this had always been practised by able and careful Mathematicians, we should have a great number of curious Remarks;[11] but besides that, these Astronomers are very unskilful, they take little care to improve that Science; and provided their Salary be paid as usual, and their Income constant, they are in no great trouble about the Alterations and Changes which happen in the Sky. But if these Phenomena's are very apparent, as when there

---

[11] Lecomte evidently had no idea as to the relative value of ancient and medieval records of celestial phenomena in China and Europe.

happens an Eclipse, or a Comet appears, they dare not be altogether so negligent.

Now the two most important features in European astronomy at the time the Jesuits began their work in China were (a) the invention and use of the telescope, and (b) the acceptance of the heliocentric theory of Copernicus. The former they transmitted, but the latter, after some hesitations, they held back. The reform of the Chinese calendar, which usually looms so large, has been exhaustively described by Bernard-Maître; in reality, it was much less significant than the two developments just mentioned. Owing to the researches of d'Elia we are now fairly well informed about what really happened. Szczesniak has said that the Copernican conflict had an even more tragic history in China than in Europe, since it lasted down to the end of the 18th century. Duyvendak has underlined the importance of the failure of the Jesuits to transmit the heliocentric system of the universe.

Ricci died in Peking in 1610, the same year in which Galileo published his *Sidereus Nuntius*. In the following winter, Christopher Clavius and other Jesuits of the Roman College repeated his telescopic observations[12] and confirmed them. But this made the Jesuits anti-Aristotelian rather than anti-Ptolemaic. Clavius, the teacher and friend of Ricci, died in 1612. The two condemnations of Galileo's Copernican views were in 1616 and 1632, and must have had considerable effect on the China Mission. The first reference to the telescope in Chinese is in the *Thien Wên Lüeh* (Explicatio Sphaerae Coelestis) by Emanuel Diaz (Yang Ma-No) of 1615, where Galileo is said to have devised it because he ' deplored the power of the unaided eye ' (*ai chhi mu li*). Venus was seen as big as the moon, and Saturn looked as if it had a hen's egg on each side, while Jupiter's satellites were clearly visible (cf. diagrams, below). In 1618 Johannes Terrentius (Johann Schreck) arrived in China; he had been the seventh member of the Cesi Academy, having been elected next after Galileo, and was an astronomer and physicist of great gifts. He brought with him a telescope, which was eventually given to the emperor in 1634, and remained in touch with Galileo, who was not very helpful, and with Kepler, who took more interest. Kepler sent out with the Polish Jesuit Michael Boym a set of the (Copernican) Rudolphine Tables in 1627, and Boym, who stayed at Macao, passed them on with enthusiastic praise to Peking.

---

12 Especially on the lunar mountains, the sun-spots, the phases of Venus, the shape of Saturn, the moons of Jupiter, the nebula in Orion, the *Praesepe* cluster in Cancer, and many stars not before visible. John Adam Schall von Bell, later to be the first European Director of the Chinese Bureau of Astronomy, was present as a young man in the hall of the Roman College in May 1611 when Galileo received a triumphant welcome from Clavius and his ' mathematicians ' after their confirmation of his discoveries.

In the previous year, Adam Schall von Bell had published a Chinese treatise on the telescope, *Yuan Ching Shuo* (The Far-Seeing Optick Glass).[13] But not until 1640, in Schall's history of Western astronomy in Chinese, were the names of Galileo, Tycho Brahe, Copernicus and Kepler actually mentioned.

It is clear that in this early period, especially before the condemnation of Galileo, the missionaries were not at one on Copernicanism. It was favoured by Boym, and taught by Nicholas Smogulęcki, another Pole, at Nanking, while Wenceslaus Kirwitzer,

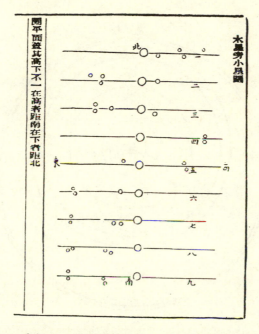

Diagrams of the moons of Jupiter (from the *Thu Shu Chi Chhêng*).

who went out with Terrentius, was definitely a Copernican, but died young in 1626. In general it may be said that Chinese books between 1615 and 1635 described the telescopic discoveries, but did not mention Copernicanism, then for a short time the heliocentric theory was described, but after news of the condemnation had reached China a curtain descended and a return to the Ptolemaic view took place. This had long before been clearly expounded in the

[13] This book included a rough picture of the Crab Nebula, though neither Schall nor his readers knew what its later importance for cosmology would be, nor that it had come from the supernova of 1054 observed only in China and Japan.

Chien Phing I Shuo (Elementary Explanations of Astronomical Instruments) by Sabbathin de Ursis of 1611.

Humanistic colleagues have sometimes expressed surprise that the Jesuits could have been so successful at preparing for the Chinese court a calendar of 'Renaissance' type while at the same time adhering to the Ptolemaic world-system and rejecting the Copernican. The first answer is that on the purely calendrical level there is nothing to choose between them. The geocentric and the heliocentric hypotheses were in strict mathematical equivalence; whether the

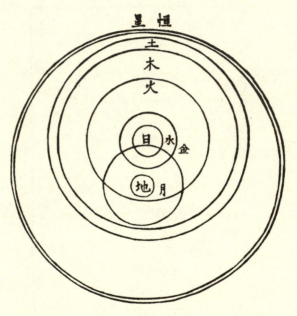

Diagram of the Tychonic theory of the solar system (from the *Thu Shu Chi Chhêng*).

earth or the sun was at rest, the lengths and angles were identical, and similar triangles had to be solved. Decision lay far beyond the frame of reference of the calendar-computer; it needed the relatively accurate observational data of the age of Cassini and Flamsteed. Secondly, the Chinese themselves had produced very good calendars for centuries before the time of the Jesuits without employing any geometrical model of the solar system at all. A calendar is only a method of reconciling terrestrial-celestial periodicities observed as carefully as possible, predicting their recurrences, and adjusting conventional human time units (months, days, etc.) to the best fit. [14] Where the Jesuits scored was in the more advanced character of their instruments and the superiority of their mathematics (old geometry indeed but quite new algebra). But it took them nearly a century to learn to profit by the great wealth of recorded Chinese celestial observations.

A curious result of the Jesuit failure to make use of the Chinese records until the time of Gaubil was that when Terrentius in 1628 expounded the telescopic discovery of sun-spots in his *Tshê Thien Yo Shuo* (Brief Description of the Measurement of the Heavens), there was no mention of the fact that they had been known for a dozen centuries before the Europeans discovered them.

Szczesniak has contrasted the situation of China with that of Japan. The effect of the closure of Japan between 1616 and 1720 was to emphasize the contribution of Dutch traders rather than that of Roman Catholic missionaries. When the first modern observatory in Japan was founded about 1725 under the direction of Nakane Genkei, Copernican ideas were fully admitted there. [15] But in China it was not until the early 19th century, with the contributions of the Protestant missionaries, such as Joseph Edkins, Alex. Wylie and John Fryer, that Copernican views really spread. Some detail of their work will be found in Szczesniak. But it is impossible to accept his contention that the main reason of the Jesuits for not propagating Copernicanism was the resistance of the Chinese to any abandonment of the geocentric world-view; this can have been only a part of the story. On the whole, one concludes that the Jesuit contribution was not an unmixed blessing.

(3) 'WESTERN' SCIENCE OR 'NEW' SCIENCE?

Nevertheless, the later work of the Society was indeed impressive. Between 1629 and 1635 the second generation of missionaries, including, besides Terrentius and Schall von Bell, James Rho, and, to a minor extent, Nicholas Longobardi, collaborating with Hsü Kuang-Chhi, Li Chih-Tsao and Li Thien-Ching, produced a monumental compendium of the scientific knowledge of the time. This

---

[14] A great deal of nonsense has been written about the calendar reform of the Jesuits in China. Cronin writes as if the Gregorian Calendar (partly the work of Matteo Ricci's teacher Christopher Clavius) adopted in Europe in 1582 was a corollary of the Ptolemaic theory. This, he suggests, had been introduced to China by the Arabs, but rejected there, so that its absence caused calendrical disorder. On the contrary, the Gregorian Calendar was simply another system of intercalation, more ingenious than its forerunners, but still arbitrary, as any such system of reconciling in commensurables must be.

[15] The growth of modern science in Japan lies outside our field. A Japanese physician (Petrus Hartsingius Japonensis, perhaps identical with Hatono Sōha) studied in 17th-century Leiden, and managed to return to his own country. An Italian missionary (Giuseppe Chiara) abandoned his mission, took a Japanese name (Sawano Chūan) and settled down to spend his life translating Dutch scientific books, especially on astronomy.

11

was entitled, upon its presentation in the latter year, the *Chhung-Chên Li Shu* (Chhung-Chên Reign-Period Treatise on (Astronomy and) Calendrical Science. Ten years later, in 1645, after the Manchus had come in, Schall von Bell attained greater favour, and the encyclopaedia was re-issued as the *Hsi- Yang Hsin Fa Li Shu* (Treatise on (Astronomy and) Calendrical Science according to the New Western Methods). Eventually it formed the basis for the *Yü-Ting Li Hsiang Khao Chhêng* (Complete Studies on Astronomy and Calendar)[16] edited by Ho Kuo-Tsung and Mei Ku-Chhêng and printed in 1723. Later on, in 1738, after much of it had been incorporated in the *Thu Shu Chi Chhêng* encyclopaedia, it was improved by the addition of astronomical tables embodying the new observations of Cassini and Flamsteed. These were the work of Ignatius Kögler and Andrew Pereira.[17]

Here we must halt a moment. The reader may have noticed nothing especially significant in the preceding paragraph, seemingly concerned only with the recitation of fact. But actually it raises certain points of extreme importance in these culture-contacts of the two great civilizations, and we must look at the facts more closely. It is vital to-day that the world should recognize that 17th-century Europe did not give rise to essentially ' European ' or ' Western ' science, but to universally valid world science, that is to say, ' modern ' science as opposed to the ancient and medieval sciences. Now these last bore indelibly an ethnic image and superscription. Their theories, more or less primitive in type, were culture-rooted, and could find no common medium of expression. But when once the basic technique of discovery had itself been discovered, once the full method of scientific investigation of Nature had been understood, the sciences assumed the absolute universality of mathematics, and in their modern form are at home under any meridian, the common light and inheritance of every race and people. Of argument about elements and humours, Yin and Yang, or ' philosophical sulphur ', there could be no end, the disputants could reach no common ground. But the mathematization of hypotheses led to a universal language, an oecumenical medium of exchange, a reincarnation of the merchants' single-value standard on a plane transcending merchandise. And what this language communicates

---

16 This formed, with the treatise on acoustics and music, *Lü Lü Chêng I*, and the companion one on mathematics, *Shi Li Ching Yün*, the three parts of the *Lü Li Yuan Yuan* (Ocean of Calendrical and Acoustic Calculations), an official and imperial publication. There is room for some doubt about the true authorship of the *Li Hsiang Khao Chhêng*, though it was certainly Chinese and not Jesuit.

17 Andrew Pereira is of particular interest to us as he was the only Englishman among all the Jesuits of the China Mission. He came of a family of the name of Jackson, settled in Oporto, doubtless connected with the wine trade and naturalized Portuguese. He seems to have been a very sympathetic character, and was a particular friend of the Yung-Chêng emperor, not otherwise an amateur of missionaries.

is a body of incontestable scientific truth acceptable to all men everywhere. Without it plagues are not checked, and aircraft will not fly. The physically unified world of our own time has indeed been brought into being by something that happened historically in Europe, but no man can be restrained from following the path of Galileo and Vesalius, and the period of political dominance which modern technology granted to Europeans is now demonstrably ending.

In their gentle way, the Jesuits were among the first to exercise this dominance, spiritual though in their case it was meant to be. To seek to accomplish their religious mission by bringing to China the best of Renaissance science was a highly enlightened proceeding, yet this science was for them only a means to an end. Their aim was naturally to support and commend the 'Western' religion by the prestige of the science from the West which accompanied it. This new science might be true, but for the missionaries what mattered just as much was that it had originated in Christendom. The implicit logic was that only Christendom could have produced it. Every correct eclipse prediction was thus an indirect demonstration of the truth of Christian theology. The *non sequitur* was that a unique historical circumstance (the rise of modern science in a civilization with a particular religion) cannot prove a necessary concomitance. Religion was not the only feature in which Europe differed from Asia. But the Chinese were acute enough to see through all this from the very beginning. The Jesuits might insist that Renaissance natural science was primarily 'Western', but the Chinese understood clearly that it was primarily 'new'.

Thus the 'Chhung-Chên treatise' of 1635 reappeared ten years later as the 'Western treatise according to New Methods'. Schall von Bell had been wanting to use the word 'Western' a long time previously. In a letter to Francis Furtado of November 1640, he said he was aiming at a Hsi Kho (Western Bureau) within the Li Kho (Department of the Calendar), but that the disadvantage of this was that it put it only on a level with the Muslim Bureau (Hui-Hui Kho) already existing. He wrote: 'The word Hsi (Western) is very unpopular (with the Chinese), and the emperor in his edicts never uses any word other than Hsin (New); in fact the former word is employed only by those who wish to depreciate us.' But after the change of dynasty Schall evidently felt that he could safely use the term 'Western'; after all, the Manchus were foreign too. So for many years printed calendars bore the title '. . . i Hsi-Yang Hsin Fa' (according to the New Western Methods). For this he was taken to task in 1661 by Yang Kuang-Hsien, and three years later formally condemned by the President of the Ministry of Rites for having used a formula ' injurious to the dignity of the empire.'[18] However, before long, Schall having died in 1666, his Belgian successor Ferdinand Verbiest was called to the Khang-Hsi emperor (who had succeeded in 1662) and spent no less than five months daily with him teaching and explaining the new mathematics and astronomy. It was then about 1669 that the encyclopaedia was reissued with again a new title, the *Hsin Fa Suan Shu* (Treatise on Mathematics (and Astronomy) according to the New Methods). The emperor's insistence united him unknowingly with that group of men at the other end of the world who exactly at the same time were meeting in the Royal Society to work out the implications of the ' new, or experimental, philosophy '—just as new for Europe as for China.

Down to the very end of the mission the Jesuits were the prisoners of their limited motive and the Chinese sought persistently to emphasize the continuity of the new science with the old. For example, in 1710 Jean-François Foucquet and others of the Society wished to make use of the new planetary tables of P. de la Hire, but the Father-Visitor would not permit it, for fear of ' giving the impression of a censure on what our predecessors had so much trouble to establish, and occasioning new accusations against our religion.' Any acceptance of Copernicanism would equally have raised doubts about all Ricci's teachings. In fact the penalty of enlisting live science in the service of fixed doctrine was to inhibit its development—Urania's feet were bound. Only in certain cases could the Jesuits move forward; for instance, the armillary sphere of 1744 was a Chinese (and therefore ' modern ') equatorial, not a Greek ecliptic, instrument; the old European co-ordinates were quietly given up. Meanwhile the Chinese were much concerned to show that the study of Nature had a continuous history. This is transparent from passages such as the following:

In the Wan-Li reign-period (1573 to 1619) the Western foreigner Li Ma-Tou (Matteo Ricci) made designs for an armillary sphere, a celestial and a terrestrial globe, etc. Li Chih-Tsao of Jen-ho wrote a discussion on the discovery, construction and use of the armillary sphere, which, though of some length, did not include diagrams. For (the new design) was not essentially different from the (long-known) apparatus constituted by the ' Component of the Six Cardinal Points ', the ' Component of the Three Arrangers of Time' and the ' Component of the Four Displacements '. The main

[18] Yang Kuang-Hsien was a scholar, amateur astronomer, and pertinacious anti-Jesuit controversialist. Associated with him was the Muslim astronomer Wu Ming-Hsüan. Schall could not remember who had originally authorized the phrase ' Western ', but it seems to have been agreed upon in the first year of the Manchu régime, when Rho was still in charge of the calendar reform, having inherited this position from Terrentius.

improvement was that whereas formerly the polar altitude was fixed in the casting, the new model was so arranged as to be adjustable for different latitudes—a very convenient thing . . .

The design and construction of astronomical instruments, and the making of observations have always been the first duty of astronomers. Those who are technically skilful can devise ingenious improvements. Thus the Westerners have many instruments with various names of which we cannot speak here, but among them the two instruments *hun kai* and *chien phing* [19] are the most refined. Reference must be made to the complete accounts for all cannot be recorded here.

And as a pendant to this consider the air-pump and its name. When Michel Benoist demonstrated this to the Chhien-Lung emperor in 1773 he termed it the *yen chhi thung* (' air-testing pipe '), but the monarch decided next day that its name should be changed to *hou chhi thung* (' air-observing pipe '), ' this word being more elegant, having served in classical writings for natural observations on the celestial bodies as well as on agricultural matters '. He was of course thinking of the antique names of the weather-vane and the seismograph, and of one of the terms for the armillary sphere.

(4) The Integration of Chinese Astronomy into Modern Science

In 1669 there began the great refitting of the Peking observatory under the care of Ferdinand Verbiest. The instruments of Yuan or Ming time were taken down from the astronomical platform on the eastern wall of the city, and a new set installed in their place, where they have remained until the present time. The Jesuit and later instruments are as follows:

(1) Simple ecliptic armillary sphere, *huang tao ching wei i*, supported on four dragon heads. Verbiest, 1673.

(2) Simple equatorial armillary sphere, *chhih tao ching wei i*, supported on the arched back of a dragon. Verbiest, 1673.

(3) Large celestial globe, *thien thi i*, encased in a horizon framework with four pedestals, and rotated by clockwork. Verbiest, 1673.

(4) Horizon circle for azimuth measurements, *ti phing ching i*, table supported on four pedestals, pointers slung from an overhead bearing. Verbiest, 1673.

(5) Quadrant, *ti phing wei i*, or *hsiang hsien i*, supported on a vertical shaft with upper and lower bearings. Verbiest, 1673.

---

[19] These are not standard names but probably refer to instruments of quadrant altazimuth type.

(6) Sextant, *chi hsien i*, on a single pedestal. Verbiest, 1673.

(7) Quadrant altazimuth, *ti phing ching wei i*, Stumpf, 1713–15.

(8) Elaborate equatorial armillary sphere, *chi hêng fu chhen i*. Kögler, 1744, assisted by von Hallerstein and Gogeisl, perhaps also by Gaubil and de la Charme.

(9) Smaller celestial globe, *hun hsiang*.

Illustrations of the first six of these were published by Verbiest under the title of *I Hsiang Thu* (Designs of Astronomical Instruments) with their description *I Hsiang Chih* (1673), and finally incorporated into the *Yü-Ting I Hsiang Khao Chhêng* (Complete Studies of Astronomical Instruments) edited by Kögler and von Hallerstein in 1744. A great deal of this, richly illustrated, had appeared in the *Thu Shu Chi Chhêng*, but the most beautiful drawings are those published by Tung Kao in the *Huang Chhao Li Chhi Thu Shih* (ch. 3) of 1759 and 1766. The Western counterpart to these publications was the *Astronomia Europaea sub Imperatore Tartaro-Synico Cam Hy* (Khang-Hsi) *appellato, ex Umbra in Lucem Revocata*, of 1687. In the same period comes the book by another Jesuit, Francis Noel, published at Prague in 1710, in which he gave for European readers much information on the stems, branches, *hsiu*, etc., with a rough correlation of Chinese and European star-catalogues, and a discussion of Chinese metrology. During the 18th century many observations on eclipses were made, largely by Jacques-Philippe Simonelli and published jointly by him with Kögler and Melchior della Briga between 1744 and 1747. A great deal of positional work was done with the new instruments, and a catalogue of 3,083 stars was included in the *I Hsiang Khao Chhêng* edition of 1757, under a preface written by the emperor himself. The astronomers responsible were Kögler and Felix da Rocha with Augustin von Hallerstein and Anton Gogeisl. These observations have all been reduced to modern expression and published in translated form by Tsutsihash and Chevalier. Another event of importance in this period was the *Huang Tao Tsung Hsing Thu* (Star-Maps on Ecliptic Co-ordinates) by Kögler, published a few years after his death in 1746.

The transmissions of the Jesuits seem to have affected a number of Chinese scholars who were more or less outside their circle. The works of Wang Hsi-Shan, for instance, deserve a special investigation. His *Wu Hsing Tu Chieh* (Analysis of the Motions of the Five Planets), published in 1640, proposed essentially what had been the system of Tycho Brahe, namely, that the sun moves round the earth but all the other planets move round the sun (1583). There is no evidence that this was not independently thought out, perhaps from a bare hint that someone in the West had conceived

16

this idea. He followed it up three years later with a larger work, the *Hsiao-An Hsin Fa* (Wang Hsi-Shan's New (Astronomical) Methods), which was an attempt to synthesize Western and Chinese ideas. So far as I can see, this astronomer was a capable man; at least he understood the Chinese system, and knew that the *hsiu* were equatorial divisions, which was more than the Jesuits did.

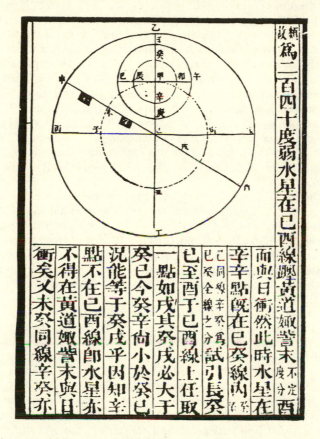

A geometrical construction from Wang Hsi-Shan's *Wu Hsing Hsing Tu Chieh* (1640) to explain the Tychonic theory of the solar system.

His contemporary Hsüeh Fêng-Tsu was more closely connected with the Jesuits, since he was a collaborator of Smogulęcki at Nanking, and therefore probably a Copernican. His *Thien Hsüeh Hui Thung* of 1650 was again a conciliation of Chinese and Western astronomy, and his treatise on eclipses *Thien Pu Chen Yuan* (True Origins of the Celestial Movements) was the first book in

Chinese to make use of logarithms. Other scholars followed tradition in being more interested in chronology, e.g. Hsü Fa, who in 1682 supported the unorthodox Bamboo Books chronology in his *Thien Yuan Li Li Chhüan Shu* (Complete Treatise on the Thien Yuan Calendar). About this time also was Shao Ang-Hsiao's *Wan Chhing Lou Thu Pien* (Study of Star-Maps from the Myriad Bamboo Tablet Studio).

As the 18th century went on, Chinese astronomers and mathematicians emancipated themselves more and more from the spell which the Jesuit apparition had woven during the decadent Ming and early Chhing times. The *Li Suan Chhüan Shu* (Complete Works on Calendar and Mathematics) of Mei Wên-Ting (1723) included much astronomy. His work stimulated a younger man, Chiang Yung, whose *Shu Hsüeh* (Mathematical Astronomy) and *Thui Pu Fa Chieh* (Analysis of Celestial Motions) both appeared about the middle of the century. This was contemporary with Shêng Pai-Erh's defence of the Tychonic against the Ptolemaic system in his *Shang Shu Shih Thien* (Discussion of the Astronomy in the Historical Classic).

At the end of the century, among several important works, mention may be made of the treatise on celestial cartography, *Kao Hou Mêng Chhiu* (Investigation of the Dimensions of the Universe), by Hsü Chao-Chün (1800). Half a century later, when Fêng Kuei-Fên gave tables of right ascensions and declinations of 100 stars, in his *Hsien-Fêng Nien Chung Hsing Piao*, Chinese astronomical science might be said to have merged at last with that of the world as a whole.

It was not to be expected that the over-emphasised, and in many respects erroneous, claims of the Jesuits for the superiority of the European science of their time would escape a strong reaction. Though this often took political and social forms, as may be read in many accounts of the period, some Chinese astronomers of the old school were actively in opposition. Thus in 1631 Wei Wên-Khuei and his son Wei Hsiang-Chhien published two books on calendrical science (*Li Yuan* and *Li Tshê*) which were so important that Schall von Bell had to write a refutation, the *Hsüeh Li Hsiao Pien*. On the other hand, the Chinese were generally open to conviction, for the following statement was signed by ten officials of the Bureau of Astronomy:

At first we also had our doubts about the astronomy from Europe when it was used in the *chi-ssu* year (1629), but after having read many clear explanations our doubts diminished by half, and finally by participating in precise observations of the stars, and of the positions of the sun and moon, our hesitations were altogether

18

overcome. Recently we received the imperial order to study these sciences, and every day we have been discussing them with the Europeans. Truth must be sought not only in books, but in making actual experiments with instruments; it is not enough to listen with one's ears, one must also carry out manipulations with one's hands. All (the new astronomy) is then found to be exact.

Unexpectedly, the Jesuit intervention led in due course to a rediscovery on the part of the Chinese of the achievements of their own civilization before the Ming decadence. In the field of astronomy there was the book of Shêng Pai-Erh just mentioned; and in 1819 the treatise of the Taoist Li Ming-Chhê *Yuan Thien Thu Shuo* (Illustrated Discussion of the Fields of Heaven), while also still Tychonic, referred to the achievements of the ancients in China. In Japan a similar movement was connected with Buddhism, as in the *Bukkoku Rekishō-hen* (The Astronomy of Buddha's Country) by Enzū (1810) described by Mikami. In Vol. 1 of our *Science and Civilization in China* (p. 48) we mentioned works composed by late Chhing scholars who sought to prove that all important inventions and discoveries had originally been made in China, for example, the *Ko Chih Ku Wei* of Wang Jen-Chün, and sometimes this was taken to considerable lengths. For instance, in his *I Shu Pien* (The Antheap of Knowledge; miscellaneous essays), Wang Ming-Shêng (1722 to 1798) maintained that much occidental calendrical science and astronomy had originated from the work of Tsu Chhung-Chih in the 5th century, which had been preserved under the Liao dynasty, and, upon its break-up in 1125, taken to Arabia (Thien-Fang) by the academicians of the West Liao State (Ta-Shih) whence it passed to Europe.

All in all, the contribution of the Jesuits, chequered though it was, had qualities of noble adventure. If the bringing of the science and mathematics of Europe was for them a means to an end, it stands for all time nevertheless as an example of cultural relations at the highest level between two civilizations theretofore sundered. Truly the Jesuits, with all their brilliance, were a strange mixture, for side by side with their science went a vivid faith in devils and exorcisms. Though some superstitions wilted in their presence, philosophers might opine that they brought as many with them. As for their judgment of the sciences of China, we know now that it was vitiated for two reasons. The Ming dynasty was a period of decline which had few exponents of indigenous tradition, and such men the Jesuits rarely met. Nor must the linguistic difficulties and the scarcity of old books be forgotten. Secondly, since the Jesuits desired to convince the Chinese of the superiority of Western religion by demonstrating the superiority of Western science in their day and

19

age, they were hardly tempted to think like historians when they came upon Chinese achievements in science or technology. Nevertheless many of the Jesuits conceived a warm enthusiasm for Chinese culture, and with the Renaissance behind them they successfully achieved a task which had proved beyond the powers of their Indian forerunners in the Thang, namely, to open communications with that world-wide universal science of Nature into which the Chinese achievements would also be built.

Making the Jesuit astronomical instruments for the Peking Observatory in 1673: a page from the *Thu Shu Chi Chhêng* showing the grinding of a bronze armillary ring.

Testing the trueness of a bronze armillary ring (from the *Thu Shu Chi Chhêng*).

15
Western Mathematics in China, Seventeenth Century and Nineteenth Century

Catherine Jami

Historians of Chinese science have proposed that the introduction of Western[1] mathematics into China took place in two waves[2]. Both of these waves may be regarded as side effects of European expansion. The first introduction of Western mathematics was due to Jesuit missionaries who entered China at the end of the 16th century and stayed there for two centuries. The second introduction took place in the second half of the 19th century, after the Opium War (1839-1842); it initiated the process of alignment of Chinese mathematical practice on Western disciplinary standards.

The purpose of this paper is to compare several aspects of these two periods: the motivations of both sides; the means of transmission of science; the institutional framework in which this transmission took place; its reception among Chinese scholars; and how the new knowledge stood in relation to previous mathematical traditions. In order to assess what was at stake in these importations of mathematical knowledge, I will give a general outline of these two waves and point to some similarities and contrasts between them.

The Jesuits

It is usually considered that at the time of the arrival of the first Jesuit missionaries, Chinese science in general and mathematics in particular were in a state of decline: the great achievements of 13th century algebrists had fallen into oblivion[3]. However, from the turn of the 17th century on there was a significant renewal of interest in "concrete studies" *(shixue)* among scholars[4]. The Jesuit missionaries who came to China at the end of the 16th century sought to arouse scholars' interest in the Christian religion by introducing some elements of European scientific knowledge, mainly in astronomy and mathematics[5]. Their aim was to be introduced at court and convert the emperor (the conversion of Constantine and the evangelization of the Roman empire were explicitly taken as a model). Their strategy was to illustrate the excellence of the Christian religion by the scientific and technical achievements of its representatives.

For their first Chinese protectors and converts, admiration for the Jesuits' scientific knowledge went together with the adoption of the Christian faith[6]. It was these converts who collaborated with the Jesuits in the translation of scientific works published at the beginning of the 17th century. The method of translation then employed was used again in the 19th century: the missionary gave an oral translation of the text, which the Chinese scholar then transcribed in classical Chinese. The translation that has attracted most attention, both among Chinese scholars of the time and among historians, is that of the first six books of Euclid's *Elements of Geometry* (1607), from Clavius' Latin version (1574), under the title[7] *Jihe Yuanben*. It was done by Matteo Ricci (1552-1610), the founder of the mission, and Xu Guangqi (1665-1633), the most famous of the Chinese converts. It is indeed very tempting to make a symbol of this translation, given that the *Elements of Geometry* were a founding text of the Western tradition. But it was rather as a book of the Renaissance and as a Jesuit textbook that it came to China: Matteo Ricci had studied with Clavius in Rome; and Clavius' works were the source of some of the first mathematical works published by the Jesuits in China. A century later, Euclid's *Elements,* which had aroused much interest and criticism among Chinese scholars, was supplanted by another book of *Elements,* written by the French Jesuit Pardiès (1671) and used as a textbook in the Jesuit colleges in France[8].

Ricci's collaborator in the translation of the *Elements,* Xu Guangqi, was a high official of the Ming court. Around 1630 he introduced the Jesuits into the Imperial Board of Astronomy to reform the Chinese calendar (which was indeed in bad need of revision[9]); they did this according to Tycho Brahe's astronomical system. In China, calendrical astronomy had always been loaded with heavy political and symbolic significance: the Board of Astronomy was subordinated to the Board of Rites. From that time on, the Jesuits were increasingly in contact with civil servants who were professional astronomers and people around the emperor, and less associated with scholars who took a "private" interest in scientific matters. They became court savants in the emperor's service. Kangxi (1662-1722), the second emperor of the Manchu dynasty (1644-1911), had a high regard for Western science and took lessons with the Jesuits; he acted as patron and arbiter of scientific knowledge[10]. It was during his reign that the French king Louis XIV attempted to break the Portuguese monopoly on the sponsorship of the Jesuit missions in the Far East[11] by sending some French Jesuits as his envoys to the Emperor with the title of "the King's Mathematicians". They were correspondents of the French *Académie Royale des Sciences* and the innovations that they tried to introduce at the Chinese court were often based on works of French Academicians. This was a source of conflict among the Jesuits of China, perceived as opposing to "French science" the scientific practice of "Portuguese" Jesuits working at the Board of Astronomy[12].

The elements of mathematics introduced into China by the Jesuits in the 17th century were mostly those necessary for the computation of the calendar according to Tycho Brahe's model[13]. These elements belong to the fields of Euclidian geometry, practical geometry, written arithmetic, and plane and spherical trigonometry. On the whole, the mathematics then spread among Chinese scholars is more reminiscent of the Renaissance than of the 17th and 18th centuries: it ignored Viète and Descartes, to say nothing about Newton and Leibniz (although the latter was very much interested in China and was in correspondence with one of the French Jesuits[14]).

The success of the scientific knowledge introduced by the Jesuits among Chinese scholars was mainly due to the latter's renewed interest in "concrete studies" *(shixue)* at the time: "Western studies" and their applications (excluding religious writings) dealt with disciplines in which more and more Chinese scholars specialized, such as mathematics, astronomy and geography. This change in Chinese scholarship was one aspect of the criticism of Neo-Confucianism that prevailed at the time. Scholars claimed that their aim was to return to "genuine Confucianism", and to its emphasis on the social concerns apparent in ancient Chinese texts[15]. Thus it was the social usefulness of mathematics and of its applications that justified its study. This argument was put forward by Ricci in his preface to the translation of Euclid's *Elements*. He mentioned the usefulness of mathematics for (among other things) state management and military art, trade and astronomy, the latter in turn being of use to agriculture and medicine[16]. This was akin to the justification of the study of mathematics (including both local and imported elements) put forward by Chinese scholars of the time[17] and fell within preoccupations that are recurrent in Chinese history. It is worth noting that Chinese scholars discriminated between what they found interesting and useful (scientific and technical writings) and what they considered dangerous as a potential factor of social disorder (religious writings) among the Jesuits' Chinese writings[18]. Chinese scholars were interested in European mathematics because it was relevant to fields of study that were considered important according to criteria pertaining to Chinese intellectual tradition.

Chinese scholars of the time looked for a language common to Chinese tradition and Western contributions in the field of mathematics. This led them to the rediscovery of their own mathematical tradition. The famous mathematician and astronomer Mei Wending (1633-1721)[19] who was one of the initiators of the rediscovery of the Chinese mathematical tradition also was one of the first advocates of the thesis of the Chinese origin of Western knowledge *(Xi xue Zhong yuan)*, which played an important role in mathematics. This thesis was not merely a chauvinistic reaction; it legitimated Western science by rooting it in Chinese antiquity. Its study was thus made part of the return to original Confucianism. The Kangxi emperor himself supported this idea. It was important for the Manchu emperor to appear as the champion of Chinese orthodoxy, and not as the upholder of "Barbarian" knowledge[20]. Kangxi, a keen student of Western mathematics and astronomy, set up new institutions and encouraged the appropriation of European scientific knowledge by Chinese scholars. It was during his reign that they started developing a creative mathematical activity, which can be characterized as a synthesis between Western knowledge and the local tradition; this activity was continued until the 19th century. At the same time the proscription of the Jesuits by the Chinese emperor in 1723 put an end to any significant Western innovation in mathematics until the middle of the 19th century.

The limits of this first transmission of European scientific knowledge in China are often emphasized, the blame being laid either on the Jesuits for not having said enough, or on Chinese scholars for not having understood the "essence" of Western science[21]. However it seems that the most important limiting factor was institutional. Chinese intellectual life of the 17th and 18th centuries was not centered at the Peking court but in the Lower Yangtze academies[22]. When they were introduced at court, the Jesuits gave up direct dialogue with the scholars that were active in the academic community, and who were less dependent on ritual and imperial sanction than court savants. However, the academics did study Western mathematics, and applied them to various fields that were of importance in the intellectual issues of the time[23].

The analysis of this transmission of Western science to China as a failure relies on the implicit assumption that what China then needed or should then have been inclined to achieve was the reproduction of the European pattern of scientific development. This assumption, which is questionable, actually stems from the interpretation of 19th century history in terms of the Chinese incapacity to face Western intrusion for lack of appropriate military technology.

The Colonial Powers

When the second wave of translation of mathematical books occurred in the later half of the 19th century, the balance of power between China and the countries from which science was imported had changed drastically. Moreover the internal situation of the Chinese empire had severely deteriorated. The Taiping rebellion (1850-1864), both a symptom of the dynastic crisis and a factor of aggravation of this crisis, had caused at least 30 million deaths and much destruction. In particular it sounded the knell of the network of academies of the Lower Yangzi area[24].

One of the first texts published then was a continuation of Ricci and Xu Guangqi's translation of Euclid's *Elements*. The remaining books, published in 1859, were translated from English by the protestant missionary Alexander Wylie (1815-1887) and the Chinese mathematician Li Shanlan (1811-1882), under the patronage of Zeng Guofan (1811-1872), the main architect of the suppression of the Taiping rebellion[25]. This translation clearly referred to the knowledge introduced in the 17th century. It opened a new era of introduction of Western mathematical works.

In the following years the translation of European and American scientific and technical works was undertaken on a much larger scale than two centuries earlier. Once again it was missionaries who together with Chinese scholars initiated the first translations. Most of these missionaries were protestants (often British); the first of them entered China following the first Opium War (1839-1842). The works they translated were often English textbooks; a number of articles of the *Encyclopedia Britannica* also served as sources for short treatises on subjects such as algebra, calculus and probability, which were new in China. These works were not systematically selected among the whole mathematical production in European languages: they were usually the books, primarily in English, that happened to come into the missionaries' possession.

Most of the Chinese institutions in which this mathematical knowledge was taught and applied were created especially for that purpose. The motive behind the acquisition of that knowledge was quite different from the issue of Western studies at the time of the Jesuits. The Chinese needed to master Western science in order to defend themselves against aggressive Western Barbarians. The core of this science was military technology. The need to train savants and engineers capable, for example, of building warships, became more and more obvious to many scholars following the defeats suffered from the Opium War on. The debate then focused on how to spread the necessary knowledge, and on how far Western science could be adopted without threatening Chinese civilisation. The creation of specialized institutions was suggested very early, and they were progressively implemented. Thus Feng Guifen (1809-1874), one of the first advocates of "self-strengthening"[26] *(ziqiang)*, wrote:[27]

"If today we wish to select and use Western knowledge, we should establish official translation offices at Canton and Shanghai. Brilliant students up to 15 years of age should be selected from these areas to live and study in these schools on double rations. Westerners should be invited to teach them the spoken and written languages of the various nations and famous Chinese teachers should also be engaged to teach them classics, history and other subjects. At the same time they should learn mathematics (Note: all Western knowledge is derived from mathematics. Every Westerner of 10 years of age or more studies mathematics. If we now wish to adopt Western knowledge, naturally we cannot but learn mathematics ...)".

This program of study was remarkably syncretic. Feng Guifen also argued that people competent in technical fields should be given the same titles and offices as those who succeeded in the traditional examination system. It was their technical competence that was vital for the defence of China, rather than knowledge of the classics and mastery of the "eight-legged essay" which were the key to official appointments[28]. This was a serious challenge to the bureaucracy, since it meant changing the content of the knowledge that legitimized their power. The response to this threat was to point to the adoption of Western science itself as the main danger for the foundation of Chinese civilization and Confucian morality. But it was also argued that coexistence between this morality and Western knowledge was possible, keeping a strict hierarchy between the two: this was epitomized by the slogan "Chinese learning for the base, Western studies for use" *(Zhong xue wei ti, Xi xue wei yong)* which Feng Guifen anticipated[29].

Despite the strong opposition of some scholars and bureaucrats, a few schools were created. In 1866, a mathematics department was added to the *Tongwenguan* (College of Interpreters), created in 1862 in Peking, which was attached to the *Zongli Yamen* (Bureau of Foreign Affairs, created in 1861)[30]. This institutional affiliation reflects the fact that mathematics and its applications were needed for reasons that had to do with foreign affairs. Later, mathematics was taught in military academies in Shanghai, Canton and Fuzhou; this teaching was always connected to that of foreign languages. In 1887 mathematics was introduced into the examination system[31].

Mathematics taught in these institutions mainly relied on recent translations. In some of the first colleges *the Nine Chapters on the Mathematical Art, Jiu zhang suan shu,* (1st century A. D., the Chinese mathematical classic[32] *par excellence)* were still taught. But by the turn of the 20th century this classic was abandoned; Euclid's *Elements* (that had played a central role in Chinese mathematics for two centuries) were hardly more favoured. On the whole the mathematics that had prevailed up to the middle of the 19th century, which was perceived as pertaining to Chinese scholarship, was replaced by "modern" mathematics that was more adapted to the main technological applications for which mathematics was then needed.

Similarities and Contrasts Between the Two Periods

The two waves of introduction of European mathematics present both striking similarities and contrasts. First, although China never was colonized in the strict sense, both waves were linked to European colonial expansion. The development of Jesuit missions in East Asia from the 16th century on relied on the Portuguese overseas expansion: the Jesuits who went to East Asia called at Goa on their way; Macao was their gateway to China where they prepared for their entry to China by learning Chinese and improving their knowledge of the sciences. The king of Portugal was the patron of all the Chinese missions. In the nineteenth century Britain was the leading colonial power in the opening of China to international trade. The books translated into Chinese reflect Jesuit teaching in the first case (including that of the University of Coimbra, but also that of other Jesuit colleges and universities of Europe[33]); in the second case, they were mostly British (and sometimes American) textbooks.

Another similarity between the two periods is that in both cases the missionaries' role was crucial in making Western mathematical knowledge available in Chinese. To these missionaries science and religion were the ways to salvation and progress, the benefits of which they sought to bestow upon China. On the other hand if the Chinese needed these intermediaries, it was because they did not see the point of learning foreign languages until compelled to do so. When they finally did, it was out of political necessity, not out of scientific curiosity[34].

In 17th century China, the interest in Western mathematics was linked to the renewal of "concrete studies"; the main application of mathematics was to astronomy. This interest was then legitimated by the claim that this knowledge belonged to Chinese tradition. The framework of reception was determined by the internal dynamics of Chinese history. Western mathematics was interesting for its content, in other words because it was mathematics. The slogan "Chinese learning for the base, Western studies for use" then went without saying: Western studies did not appear as a threat to Chinese learning, but as part of it. When the slogan was stated in the 19th century, it was crucial to make it explicit that the foundations of learning lay in the Confucian tradition. This became even truer as Confucian learning was threatened as a source of legitimacy of power, because of the need to appropriate Western knowledge. By then the interest in Western mathematics was linked to the "self-strengthening" movement: the Chinese were compelled to study it in order to turn the Westerners' weapons against them. Western mathematics was then included in the learning of imported technology because it was regarded as a key to military power. This learning was linked to Western intrusion, not to "internal" Chinese factors. Western mathematics was vital because it was Western. It was regarded as part of a corpus of knowledge that was essentially foreign. At the same time, the Chinese mathematical tradition was depreciated and gradually abandoned, being regarded as one of the causes of Chinese military inferiority. This marked the end of a specific mathematical tradition in China, in contrast with the first wave of introduction of Western mathematics which had nurtured and renewed this tradition.

Centre National de la Recherche Scientifique (REHSEIS), Paris

Notes

[1] The term "Western" used in this paper corresponds to the Chinese category of *Xixue,* "Western learning", a term that was used from the 17th century on to refer to all the knowledge brought in by the Europeans.

[2] Li Yan and Du Shiran, *Chinese Mathematics. A Concise History.* Oxford, Clarendon Press, 1988; p.190-266; Wang Ping, *Xifan lisuanxue zhi shuru* (The Introduction of Western Mathematics and Astronomy). Taipei, 1966.

[3] On 13th century mathematics, cf. Li and Du, *op. cit.,* p.109-174.

[4] Concrete studies *(shixue)* were opposed to the emphasis on self-cultivation that prevailed in Neo-Confucianism. They included fields such as mathematics, astronomy, water control and land reclamation. Up to then such "technical fields" were hardly regarded as suitable concerns for a scholar. Cf Benjamin A. Elman, *From Philosophy to Philology. Intellectual and Social Aspects of Change in Late Imperial China.* Cambridge, Mass., Harvard University Press, 1984, p.46.

[5] Jacques Gernet, *Chine et christianisme. Action et réaction.* Paris, Gallimard, 1982; p.32-35.

[6] Two of the most famous converts, Xu Guangqi and Li Zhizao, contributed to the translations of mathematical works. Li an Du, *op. cit.,* p.191-201.

[7] Pasquale D'Elia, "Presentazione della prima traduzione cinese di Euclide", *Monumenta Serica* XV-1: 161-202 (1956).

[8] A Chinese adaptation of I.G. Pardiès' *Elémens de Géométrie* (Paris, 1671) was published in 1723 in the famous imperial mathematical encyclopedia *Yu zhi shu li jing yun* (Imperially commissioned collected basic principles of mathematics). Li and Du, *op. cit.,* p.219.

[9] There had already been several attempts to reform it in the late Ming; Willard Peterson, "Calendar Reform Prior to the Arrival of Missionaries at Ming Court", *Ming Studies* 21: 45-61 (1986).

[10] Rita H. Peng, "The Kangxi Emperor's Absorption in Western Mathematics and Astronomy and His Extensive Application of Scientific Knowledge", *Lishih Hsüehpao* 3: 349-422 (1975).

[11] This Portuguese monopoly was a consequence of the treaty of Tordesillas (1494) between Spain and Portugal which divided the world in two zones, the East being allotted to the Portuguese.

[12] Catherine Jami, "The French Mission and Verbiest's Scientific Legacy", forthcoming in *Proceedings of the Ferdinand Verbiest Conference,* Louvain, 1988.

[13] Henri Bernard-Maître, "Les adaptations chinoises d'ouvrages européens: bibliographie chronologique", *Monumenta Serica* X: 1-57 et 309-388 (1945) et XXV: 349-383 (1960).

[14] Etiemble, *L'Europe chinoise.* Paris, Gallimard, 1988-89 (2 vol); **vol.1,** p.370-436.

[15] Elman, *op. cit.*

[16] D'Elia, *op. cit.,* p.179-185.

[17] Catherine Jami "Learning the Mathematical Sciences in the Early and Mid-Ch'ing" in *Education and Society in Late Imperial China,* B. Elman and A. Woodside eds, forthcoming, University of California Press.

[18] Gernet, *op. cit.,* p.85.

[19] Li and Du, *op. cit.,* p.212-216.

[20] Lawrence Kessler, *K'ang-hsi and the Consolidation of Ch'ing Rule. 1661-1684.* Chicago, Chicago University Press, 1976; pp 137-166.

[21] Joseph Needham, *Science and Civilisation in China.* Cambridge, Cambridge University Press, 1954-, 7 vol.; **vol.III,** p.442-447; Jean-Claude Martzloff, *Histoire des mathématiques chinoises.* Paris, Masson, 1987; p.100-108.

[22] Elman, *op. cit.,* p.7-13

[23] For an example of problems of chronology raised by the development of rigorous methods in history and philology, which was the main trend of Chinese scholarship at the time, see, Elman, *op. cit.*

[24] Frederic Wakeman, *The Fall of Imperial China*. New York, The Free Press, 1975; p.143-156.

[25] Li and Du, *op. cit.*, p.257.

[26] On the theory of self-strengthening, cf. Ssu-yü Teng and John K. Fairbank, *China's Response to the West. A Documentary Survey*. Cambridge, Mass., Harvard University Press, 1954; 2nd ed. 1979; p.46-59.

[27] Teng and Fairbank, *op. cit.*, p.51. This was written in 1860.

[28] Teng and Fairbank, *op. cit.*, p.52.

[29] This was the slogan of the Chinese reformers of the last decade of the 19th century. Ssu-yü Teng and John K. Fairbank, *op. cit.*, p.169.

[30] Li Shanlan, the translator of the last books of Euclid's *Elements*, was the first Chinese to teach mathematics there.

[31] Frank J. Swetz, "The Introduction of Mathematics in Higher Education in China, 1857-1887", *Historia Mathematica* 1: 167-179 (1974).

[32] Li and Du *op. cit.*, p.33-56.

[33] Ricci and other Italian Jesuits transmitted the teaching of the Collegium Romanum, where Clavius' influence had been predominant.

[34] This was in strong contrast to the Japanese situation: the first Japanese interested in Western medicine in the 18th century learned Dutch and made adaptations of Western works themselves. cf. Donald Keene, *The Japanese Discovery of Europe. 1720-1830*. Stanford, Stanford University Press, 1969; p.17-30.

16

Ottomans and European Science

Ekmeleddin Ihsanoglu

It may be said that the environment with which Western science first came into contact, outside its milieu, was the Ottoman world. The close interaction, geographical proximity and active relations of the Ottomans with Europe, made the Ottomans aware of the novelties and discoveries in Europe. Throughout the history of the Ottoman State which lasted 600 years, the Ottomans naturally took an interest in the developments of Western science and technology. To understand the context and nature of this interest, we have to go back to the 15th century when the features were different from what happened in the 20th century. This would clarify an important subject of Ottoman history; at the same time, it would add a new dimension to the theories put forward about the spread of Western science.

Evidently, the theories of Basalla[1] and Pyenson[2] about the spread of Western science, which cite various examples, are not valid for the Ottoman case, since there is no center-periphery and colonial power-recipient pattern. The matter discussed here is the attitude of a powerful empire towards the occurring developments outside its domain. That is to say, with the exception of the missionary activities of the French and American schools which were founded in Beirut in the second half of the 19th century, the matter is not a question of the influence of the West on the Ottoman State, but rather the interest of Ottomans in the West. For these reasons, construction of the theoretical model for the relationship of Ottomans with Western science would mean to construct a sui generis model or a paradigm.

In order to understand the attitude of the Ottomans towards Western science and technology, we have to bear in mind the Ottomans' general outlook towards the West as well as the state of their own scientific institutions when they faced the necessity to answer new needs.

Their attitude was not any different from their outlook on the Western world. During the first centuries of their history, the Ottomans considered themselves to be morally and materially superior to the Europeans. This consciousness was due to the fact that their economy and finances were sound, they had rich mining sources and military power and were victorious in warfare. Moreover, being heirs of the rich

Islamic civilization of the middle ages and their belief in Islam, as the last and truest faith, were among underlying reasons for this feeling of superiority. In our opinion, while examining Ottoman-Western relationship, the factor of superiority may give us better understanding of the Ottomans' attitude towards Western science.

Moreover, in that period, the cultural and scientific autarchy of the Ottoman State must be considered when evaluating its attitude towards Western science. The *medreses* which were the most important educational and scientific institutions in the Ottoman State were organized to meet the social and cultural needs of people and solve the various problems which they faced. Their own sciences were adequate for the Ottomans in that they were able to find the basic solutions regarding the matters which they needed and their educational system was organized to fulfill this aim. For this reason, they did not need the science of contemporary European countries and did not consider it indispensable. Likewise, the fact that the Ottomans were economically more advanced than the contemporary European and other muslim states, shows that the Ottomans also had a self-sufficient economic system. This self-sufficiency, however, did not prevent the Ottomans from receiving the novelties from the West which they did not possess but considered necessary.

Contacts with the West in the 15th and 16th Centuries

The feeling of superiority and autarchy in the Ottoman State prevented the Ottomans from realizing the importance of the newly developing intellectual and scientific trends of the Renaissance and Scientific Revolution. They did not realize the consequences that would arise from these new developments either. But this did not mean that they were not aware of the technical developments and geographical discoveries of the 15th and 16th centuries. These developments were followed in the Ottoman State in different ways and means, selectively in the fields of warfare, mining technology, geography and medicine.

Direct geographical contact with Europe was an important factor in following the Western developments. Ottoman lands stretched from Rumelia to the middle of the Continent, reaching to the borders of European countries and they also reigned in North Africa and the Mediterranean. Their close geographical proximity with European countries enabled the Ottomans to obtain information about the developments in Europe. At the same time, the Ottoman State had an attraction for Europeans who, one way or another, found a means of arriving in the country. Other means of contact with the West were provided by the diplomats, Europeans who accepted Islam *(muhtedis)*, travellers, merchants, sailors and war prisoners, immigrants, especially the Jews and Morisques who ran away from the religious oppression in Europe. These people were instrumental in transferring a lot of scientific and technical information to the Ottoman State as well as new skills and knowledge.

Geography: In examining maps used by the Ottomans[3] of the 15th century and the geography books such as *Kitab-i Bahriye* (1521)[4] and *Tarih-i Hind-i Garbî* (1580)[5] of the 16th century, European influence is easily recognized. These works show that new elements were transferred from European geography sources in addition to the classic Islamic knowledge of geography. As well as mentioning new geographical discoveries, they gave information gained as a result of these discoveries. It is evident that Ottoman seamen were aware of the developments in cartography and followed the geographical discoveries of this period. An examination of *Kitab-i Bahriye* by Pirî Reis indicates vividly that he supplemented his own observations and findings with information from the West. *Tarih-i Hind-i Garbî* which was prepared around 1580 was based on Spanish and Italian geographical references[6]. It mentions the discovery voyages made to America from 1492 through 1552, giving information backdated thirty years, thus is a measure of the interval with which the Ottomans followed some of the developments in the West.

War technology: Developments regarding the use of firearms and gunpowder in the West were also followed in a similar manner. Ottomans gradually started using firearms at the end of the 14th century, fifty years after the firearms were first used in Europe. Towards the middle of the 15th century, great progress was seen in the Ottoman artillery. Gunsmiths from Italy, Germany and Hungary worked together with the local masters in casting guns. When Bosnia and Serbia were annexed to the Ottoman State, many munition factories and a large number of guns were taken over[7].

Mining: In the 16th century, Ottomans used the same techniques as the Europeans. They were aware of the techniques explained in Agricola's book *De Re Metallica* printed in 1556. Mehmet Ashik, an Ottoman traveller who visited one of the big Ottoman mines of Siderokastron, in the Thrace region, wrote about the equipment and techniques used in the mine which were similar to those defined by Agricola.

Medicine: The Renaissance medical science was brought to the Ottoman State by Spanish, Portugese and Italian physicians of Jewish origin who took refuge in the Ottoman State after 1492[8]. As these physicians were familiar with the new developments in Europe as well as the classic Islamic medicine, they offered their services to the Court and were able to distinguish themselves. Some even became personal physicians of the Sultan. It is interesting to note that besides religious tolerance, the Ottomans also expressed their appreciation for this group, in other ways. Jewish physicians were exempt from some taxes and certain privileges were given to them.

Ottomans' first contact with the Renaissance medicine started with physician Jacopo of Gaeta, a Jew of Italian origin, who entered the service of Murad II (1421-1451). He became personal physician to Sultan Mehmed II and later was favoured with the rank of Chief Physician and Minister. Starting with this Italian physician at the end of the 15th century, the Ottoman State was able to follow the Renaissance medicine in the 16th century, through the Jewish physicians.

Contacts with Western Sciences in the 17th, 18th, and 19th Centuries

As a result of our studies to this day, it appears that from the 17th century to the beginning of the 19th century, Ottoman contacts with the West were realized through three main channels. Firstly through translations made from European languages, secondly via personal observations of Ottoman ambassadors who paid official visits to Europe, and thirdly through modern educational institutions which were established in the Ottoman State at the end of the 18th and at the beginning of the 19th century. From the third decade of the 19th century Ottoman State initiated a new mechanism of acquaintance with Western science by sending students to study in Europe. In the beginning of the 20th century, a Faculty of Science was established within the University of Istanbul *(Dârü'l-fünûn)*, hence a new mechanism of scientific transfer started in Ottoman educational institutions. This was different from the scientific transfer applied in institutions established in the 18th and 19th centuries in the Ottoman history of science. In this paper, we shall try to clarify the nature of the Ottoman attitude toward Western sciences, as a result of our researches on these channels of transfer.

Translations: Though we have many examples of translations in different branches of Western sciences from 17th century onwards, we shall confine ourselves to translations on astronomy which we think will more effectively illustrate the Ottoman attitude to science.

As far as we could establish, the first work of astronomy translated from European languages is astronomical tables entitled *Ephemerides Motuum Celestium Richelianae ex Lansbergii Tabulis* (Paris, 1651) by the French astronomer Noël Duret (d.1650). The translation was made by the Ottoman astronomer Tezkereci Kose Ibrahim Efendi *(Zigetvarli)* in the year 1660 under the title of *Sajanjal al-Aflak fi Ghayat al-Idrak*. Examination of this work shows that within the psychology of Ottoman superiority, the first reaction of the *müneccimbashi* (chief astronomer of the Sultan) was to declare the book to be a "European vanity", but after learning its application and checking with Ulug Bey's *Zij*, he realized its practical use and value and rewarded the translator. This was an indication of the fact that Ottomans were not yet ready to accept the superiority of the West in the field of science. On the other hand, it shows that they were capable of following the developments in the West without a great time lapse.

This translation is also the first book in Ottoman literature which mentions Copernicus. Copernicus' heliocentric theory which caused a controversy in Europe, was taken as an alternative technical detail by the Ottoman astronomers and it was not made a subject for polemics. One probable reason may be that there were no religious dogmas concerning the system of the cosmos.

Other astronomy books translated from European languages, which followed this book, were mostly astronomical tables. Whereas many important works of this period, written by Copernicus, Tycho Brahe, Kepler, and Newton which changed the main principles of the science of astronomy did not interest the Ottoman astronomers.

Translation of the necessary astronomical tables, which were the focus of interest in Ottoman astronomy, instead of the major works of above-mentioned pioneers of modern science, characterize the practical aspect which dominated the Ottoman science. Hence, the Ottomans' interest was not in the science of astronomy, but in the developments concerning calendar making and timekeeping which were necessary for the State and religious affairs and daily life. Ottomans were only interested in and used the things they needed. In other words, theirs was a selective transfer. Their approach to astronomy was an example of what they expected from the West[9].

In examining the scientific literature in Turkish, the astronomical tables in particular, one can easily see that after overcoming their feeling of superiority, new concepts and information and techniques were readily accepted by the Ottoman scientists. The State had a positive outlook and the *"ulema"* (religious circles) did not display a negative attitude. There was no conflict of science and religion at this stage.

Publication of science books began with the establishment of the first official printing house in 1727. Bibliometric studies of these books and the analysis of the contents showed that the objectives of transferring Western sciences changed according to political developments. Books which were printed before 1839, date of the proclamation of the reformation movement known in the Ottoman history as the *Tanzimat,* mostly aimed at realizing military objectives. Books printed after this date generally aimed at developing the civil and social life and other areas of modern science which took up the public interest. There was an increase in the number of books on medicine and mathematics while the number of publications on geography, military art and sciences and astronomy decreased relatively[10].

Ambassadors' Reports *(Sefaretnames):* These reports are exclusive sources that indicate what was most interesting to the Ottoman ambassadors in Europe and what they sought, as well as expressing the Ottoman psychology towards Europe.

Ambassadors, who were very protocol-conscious, concentrated their attention on sites of military significance on their route, the organization of the armies and firearms. The first contact between the ambassadors and European science began with their visits to scientific institutions.

In the 18th century, Ambassador Shehdi Osman Efendi went to the Russian Academy of Sciences in Petersbourg, where he visited the museum of natural history which he called *"acayiphane"* (house of wonders), the library and the printing house. Of these three, he was most interested in the printing house. As to research orientated activities of the Academy of Sciences, he did not report on this as he apparently did not find it worth mentioning. This was not only important in reflecting the subjects in which the ambassador took an interest, but also a conspicuous example that the Ottomans did not take into account the "research-oriented" aspect of Western science which would play an important role in the transfer and establishment of science.

Most notable visits were made to the observatories. We know that two ambassadors paid visits to Paris and Vienna Observatories in the first half of the 18th century. In 1721, Yirmisekiz Mehmed Chelebi visited the Observatory and the Botanical Gardens *(Le Jardin du Roi)* in Paris, while in 1748 Hattî Mustafa Efendi visited Vienna Observatory. Mehmed Chelebi's visit was a significant event for Ottoman science in that besides his personal interest in astronomy, he brought back to Istanbul the astronomical tables presented to him by the director of the Observatory, J. D. Cassini, and gave them to the Ottoman astronomers[11].

Educational Institutions: The main channel through which modern science was introduced to the Ottoman Empire was the new type of educational institutions established at the end of the 18th and the beginning of the 19th century. These institutions were established for more practical reasons such as organizing and making reforms in the army and to provide technically educated officers *(mütefennin zabit),* in order to hold their own against the European armies equipped with the latest techniques. *Hendesehane* (School of Mathematics) which was opened in 1733 was followed by the *Mühendishane-i Bahri-i Hümayun* (Imperial School of Naval Engineering) in 1773. The *Mühendishane-i Berri-i Hümayun* (Imperial School for Military Engineering) which started functioning in 1795, provided to a certain degree, a systematic scientific education[12].

The Ottoman *ulema,* together with foreign experts and engineers, taught lessons in these institutions of modern science. Theoretical science courses were taught by the teachers from the *medreses* while applied sciences were taught by Europeans, mainly French. Thus teachers from these classical educational institutions supported this new movement of modernization in education. After the *Tanzimat* period in the middle of the 19th century, the number of *ulema* teaching in modern schools gradually decreased and they were replaced by engineers and officers who had graduated from these new institutions.

Mühendishane was the first example of the Western-Ottoman synthesis in the framework of institutions. The synthesis is seen in the educational organization such as the formation of classes, system of grading and graduation as well as in the educational staff, curriculum and textbooks. Translation of science books of Western origin gained momentum in the time of Chief Instructor Ishak Efendi. Books compiled by him from the French sources[13] were used as basic educational books in the *Mühendishane.*

In the 19th century, in addition to the *Mühendishanes,* two other modern schools were founded. These were *Mekteb-i Harbiye-i Shahane* (Imperial Military School) founded in 1834[14] and the *Mekteb-i Tibbiye-i Adliye-i Shahane* (Imperial School of Medicine) founded in 1839.

Mahmud II of this period emphasized the importance of these schools by visiting them and favouring the staff.

With the proclamation of the *Tanzimat* reformation movement in 1839, the foundations of radical changes were laid. Though the *Tanzimat Firman* did not include an article on education, the educational policy of the Ottoman State, which was directed at military objectives underwent a transformation and was replaced by public education with a view to raise the educational and cultural level of the people and establish Western style modern educational institutions. Within this understanding, three unsuccessful attempts to open an institution of higher learning namely the *"Dârü'l-fünûn"* (University) were made until the end of the century.

Within the *Tanzimat* period, the educational policy was run by the Council of Public Instruction. *(Meclis-i Maarif-i Umumiye)* and the Ministry of Public Instruction *(Maarif Nezareti)*. In 1869, a commission which was entrusted with the task of studying the French educational system[15] prepared the general educational regulations[16] called the *Maarif-i Umumiye Nizamnamesi*. However, they were not completely successful in implementing many of the articles, especially those regarding the *Dârü'l-fünûn*.

Europeans in Ottoman Lands, Ottomans in Europe

When one considers the role of the Europeans in the transfer of sciences to the Ottoman world, a similar paradigm comes to surface. The influence of the Europeans who were employed by the State from the 16th to 19th centuries may be summarized as follows.

There was a group of Europeans called *Taife-i Efrenciyan* who were employed in the Ottoman Palace to help transfer European war techniques[17]. In the 18th century, we find European experts employed in the Ottoman army who were instrumental in introducing some elements of modernization in the first half of the century. In the second half of the 18th century, foreign teachers, especially French engineers, were employed in the new type of educational institutions founded in this period. These teachers wrote books concerning their subjects and were also employed actively in the fields of gunnery, naval and military engineering.

In the 19th century, physicians were called from Europe to teach in the modern medical schools which were opened in addition to the engineering schools. The French surgeon Sat de Gallière (in 1832)[18] then the Austrian physician C. Ambroise Bernard in 1839 , contributed to the modernization of the medical school in Istanbul. Modern medical education was carried out more systematically in Bernard's time. However, in the trials to establish the *Dârü'l fünûn*, no attempt was made to bring teachers or scientists from Europe.

Apart from those who were employed in State services, there is no evidence that European scholars who applied for entry to the Ottoman State, mostly for archaeological studies or scientific field researches, were functional in the transfer of Western sciences into the Ottoman world. We may briefly say that the role of the Europeans was to fulfill the services required by the State and was subject to the initiative of the statesmen. Naturally, the situation of Western teachers who worked in the French and American educational institutions, established in the second half of the 19th century as part of the missionary activities in Beirut, constitute a separate subject outside the above generalization.

A new episode in the introduction and transfer of Western sciences started in the 19th century with the influx of students who were sent to Europe for training. This practice which started in the period of Mahmud II (1808-1839) was confined to military education. After the proclamation of the *Tanzimat* in 1839, students also received training in other disciplines in Europe. Between the years 1864-1876, 93 students were sent to France, of these 42 were officers and military physicians. The rest received their training in different professions, such as lathe operators, carpenters, upholstery workers, etc[19]. Here we also observe that the *Tanzimat* movement caused a shift in the transfer of Western sciences from military to civilian ends and also in the objectives of science and learning.

Conclusion

Following is the general conviction which we deduce from an examination of the contacts and attempts related to Ottoman-European relationship in the field of science.

The Ottomans did not consider it necessary to deal with the process of the transfer of Western science as a whole. At the beginning, the Ottomans' feeling of superiority and the autarchy of the Ottoman State led them to implement this transfer process only in the necessary fields. One can say that this process, which can be called a functional transfer, was carried out in two categories as before and after the *Tanzimat*, both categories having the same characteristics.

Before the *Tanzimat* period, the State had need of the army and military techniques, while medicine, astronomy and others were necessary for the administration and the needs of the public. The Ottomans required the immediate transfer of science and techniques concerning the former subjects while this movement did not extend beyond practical purposes. After the *Tanzimat,* this transfer was made with the objective of serving the public needs. The change in the objectives of the State was also reflected in the field of science, and the transformation from military to civilian objectives is observed in what was expected from science.

In conclusion we may say that the Ottomans did not consider the Western science as a whole. The new concepts and mentality arising from the scientific revolution, that is, research of matter, space, time, movement and nature, as well as the essence of research and detailed study, escaped their attention.

Perhaps, it would not be an exaggeration to say that Ottomans' principal interest was oriented towards practical ends and the application of scientific discoveries while the three main aspects of science, namely theory, experiment and research were not taken into consideration. This understanding was reflected in the educational and "scientific" policy of the Ottoman State before and during the *Tanzimat* period and no attempt was made to include scientific research per se in the curriculum of the educational institutions. For this reason, institutions established for the transfer of Western sciences were not as successful as their counterparts in Russia and Japan.

Naturally the determination of every aspect of Ottoman-Western science relationship depends on new researches. As stated above, however, the feeling of superiority and autarchy which was dominant among the Ottomans, explains one aspect of this relationship until the middle of the 18th century.

The paradigm of "Ottoman-European Science" relationship which we examined in a broad sense from its beginning to the middle of the 19th century, continued after the middle of the century without changing its main traits. The greatest exception in the 20th century was that the Faculty of Science established in 1900 in the University of Istanbul aimed to teach science itself instead of the previous practice where science was taught as an auxiliary course for civilian and military professions. Meanwhile, we may say that the subsequent increase in scientific activities created some new factors and developments which had controversial effects, especially from intellectual and social viewpoints. An analysis of these developments could be the subject of another study.

Research Center for Islamic History, Art and Culture (ICIRCA), Istanbul

Notes

* The well known works (Bernard Lewis, *The Emergence of Modern Turkey*, 2nd ed. London 1968; Sherif Mardin, *The Genesis of Young Ottoman Thought*, Princeton 1962; Niyazi Berkes, *The Development of Secularism in Turkey*, Montreal 1964; Roderic H. Davison, *Reform in the Ottoman Empire, 1856-1876*, New York 1973), which treat the relation of the Ottomans with the West, have dealt more with the political and cultural aspect of the subject. Lewis has treated the subject as a separate chapter in his work entitled *The Muslim Discovery of Europe* (1982). His evaluations are based on the studies on History of Science up to that point and on the widespread opinions about the subject. The most important opinion among them is the one which states that the *ulema* are opposed to European science and technology. As a result of the studies conducted in the last ten years, this opinion is now changed (See E. Ihsanoglu, *Annotated Bibliography of Turkish Literature of Chemistry: Printed Works 1830-1928*, Istanbul 1985, in Turkish; *The Ottoman Scientific and Professional Associations* (ed. Ihsanoglu), Istanbul 1987, in Turkish; "Some critical notes on the Introduction of Modern Sciences to the Ottoman State and the Relation Between Science and Religion up to the End of the 19th Century", *Varia Turcica IV*, Comité international d'études pré-ottomanes et ottomanes, VIth Symposium, Cambridge, 1-4 July 1984, Proceedings, Istanbul-Paris-Leiden 1987, p.235-251.

  In the current paper, some results deduced from our studies on Ottoman understanding of science are presented in short notes. It may not be possible to give the whole picture here due to lack of space, but we tried to delineate the main lines of the subject. Our study, which treats the relations of Ottomans with Western science, more extensively, is in press (See. E.Ihsanoglu, "Tanzimat Oncesi ve Tanzimat Donemi Osmanli Bilim ve Egitim Anlayisi", *Tanzimat II*, Türk Tarih Kurumu, Ankara 1991, in press).

[1] G. Basalla, "The Spread of Western Science", in *Science*, vol.156, n°3775, 1967, p.611-622.

[2] Lewis Pyenson, "Pure Learning and Political Economy: Science and European Expansion", in R. P. W. Visser, H. J. M. Bos, L. C. Palm, H. A. M. Snelders (eds.), Proceedings of the Utrecht Conference, *New Trends in the History of Science*, Amsterdam, 1989, Rodopi.

[3] Maps prepared by Ibrahim Kâtibî in 1416; by Mürsiyeli Ibrahim in 1461; and map made by Pirî Reis, drawn on Colombus' map dated 1489 and presented by Pirî Reis to Yavuz Sultan Selim in 1513.

[4] Pirî Reis, *Kitab-i Bahriye*, facsimile edition published by Türk Tarihi Arashtirma Kurumu, Istanbul 1935.

[5] *Tarih-i Hind-i Garbi ve Hadis-i Nev*, facsimile edition published by T. C. Kültür ve Turizm Bakanligi, Istanbul 1987.

[6] Thomas D. Goodrich, *The Ottoman Turks and the New World, A Study of Tarih-i Hind-i Garbi and 16th Century Ottoman Americana*, Wiesbaden 1990.

[7] V. J. Parry, "Barud", *Encyclopaedia of Islam* (EI2), vol.I, Leiden-Brill 1979, p.1060-66; Djurdjica Petrovic, "Firearms in the Balkans on the Eve of and After the Ottoman

Conquests of the 14th and 15th Centuries", *War, Technology and Society in the Middle East*, ed. V. J. Parry and M. E. Yapp, London 1975, p.164-194.

[8] Avram Galante, *Türkler ve Yahudiler*, 2nd ed., Istanbul, 1947, p.101-102; A. Galante, "Médecins Juifs au Service de la Turquie", *Histoire des Juifs de Turquie*, vol.IX, n.d., ed. ISIS, p.71-117.

[9] E. Ihsanoglu, "Introduction of Modern Astronomy to the Ottoman State: 1660-1860", 1st International Symposium on Modern Science and the Muslim World, Istanbul, Sept.1987, *Proceedings* (ed. E. Ihsanoglu), in press.

[10] Feza Günergun, "A General Survey on Turkish Books of Science Printed During the Last Two Centuries of the Ottoman State", paper presented at the XVIIIth International Congress of History of Science, Hamburg-Munich, 1-9 August 1989, (unpublished paper).

[11] E. Ihsanoglu, "Tanzimat Oncesi ve Tanzimat Donemi Osmanli Bilim ve Egitim Anlayishi", *Tanzimat II*, Türk Tarih Kurumu, Ankara 1991, in press; for the French edition of Mehmed Chelebi's report see *Le paradis des Infidèles, un ambassadeur ottoman en France sous la Régence*, éd. Gilles Veinstein, Paris 1981.

[12] Cavid Baysun, "Eski Mühendishanelerin Kurulushuna Ve Bazi Hocalara Dair", Istanbul Teknik Okulu Yilligi, Istanbul (1952), p.52-54.

[13] E. Ihsanoglu, *Bashhoca Ishak Efendi, Türkiye'de Modern Bilimin Oncüsü (Chief Instructor Ishak Efendi, Pioneer of Modern Science in Turkey)*, Kültür Bakanligi Kaynak Eserler Dizisi, Ankara 1989, (with a summary in English).

[14] Osman Nuri Ergin, *Türkiye Maarif Tarihi*, vols.1-2, Istanbul 1977, p.354-368.

[15] Mehmed Galip Bey, *Sadullah Pasha Yahud Mezardan Nida*, 1909, Ebüzziya Press, p.26-28.

[16] E. Ihsanoglu, "Dârü'l-fünûn Tarihçesine Girish: Ilk Iki Teshebbüs", *Belleten*, vol.LIV, n°210, 1990, p.699-738.

[17] Rhoads Murphey, "The Ottoman Attitude Towards the Adoption of Western Technology: the Role of the Efrenci Technicians in Civil and Military Applications", *Contributions à l'Histoire Economique et Sociale de l'Empire Ottoman*, Collection Turcica III, Editions Peeters, Louvain (Belgique), 1983, p.287-298.

[18] *Takvim-i Vakayi*, n°11, 11 Shaban 1247 (15 January 1832), p.2, col. 3; No information was available about the identity of Sat de Gallière who is said to be a French surgeon.

[19] Adnan Shishman, *Tanzimat Doneminde Fransa'ya Gonderilen Osmanli Ogrencileri*, Ph. D. diss., Istanbul University, 1983.

Index

Abbeville, Nicolas Sanson d', geographer, 236
Academia del Cimento, 14
Académie des Sciences, 14, 35, 63
Adanson, Michel, botanist, 6, 40
Admiralty, British, 116–17, 120, 123
Adriansz, Pieter, 192–3
aeroplane, 17th-century anticipation of, 286
Africa
  cartography, 165
  scientific expeditions in, 5, 40
Agassiz, Louis, 13
Agemaryo, Brahman medical practitioner, 248
agraharas, 248
Agricola, *De Re Metallica*, 317
air-pump, 297
Airy, George, astronomer, 42
Alarcón, Hernando, explorer, 145, 219
Aleni, Giulio, S.J., cartographer, 202–3, *203*,
  205
Aleutian Islands, 103
algebra, Chinese and, 283
Algiers, 65
Amane, Nishi, 277
Amazon river basin, English surveys of, 181–
  93, *182*, *184–5*
America(s)/New World, *see also* United States
  European colonization, 112, 140, 173–4
  European trade with, 115, 117, 181
  exploration, 104–5
  mapping, *see* cartography, of Amazon river
    basin; cartography, of North America
  spread of modern science in, 3–4, 8, 32–4,
    38–43
American Indians, *see also* Hohokam;
  Totonteacs; Trincheras; Zuni
  contributions to mapping of North America,
    211–17, *214*, 219–45
  observation by European explorers,
    historiographic considerations, 140–1,
    146–52
  in southwestern North America, 140–52
American Revolution, 75
Amery, Lord, 47
anatomy, studied in Japan, 264
Annual Magazine of Natural History, 42
Ansai, Yamazaki, 264
Anson, George, navigator, 68, 99, 106, 116,
  119–20
Antarctica, scientific expeditions in, 4
anthropology, 2, 125, 140–1, 146–52

Antilles, scientific expeditions in, 63
Antunes, Francisco, physician, 255
archaeology, 2, 149
Archer, Gabriel, British captain, 212, 214–15
Areche, José Antonio, inspector in Peru, 64
armillary sphere, 296–7, *303*
Arriaga, Juliàn, minister of Indies and
  Marine, 64
Ashik, Mehmet, traveler, 317
Asiatic Society of Bengal, 39
astronomical instruments
  design and construction, 296–7
  in Peking observatory, 297–8, *303*
astronomy, 2, 17, 63, 65
  Chinese, 284–8, 306, 312; European
    accounts of, 288–90; integration into
    modern science, 297–302; Jesuits' role
    in, 283
  European, 290
  Japanese, 261, 263–5, 267–70, 293, 301
  Ottoman, 319–21
Auchagah, cartographer, 220, 224, 228, 230,
  234
Australasian Association for the Advancement
  of Science, 45
Australia, 74, 94–5, 118; *see also* New South
  Wales
  science in, 13, 40–2
  scientific expeditions in, 4, 81
Austria, 1
Auteroche, Chappe d', director of Hispanic
  French Commission, 59, 63
autopsy, in Japan, 264–5
awards, in scientific communities, 12, 14, 30,
  45, 122–3
Ayurveda, 247–57
Azara, 63
Azevedo, Simão de, physician, 255

Bacon, Sir Francis, philosopher, 2, 89
Baja California, 63
Banks, Sir Joseph, naturalist, 4, 38, 48, 72,
  76, 81, 102, 124
Bansha no Goku incident, 270–2, 280–1
Bantô, Yamagata, merchant/scholar, 268
Barcaztegui, 63
Barreto, António Moniz, Governor of Goa,
  250
Bartram, John, scientist, 3
Bartram, William, scientist, 3

Basalla, George, historian, 1–18, 30–3, 35
Batavia, 94–5, 100–1
Bateson, William, geneticist, 17
Baudin, Nicolas, navigator, 80–1
Beaglehole, John C., historian, 123
Beagle, ship, 38
Beauchesne, navigator, 106
Beauharnois, Marquis de, governor general of
    New France, 220, 224, 226–7, 231
Bellin, Jacques Nicolas, geographer, 225, *226*,
    227, 234, 241–2
Bello, Andrés, educator, 11
Benoist, Michael, 297
Bering, Vitus, navigator, 86, 103
Bernard, C. Ambroise, physician, 322–3
Bernard-Maître, 290
Betagh, William, traveler, 58
Bhātta, Apu, Brahman physician, 255
Bhātta, Ranga, Brahman physician, 255
Bhāva Prakāsa, 249
Blaeu, Willem, cartographer, 167, 172, 209
Blanchardière, traveler, 59
Block, Adriaen, cartographer, *222*, 243
Blunt, Winfred Scawen, 46
Board of Longitude, 122
Bodega, 63
Boer War, 45
Bonaechea, 62
Bonpland, Aime, 58
book publishing, Ottoman, 320
Boston, as scientific center, 4
Botanical Gardens of Guatemala and Mexico,
    65
Botanical Gardens of Paris, 320–1
Botanic Gardens at Calcutta, 5
botany, 2, 4–5, 58, 61, 65
    Indian, 255–7
Botany Bay, 76, 78
Boto, Rama, Hindu physician, 253
Bougainville, Louis de, explorer, 69, 71, 86,
    118, 120, 123, 125–6
Bouger, Pierre, 59
Boumois, *see* Vérendrye, Pierre Gaultier de
    Varennes et de la
Bouvet, De Lozier, statesman, 119
Boxer, Charles R., historian, 252
Boym, Michael, Jesuit missionary, 290–1
Brahe, Tycho, astronomer, 284, 291, 306–7
brahmapuris, communities of learned
    Brahmans, 248
Brahm, William Gerard, surveyor, 216–17
Brazil, 109
    modern science in: Dutch rule and, 8;
        social factors, 13, *16*

Brisbane, Sir Thomas, astronomer, 38, 41
British Department of Scientific and Industrial
    Research, 48
British East India Company, 5, 103, 114
British Empire League, 47
British Royal Navy, 108, 116–17
British Science Guild, 46–7
Brosses, Charles de, *Histoire des Navigations
    aux terres australes*, 118–19
Brouwer, Hendrick, Dutch commander, 104
Brown, Robert, *Prodromus florae novae
    Hollandiae et insulae Van-Diemen*, 4
Bruno, Giordano, *De Infinito Universo*, 285
Bry, Theodore de, 172
Buache, Philippe, geographer, 225
buccaneers, 105
Buchan, Alexander, technical artist, 72
Bud, British captain, 188
Butler, A. G., 48
Byron, John, British captain, 68–9, 116, 118–
    19

Caamano, 63
Cadiz, 62
Caille, Nicola Louis de la, traveler, 59
Caldwell, William, scientist, 43, 51
calendar
    Chinese, 290, 292–3, 295–6, 306–7
    Japanese, 263–4, 267–70
Canada, 79
Canary Islands, 63
Cape Horn, 98–9, 107, 116
Careri, Giovanni Francesco Gemelli,
    physician/traveler, 254
Carteret, Philip, navigator, 116, 119
Cartier, Jacques, explorer, 219
cartography, 2, 125, 169
    of Amazon river basin, 181–93, *182*, *184–5*
    in Asia, Ricci's influence on, 198–210, *200*
    historiographic considerations, 174–5, 243–4
    of North America: American Indian
        contributions to, 211–17, *214*, 219–45;
        historiographic considerations, 211
    omissions in, 161–75; classification, 161–2,
        169–70; economic aspects, 165–9;
        epistemological aspects, 169–74;
        political aspects, 161, 163–75;
        religious aspects, 170–2, *171*; scientific
        aspects, 169–70; social aspects, 170–2;
        strategic aspects, 164–5
    Ottoman, 317
    philosophical considerations, 162–3, 170
Casa de Contratación, board of trade, 165–6,
    169

Cassini, J.D., astronomer, 321
Castile, *see* Spain
Catesby, Mark, scientist, 3
Ceballos, 63
censorship, in cartography, 163–5
Cevallos, Pedro, minister to Charles IV, 64
Chamberlain, Neville, statesman, 46
Champlain, Samuel, explorer, 211, 237
Chang Heng, astronomer, 204
Charaka *samhita*, 247
Charles II, king of England, 105
Charles III, king of England, 110
Charles III, king of Spain, 64
Charles IV, king of Spain, 65
Charles V, king of Spain, 168
Chegeree, cartographer, 216
Chekhov, Anton, writer, 18
chemistry, Japanese, 272
Chesapeake Bay region, mapping, American
    Indian contributions to, 212–15, *213*
Chevalier, Jean-Baptiste, 72
Chhung-Chên Li Shu (Chhung-Chên Reign-
    Period Treatise on (Astronomy and)
    Calendrical Science), 294–5
Chiang Yung, astronomer, 300
Chile, 59, 63–4
China
    academies of Lower Yangtze area, 308–9
    Board of Astronomy, 306–7
    Board of Rites, 306
    cartography in, 198–205
    cosmology, 284–8; cartography and, 203–4
    European trade with, 102, 104
    Ming period, 288–9, 301
    spread of modern science in, 3–4, 283–97
    western mathematics in, 305–12
Chinese learning, influence in Japan, 261–6
Chôei, Takano, 271
Chomel's Encyclopedia, translation into
    Japanese, 274–5, 279
Chüan Chin, cartographer, 199
Chu Hsi, Confucian, 261–2
Churruca, 63
Chûtoku, Ishiguro, 276
Cibola, 140–51
Cipolla, Carlo, *European Culture and
    Overseas Expansion*, 28
Ciudad-Rodrigo, Antonio de, friar in Mexico,
    144
civilization-savagery myth, 151
Clairac, 63
Clark, William, explorer, 4, 211
Clavius, Christopher, Jesuit astronomer, 290,
    306

Clayton, John, scientist, 3
Cleyer, Andreas, botanist, 4
cochineal, 59
Cohen, I. Bernard, historian, 29
Colégio de São Paulo, Jesuit college in Goa,
    250
College of Chinese Mathematicians, 199
colonies, modern science in, 6–18, 29, 38–43
    dependence on Western Europe, 8–12, 29–
        31, 39, 41–2
    economic aspects, 32–4
    historiographic considerations, 26–7, 31–4
    independence from Western Europe, 12–18
    political aspects, 34, 39
Columbus, Christopher, explorer, 90–1, 211
Comberford, Nicholas, cartographer, 190
Commerson, Philibert, naturalist, 59, 71
Compagnie de la Chine, 106
Compagnie de la Mer Pacifique, 106
Compania de Filipinas, 57
*Compendio y descripción de las Indias
    Occidentales*, 58
Condamine, Charles Marie de la, 59, 63–4
Confucianism
    and Chinese science, 307–8
    influence in Japan, 261–6
    and modern science, 12–13
Conrad, Joseph, author, 87
Consulado de La Habana, 57
Cook, Captain James, navigator, 4, 72–5, 77–
    8, 86–8, 116, 119–20, 123, 125–6
Cooke, Edward, privateer, 105
Copernicus, Nicolas, astronomer, 204, 319
    heliocentric theory, 284, 290–3
Coronado, Francisco Vásquez de, conqueror,
    143–7
Coronelli, Vincenzo Maria, geographer, 235, *238*
Correia, Gaspar, historian, 250
Cortés, Hernando, conqueror, 145
cosmology, Chinese, 284–8
    cartography and, 203–4
Costa, Dom Rodrigo da, Governor of
    Portuguese India, 255
creation, scientific views on, 40, 42
crystalline spheres, dissolution, China and,
    283–8
Cuellar, 58, 63, 65
Cunningham, Peter, 42

Dalrymple, Alexander, historian, 115
Dampier, William, navigator, 86, 88, 100, 105
Daniel, John, cartographer, 190
Darwin, Charles, naturalist, 3, 9
    theory of evolution, 6

Das Deutsche Kolonialreich, 5
David, Sir Percival and Lady, benefactors, 198, 203
Deakin, Alfred, prime minister of Australia, 47
Defoe, Daniel
  The Consolidator; or Memoirs of Sundry Transactions from the World in the Moon, 286
  Robinson Crusoe, 85–6
della Briga, Melchior, 298
Dellon, Gabriel, French physician, 254
Denison, Sir William, 43
Dias, Manuel, S.J., cartographer, 198, *201*, 202, 204
Diaz, Emanuel, *Thien Wên Lüeh* (Explicatio Sphaerae Coelestis), 290
diseases
  European, effect on American Indians, 140–1, 148
  search for cures for, 46
Dolphin, ship, 70, 73
Dombey, N., scientist, 64
Dom Pedro II, King of Portugal, 255
Drake, Sir Francis, navigator, 165, *166*
Dudley, Robert, *Arcano de Mare*, 183, 186, *186*
Dupaix, 63
Duret, Noël, astronomer, 319
Dutch
  in Amazon basin, 183, 186, 189–93
  in Brazil, 8
  and spread of modern science, 1
Dutch East India Company, 4, 93–7, 100–1, 114
  cartography and, 166–7
Dutch West India Company, 94–6, 100, 104, 189
Duyvendak, 290

Easter Island, 63
eclipses, prediction
  Chinese methods, 283–4
  European methods, 283
economy
  and exploration of Pacific Ocean, 88, 92, 95–6, 101–5, 113–19
  and spread of modern science, in New World colonies, 32–4
Edkins, Joseph, Protestant missionary, 293
Edo, Japan, importation of western culture through, 259–60
education
  and development of modern science, 8–9, 13–14
  Ottoman, 321–2
Egmont, Earl of, 116, 120

Egypt, Napoleonic campaign in, scientific aspects, 5, 14
Egyptology, 5
Ekken, Kaibara, scholar, 261
elements
  Aristotelian, 284
  Chinese, 284
Elia, Pasquale d', 290
Elizalde, 63
Endeavour, ship, 72
England, *see* Great Britain
Entrecasteux, Joseph-Antoine Bruni d', navigator, 79–81
Enzu, Buddhist astronomer, 301
episteme, 162–3, 169, 172, 174
Escobedo, Jorge, inspector in Peru, 64
Espinosa, Antonio Vazquez de, scientist, 58
Esteban, slave, 141, 143–6
ethnology, 2, 140–1, 146, 149–51
Euclid's *Elements of Geometry*
  Pardiès' translation, 306
  translated into Chinese, 306–7, 309, 311
Europe, *see* Western Europe
evolution, Darwinian theory, 6, 42

Falkland Islands, 68–70, 99, 110, 116, 120
Feng Guifen, *see* Fêng Kuei-Fên
Fêng Kuei-Fên, astronomer, 300, 310
Ferdinand VI, king of Spain, 64, 110
Feuillée, Louis, traveler, 58–9
Fidalgo, 63
Field, Barron, 40
firearms, in Ottoman State, 317
Fleming, Donald, historian, 29, 39
Fleury, André-Hercule de, cardinal and statesman, 108
Flinders, Matthew, British explorer, 81
Flood, Captain, 189
Florida, 65
Fontenelle, B. de, *Entretiens sur la Pluralité des Mondes*, 287
Forrest, Jesse de, traveler, 190–1
Forster, Johann Reinhold, scientist, 74–5
Foster, John, cartographer, 239, *244*
Foucault, Michel, philosopher, 162–3, 172
Foucquet, Jean-François, 296
France
  exploration of Pacific Ocean, 69, 71–2, 75–6, 79–81; political aspects, 106–8, 110, 119–20; scientific aspects, 71, 79–81, 124
  naval power, 118–19, 121
  science in, 1, 9, 14–15, 124; cooperation with Spain, 63

Franklin, Benjamin, statesman and scientist, 9, 11
Franklin, Sir John, explorer, 39
free trade, 114
French East India Company, 104
Fresne, Marion du, navigator, 72
Freycinet, Louis de, navigator, 81
Frézier, Amédée François, traveler, 58–9
Fryer, John, Protestant missionary, 293
Fry, Roger, British captain, 190
Furtado, Francis, 295

Galileo Galilei, scientist, 204, 284, 290–1
Gallière, Sat de, surgeon, 322–3
Gálvez, José, inspector in New Spain, 64
Gama, Vasco da, explorer, 28
Garden, Alexander, scientist, 3
Gaultier, Pierre, see Vérendrye, Pierre Gaultier de Varennes et de la
Gemboku, Itô, scholar, 271–3
Gempaku, Sugita, scholar, 260–2, 265–6, 280
Gen'i, Nagoya, physician, 261–2
Genkei, Nakane, astronomer, 265, 293
Genkyô, Hirose, scholar, 272
Genseki, Habu, 270
Gentaku, Otsuki, 266, 268, 271
Genzui, Uragawa, 271
geography, 2, 97–9, 101, 105, 121, 124–5; see also cartography
Ottoman, in 15th and 16th c., 317
geology, 2, 64
geophysics, 2
Germany, 1, 5, 9
colonial wealth, 5
Gibbs, Josiah Willard, mathematician and physicist, 9
Gila Polychrome, pottery, 150–1
Gilbert, John, ornithologist, 43
Gilbert, William, De Magnete, 285
glassmaking, Japanese, 278
Goa, Portuguese territory, 311
Arab settlements in, 248–9
Ayurvedic medicine in, 247–57
Christianization, 249–55
conquest by Portugal, 247–8
Konkani language, 255
Godin, Louis, 59
Godoy, 64
Godwin, Francis, The Man in the Moon; or, A Discourse of a Voyage Thither, by Domingo Gonsales, the Speedy Messenger, 286
Gogeisl, Anton, astronomer, 298

gold, 142–3
Gonçalves, Sebastião, Jesuit missionary, 253
Gôryû, Asada, scholar/astronomer, 269
Gosnold, Bartholomew, navigator, 211
gravity, Chinese theory, 204
Great Britain
cartography in, 164, 167
exploration of Pacific Ocean: economic aspects, 88, 103–5, 113–19, 123; political aspects, 67–8, 72–81, 86, 100–1, 106, 108, 110, 114, 119–20; rivalry with other European powers, 69–70, 77, 79–81, 100–1, 108, 120–1; scientific aspects, 70–2, 74–6, 79, 81, 104–5, 120–3, 165
imperial expansion, science and, 1, 5, 27, 35–51, 124
naval power, 108, 116–17, 119–21
relations with Spain, 108–10, 120
Great Lakes, mapping, 220–8, 223–224, 228, 241–2
Green, Charles, 72
Grimaldi, Jeronimo, 64
Guatemala, 61
Guhalla-dēva, Brahman king, 248
Guiana, English surveys, 181–93, 182, 184–185
Guinal, 62–3
Guzmán, Diego de, explorer, 145–6
Guzmán, Nuño de, explorer, 145

hakims, Muslim physicians, 249
Hakuseki, Arai, Japanese official, 205
Half King, native American leader, 216
Halley, Edmund, astronomer, 122
Hanke, Tadeo, scientist, 64
Harcourt, Robert, 186–7, 189
Harlow, Vincent, historian, 112–15
Harriot, Thomas, traveler, 3
Harrison, purser, 71
Harumi, Shibukawa, astronomer, 261, 263–4
Hatti Mustafa Efendi, Ottoman ambassador, 321
Hector, Sir James, scientist, 45
Henderson, John, 41
Hennepin, Jean-Louis, explorer, 235
Hernandez, Francisco, traveler, 58
Herschel, Sir John Frederick William, astronomer, 38
Heuland brothers, scientists, 58, 63–5
Hire, P. de la, 296
Hirobumi, Itô, Meiji Prime Minister, 277
Hohokam, native Americans, 141, 149–51
Ho Kuo-Tsung, 294

Holland, cultural exchange with Japan, 259–82
Hooker, Sir Joseph Dalton, *Flora Indica*, 5
Hooker, W.J., botanist, 40, 42
Hoshû, Katsuragawa, 271
Howe, Richard, 1st Earl, admiral, 76
Howes, Edmund, chronicler, 181–3
Hsin Fa Suan Shu (Treatise on Mathematics (and Astronomy) according to the New Methods), 296
Hsi-Yang Hsin Fa Li Shu (Treatise on (Astronomy and) Calendrical Science according to the New Western Methods), 294–5
Hsü Chao-Chün, astronomer, 300
Hsüeh Fêng-Tsu, astronomer, 299
Hsü Fa, 300
Hsü Kuang-Chhi, *see* Hsü Kuang-ch'i
Hsü Kuang-ch'i, scholar, 202, 293
Hudson's Bay Company, 220
Humboldt, Alexander von, 58
Huxley, Thomas Henry, biologist, 44
Huygens, Christian, 286
Hyam, Ronald, historian, 25
hydrography, 2, 63, 165–6, *230*

iasak, tax, 103
Idea del Reino de la Nueva España, 58
imperialism
    relation to science, 23–51; historiographic considerations, 25–7, 31–4, 49–51, 126; political aspects, 34, 39, 46–51; World War I and, 48
    technology and, 28, 125
India
    British control, 114
    European trade with, 102–3
    modern science in, 3–5, 38, 40, 48
    syphilis introduced into, 249
Indian Ocean, 90, 94
Indian Science Congress, 48
indigo, 59
Institut d'Egypte, 14
interplanetary travel, 17th-century romances about, 286
Ishak Efendi, Ottoman educator, 321
Isle, Guillaume de l', cartographer, 224, 227, 233, 242
Institut de France, 14
Italy, and spread of modern science, 1
Iturriaga, 62

Jacopo of Gaeta, physician, 318
Jakusui, Inô, scholar, 261

Jamal-ud-Din, astronomer, 199, 202
Japan
    bureau for translation of Dutch books, 274–5
    cartography in, 198–9, 205–10
    European trade with, 95, 101–3
    first contact with Europeans, 259
    Meiji government, 258, 273, 276–7
    modern science in, 2, 4, 8–11; government and, 13, 276–7; pre-history of, 258–82
    Office for the Inspection of Foreign Books, 275
    Tokugawa Shogunate: importation and assimilation of western science during, 258–9, 261; policy of seclusion, 258–9, 269–70, 274, 281
    western learning in, 274–5, 279–82; Echizen fief and, 278; Matsushiro fief and, 278; Môri fief and, 277; Nabeshima fief and, 278; Nagato fief and, 277–8; Satsuma fief and, 277–8
Jayakēsi I, Kadamba King of Goa, 249
Jesuits, *see also* missionaries
    in China, 4, 198–205, 283–303, 305–9, 311–12
    Christian converts in China, 306
    in New World, 141, 148, 151
    and spread of modern science, 4, 198–210, 283–303, 305–9, 311–12
Jinsai, Itô, Confucian, 262
Jirô, Numata, historian, 280
João II, king of Portugal, 165
Jolliet, Louis, explorer, 235
journals, scientific, 14
Jussieu, Laurent de, botanist, 80

Kaempfer, Engelbert, botanist, 4
Kagesuke, Shibukawa, astronomer, 270
Kageyasu, Takahashi, astronomer, 266, 269–70, 275
Kaikô, Yamaji, astronomer, 270
Kaitai Shinsho, 260–1, 265–71
Kalm, Peter, scientist, 3
Kamala-dēvi, Kadamba Queen of Goa, 248
Kangxi, Manchu emperor, 306–8
Kanrin Maru, Japanese vessel, 276–7
Kaoru, Inoue, 277
Kazan, Watanabe, 280–1
Kennedy, Edmund, surveyor, 43
Kepler, Johannes, astronomer, 290–1
Keynes, John Maynard, economist, 88
Kikai Kanran, 272
King, P.D., geographer, 40
King, Philip Gidley, British administrator, 80–1

King, Thomas, British captain, 181, 183, *185*, 187, 190–2
Kirwitzer, Wenceslaus, 291
Knox, Sir Thomas, anatomist, 41
Kôan, Ogata, physician, 271, 273
Kögler, Ignatius, 294, 298
Kôgyû, Yoshio, interpreter, 266
Kôjô, Hashimoto, 276
Kôkan, Shiba, painter/scholar, 268
Kômin, Kawamoto, scholar, 272
Konkani, language of Goa, 255
Kon'yô, Aoki, scholar, 260, 265
Konzan, Gotô, physician, 261–2, 264
Kôsei Shimpen, 275
Kublai Khan, 199
Kuo Shou-Ching, 288

Laet, Jan de, historian, 189
Laet, Samuel de, 189
Lahontan, traveler, 216
Lake Superior, 224, 229, 233–4, 239
Lake Winnipeg, 228–30, 234, 241
Langara, 63
La Pérouse, Comte de La, navigator, 75–6, 79–80
La Salle, Robert Cavelier Sieur de, explorer, 211
Las Casas, Bartolomé de, historian, 146
latitude, five zones, 199, 203
Lavradio, Marquis of, 73
Law of the Americas, 69
Lawrence, Robert, botanist, 40
Lawson, John, "Account of the Indians of North Carolina," 215–16
Lecomte, 289–90
Lederer, John, explorer, 217
Leggatt, John, explorer, 183
Leibniz, Gottfried Wilhelm, philosopher/mathematician, 307
Leon, Joaquin Velazquez de, 63
Léry, Chaussegros de, cartographer, *224*, 224–7, *225*, 231, 233–4, 241–2
Lewis, Meriwether, explorer, 4, 211
Li Chih-Tsao, scholar, 202–3, 293, 296
Li Ma-tou, *see* Ricci, Matteo
Li Min-Chhê, Taoist, 301
Linnaeus, Carolus, botanist, 72
Li Shanlan, mathematician, 309
Li Thien-Ching, 293
Li Tse-min, cartographer, 199
Liversidge, Archibald, 51
Löeffling, Peter, botanist, 62, 64
Lomonosov, Mikhail V., chemist, 9
longitude, determination, 122, 125

Longobardi, Nicolo, S.J., cartographer, 198, *201*, 202, 293
Louis XIV, king of France, 307
Lyell, Sir Charles, *Geology*, 42

Macao, 311
Magellan, Ferdinand, navigator, 90
Magellanica, 199, 202
Mahmud II, Ottoman emporer, 322–3
Maire, Jacob, navigator, 98
malaria, 46
Malaspina, Alejandro, explorer, 61, 63–5, 78–9
Malay Archipelago, 4
Manila galleon, 90, 92
Manson, Patrick, scientist, 44
Mantri, Madhava, Governor of Goa, 248
Manucci, Niccolo, 254
maps, *see also* cartography
    historiographic considerations, 174–5, *243–4*
    mosaicing, 229, *233*
    omissions in, 161–75; classification, 161–2, 169–70; economic aspects, 165–9; epistemological aspects, 169–74; political aspects, 161, 163–75; religious aspects, 170–2, *171*; scientific aspects, 169–70; social aspects, 170–2; strategic aspects, 164–5
    philosophical considerations, 162–3, 170
Marcos de Niza, *see* Niza, Marcos de
Marquette, Jacques, explorer, 235
Marteblanche, cartographer, 230, 239
Martinez, José Longinos, 61
Martinez, Spanish commodore, 78
Massa, Isaac, merchant, 164
Masson, Francis, botanist, 76
mathematics
    Chinese, 288, 305–12
    education in, in China, 311
    Japanese, 261, 263, 267
    technological uses in China, 310–12
    western, in China, 305–12
Mboya, Tom, 47
medical knowledge, exchange between India and Portugal, in Goa, 247–57
medicine, *see also* Ayurveda
    Arabic, 248–9
    Indian, European discovery of, 247–57
    Japanese, 275–6
    Ottoman, 322–3; in 15th and 16th c., 318
    western, transmission to Japan, 259–72
Mehmed Chelebi, Yirmisekiz, Ottoman ambassador, 320–1
Meiji Restoration, 2, 9, 11, 258, 264, 273, 281–2

Mei Ku-Chhêng, 294
Mei Wending, *see* Mei Wên-Ting
Mei Wên-Ting, astronomer, 265, 300, 308
Melendez, 63
Mendaña, explorer, 91–2
Mendizabal, 63
Mendoza, Antonio de, viceroy of New Spain, 142–5
Menonville, Nicolas Thiery de, 59–60
Mercator, Gerardus, geographer, 169–70, 199
meteorology, and spread of modern science, 2
metropolitan science, 24, 26–7, 29–30, 35–8, 41–2
military science
    Chinese, 310, 312
    Japanese, 271–2, 274–5, 278
    Ottoman, 317, 322
Milner, Lord, 47
mining, Ottoman, in 15th and 16th c., 317
Misra, Bhāva, 249
missionaries, 4, *see also* Jesuits
    in southwestern North America, 141–52
    translations of European and American
        works into Chinese, 306–7, 309, 311
Mitsuyoshi, Yoshida, mathematician, 263
Mocino, José Mariano, 61–2, 64
models, use in history, 34–5
monopolies, 165, 168
    in Pacific Ocean: Dutch, 97–8, 102; French, 104; Spanish, 97–8, 102, 106–8
Mopox, 63
Moraleda, 63
Morse, Edward S., zoologist, 9
Morton, Matthew, navigator, 181, 183, 187–91
Murad II, sultan, 318
Mutis, 62–3, 65

Nagasaki, Japan
    importation of western science through, 259, 266–7
    naval training establishments at, 275–6, 278
Nag Devaryo, Brahman medical practitioner, 248
Napoleon Bonaparte, emperor of France, 5, 14, 60, 80
Narborough, John, British captain, 104–5
Narváez, Panfilo de, explorer, 141
nationalism, role in spread of modern science, 11–12
national scientific associations, 14, 35–8, 50, 124
    problems posed by, 35–7, 122–4
naturalists, role in spread of science, 3–6

Navarrete, Domingo, friar, 205
navigation
    in Pacific Ocean, 121–2; motives for, 87–8, 90–5, 103–5, 113, 119, 122–3
    as science, 122
Navigation Acts, 117
Née, Louis, scientist, 64
New South Wales, 74, 76–8, 117–18
Newton, Sir Isaac, scientist, 18
New World, *see* America(s)/New World
New Zealand, 74–6
Nieuwhoff, 288
Nighantu, dictionary of Ayurvedic terms, 250–1
Niza, Marcos de, explorer
    chronicles, 140–51; criticism, 144; historiographic considerations, 140–1, 146–51; reliability, 143–4
    travel route, *142*, 144–6
Nodal brothers, navigators, 93
Noel, Francis, Jesuit, 298
Nootka Sound, 78–9
Nordenflycht, Timoteo, 64–5
Norden, John, cartographer, *171*
North America, *see* America(s)/New World; Canada; United States
North, Roger, British captain, 181, 183, 191
Northumberland, Earl of, 188
Nueva Galicia, 143

Oaxaca, 59
O'Brien, Bernard, adventurer, 191
observatories, 65, 122
O'Crowley, Pedro Alonso, 58
Onorato, friar in Mexico, 143–4
Opium Wars, 309
Oppenheimer, J.R., physicist, 17
Orinoco River, 181
Orta, Garcia d,' Portuguese physician, 251–2
Ortelius, Abraham, *Theatrum Orbis Terrarum*, 199, 202
Ottoman State
    autarchy, 316
    contacts with West: in 15th and 16th century, 316–18; in 17th–19th century, 318–22
    educational institutions, 321–4
    and European science and technology, 315–25
    outlook on Western world, 315–16
    scientific transfer in: via ambassadors' reports *(sefaretnames)*, 320–1; via educational institutions, 318, 321–2; via Europeans, 322–3; via students in Europe, 322–3; via translations from

European languages into Turkish, 318–21

Ottoman State continued
  ulema (religious circles), 320–1
Owen, Richard, naturalist, 42–3
Oxley, John, scientist, 40

Pacific Ocean
  exploration: 1510 through 1640s, 90–6;
    1640s through 1760s, 96–111; 1760s
    onward, 111–26; funding for, 88, 94–6,
    101, 122; geographic considerations,
    97–9, 101, 105, 121, 165;
    historiographic considerations, 96–7,
    111; lapse in, 86, 96–111; motives for,
    87–8, 90–5, 97–9, 101–5, 113, 115–
    23; political aspects, 97–101, 112–13,
    118–19, 121
  scientific expeditions in, 63, 86–7, 121–6;
    historiographic considerations, 67–8,
    126; political aspects, 67–81, 88–9,
    120–2
Page, Pierre Marie de, traveler, 59
Panama, 63
Pandita, Vinayaka, Brahman physician, 255
panditos, Hindu physicians, 249–55
Pando, 63
Paraguay, 63–4
Pardiès, I.G., translation of Euclid's *Elements*,
  306
Paris Observatory, 320–1
Parkinson, Sydney, technical artist, 72
Parra, botanist, 58, 63, 65
Patagonia, 63–4
Pavon, botanist, 65
Peking observatory, 297–8, *303*
Percy, George, British Captain, 188
Pereira, Andrew, Jesuit missionary, 294
Perez, 63
Perler, 63
Permadi, Kadamba King of Goa, 248
Pérouse, *see* La Pérouse
Perry, Matthew, US naval officer, 274–5
Peru, 59, 63–4, 104–6, 143
Peter I, "the Great", emperor of Russia, 103
Phelypeaux, Jean Frédéric, minister of marine,
  224
Philadelphia, 4
Philip II, king of Spain, 241
Philip V, king of Spain, 64
Philippines, 62–3, 90
Phillip, Arthur, British captain, 76–7
Philosophical Magazine, 9
Philosophical Society of Australasia, 39

*Philosophical Transactions of the Royal
  Society of London*, 14
philosophy
  and attitudes toward modern science, 12–
    13, 203–4
  in Japan, 277
Physical Review, 9
physics, Japanese, 272
pirates, 105
Pitt, William, statesman, 110
Plancius, Peter, cartographer, 167, 202
plantations, 181
Plumier, Charles, traveler, 58–9
Portugal
  cartography in, 165–6, 168
  exploration of Pacific Ocean, 90–1
  role in spread of modern science, 4–5, 8
  South American colonies, 186, 191, 193
  territory of Goa, *see* Goa
  trade relations, 109
pouvoir savoir, *see* power-knowledge
Powell, John Wesley, geologist and explorer, 4
power-knowledge, 162–3, 168, 174
progress, 124–6
  science and, 89, 124, 169
Ptolemaic world-system, 291–2
Purcell, James, trader, 191
Purcell, Philip, trader, 191
Purchas, Samuel, chronicler, 183

Queiroz, Fernão de, 254
Quiroga, 64
Quiros, explorer, 91–2
Quite, 63–4

Rabi, I. I., physicist, 17
Ragapo, Leonard, chief, 187
Raleigh, Sir Walter, navigator, 168, 181, 183,
  187, 212
Ramsay, Sir William, chemist, 46
Rangaku, "Dutch learning", 260–1, 265, 269–73
Rangaku Kaitei, 266
Rangaku Koto-hajime, 260, 265
Rattlesnake, ship, 38
Reis, Pirî, cartographer, 317
Rekishô Shinsho, 268
Relacion de Nueva España, 58
religion
  and modern science, 12, 202
  role in European expansion, 28
Rho, James, S.J., missionary, 293
Ricci, Matteo, S.J., missionary, 263, 265, 284,
  288, 290, 296, 306–7
  cartographer, 163

Ricci, Matteo, continued
  influence on Asian cartography, 198–210,
    200
Rigada, 63
Rigaku Teiyô, 272
Rikkei, Sugita, translator, 275
Rinsô, Aoji, scholar, 272, 275
Rintarô, Katsu, 275–6
Rio de la Plata, 63
Robinson, Philip, collector, 199
Rocha, Felix da, astronomer, 298
Roe, Sir Thomas, courtier, 181, 183, 187–9,
  191
Roggeveen, Jacob, navigator, 86, 100, 107
Ross, Ronald, 47
Royal Geographical Society, 199
Royal Observatory at Greenwich, 122
Royal Society of London, 14, 35, 38–9, 41–2,
  44, 120, 124–5, 296
Royal Society of New South Wales, 45
Ruiz, botanist, 65
Russell, H.C., astronomer, 45
Russia, *see also* Soviet Union
  expansion, in Pacific Ocean, 77–8, 102–3,
    121
  modern science in, 8, 17
Rutherford, Ernest, physicist, 47
Ryôei, Motoki, interpreter, 267–8
Ryôjun, Matsumoto, 276
Ryôkai, Shiba, scholar, 276
Ryôtaku, Maeno, scholar, 260

Sabine, Sir Edward, scientist, 38
Sadano, Arab prime minister of Goa, 249
Sagasti, Francisco, economist, 32–3
Saint-Hilaire, Geoffroy, naturalist, 5
Saint-Malo, 106–7
Saint-Mary, Frédéric Moreau de, traveler, 58
Salle, *see* La Salle, Robert Cavelier Sieur de
samhita, medical textbook, 247
San Miguel de Culiacán, 143
Sanson, Nicolas, cartographer, 236, *240*
Santa Lucia, ship, 183
Sassetti, Filippo, Italian traveler, 250–1
Saxton, Christopher, surveyor, 164, 169
Scandinavia, and spread of modern science, 1
Schall von Bell, John Adam, Jesuit
    missionary, 294–6
  Yuan Ching Shuo (The Far-Seeing Optick
    Glass), 291
Scheiner, Christopher, 288
Schreck, Johann, *see* Terrentius, Johannes
science
  education and, 8–9, 13–14
  government influence in, 13, 33, 121–3,
    163–6
  and idea of progress, 89, 124–5, 169
  imperialism and, 25–51, 121–2;
      historiographic considerations, 25–7,
      31–4, 49–51, 126
  international competition in, 37, 122
  journals, 14
  modern, universal validity, 294–5
  national societies and associations, 14, 35–
    8, 41, 44, 50, 124; problems posed by,
    35–7, 122–4
  and political power, 89, 121–2, 161–75
  spread: in civilizations with existing
      scientific traditions, 3; historiographic
      considerations, 2, 18; to Ottoman
      world, 315–25; political aspects, 34,
      39, 41–2, 44, 46–7, 119–22, 124–5;
      three-stage model for, 1–18, *3*, 30
  statecraft and, 25, 311
  technology and, 15, 125, 169
  trade and, 24, 165–9
science books, Ottoman, 320
scientific culture, 8, 11–12
scientific method, 46–7, 294
Scientific Revolution, in Western Europe, 1,
  17
scientific romances, 17th-c., 286
scientists, social status, 13
Scott, John, historian, 192–3
seapower
  British, 108, 116–17, 119–21
  French, 118–19, 121
  relation to science, 89
secrecy, in cartography, 161–75
Seikei, Sugita, translator, 275
Seimi Kaisô, 272
Sensai, Nagayo, 273, 275
Sesse, Martin de, botanist, 65
Seven Years' War, 110
Shao Ang-Hsiao, 300
Sharp, Bartholomew, buccaneer, 105
Shehdi Osman Efendi, Ottoman ambassador,
  320
Shelvocke, George, British captain, 119
Shêng Pai-Erh, astronomer, 300–1
Shigeki, Tôyama, historian, 280–1
Shigetomi, Hazama, merchant, 269
Shindô, Tsuboi, scholar/teacher, 271
Shin'ichi, Takahashi, historian, 280
Shintoism, in Japan, 264
shipbuilding, Japanese, 278
Shôchû, Satô, physician, 275
Shoho world map, 198, 205, *206–7*, 208–9

Shokugaku Keigen, 272
Shôsendô, 271–2
Shôsuke, Satô, historian, 280–1
Shôzan, Sakuma, scholar, 278–9
Shûhan, Takashima, gunner, 278
Shûseikan, 278
Siebold incident, 269–70, 272, 280
silence
   definition, 162
   in maps, 161–75
silver, 91–2, 106, 143
Simonelli, Jacques-Philippe, 298
Sivachitta, Kadamba King of Goa, 248
Smith, Adam, *Wealth of Nations*, 126
Smith, John, governor of Virginia, 172, *173*,
   211–12, *213*, 215, 217, 220
Smith, Sir James E., botanist, 6, 40, 76–7
Smogulecki, Nicholas, 291
Sôkichi, Hashimoto, physician, *10*, 11, 269
Solander, Daniel, naturalist, 72, 76
Solano, José, 63
Sorai, Ogyû, Confucian, 262, 280
Soto, Hernando de, explorer, 145
Sousa Coutinho, Cristóvão, 255
Sousa, Francisco de, Jesuit father, 250
Sousa, Martim Afonso de, Governor of Goa,
   250
South Africa, European settlements in,
   scientists in, 5
Southwest, region of North America,
   aboriginal cultures in, 140–52
   historiographic considerations, 146
Soviet Union, *see also* Russia
   science in, 17
Spain
   cartography in, 165–6, 168
   exploration of Pacific Ocean, 68–70, 77–9,
      98–9, 101; motives for, 90–3
   New World colonies, 68–70, 93, 104–7,
      141–52
   relations with Great Britain, 108–10, 120
   scientific expeditions, 8, 56–8, 61, 63–4;
      cooperation with France, 63
   war of succession, 105–6
spice trade, 96, 102–3
Spinola, Carlo, S.J., mathematician, 205
Spöring, Herman, naturalist, 72
Sprat, Thomas, historian, 5–6, 30–1
statecraft, relation to science, 25, 311
Stow, *Annales*, 181
sugar, 181
sun-spots, 293
surgery, western: introduced into Japan, 271
Surville, Jean de, 72

Sushruta *samhita*, 247
Swift, Jonathan, author, 23, 85
syphilis, introduction into India, 249
Szczesniak, 290, 293

Tadao, Shitsuki, scholar, 266, 268
Tadataka, Inô, cartographer, 269
Tahiti, 71–2, 74
Taiping rebellion, 309
Takakazu, Seki, mathematician, 261, 263, 267
Tamar, ship, 70
Tanzimat, 320–4
Tarôzaemon, Egawa, Commissionar at
   Shimoda, 274
Tasaburô, Itô, historian, 279–80
Tasman, Abel Janszoon, navigator, 94, 99,
   167
Tatton, Gabriel, cartographer, 183, *184*, 186,
   187, 187–91
Tavernier, Jean Baptiste, 254
technology
   relationship to science, 15, 125, 169
   role in European expansion, 28, 125
Teiyû, Baba, interpreter, 266, 269
Tekijuku, 271–3
telescope, 290–2
Terra Australis, search for, 70, 73–4, 100, 118
terra incognita, 219–20, 226, 234
Terrentius, Johannes, astronomer/physicist,
   290, 293
tetsugaku, philosophy, 277
Tezkereci Kose Ibrahim Efendi, translator, 319
Thornton, Robert, explorer, 183
Thunberg, Carl Peter, medical officer, 4
Thu Shu Chi Chhêng, Chinese encyclopedia,
   294
T'ien-ch'i, Chinese emperor, 203
Timor, 100
tobacco, 181, 193
Tocqueville, Alexis de, author, 29
Tokyo Imperial University, 275
topography, and spread of modern science, 2
Torres, Luis Vaez de, explorer, 91–3, 202
Totonteacs, native Americans, 150–1
Tôyô, Yamawaki, anatomist, 264
trade
   and exploration of Pacific Ocean, 90–3,
      101, 104–5, 108, 113–14, 119, 123
   free, 114
   monopolies, 165, 168; British, 103–4;
      Dutch, 97–8, 102; French, 104;
      Spanish, 97–8, 102, 106–8
   relation to science, 3, 24, 72–3, 77, 122,
      165–9; Marxist theory, 28

Traite de la culture de nopal et l'education de la cochenille, 59
Transit of Venus expeditions, 26, 37, 73, 120, 123
translations
    of European and American works into Chinese, 306–7, 309, 311
    from European languages into Turkish, 318–21
Treaty of Friendship between Japan and America, 274–6
Treaty of Tordesillas, 89
Treaty of Utrecht, 69
Trigault, 288–9
Trincheras, native Americans, 141, 149
Tsu Chhung-Chih, astronomer, 301
Tsûshi, 259–60

Ulloa, Antonio de, 58–9, 63
Ulug Bey, astronomer, 319
United States, development of modern science in, 9, 17, 29–30
Ursis, Sabbathin de, astronomer, 283
    Cheng Phing I Shuo (Elementary Explanations of Astronomical Instruments), 291–2
Urville, Jules Dumont d', navigator, 81
U.S.S.R., *see* Soviet Union

Vaca, Cabeza de, explorer, 141–5
Vagbhāta *samhita*, 247
vaidyas, Hindu Ayurvedic physicians, 247, 249
Valdelirios, Marques de, 63–4
Vancouver, George, navigator, 79
Van Diemen, Anthony, governor-general of Batavia, 94
Van Draakenstein, Henricus Van Rheede, Governor of Malabar, *Hortus Indicus Malabaricus*, 255–7
van Linschoten, Jan Huyghen, Dutch voyager, 250
van Meerdervoort, Pompe, 273, 276
van Sype, Nicola, cartographer, *166*
Varennes, Jacques-René Gaultier de, 220
Velasco, Don Alonso de, cartographer, 220, *221*, 241–2
Venezuela, 63
Verbiest, Ferdinand, astronomer, 296–8
Vérendrye, Pierre Gaultier de Varennes et de la, explorer, 220, *221*, *224*, 224–31, 236–42
Véron, Pierre, astronomer, 71
Vienna Observatory, 320–1

Virginia, *173*, 212–15, *213*
Virginia Company, 212
von Hallerstein, Augustin, astronomer, 298
von Humboldt, Alexander, scientist, 3
von Mandelslo, Johann Albrecht, 253
von Siebold, Philipp Franz, physician and botanist, 4, 266–7, 271

Wallace, Alfred Russell, naturalist, 4
Wallis, Samuel, British captain, 70–1, 73, 116, 119
Walpole, Sir Robert, British minister of state, 108
Wang Hsi-Shan, astronomer, 298–9
Wang Jen-Chün, 301
Wang Ming-Shêng, 301
Wang P'an, scholar, 199
Wang Yang-ming, Confucian, 262
War for American Independence, *see* American Revolution
War of Spanish Succession, 105–6
war technology, *see* military science
Washington, D.C., 4
Washington, George, U.S. president, 216
Wei Hsiang-Chhien, astronomer, 300
Wei Wên-Khuei, astronomer, 300
Western Europe
    birth of modern science in, 1
    exploration of Pacific Ocean by, *see* Pacific Ocean
    influence on scientific culture, 8
White, John, artist, 172
Wilkins, John, *Discovery of a World in the Moon, tending to prove that 'tis probable that there may be another habitable World in that Planet*, 286
William III, king of England, 100
Williams, Wells, 288
Wilson, Miles, *History of Israel Jobson, the Wandering Jew*, 286–7
Wood, William, 172
World War I, effect on imperial science, 48
Wylie, Alexander, Protestant missionary, 293, 309
Wytfliet, Cornelius, cartographer, 236, *241*

Ximénez, Gerónimo, friar in Mexico, 146
Xingú River, 188–91
Xu Guangqi, Christian convert, 306

Yang Kuang-Hsien, scholar/astronomer, 295
Yang Ma-No, *see* Diaz, Emanuel
Yang T'ing-yün, scholar, 203
Yasusada, Miyazaki, scholar, 261

Yin and Yang, 203–4
Yôan, Udagawa, scholar, 272
yôgaku, western learning, 274–5, 277–82
Yoshimune, Tokugawa Shogun, 265
Yoshitoki, Takahashi, astronomer, 269
Yukichi, Fukuzawa, educator, 271–3, 277

Zembei, Iwabashi, telescope maker, 269
Zeng Guofan, 309
zoology, 2, 42
Zumárraga, Juan de, bishop of Mexico, 143, 146
Zuni, native Americans, 141, 143, 146–9